Intuition in Business

Intuition in Business

Eugene Sadler-Smith

Great Clarendon Street, Oxford, OX2 6DP,
United Kingdom

Oxford University Press is a department of the University of Oxford.
It furthers the University's objective of excellence in research, scholarship,
and education by publishing worldwide. Oxford is a registered trade mark of
Oxford University Press in the UK and in certain other countries

© Eugene Sadler-Smith 2023

The moral rights of the author have been asserted

Impression: 1

All rights reserved. No part of this publication may be reproduced, stored in
a retrieval system, or transmitted, in any form or by any means, without the
prior permission in writing of Oxford University Press, or as expressly permitted
by law, by licence or under terms agreed with the appropriate reprographics
rights organization. Enquiries concerning reproduction outside the scope of the
above should be sent to the Rights Department, Oxford University Press, at the
address above

You must not circulate this work in any other form
and you must impose this same condition on any acquirer

Published in the United States of America by Oxford University Press
198 Madison Avenue, New York, NY 10016, United States of America

British Library Cataloguing in Publication Data

Data available

Library of Congress Control Number: 2022950785

ISBN 978–0–19–887156–9

DOI: 10.1093/oso/9780198871569.001.0001

Printed and bound by
CPI Group (UK) Ltd, Croydon, CR0 4YY

Links to third party websites are provided by Oxford in good faith and
for information only. Oxford disclaims any responsibility for the materials
contained in any third party website referenced in this work.

To my mother Winifred Sadler-Smith; easily the most intuitive person I have ever known.

Preface

Intuition in Business is my third book on the subject of intuition. When I first approached this subject in the early 2000s, intuition was to me, along with many other management researchers, an interesting and unusual new topic. I have always believed that the best way to understand something new and challenging is to write about it and/or try to teach it. In order to come to a better understanding of intuition I wrote *Inside Intuition* (Routledge, 2008). At around the same time I also dipped my toe in the water of teaching intuition to the challenging audience of executive MBA students. My second book, *The Intuitive Mind: Profiting from the Power of your Sixth Sense* (John Wiley and Sons, 2010) was my attempt to communicate the topic of intuition, which managers seem to find perennially fascinating, to a practitioner audience. *Intuition in Business* presents my perspective on the topic of intuition with the benefit of the best part of two decades of researching and writing about intuition in business and management. It seeks to be retrospective (asking 'where have we come from?'), current ('where are we now?'), and prospective ('where are we headed?') and to communicate a body of knowledge to specialists and non-specialists alike in the various sub-fields of management and leadership. The book's core idea is that intuition is a uniquely human *sensing* capability which supports decision-making under uncertainty and complements the *solving* capabilities of rational analysis in problem-solving and decision-making, moral and social judgements, and creativity.

In the years that have elapsed since the publication of *Inside Intuition*, much has changed in the intuition landscape in business and beyond. The number of books and articles on the subject has flourished and intuition has entered the mainstream of business management research and practice. Conferences on the subject have been held, intuition symposia at leading management conferences regularly take place, whole handbooks devoted exclusively to the topic of intuition have been published, and I for one teach intuition in my leadership and decision-making courses to both undergraduate and postgraduate business school students in the UK and abroad. Business school students whoever and wherever they are certainly seem to enjoy the topic and as a result of studying it they will hopefully enter the world of work better-prepared to cope with the ambiguities, complexities, and uncertainties of organizational life which they will surely face. In the behavioural sciences more broadly, the study of intuition has come on in leaps and bounds, not least as a result of remarkable progress in fields such as social cognitive neuroscience, supported by astonishing developments in techniques for studying the inner workings of the intuitive mind using functional brain imaging. Intuition is no longer confined Cinderella-like to the margins of the behavioural sciences; it has accumulated its own body of knowledge.

Intuition in Business is a comprehensive introduction to the science of intuition which will be of benefit to students, researchers, and practitioners.

Looking to the future, we are compelled to ask ourselves questions about what the future holds for human intuition in the age of artificial intelligence. Could an 'artificial intuition' be the next or perhaps even the ultimate AI? Could an artificial intuition ever replace human intuition's phenomenal sensing capabilities? Perhaps artificial intuition is an impossibility precisely because intuitions are embedded in our physical bodies and as such are central to the experience of being human and part of who we are as individuals and therefore cannot be replicated in a machine. These are important questions for the not-too-distant future. The pressing issue for the present is how the extensive knowledge of intuition, not available twenty years ago but which we are now in the fortunate position of being privy to, can be used to create positive change that will have a beneficial impact on individuals, organizations, the economy, and wider society. The aim of this book is to provide readers with knowledge to support them in making a positive impact through intuition both in their professional and personal lives.

Acknowledgements

I first published on the subject of intuition in 2004 in an article in the *Academy of Management Executive*. Since then, it has been my pleasure and privilege to work with many remarkable people in researching and publishing on this important and interesting topic. *Intuition in Business* is the culmination of the best part of twenty years work on intuition in business, none of which would have been possible without the following outstanding scholars who took the risk of working with me and I am privileged to be able to call my colleagues; to them I extend my utmost respect and gratitude (they are listed in alphabetical order and with requisite apologies for any omissions): Cinla Akinci (for research into intuition in police work, collective intuitions, and much else besides); Vita Akstinaite (linguistic markers of intuition and insight and much else besides); Chris Allinson (cognitive styles); Steve Armstrong (cognitive styles); Lisa Burke-Smalley (intuition in management learning and education); Guy Claxton (intuition and creativity and hubris as unbridled intuition); Eva Cools (cognitive styles); Julie Gore (different types of intuition); John Hayes (cognitive styles); Ann Hensman (intuition in banking and finance); Gerard Hodgkinson (cognitive styles, dual-processing and much else besides); Josh Keller (intuition and paradoxes); Janice Langan-Fox (intuition); Steve Leybourne (intuition in project management); Andrew Miles (intuition in human resources); Lord David Owen (hubris as unbridled intuition); Ceyda Paydas Turan (intuition and hybrid intelligence); Richard Riding (cognitive styles); Erella Shefy (who helped to demystify intuition); Marta Sinclair (cognitive styles and for editing an outstanding series of intuition handbooks); Paul Sparrow (intuition in business strategy and decision-making). Thank you Sarah Sadler-Smith for drawing the pictures. I thank the team at Oxford University Press, Vicki Sunter and Nandhini Saravanan, who saw *Intuition in Business* through to final completion. Last and most certainly by no means least, my sincere thanks go to Adam Swallow, Commissioning Editor at Oxford University Press, without whose encouragement and support *Intuition in Business* would never have seen the light of day.

Contents

List of Figures   x
List of Tables   xi

1. Making Sense of Intuition   1
2. How Intuition Sometimes Gets It Wrong: Heuristics and Biases   32
3. How Gut Feeling Sometimes Gets It Right: Fast and Frugal Heuristics   56
4. Why Intuition Often Gets It Right: Recognition-Primed Decision-Making   80
5. The 'Two-Minds' Model   103
6. Core Processes of Intuition   134
7. The Expert Sense   163
8. The Moral Sense   189
9. The Social Sense   208
10. The Creative Sense   229
11. Making an Impact through Intuition   260

Index   296

List of Figures

4.1.	Recognition-based intuition	94
4.2.	Intuition-based inquiry	95
4.3.	Traffic light model for intuition and analysis	98
6.1.	Kanizsa triangle illusion	138
6.2.	Gestalt closure task: meaningful (left) and non-meaningful (right) arrangements of the same visual elements	139
6.3.	Approximate location of orbitofrontal cortex; associated with perceptions of coherence	140
6.4.	Approximate locations of precuneus associated with pattern recognition and caudate nucleus associated with generation of best next-move	144
6.5.	Approximate location of ventro-medial prefrontal cortex and amygdala; associated with somatic markers	147
6.6.	Approximate location of anterior insula; associated with interoceptive awareness	151
6.7.	Approximate locations of mirror neurons; associated with mirror mechanism	154
9.1.	Neural correlates of the C-system (refle$c$tive cognition) and X-system (refle$x$ive cognition)	222
10.1.	The right hemisphere aSTG associated with solving laboratory insight problems	233
10.2.	Five stages of the creative process in terms of different levels of consciousness	236
11.1.	Four cognitive styles	269

List of Tables

3.1. Predictors of future job performance   69
11.1. Questions for diagnosing your analysis/intuition cognitive style   268

1
Making Sense of Intuition

Overview

The main idea of this chapter is that intuition 'senses' whilst its counterpart, analysis, 'solves'. The power of intuition's sensing function is illustrated with the example of the 2008 credit crunch which brought the world financial system to its knees. The example of business venturing illustrates how experienced investors, so-called 'business angels', blend intuitive sensing and analytical solving to take high-risk decisions in the volatile world of entrepreneurship. The concepts of risk and uncertainty demonstrate the limits of rationality (that it is 'bounded') and illustrate how informed intuition expands experienced decision-makers' capabilities especially when rationality reaches its limits. The history of these ideas is traced back to one of the book's central figures, the Nobel Laureate Herbert Simon, and beyond to his intellectual forerunner, the intellectually curious business executive Chester Barnard. Intuition is defined. The differences between intuition and instinct are explained. A caveat is offered for those who are tempted to trust their intuition unreservedly. As well as helping us to take decisive and incisive action, intuition helps us to make sense of situations that initially do not make sense. Opening evidence is offered for how and why managers use intuition to take decisions; the conditions under which it is likely to be successful are discussed, and this idea is developed throughout the book. The chapter concludes with a discussion of intuition in the age of artificial intelligence (AI) and speculates on the prospects for an 'artificial intuition' as a new, and perhaps ultimate, form of AI.

Shadow Banking

Few executives or experts in the finance industry sensed the calamitous events that unfolded in the 2008 financial crash. This shortcoming prompted Her Majesty Queen Elizabeth II in a visit to the London School of Economics in November 2008 to inquire, with regal understatedness, why no one had noticed that the credit crunch was on its way. In the letter of reply to Buckingham Palace which followed—signed by over thirty eminent scholars, civil servants, and business leaders — the humble response to Her Majesty was that the crisis was hard for them to foresee because, engrossed and preoccupied as they were with mathematical detail, they, the experts, simply lost sight of the bigger picture.[1] In any crisis, prevention is always better than

Intuition in Business. Eugene Sadler-Smith, Oxford University Press. © Eugene Sadler-Smith (2023).
DOI: 10.1093/oso/9780198871569.003.0001

2 Making Sense of Intuition

cure but did anyone in the industry have a feel for the bigger picture and a sense for the calamitous events that lay ahead? Were there any faint, which is not to say weak, signals that an impending global financial meltdown was about to take place; could the experts have used these to make sense of and avoid this catastrophic financial black swan?[2]

In the *Silo Effect: Why Putting Everything in its Place Isn't Such a Bright Idea* (2015) leading financial journalist and Cambridge-educated anthropologist Gillian Tett recounted how in 2007 leading macroeconomic and monetary policy experts, including some of the best financial brains in the world, sensed that something in the 'shadows' was causing the world economy to be tilted out of true. But they were unable to say what it was and why it gave them such cause for concern. The then Deputy Governor of the Bank of England, Paul Tucker, gave a speech in April 2007 to a conference for hedge fund managers organized by Merrill Lynch in London.[3] Tucker presented a seemingly upbeat account of robust growth, containment of inflation, and, most importantly for the audience, healthy returns for their sector.

However, against this optimistic assessment Tucker also felt a pointed unease: 'the dials on the economic instrument board did not seem to be moving in the normal way.' In the bigger picture, money was swirling around the economy at pace that did not make sense either to the policymakers or the economists.[4] Tucker suspected that the source of these incongruities and inconsistencies lay somewhere outside of the banks. But 'it was one thing to have a hunch … it was much harder to actually prove that something was wrong when there was so little data.'[5] Part of the problem was that the algorithms that were the engines of modern mathematical finance had become so complex that many of the brightest brains in banks, equities, and hedge funds even had trouble understanding their creations; as a result, they were quite simply getting their 'sums wrong'.[6] To make the point, Tett likened the multiple use of a single asset, such as a mortgage loan, to create new trading and hedging opportunities to a spinning out a single strand of sugar to make an enormous but insubstantial cone of candy floss.[7]

To make matters worse, the experts themselves lacked a language with which to even name the exotic financial innovations that Tucker intuited to be a root cause of his unease. When meltdown eventually came it was accompanied by the invention of the new, but now widely used, term 'shadow banking'.[8] Shadow banking was outside the known banking world. The shadow metaphor captured perfectly the intuitive 'felt-sense'[9] of disquiet and foreboding felt by a small group of financial experts. Tucker sensed that something about the system itself did not add up. He had an intuition, albeit only partially formed, that the problem was lurking in the shadows in the high-stakes world of high finance. The problem was intuitively sensed, but unfortunately it could not be analytically solved by the intervention of the central banks before it was too late. Tucker did not have extrasensory perception, but he did have an expert's intuition, which led him to sense that the road ahead was likely to give the global financial system a very bumpy ride. It did, and the effects are still being felt to this day, for example, in lower economic growth, increased income inequalities and government debt.

Intuitive Angels

The 'sixth sense' and self-help intuition literatures are full of exotic interpretations of intuition's magical powers. These range from intuition-as-ESP[10] through to intuitive 'angels' with supernatural powers of intercession in human affairs.[11] The intuitions, and intercessions, of a different kind of angel are vital for aspiring entrepreneurs in the fast-moving, risky, and uncertain world of business venturing. The decision to try and found a successful start-up business means accepting the risk of failure. In the UK, around 20 per cent of start-ups fail within their first year, and at the end of three years around 60 per cent will have gone bust.[12] Starting up a business, especially in high-growth, fast-moving areas such as high-technology, requires a significant financial investment. Some of the largest sources of venture capital for tech entrepreneurs are low-profile, wealthy individuals, first referred to in the 1980s by William Wetzel as 'business angels'. Business angels provide capital directly to small, private, often start-up firms operating in conditions of high risk and extreme uncertainty. The have been made famous by TV shows such as 'Dragon's Den' in the UK and 'Shark Tank' in the USA. But how do business angels decide which business ventures are worth risking their hard-earned cash on?

Entrepreneurship researchers Laura Huang and Jone Pearce compared how much angel investors relied on hard analytics (such as financials and an entrepreneur's business plan) versus soft intuitions (such as their intuitive assessment of the opportunities and risks). They discovered that experienced business angels—who stood to make substantial losses if the venture failed—did rely on their intuition, but they used it in a complex and highly nuanced way far removed from the 'go-with-your-gut-instinct' exhortations so beloved of business biographies.[13] For successful angel investors, intuition is a skill that is absorbed, cultivated, and sharpened by constantly paying attention to experienced-based prototypes of what constitutes a potentially successful business venture, including market information, financials, product prototypes, etc. But the angels did not shy away from entering into high-risk investments by also relying on their gut feelings. They used their intuition as a way of managing uncertainties that were so extreme as to qualify as unknowable. One angel commented that investing is not about avoiding uncertainly but rather of embracing it: '[it is OK to] be uncertain. Bear the uncertainty. Embrace it. Go with it. Let that lead you to the interesting stuff. That's how I make my huge profits.'

The angels used their heads and their hearts by combining hard 'business viability data' (BVD) such as market size and business growth projections with softer 'person perceptions' of the founding entrepreneur. This intuitive assessment of the person was described by one investor as 'noticing right away, sometimes within five seconds of meeting the entrepreneur, how you feel about them and what your overall sense is for them as a person'.[14] But the angel investors did not allow their subjective person perception to overwhelm the objective BVD, or vice versa. They had clear goals in pursuit of which they were prepared to take a risk, acknowledging the possibility that they could lose their entire investment. They relied on a combination of intuitive expertise and formal analysis to pick winners and predict extraordinarily profitable investments.

The stories of shadow banking in the credit crunch and business angels in business venturing illustrate two fundamental points about intuition. First, human beings possess a dual system of thinking: an 'analytical system' which is designed (by evolution) and adapted (by experience) for the general purpose of 'solving'; an 'intuitive system' which is designed and adapted (by evolution and experience) for the general purpose of 'sensing'. In the shadow banking case, the intuitive system was able to sense that something in the financial system was out of kilter without being able to say why precisely. Second, the intuitive system and the analytical system work best when their complementary sensing and solving capacities are used jointly and cooperatively. In the business angels' case, objective business viability data was used to solve and subjective person perception was used to sense; in combination, analytical solving and intuitive sensing provided an answer to the conundrum of whether or not to invest. The synergy of sensing and solving can result in extraordinary achievements not only in business but, as we shall see, in many other professional fields as well as in the arts, technology, and the sciences.

Decision-Making under Risk and Uncertainty

Shadow banking in high finance and the activities of angel investors in small firm start-ups occupy opposite ends of the business spectrum. However they both illustrate the challenges that decision-makers are confronted by with the uncertainty that characterizes the twenty-first century business environment. They also show how an informed and intelligent use of intuition is one way—and sometimes the only way—in which decision-makers can make sense of and take decisive actions in the face of risks that are hard to quantify and uncertainties so extreme as a to be unknowable.

In the 1920s the University of Chicago economist Frank Knight elucidated the distinction between risk and uncertainty; the term 'risk' refers to those situations where we do not know the outcome but can measure the odds (for example an airline can calculate the chances of a plane crash). Uncertainty, or 'Knightian uncertainty', on the other hand, refers to those situations where we cannot know all the information we need in order to set accurate odds in the first place (for example, the prospects for the airline business in fifty years' time on the other hand is incalculable).[15]

A little later, another of the most influential economists of the twentieth century, John Maynard Keynes, writing in 1937, illustrated the distinction between risk and uncertainty by reference to games of chance. In situations of risk the possible alternatives, their consequences and their probabilities are known. In such situations mathematical probability can be a helpful decision aid. For instance, the odds of a winning ticket in the UK's National Lottery can be expressed in probabilistic terms; the chances of a particular set of numbers coming up can be computed and expressed as a risk (for example, one in 45 million for the jackpot). However, arriving at a similar assessment of probability is not possible in the complex, ambiguous, and dynamic environment in which many of our consequential personal and professional decisions are taken. To illustrate the difference between risk and uncertainty, Keynes, who was writing shortly before the outbreak of the Second World War, observed that 'the prospect of a European war is uncertain' and about this matter 'there is no scientific basis on which to form any calculable probability whatsoever. We simply do not know.' Decision-making under uncertainty is not the same as decision-making under risk. In risk, the probabilities of outcomes are knowable and optimum choices can be computed (for example, one in 45 million); under uncertainty, probabilities are not knowable (for example, the probability of a war between the USA and China) hence it is not possible to compute an optimum choice. Such choices can, however, be sensed.

In a speech to the Economic Club of Washington in 2018 Jeff Bezos described how Amazon made sense of the conundrum of if and how to design and implement a loyalty scheme for its customers. This consequential decision was taken under uncertainty. For some time, Amazon had been searching for an answer to the question of 'what would a loyalty program for Amazon look like?' A junior software engineer came up with the idea of fast, free shipping. But a big problem was that shipping is expensive. Also, customers like free shipping so much that the big eaters at Amazon's 'buffet' would take advantage by free-shipping low-cost items, which would not be good for Amazon's bottom line. When the Amazon finance team modelled the idea of fast, free shipping the results 'didn't look pretty'. In fact, they were nothing short of 'horrifying'. But Bezos is experienced enough to know that some of his best decisions have been made with 'guts ... not analysis'. In his speech he reminded his audience that 'if you can make a decision with analysis, you should do so. But it turns out in life that your most important decisions are always made with instinct and intuition, taste, heart.'[16]

In deciding whether to go with Amazon Prime, the analysts' data could only take the problem so far towards being solved. As a seasoned executive and experienced entrepreneur, Bezos sensed that the Prime idea would work. Prime was launched in 2005. It has become one of the world's most popular subscription services, with over 100 million members who spend on average $1400 per year compared to $600 for non-prime members.[17] The launch of Amazon Prime is a prime example of a CEO's informed and intelligent use of intuition paying off in decision-making under uncertainty. The customer loyalty problem for Amazon was uncertain because probabilities and consequences could not be known at the time. No amount of analysis could reduce the fast, free-shipping solution to the odds of success or failure. Under these circumstances Bezos had to go with his gut. This is not an uncommon CEO predicament. In business, decision-makers often have to act instinctively, even though they have no way of knowing what the outcome is likely to be. Bezos did not know whether Prime would work or not, nonetheless he used his intuition to sense what the likely outcome might be and make his judgement call. In the case of Amazon Prime, going with his gut worked out well.

Decision-Making under Radical Uncertainty

Oxford economist John Kay and former Bank of England Governor Mervyn King in their book *Radical Uncertainty: Decision-making for an Unknowable Future* (2019), distinguished further between two types of uncertainty: 'resolvable uncertainty' and 'radical uncertainty'. Resolvable uncertainty can be looked up; for example, to resolve any uncertainty regarding 'what is the capital of Mongolia?' the answer, Ulaanbaatar, is discoverable and resolvable quickly and easily at the click of a mouse. However, radical uncertainty cannot be resolved in any similar way because radically uncertain situations tend to be volatile, uncertain, complex, and ambiguous. The problems that abound in a radically uncertain world, unlike the problem-solving puzzles that are studied in many psychology laboratories, tend to be ill-defined and loosely structured. As a consequence, under conditions of radical uncertainty a decision-maker will often have to admit that they simply 'do not know' but have nonetheless to take decisions, even though they do not know what the outcomes of their actions are likely to be.

Kay and King described the decision-making dilemma faced by President Barack Obama on whether or not to storm the compound in Abbottabad where the al Qaeda leader Osama Bin Laden might have been hiding as a classic case of radical uncertainty. The CIA's team leader put the probability of Bin Laden being in the compound at 95 per cent. Other advisers put it as low as 30 per cent. Averaged out, the decision was 50:50. Obama's challenge was that probabilities were being used by his aides to disguise uncertainty. The president was the one who had to sense what the outcome might be. He had to take the decision of whether or not to storm the compound. This was in spite of the fact that at 50:50, the probabilistic risk assessment that Bin Laden was in there was not much better than flipping a coin. Obama 'made his peace with 50:50'. He approved the raid.[18] It took place on 2 May 2011. As we know, Bin Laden was killed by a team of US Navy Seals. His body was buried at sea from the USS Carl Vinson later that same day.

In his autobiography, *A Promised Land* (2020), Obama related how he often relied on his intuition when taking consequential decisions. For example, when deciding whether to run for president or to go back to being a law school professor he remarked that he had to 'decipher what I was feeling in my gut'.[19] When deciding whether to go with Joe Biden as his running mate his 'gut' told him that 'Joe was decent honest and loyal'.[20] In choosing Timothy Geithner for treasure secretary his instinct was that 'Tim had a basic integrity, a steadfastness of temperament, and an ability to problem-solve unsullied by ego or political considerations.' Obama quickly realized that formal processes and mathematical probabilities can only take a president so far. The same is true of a CEO. The problems that make it to the president's, or CEO's, desk are by their nature complex and messy. If this was not so, then someone lower down the chain of command would have solved them already or could be delegated to do so. But Obama also recognized a conundrum: the pursuit of the perfect could can lead to paralysis-by-analysis, whilst 'going with your gut too often meant letting preconceived notions or the path of least political resistance guide a decision—with cherry picked facts used to justify it.'[21] The president's dilemma illustrates perfectly the challenge that sooner or later confronts many decision-makers who have to take consequential decisions under uncertainty: decisions often have to be taken under significant constraints which sometimes severely limit how rational they can actually be even when they aspire, or claim, to be fully rational.

Managers, as well as presidents, often find themselves in situations that are highly uncertain. This might be where no further data are available, not enough time or resources are available to gather more data, first-mover advantage has to be secured, there is little previous precedent to go on, the territory is uncharted and there are no maps, or there are a number of equally compelling solutions that cannot be discriminated between using analytics. In such situations, making a gut call may be the only way to move the situation forward. In describing how his company responded to the challenges of doing business in the radically uncertain and uncharted territory of the aftermath of the 2008 financial crisis, the CEO of one of the world's largest engineering professional services firms remarked that: 'In a recession, you don't necessarily know what you're up against, but you still have to be decisive, which means you'll find yourself making decisions based on gut feel rather than just the facts and accepting that sometimes you'll get it wrong.'[22]

Rationality Is Bounded

The psychological processes that are at work in decision-making under uncertainty were the focus of attention for one of management's most original and influential thinkers: the 1978 Nobel Laureate Herbert Simon (1916 to 2001) of Carnegie-Mellon University. Simon's work is pre-eminent in intuition research in business and management; it is on his shoulders that subsequent generations of decision-making researchers have stood, so much so that someone once commented, not disparagingly, that much of intuition research in business is a footnote to Simon.[23] Three of the theories of intuition discussed in this book ('heuristics-and-biases' in Chapter 2, 'fast-and-frugal' heuristics in Chapter 3 and 'recognition-primed decision-making' in Chapter 4) are so strongly influenced by Simon's work that they can be thought of as extensions and elaborations of his original theory of 'bounded rationality'.

Simon described management as the 'art of getting things done' by 'insuring incisive [penetrating and insightful] action'. He also reminded us that incisive action must be preceded by making sense of a situation in order to decide what needs to be done before doing it. However, incisive and decisive action in business as well as in any other walk of life often has to be taken under constraints of information and time, a lack of knowledge of the consequences of one's actions, and using an information processing system (the human brain) that has limited processing capacity. For these reasons Simon described rationality as 'bounded'. This is also why Simon considered the idealized 'classical' rational model of decision-making favoured by many economists a somewhat 'dubious way of describing human choice'.[24]

The classical/rational model of decision-making typically involves the identification of various options and attributes—for example their 'pros' and 'cons'—and assigning values to them in order to compute a utility analysis. However, as Simon realized, managers' rational and analytical decision-making capabilities are bounded not only by their knowledge of the available alternatives and the consequences of their actions—which are intrinsically uncertain—but also by the human mind's inherent computational limitations.[25] The challenge is compounded when decisions have to be taken under time pressure. The classical/rational model assumes that managers have a knowledge of the future that is quite different from that which they, as human beings, are actually able to possess. These are some of the reasons why Simon considered managers to be boundedly rational actors and management to be an 'art' that is inherently intuitive and judgemental.[26] We will return to a more detailed analysis and appreciation of Simon's theory of bounded rationality in Chapter 2.

The models of decision-making that managers are taught typically in business schools are based on the economic principles of logic and rationality. It is these principles that managers are expected to follow. We also tend to live our lives more generally as though the world is rational. When this turns out not to be the case, we find it unsettling. In these circumstances intuition is one way of making sense of and taking action in an uncertain world that is not as rational as we may have been led or might like to believe that it is. This endows intuition with an element of strangeness that many people find both alluring and mystifying, and which some even mistake for magic. Unpacking intuition's strangeness, allure, and mystique begins by stripping intuition down to its essentials, and that means defining it.

Unpacking Intuition

History matters. One of the earliest and to this day most insightful analyses of the role of intuition in management decision-making is *The Functions of the Executive* by Chester Barnard published in 1938. Barnard (1886 to 1961) was not only an intellectually curious business executive of a major US corporation (president of New Jersey Bell Telephone Company, now part of Verizon) he was also a pioneering and perceptive writer on the subject of management.[27] *The Functions*, which is still in print, is Barnard's magnum opus. It is one of the most thought-provoking books on organization and management ever written by a practising executive.[28] Barnard's work has made an enormous, if not always explicitly acknowledged, 'impact on both the academic and business community'.[29]

The roots of modern intuition research are to be found not in the main body of *The Functions* but in its appendix entitled 'The Mind in Everyday Affairs'.[30] Barnard's cogent and concise exposition, which runs to just over twenty pages, is foundational not least because of the influence it had on intuition researchers who followed in his footsteps, most notably Herbert Simon. In 'The Mind in Everyday Affairs', Barnard drew a straightforward distinction between 'logical mental processes' and 'non-logical mental processes'. Logical processes are those thoughts 'that can be 'expressed in words or other symbols'.[31] On the other hand, non-logical processes are those mental processes 'not capable of being expressed in words or as reasoning, which are only made known by a judgement, decision or action'. Non-logical processes are 'unconscious' and so 'complex' and 'rapid, often approaching instantaneous', that they 'could not be analysed by the person within whose brain they take place'. Barnard attributed them to factors in the physical and social environment 'mostly impressed upon us unconsciously or without conscious effort on our part' in addition to the 'mass of facts, patterns, concepts, techniques and abstractions' which are 'impressed on our minds ... by 'conscious effort and study'.[32] Based on this clear and common-sense way of thinking, Barnard defined intuition as:

A complex and rapid mental process not capable of being expressed in words or as reasoning or analysed by the person within whose brain it takes place and manifesting in judgement, decision and action.[33] (Definition 1)

Barnard's is the first of three definitions of intuition which are cornerstones of intuition research in business. Barnard pointed out that the logical and non-logical mental processes are characteristic of different types of work, for example, logical characterizes the work of accountants and non-logical characterizes that of '"high pressure" trading', 'salesmanship', and 'in much of the work of business men [*sic*] or executives'.[34] He also argued that logical reasoning—that source of the 'incessant din of reasons'[35] that can sometimes obscure intuitions—does not necessarily denote a higher order of intellect than the non-logical processes that underlie quick judgements (i.e. 'handling of a mass of experience or complex of abstractions in a flash'). His unequivocal position is that without this capacity, which is so 'unexplainable that we call it "intuition"', managers 'could not do *any* work'.[36]

Barnard's use of accountancy as an example may be somewhat surprising and contradictory given what he said about the suitability of logical and non-logical processes for different business functions. But he argued that experienced accountants can take a complex balance sheet and within minutes or even seconds 'get a significant set of facts from it' which do not 'leap from the paper and strike the eye [of the novice]' but which 'lie between the figures in the part filled by the mind out of years of experience and technical knowledge'. The intuitable aspects of a complex balance sheet provide 'something to which then reason can usefully be applied'.[37] With impressive foresight (given later discoveries about human cognition, see Chapters 5 and 6) Barnard hints at the complementarity of the two processes: the function of the non-logical processes is 'sensing' those things which do not leap out at the eye, whilst the logical processes 'solve' through the application of reason.

Ultimately, Barnard's choice of accountancy as an example need not be problematic since it highlights the important idea that logical (analytical) and the non-logical (intuitive) processes are complementary and both are required by most if not all management functions, no matter how quantitative (or qualitative) the demands of a specific task might be. It has taken some time for management educators and researchers to accept that intuition has a vital role to play in managerial work, even though most managers would accept this as self-evident.[38] Intuition has tended to be denigrated in the social sciences more generally, which is in contrast to its status in the arts and physical sciences where it is lauded. For example, Einstein is reputed to have said: 'The intuitive mind is a sacred gift and the rational mind is a faithful servant. We have created a society that honours the servant and has forgotten the gift.' Intuition and analysis are qualitatively different ways of thinking, deciding, and problem-solving. Each is more or less appropriate depending on the task, person, and context. The most successful managers and business people have perfected the art of amalgamating, balancing, and reconciling Barnard's logical and non-logical processes, for example, 'business viability data' and 'person perception', as in the case of the business angels discussed earlier.[39]

Following Barnard's groundbreaking work in the 1930s, a further milestone in the study of intuition came several decades later in Simon's work. This culminated in his 1978 Nobel Prize in economic sciences awarded for 'his pioneering research into the decision-making process within economic organizations'.[40] It is ironic that Simon's Nobel Prize was in economics (since there is no prize in psychology) given that his theory of bounded rationality was a direct assault on classical economic models of decision-making. It marked the inception of the field of behavioural decision theory (BDT). Incidentally, but not unimportantly, the Foreword to the first edition of Simon's magnum opus, *Administrative Behaviour: A Study of Decision-Making Processes in Organizations* (first published by Macmillan in 1947 and still in print), was written by Chester Barnard. This is a testament to the influence that Barnard's writing had on Simon. Simon was impressed greatly by Barnard's account. But he was also 'troubled' by it as an explanation of intuition because it did not give any clues as to how the subconscious processes themselves operate in the lead-up to an intuitive judgement.

Simon, in his own estimation, arrived at a 'solid understanding' of what those processes are via his research on expertise in chess, most notably with his colleague William Chase. This groundbreaking work was based on the proposal that a chess grand masters' memories hold two vital pieces of information which helps them to judge whether a particular move is better executed or avoided: the first is a set of meaningful patterns that represent the arrangement of the pieces on the board; the second is information about each pattern in terms of the opportunities and threats posed. Simon's theory offered an explanation as to why chess grand masters can play several games simultaneously and make significant moves intuitively often in 'only a few seconds'.[41] He estimated that a chess master's long-term memory contains in the order of 50,000 'familiar patterns' built up over many years of learning and experience. Simon's interpretation was corroborated by World Chess Champion Garry Kasparov, who claims to be able to think up to fifteen moves ahead. Kasparov remarked that 'the total number of possible different moves in a single game of chess is more than the number of seconds that have elapsed since the big bang' and that in the chess universe 'intuition is the defining quality of a great chess player.'[42]

Simon extrapolated from research in chess to the practice of management. He argued that the intuitive skills of experienced managers depend on 'the same kinds of mechanisms as the intuitive skills of chess masters or physicians'.[43] Moreover, he remarked that it would be 'surprising if it were otherwise'[44] on the basis that the underlying processes of pattern recognition are widely applicable to judgement and decision-making (i.e. they are 'domain general' rather than being confined purely to chess).[45] Simon defined intuitions succinctly as:

> Analyses frozen into habit and into the capacity for rapid response through recognition.[46] (Definition 2)

In this view, despite appearing 'spontaneous and non-deliberative', intuition is essentially a rational rather than an irrational process. As such it 'needs no veil of mystery'.[47] Simon described intuition's best effect as being when it is 'backed up by whole volumes of knowledge … preserved in a frozen state in long-term memory until thawed by the act of recognition'.[48]

Contrary to the Swiss psychoanalyst Carl Jung's theory of psychological types,[49] Simon doubted that people, including managers, fall into stereotypical intuitive or analytical types. He thought it much more likely that managers, or at least effective managers, do 'not have the luxury of choosing between "analytic" and "intuitive" approaches to problems'.[50] Good management—indeed the 'art' of management[51]— involves an 'intimate combination'[52] of intuitive sensing and analytical solving. In the same way that Simon was troubled by Barnard's work,[i] Simon's work is also troubling in that it tends to gloss over the more affective (i.e., feelings-based) aspects of intuition—gut feelings, hunches, and vibes[53]—which Barnard himself referred to as 'this feeling in our "marrow"'.[54] This is important because intuition is unique in that it exists at the nexus of cognition (thinking) and affect (feeling).[55]

Two decades after Simon's seminal article in 1987 on the role of intuition in management decisions,[56] American management researchers Erik Dane and Michael G Pratt identified three blockages to a productive discourse on intuition in business. Firstly, considerable confusion about what intuition is. Secondly, failure to distinguish between the process of intuiting and the outcome of that process, intuition. Thirdly, a lack of understanding of the conditions that foster the effective use of intuition, and hence disagreements about if and when it can be trusted.[57] They described the process of intuiting as 'nonconscious' (i.e. outside of conscious awareness), involving 'holistic associations' (meaning that cues in the environment are matched with patterns in long-term memory), and 'rapid' (or comparatively so compared with the operations of the rational system). The outcome of intuiting—the intuitive judgement itself—is 'affectively charged' (involves cognitive feelings, gut feelings, gut instincts, etc.) which give rise to feelings of knowing, even though the knower may not know exactly how they have come to know. In the words of the philosopher Michael Polanyi they 'know more than they can tell'. Dane and Pratt produced what has become for many intuition researchers the consensus definition:

---

[i] Because it failed to offer any explanation for the underlying cognitive mechanisms for non-logical processes.

Intuitions are affectively charged judgments that arise through rapid, nonconscious, and holistic associations.[58] (Definition 3)

In formulating this description, they successfully addressed two of their three barriers, i.e. confusion about what intuition is and the failure to distinguish between intuiting and intuition. The third barrier—lack of understanding of the conditions that foster the effective use of intuition—is one of the focal points of intuition research. The question of not 'if' but 'when does intuition work best?' is the subject of ongoing inquiry and of much of this book.

The seminal contributions of Barnard, Simon, and Dane and Pratt provide an answer to the question 'what is intuition?'

Intuition is an involuntary, difficult-to-articulate, affect-laden recognition or judgement, based on prior learning and experiences and arrived at rapidly without deliberate or conscious rational thought.[59]

A shortish answer to the question of 'when does intuition work best?' is that intuition works best when it is exercised by the right person, at the right time, under the right circumstances. A useful starting point in trying to understand why this is the case is to try to get closer to the subjective experience of intuition itself.

The 'Sixth Sense'?

In terms of its proximity to consciousness,[60] the unconscious process of intuiting leads to a conscious outcome, intuition. This outcome manifests as bodily sensations referred to variously as gut feelings, hunches, vibes, etc. Intuiting is both 'embrained' (in that there are cognitive processes—albeit unconscious—which lead to the outcome) and 'embodied' (in that awareness of it is experienced as a 'felt-sense').[61] Evidence for intuition as a universal and embodied phenomenon is to be found in the words used to describe it across human languages and cultures. 'Gut feeling' in Greek is 'éntero' (έντερο), in Chinese it is 'Zhíjué' (直觉), in Hindi it is 'saahasee bhaavana' (साहसी भावना), and in Korean it is 'jiggam' (직감).[62]

Although the person experiencing the intuition (the intuitor) cannot comprehend fully where their gut feelings emanate from, they are nonetheless aware of the outcome in the form of an intuitive felt-sense.[63] That said, as we shall see in Chapter 6, there are certain circumstances in which our decisions can be influenced by our intuitions without us necessarily being aware that our 'gut', and not our head, appears to be the one that is in charge.[64] Irrespective of how the process operates (and more of that in the subsequent chapters) the result is that the person experiencing the intuition feels or thinks, via a gut feeling or a hunch, that they 'know without knowing how or why they know'.[65]

But what does it feel like to know without knowing how or why you know, or to put it another way 'what happens when you intuit?' In my own research I asked a sample of 127 human resource (HR) managers to answer the question 'what happens when you intuit?' As far as the process of intuiting itself was concerned, HR managers' prior experiences (for example, 'elements of my experience come together to shape my thoughts and actions') and perception of cues ('I recognize cues') resulted in a process that was automatic ('I feel something to be true without analysing it'), fast ('I make a decision quickly'), and subconscious ('it feels as though an answer appears from nowhere'). In terms of outcomes, the HR managers distinguished between bodily awarenesses as feelings ('a whole body feeling') and gut reactions ('I get feelings in my stomach'), and cognitive awarenesses, for example, as mental imagery (an aural image 'I listen to that small voice in my head'). The outcomes manifested as insights ('connections between previous unconnected or apparently unrelated ideas') and as both positive signals ('something clicks inside that I recognize as clearly right') and negative signals ('I know something is wrong'). Managers used these signals for anticipating ('I sense that someone is going to say something'), deciding ('guides me towards concrete direction, decision or action'), judging ('I cannot rationalize an absolute decision so I make a casting vote based on intuition'), and questioning ('I ask myself what's really going on here').[66]

The aim of this research was to try and get close up to managers' subjective experiences of intuition; it illustrates a number of important general points about intuition as a 'sense'. Intuition is sometimes referred to metaphorically as a 'sixth sense'; this is not a wholly inappropriate way of thinking about it given that intuition works by interpreting information provided by the other five sense perceptions. For example, wine experts use taste and smell to intuitively identify the year, the grape, and sometimes even the exact vineyard where a particular wine was produced. Expert firefighters are able to use the sound of the blaze and the sponginess of a surface to judge whether a burning building is about to collapse. Art experts are able to judge instantaneously from the merest glimpse whether a work of art is a fake. The five sense perceptions work from outside to inside; cues from the outside world are perceived and processed. Intuition, on the other hand, works from the inside to outside; signals from the inside world (in the form of an intuitive felt-sense) are presented to us from within and inform our thoughts, actions, and behaviours. But even as a metaphorical 'sixth sense', no paranormal explanation of intuition is necessary.

If and how this information is interpreted and whether it leads to an accurate judgement depends on the person's prior knowledge and experiences (some people have much more experience than others on which to base their intuitions) as well as on the situation (some situations are more amenable to being judged intuitively than others). This means that not everybody will arrive at the same intuition even though they experience the same cues; for example, a novice who tastes and smells a vintage wine or sees a genuine work of art is likely to come to a quite different, less informed, and more hit-or-miss interpretation compared to that of an expert, even though they will be drinking the same drink and looking at the same image. Experts, whether it be in wine or art connoisseurship, chess, firefighting, or management, see and interpret the world quite differently from non-experts. Experts, by dint of their know-how, are able to come up with gist-based interpretations which help them to navigate their world intuitively.⁶⁷ Intuitive expertise may be marvellous in terms of what it can achieve, but it does not require mystical, magical, or paranormal explanations to account for how it works.

Incidentally, the question of whether intuition operates at the level of a 'supra-consciousness' was alluded to by intuition researchers Marta Sinclair and Neal Ashkanasy. They speculated that in future it might be necessary to depart from conventional psychology to explain intuition, for example by reference to transpersonal psychology and other spiritual and transcendental perspectives that acknowledge the possibilities for 'alternate realities'.⁶⁸ A 'spiritual intuition' has been mooted which offers holistic perception of reality that transcends rational, dualistic ways of knowing and gives the individual a 'direct transpersonal experience of the underlying oneness of life'.⁶⁹

Intuition Makes Sense

Police work is a demanding business. Police officers often have to make sense of situations that initially do not make sense in order to take sometimes urgent and often consequential decisions in uncertain, ambiguous, complex, and fast-moving environments. Much police work involves situations in which officers are required to use their experience to take actions spontaneously to resolve a situation, for example, a person who is in the precarious position of having fallen into a fast-flowing river and has to be rescued immediately. Other aspects of police work cannot be resolved so instinctively, for example, when a mother calls to make a complaint of a domestic dispute involving a child but when the officers arrive the mother claims that everything is now okay, despite the fact that her partner is nowhere to be seen and the child appears to be brooding and withdrawn.

In the first example of the river rescue, it is clear what the circumstances are and what needs to be done: officers have to see and respond. In the second example of the domestic dispute, the circumstances are ambiguous and perplexing; what needs to be done next is not clear, and officers have to sense, inquire, interpret, and respond. Skilled police officers make sense of such situations by interpreting the observable cues in terms of their previous experiences so as to develop a plausible meaning that can be used as a basis for action. Their intuition tells them that the situation does not look right and therefore they need to find out why and then act accordingly. They intuit their way into sense.⁷⁰

Sense-making is the act of developing ideas that make the explanation of ambiguous, equivocal, or confusing events possible.⁷¹ People use sense-making when they are initially confused and cannot choose between different interpretations of an ambiguous situation and decide what the best course of action is likely to be.⁷² In intuitive sense-making, someone notices something as surprising because the cues do not fit with an established pattern which makes it 'out of kilter' with their experiences and expectations. The initial intuitive response is likely to be experienced bodily through gut feelings and hunches and intellectually through puzzlement and perplexity. Intuitions are activated as a result of cues, such as a person's verbal and non-verbal behaviours, violating expectations and causing surprise. Things not making sense prompts the making of sense. In such situations it is necessary to come up with a plausible explanation in order to respond with a reasonable and justified action; moreover, it is not possible to simply edit intuition out of the decision-maker's lived experience.[73]

In the domestic dispute example above, officers engaged in a process of sense-making by the rational process of inquiring (see Chapter 4). The officers were 'thrown' via their intuitions into inquiring, rather than into acting, by the uniqueness of the situation.[74] They had to inquire because their initial sense that was personal, partially formed, intuitive, tacit, and complex needed to be turned into something that was simpler, fully formed, more ordered, and could be articulated so as to be usable by other stakeholders (in the police example these were the participants, colleagues, and the judiciary).[75] In the process of sense-making, intuition acquires new properties: it transitions from being tacit, ineffable, and nebulous to explicit, detectable, and solid. As the eminent organization theorist Karl Weick commented: 'Intuiting, rather than intuitions, is what moves an initial tacit, intimate, and complex sense into a public, simpler, ordered sense.'[76]

In acquiring new properties, for example by becoming more solidified, intuitions can become not only explanatory (explaining ambiguous events), but they can also become generative (creating new ideas). As such they assist in the process of foreseeing. Innovation and new product development (NPD) is the life blood of growth in high-tech firms but the front end of the process is typically fuzzy, and effort and resources can go to waste. One of the reasons for this is that the critical success factors (CSFs) which influence idea screening at the NPD front end and help to weed out unpromising ideas can often be tacit, ineffable, and nebulous. Managers may know the CSFs when they see them and take them for granted. Carnegie Mellon University Software Engineering Institute's 'CSF Method' taps into managers' intuitions by making their 'sixth sense' explicit so that the organization can use it.[77] The CSF method is based on the idea that every organization already has a set of CSFs, but these are often tacit, hence it may not 'know that it knows'. The former CEO of Hewlett Packard (HP), Lew Platt, is reputed to have said that 'If HP knew what HP knows, we'd be three times more productive.'[78] In the medical device industry, which thrives on NPD, the CSF method has been used to glean a set of simple and seemingly obvious rules of thumb that are sometimes taken for granted but when harvested and articulated can be used to make the NPD process far smarter, for example: 'resource requirements are clearly documented', 'the project has the ability to meet customer needs', 'the right people are active in the right place at the right time', 'criteria are established to promote or kill the project', 'competitive advantage from the project is clear', etc. Identifying CSFs makes explicit those things that the skilled manager knows intuitively but which must be interpreted, integrated, and institutionalized in order to guide and direct the process of organizing. Making sense of CSFs that experienced managers rely on intuitively makes the fuzzy front end of the NPD process more efficient by reducing the time taken, having fewer failures, being less wasteful of resources, and, ultimately, increasing the chances of success.[79]

Sharing individual managers' intuitions, for example by encoding them as simple rules, is one way to build what have become known as 'collective intuitions'.[80] Strategic management researchers Christopher Bingham and Kathleen Eisenhardt documented numerous simple rules based on collective intuitions that were a source of competitive advantage for technology-based ventures that were seeking to internationalize, for example 'enter one continent at a time', 'sell through partners first, then build direct channels', 'place greatest emphasis on government accounts', etc. Once captured, these rules seem like common sense, but only once they are distilled from the experiences and intuitions of individual managers.[81]

Instinct or Intuition?

A no-nonsense perspective on intuition in business is to be found in the autobiography of Jack Welch (1935 to 2020 and former CEO and Chairman of General Electric from 1981 to 2001) which is entitled *Straight from the Gut* (2001). For Welch a 'tin gut' (analogous to the metaphorical 'tin ear') can incapacitate managers; on the other hand strong and effective leaders have 'an instinct for business—a "gut" that guides them well'.[82] Likewise, Bill Gates in articulating his 'grudging respect' for Steve Jobs, commented that although 'He [Jobs] never really knew much about technology … he had an amazing instinct for what works.'[83] Sir Richard Branson in his autobiography *Losing my Virginity* commented that he relies 'far more on gut instinct that researching huge amounts of statistics'.[84]

Sometimes following your instinct means going out on a limb and against the grain. There are plenty of examples in the popular business press of executives who did so and it paid off. Henry Ford is reputed to have used his business instinct in 1914 to meet the challenge of falling demand for his vehicles and high employee turnover. His instinct was to double his employees' wages. Many in the industry thought he had made a grave error, however, within a year employee turnover had fallen by 20 per cent, productivity doubled, and demand for Ford motor vehicles doubled partly because employees could now afford the cars they were making.[85] Boeing CEO Bill Allen's instinctive decision in the 1950s to expand out of the military aircraft market and into commercial airliners in the project to develop the Boeing 707, which could hold up to 190 passengers, was met with howls of derision, but it ended-up transforming both his own company and the business of air travel.[86] Chrysler CEO Bob Lutz's decision to go with his gut to develop a 'muscular, outrageous sports car that would turn heads and stop traffic' was opposed vehemently by the 'naysayers' and 'bean counters'. The Dodge Viper was a product of Lutz's executive instinct, in his own words 'a visceral feeling [that] just felt right' which turned out to be a commercial success.[87]

'Gut instinct', 'business instinct', or 'executive instinct' are often endorsed by business biographers and the popular press as desirable management and leadership attributes. But whilst instinct might be an appealing and catchy metaphor for how senior managers, usually male, take decisive actions, it is potentially unhelpful in arriving at a scientific understanding of intuition in business decision-making. In its proper sense, instinct is a biological term that is best confined to behaviours and responses that are pre-programmed genetically into an organism. Such behaviours include a baby's grasping reflex and other hardwired behaviours such as the homing instinct in pigeons. Instinct in the context of intuition in business is a metaphor. How expert executives and managers come to be able to intuitively, and on the face of it 'instinctively', navigate the risky and uncertain world of business world is much more likely to be a product of their experiences and their situation than any hardwired instinct or genetic predisposition. For these reasons gut instinct is a term that is perhaps best avoided. The seemingly related term 'insight' is, likewise, not the same thing as intuition even though intuition and insight are sometimes used interchangeably. The differences between them are explored in Chapter 10.

The Science of Intuition in Business

The business of intuitive judgement—and whether intuition should be trusted or not—is a complex and contested matter. Behavioural and brain scientists have expended a great deal of effort both in the laboratory and in the field in order to understand the conditions under which intuition helps or hinders decision-making. Common sense tells us that it is less a question of *if* intuition can be trusted, and more a question of *when* intuition can be trusted.[88] Is there a key ingredient that separates good from bad intuitions?

Research into expert performers in areas as diverse as chess, firefighting, policing, medicine, and management conducted over the best part of half a century consistently shows that being able to make sense of and respond intuitively and effectively in complex and uncertain situations is very much a matter of not only the quantity but also the *quality* of one's experiences.[89] Extensive high-quality learning and experience helps mind *and* body adapt to what is required in a specific situation[90] and builds the capacity for rapid response through recognition.[91] Experienced decision-makers know without necessarily knowing how or why they know; their intuitive knowledge is hard to articulate or 'tacit' (from the Latin *tacēre* meaning 'to be silent').[92]

In the early years of this century only a small handful of scientific works existed on the subject of intuition in business decision-making. By contrast, there was a plethora of popular self-help books by advocates of intuition, for example *Intuition and Beyond*[93] claims benefits of 'more abundance' and 'greater financial freedom', *Awakening Intuition*[94] promises to help readers use their 'mind-body network for insight and healing', and *Intuition by Design* is based on 'subtle energy geometrics'. Managers who wondered whether intuition could add value to business decision-making could be excused for being confused. There was little in the way of hard evidence for where and how intuition worked over and above general discussions of the benefits of using intuition (for example, it expedites and improves decision-making)[95] and suggestions for how to use intuition (for example, 'getting a feel for your intuitive batting average' and 'getting good feedback' on your intuitive decisions).[96] This early work, whilst doing much to raise the profile of intuition in business, was based more on conjecture than on substantive research evidence. To move the scientific study of intuition in business forward, more was needed than anecdotes and advice. Fortunately, a considerable body of empirical evidence has accumulated over the past two decades. This work, rather than being mere advocacy for intuition, takes an objective view and shows that intuition works well, but only under certain conditions, and consequently has the potential to both be the managers' friend and a foe in the complex and uncertain business environment of the twenty-first century.[97]

One of the groundbreaking studies of intuition in business was conducted by Naresh Khatri and Alvin Ng in the early 2000s. They set out to explore if there were particular conditions under which strategic intuitive decisions are more likely to work well. They looked at how the interaction between intuitive decision-making and the stability of a firm's business environment affected financial performance (for example, profits and growth) and non-financial performance (for example, operational efficiency). Did intuition work best in stable or unstable conditions? Khatri and Ng's proposition was that in fast-moving, unstable environments boundedly rational managers must combine real-time information about their environment gleaned from multiple sources (for example, markets, finance, competition, technology, policy, etc.) and integrate this into a holistic, intuitive assessment of how to act. They surveyed managers in three contrasting industries that varied in terms of competition, technology, and government regulation: the computer industry characterized by high instability; banking, moderate instability; public utilities, low instability.

Khatri and Ng found that the use of intuition in strategic decision-making was positively related to organizational performance in an unstable environment (i.e. the computing industry) whereas intuition was negatively related to performance in a stable environment (i.e. the public utilities industry). Their results showed that intuition is advantageous in fast-moving sectors and markets which tend to be more unstable and where creativity, innovation, and first-mover advantage are important. However, they also concluded that intuition needs to be used cautiously and much less often in stable and moderately unstable environments.

I extended this work a few years later in a longitudinal study of decision-making in the fast-moving entrepreneurial environment of small business management in the UK. I found that intuitive decision-making was associated with superior financial performance (sales growth, objectively measured) and non-financial performance (efficiency, reputation, and product and service quality) both over the shorter and longer terms.[98] In the years since Khatri and Ng conducted their groundbreaking study, the business environment in general has become more unstable. It is not unreasonable to assume, therefore, that across businesses the ability to sense intuitively as well as solve analytically are likely to be key ingredients of organizational resilience and sustainability.[99]

By the end of the first decade of the twenty-first century, management researchers had built a solid framework which offered empirical evidence for intuition's role in business decision-making, especially in fast-moving environments. A study by

Mark Fenton-O'Creevy and colleagues of the use of intuition by traders in four leading investment banks in the City of London found that higher-performing traders reported that they often relied on their intuition. Unsurprisingly, given what has already been said, higher-performing traders did not just 'go with their gut'. Instead they tended to weigh their gut feelings critically alongside other evidence and to introspect about the whys and wherefores of their gut feelings in order to pin down what their instincts were telling them.[100] One experienced higher performing trader remarked that 'there are very good traders that say they're trading off gut feel ... but perhaps they're not analysing what they're actually thinking ... they're seeing a lot of customer flow and a lot of buyers and they probably don't necessarily realize the reasons why they want to buy.' The knowledge that these experienced high-performing traders were using was acquired experientially and used intuitively. In contrast with the intelligent use of intuition by experienced high-performing traders, lower-performing traders tended to rely exclusively on gut feelings and were less disposed towards thinking critically about their hunches. Somewhat worryingly, one low-performing trader remarked, 'It's almost like a sixth sense. Something comes over you and you feel like—yes I know they're going to be looking to buy these later on or looking to sell these later on.'

Fenton-O'Creevy's research suggests that there is more to making effective use of intuition than simply having a quantity of experience. He and his team found that use of intuition increases quantitatively with traders' experience (i.e. they became more intuitive over the years), however, the way that experienced traders used their intuition varied qualitatively between the higher and lower performers. High-performing traders consciously tried to make sense of their intuitions before acting on them, this involved the skill of engaging with intuitions 'meta-cognitively', i.e. they thought critically about their intuitive thinking processes.[ii] Managers, such as the traders in this study, must be able to make sense not only of the problems they have to solve and the decisions they are required to take but also make sense of their intuitions in order to be able to determine if and when they are to be trusted.

Caveat Emptor

Because our 'intuitive mind' works automatically and effortlessly, we typically do not have to ask it what it 'thinks'—it tells us, whether we want it to or not. 'Intuitive hits' such as those of Jack Welch at General Electric or Bob Lutz at Chrysler are highly visible. They get promulgated and perpetuated in the business press and CEO biographies, end up being part of business folklore, and perpetuate a macho 'go-with-your-gut' myth. What are less well known are the 'intuitive misses' and the potential that intuition has for getting it wrong. In areas of business, from strategic planning through human resources to finance and accounting, managers regularly have to

---

[ii] Meta-cognition is 'thinking about thinking'. Hence engaging with one's intuitions 'metacognitively' means thinking about one's intuitive thinking processes.

decide whether not they should trust their intuitions when they take important, and potentially career- and business-changing, decisions. It is tempting to 'go with your gut' when time and information are scarce. However, problems are likely to follow when an intuitive sense of 'feeling good' about something is conflated with accuracy of judgement. Obviously, simply because a decision *feels* right does not mean that it *is* right. For example, a popular mantra in many intuition self-help books is that intuition 'always shows the best route'.[101] Decades of research in the behavioural sciences into the biases that bedevil human judgement tell us that this statement cannot possibly be true (more of this in Chapter 2). Therefore, following your intuition indiscriminately could be the first step on the slippery slope of an undiscerning, uninformed, and ultimately unintelligent, use of intuition. It is worth reiterating: the conditional statement '*if* I simply feel good about a judgement, *then* I must be right about it' does not hold true.[102] Simply feeling right about a business decision can be a short cut to errors and biases and opens the door to naïve and wishful thinking and false hopes. It can, more perniciously, lead to prejudice and discrimination. One of intuition's more perilous features is that it is sometimes wrong but rarely in doubt.

A case in point is employee selection decisions. HR practitioners have been criticized for a 'stubborn' over-reliance on intuitive judgements despite the availability of rigorously researched scientific approaches to decisions about hiring.[103] Nonetheless many managers will testify, quite genuinely and sincerely, that going with their gut has served them well in making new hires.[104] However, one of the problems of going with your gut in such situations is that as human beings we engage automatically in intuitive categorizations based on stereotypes in a fast, automatic process of impression formation.[105] For example, it has been long established that we intuitively like and are attracted to people who we perceive to be like us and hence are more likely to hire them. Unfortunately, the fact that we may be doing so, and reasons for it, may not be known immediately to us or open to introspection—the result can be an unconscious bias.[106] The intuitive mind operates on the basis of implicit categorization processes[107] and when intuition is used indiscriminately, for example in hiring decisions, managers run the risk of violating principles of fairness, justice, and equity as well as their own professional standards. They may also create an echo chamber of their own making which reproduces and replicates their own beliefs and values.[108]

Deciding whether to go with your gut is surrounded by tensions, contradictions, and paradoxes. The challenge for managers is not to simply 'feel' right about their intuitions and go with them because they feel good. The challenge is to find ways to build intuitive 'muscle power',[109] develop strategies for integrating and reconciling the sometimes contradictory voices from their intuitive and analytical minds, and ultimately to develop an informed intuitive intelligence. Until relatively recently, the expectation had been that when managers take decisions they leave their intuitions at home or consign them to the closet ('Don't trust your gut'[110]) and exercise choices in ways that are consistent with economic principles such as 'optimization' and 'maximizing utility' (more on these concepts in the next chapter). This is likely to be in line both with societal expectations and with what managers are likely to have been taught in training courses and business schools. However, the reality of decision-making in a world that is often unknowable and radically uncertain is somewhat different.[111] It is also against our human nature. Intuition does have a place in business decision-making, and intuitive intelligence begins with a solid understanding of the science of intuition and an appreciation of its powers and perils.

Artificial Intuition: The New AI?

In the middle of the last century the psychologist Paul Meehl in his book *Clinical Versus Statistical Prediction* (1954) compared how well the subjective predictions of trained clinicians such as physicians, psychologists, and counsellors fared when compared with predictions based on simple statistical algorithms.[112] To many people's surprise, Meehl found that experts' accuracy of prediction, for example trained counsellors' predictions of college grades, was either matched or exceeded by the algorithm. The decision-making landscape that Meehl studied has been transformed radically by the technological revolutions of the 'Information Age'.[113] Computers have exceeded immeasurably the human brain's computational capacity. Big data, data analytics, machine learning (ML), and artificial intelligence (AI) have been described as 'the new oil'.[114] They have opened up possibilities for outsourcing to machines many of the tasks that were until recently the exclusive preserve of humans.[115] The influence of AI and machine learning is extending beyond relatively routine and sometimes mundane tasks such as cashiering in supermarkets. AI now figures prominently behind the scenes in things as diverse as social media feeds, the design of smart cars, and online advertising. It has extended its reach into complex professional areas such as medical diagnoses, investment banking, and even in scriptwriting for advertisements.[116]

There is nothing new in machines replacing humans: they did so in the mechanizations of agriculture and industry in the agricultural and industrial revolutions and since the 1980s many blue collar jobs are now performed by robots. We now find ourselves in the fourth industrial revolution, but Daniel Suskind, author of *World without Work*, thinks the current technological revolution is different. The power with which robots and computers are able to perform tasks at high speed, with high accuracy, at scale using computational capabilities are orders of magnitude greater than those of any human or previous technology. This is one reason why this revolution is different and why it has been referred to as nothing less than the 'biggest event in human history' by Stuart Russell, founder of the Centre for Human-Compatible Artificial Intelligence at the University of California, Berkeley.[117]

The widespread availability of data, along with cheap, scalable computational power, and rapid and ongoing developments of new AI techniques such as machine learning and deep learning have meant that AI has become a powerful tool in business management.[118] Examples include Amazon's Prime Air, which delivers packages using autonomous, small drones; McDonald's use of voice-based AI for ordering at drive-throughs; and Macy's On Call personal in-store assistant which gives shoppers customized answers to the kind of questions they would normally ask a sales associate face to face.[119] The financial services industry deals with high-stakes, complex problems involving large numbers of interacting variables. It has developed AI that can be used to identify cybercrime schemes such as money laundering, fraud, and ATM hacking.[120] By using complex algorithms, 'fourth generation AI' can uncover fraudulent activity that is hidden amongst millions of innocent transactions and alert human analysts with easily digestible, traceable, and logged data to help them to decide whether activity is suspicious or not and take the appropriate action.[121] There are few areas of business which are likely to be exempt from AI's influence.

Creativity is vitally important in many aspects of business management. It is perhaps one area in which we might assume that humans will always have the edge. However, creative industries, such as advertising, are using AI for idea generation. The car manufacturer Lexus used IBM's Watson AI to write the 'world's most intuitive car ad' for a new model, the strapline for which is 'The new Lexus ES. Driven by intuition'.[122] The aim was to write the ad script for what Lexus claimed to be 'the most intuitive car in the world' using a computer. To do so Watson was programmed to analyse fifteen years'-worth of award-winning footage from the prestigious Cannes Lions international award for creativity using its 'visual recognition' (which uses deep learning to analyse images of scenes, objects, faces, and other visual content), 'tone analyser' (which interprets emotions and communication style in text), and 'personality insights' (using data to make inferences about consumers' personalities) applications.[123] Watson AI helped to 're-write car advertising' by identifying the core elements of award-winning content that was both 'emotionally intelligent' and 'entertaining'. The script outline was literally written by Watson. It was then used by the creative agency, producers, and directors to build an emotionally gripping advertisement.

Even though the Lexus-IBM collaboration reflects a breakthrough application of AI in the creative industries, IBM's stated aim is not to attempt to 'recreate the human mind but to inspire creativity and free up time to spend thinking about the creative process'.[124] The question of whether Watson's advertisement is truly creative in the sense of being novel, as well as useful, is open to question given that it was based on human works that were judged to be outstandingly creative by human judges at the Cannes festival. Another example of area in which fourth-generation AI is making inroads is in the emotional and interpersonal domains. The US-based start-up Luka has developed the artificially intelligent journaling chatbot 'Replika', which is designed to encourage people to 'open up and talk about their day'.[125] Whilst Siri and Alexa are emotionally 'cold' digital assistants, Replika is claimed to be more like your 'best friend'. It injects emotion into conversations and learns from the user's questions and answers.[126]

The fact that computers are making inroads into areas that were once considered uniquely human is nothing new. Perhaps intuition is next. The roots of modern intuition research are in chess, an area of human expertise in which grand masters intuit 'the good move straight away'.[127] But in 1997, IBM's Deep Blue beat Russian chess grand master and world champion Garry Kasparov. Does this mean that

IBM's AI is able to out-intuit a human chess master? The strategy that Deep Blue used to beat Kasparov was fundamentally different from how another human being might have attempted to do so. Deep Blue did not beat Kasparov by replicating or mimicking his thinking processes, in Kasparov's own words: 'instead of a computer that thought and played like a chess champion, with human creativity and intuition, they [the "AI crowd"] got one that played like a machine, systematically, evaluating 200 million chess moves [greatly surpassing Simon's 50,000 "familiar patterns"] on the chess board per second and winning with brute number-crunching force.' Nobel laureate in physics, Richard Feynman, commented presciently in 1985 that it will be possible to develop a machine which can surpass nature's abilities but without imitating nature.[128] If a computer ever becomes capable of out-intuiting a human, it is likely that the rules that the computer relies on will be fundamentally different to those used by humans[129] and will use a very different mode of reasoning to that which evolved in the human organism over many hundreds of millennia.

But AI can also be surprisingly dumb. In medical diagnoses, even though the freckle-analysing system developed at Stanford University does not replicate how doctors exercise their intuitive judgement through 'gut feel' for skin diseases, it can nonetheless through its prodigious number-crunching power diagnose skin cancer without knowing anything at all about dermatology.[130] But as Stuart Russell remarked, the deep learning that such AI systems rely on can be quite difficult to get right, for example some of the 'algorithms that have learned to recognise cancerous skin lesions, turn out to completely fail if you rotate the photograph by 45 degrees [which] doesn't instil a lot of confidence in this technology.'[131]

Although nowhere near as humanly consequential as medical diagnoses, the credit rating decisions taken by managers in banks are nonetheless financially significant. The credit risk assessment process begins with compiling data for analysis, which is then inputted to a bank's proprietary model (e.g. a simple logistic regression equation) and which then generates an output of a preliminary rating in the form of a scorecard. The scorecard summarizes the potential borrower's likelihood of defaulting on a loan. This preliminary risk rating is then reviewed in the light of all other information about the borrower. The process of adjustment to give the final rating by the loan officer is called 'notching' and is based on their experience of making loans and their intuitions about the loan applicant. The final credit risk judgement is based on the statistical analysis plus the notching. In practice, the human assessment is typically several notches lower (i.e. judged riskier) than the computer assessment, suggesting that human intuition errs on the side of caution when judging credit worthiness.

Matthew Harding of University of California Irving and Gabriel Vasconcelos of the Brazilian Bank of Communications investigated whether it was possible to replicate this entire process using a machine learning algorithm capable of both the statistical analysis and the subjective assessment. They constructed several different algorithms which incorporated quantitative variables (e.g. company cash flow, total assets, and profit after tax) and qualitative variables (e.g. ratings of management quality, firm's outlook in the market, and vulnerability to changes in business environment). When they ran the analysis, they found that the best of the machine learning algorithms could match the final risk rating based on the computer's statistical analysis and the manager's subjective assessment with a degree of accuracy of 95 per cent. It seems as though a relatively simple machine learning algorithm can replicate almost perfectly the risk assessment made by highly skilled human judges.[132] They concluded that it could be much quicker and cheaper for banks to process loan applications using a machine instead of a human and that with additional data and computational power the algorithms could be improved even further. However, as some commentators have noted, although analysis is easy to automate, human accountability, with its various social, ethical, and political ramifications, is not and cannot be reduced to an algorithm.[133] For example, how might a machine learning algorithm rate a loan application from a financially robust terrorist group in order to finance the development of a novel, first-to-market weapon of mass destruction?

Is the balance of how we comprehend situations and take business decisions shifting inexorably away from humans and in favour of machines?[134] Is 'artificial intuition' inevitable and will it herald the demise of 'human intuition'? If an artificial intuition is eventually realized that can match that of a human, it will be one of the pivotal outcomes of the fourth industrial revolution—perhaps the ultimate form of AI. More apocalyptically, could the creation of artificial intuition be the 'canary in the coalmine', signalling the emergence of Vernor Vinge's 'technological singularity', wherein large computer networks and their users suddenly 'wake up' as 'superhumanly intelligent entities'.[135] Could such a development turn out to be a Frankenstein's monster with unknown but potentially negative, unintended consequences for its makers? The potential and the pitfalls of AI are firmly in the domain of the radically uncertain.

Making any predictions about what computers will or will not be able to do in the future is a hostage to fortune. For the foreseeable future, most managers will continue to rely on their own rather than a computer's intuitive judgements when taking both day-to-day and strategic decisions. Therefore, until a viable 'artificial intuition' arrives that is capable of out-intuiting a human, the more pressing and practical question is what value does human intuition add in business? The technological advancements of the information age have endowed machines with the hard skill of 'solving' which far outstrips this capability in the human mind. The evolved capacities of the intuitive mind have endowed managers with the arguably hard-to-automate, or perhaps even impossible-to-automate, soft skill of 'sensing'. This is the essence of human intuition.

Summary

1. The main idea of this chapter has been that human beings possess two complementary modes of thinking: intuitive (which 'senses') and analytical (which 'solves').

2. Intuition is an involuntary, difficult-to-articulate, affect-laden recognition or judgement, based on prior learning and experiences and arrived at rapidly without deliberate or conscious rational thought.
3. Human intuition is both powerful and perilous; it may help or hinder managers in making sense of situations, making decisions, and taking action.[136]
4. Naïve intuitive judgements can result in logically flawed short cuts that can lead decision-makers down blind alleys and to biased judgements.
5. Informed intuition can help managers to take quick decisions based on prior experiences (expert intuition), decipher the motives, intentions, and behaviours of others (social intuition), locate their moral compass (moral intuition), and sense novel and useful ways of solving problems (creative intuition).
6. Informed intuitions help managers to make sense of confusing situations; in the sense-making process intuitions themselves transition from being tacit, ineffable, and nebulous to explicit, detectable, and solid.
7. Intuition might also be a window into some of the more intangible and ineffable aspects of human experience.

Endnotes

1. British Academicians Letter to The Queen, 22 July 2009. Available online at: https://www.ma.imperial.ac.uk/~bin06/M3A22/queen-lse.pdf Accessed 07.02.2022.
2. Taleb, N. N. (2007). *The Black Swan: The Impact of the Highly Improbable*. London: Random House.
3. Tucker P. (2007). *A Perspective on Recent Monetary and Financial System Developments*. London: Bank of England. Available online at: https://www.bankofengland.co.uk/-/media/boe/files/news/2007/april/a-perspective-on-recent-monetary-and-financial-developments-speech-by-paul-tucker. Accessed 07.02.22.
4. Tett, G. (2015). *The Silo Effect: Why Putting Everything in Its Place Isn't Such a Bright Idea*. London: Little Brown, p. 123.
5. Tett op. cit., p. 124.
6. Barber, L. (2020). *The Powerful and the Damned: Private Diaries in Turbulent Times*. London: W. H. Allen, p. 113.
7. Barber op. cit., p.45
8. Invented by Californian asset manager Paul McCulley, see Tett op. cit., p. 126.
9. Gendlin, E. T. (1969). Focusing. *Psychotherapy: Theory, Research & Practice*, 6(1): 4–15.
10. Bartlett, J. (2018). *Led by Light*. Eugene, OR: Alight Press
11. Richardson, T. C. (2018). *Angel Intuition: A Psychic's Guide to the Language of Angels*. Woodbury, MN Llewellyn Publications:
12. Fundsquire (2020). *Business start-up statistics*. Available online at: https://fundsquire.co.uk/startup-statistics/ Accessed 07.02.2022.
13. Welch, J. (2003). *Straight from the Gut* (with John A. Byrne). London: Hodder Headline.

14. Huang, L., & Pearce, J. L. (2015). Managing the unknowable: The effectiveness of early-stage investor gut feel in entrepreneurial investment decisions. *Administrative Science Quarterly*, 60(4): 634–670, p. 644.
15. Dizikes, P. (2010). Explained: Knightian uncertainty. *MIT News*, 2 June 2010. Available online at: https://news.mit.edu/2010/explained-knightian-0602 Accessed 19.04.2022.
16. Hamilton, I. A. (2018). Jeff Bezos explains why his best decisions were based off intuition, not analysis. *Inc*. Available online at: https://www.inc.com/business-insider/amazon-ceo-jeff-bezos-says-his-best-decision-were-made-when-he-followed-his-gut.html; The Economic Club of Washington: Milestone Celebration Event, Jeff Bezos, 13 September 2018. Available online at: Jeff Bezos| The Economic Club of Washington D.C. Accessed 07.02.2022. https://www.economicclub.org/events/jeff-bezos
17. Patrick, M. (2019). Amazon Prime: Integral part of Amazon's success story. *Market Realist*. Available online at: https://marketrealist.com/2019/08/amazon-prime-integral-part-of-amazons-success-story/ Accessed 07.02.2022.
18. Bowden, M. (2012). The hunt for 'Geronimo'. *Vanity Fair*, 12 October 2012 Available online at: https://www.vanityfair.com/news/politics/2012/11/inside-osama-bin-laden-assassination-plot Accessed 07.02.2022.
19. Obama, B. (2020). *A Promised Land*. New York: Crown, p. 30.
20. Obama op. cit., p. 165
21. Obama op. cit., p. 294.
22. Jones, S. (2019). When following your gut is the only choice. *Management Today*, 7 November 2019. Available online at: https://www.managementtoday.co.uk/when-following-gut-choice/leadership-lessons/article/1665038 Accessed 21.02.2022.
23. In the same way that the British philosopher A. N. Whitehead once commented that the European philosophical tradition is a footnote to Plato.
24. Simon, H. A. (no date). The limits or the bounds of rationality. Available online at: https://www.youtube.com/watch?v=ErnWbP_Wztk Accessed 07.02.2022.
25. See Simon's concept of 'bounded rationality' in the commentary to Chapter V of: Simon, H. A. (1997) *Administrative Behaviour*. New York: Free Press.
26. Simon (1997) op. cit., p. 354.
27. Frantz, R. (2003). Herbert Simon. Artificial intelligence as a framework for understanding intuition. *Journal of Economic Psychology*, 24(2): 265–277, p. 267
28. Andrews, K. R. (1968). Introduction to the 30th Anniversary Edition of Functions of the Executive. *The Functions of the Executive*, Cambridge, MA: Harvard University Press, p. xxi.
29. Isomura, K. (2020). *Organization Theory by Chester Barnard: An Introduction*. Singapore: Springer, p. 3.
30. Appendix to the book and transcript of a 'Cyrus Fogg Bracket Lecture before the Engineering Faculty and Students of Princeton University, March 10, 1936'.
31. Barnard, C. I. (1938). *The Functions of the Executive*. Cambridge, MA: Harvard University Press, p. 302.
32. Barnard op. cit.
33. This definition is synthesized directly from Barnard's own writings.
34. Barnard op. cit., p. 303.
35. Barnard op. cit., p. 305.
36. Barnard op. cit., emphasis added.
37. Barnard op. cit., p. 306.

38. Bonabeau, E. (2003). Don't trust your gut. *Harvard Business Review*, 81(5): 116–123.
39. Huang & Pearce op. cit., p. 644.
40. The Nobel Prize. Press Release, 16 October 1978. Available online at: https://www.nobelprize.org/prizes/economic-sciences/1978/press-release/ Accessed 17.02.21.
41. Simon, H. A. (1997) *Administrative Behaviour*. New York: Free Press, p. 133
42. Matzler, K., Bailom, F., & Mooradian, T. A. (2007). Intuitive decision making. *MIT Sloan Management Review*, 49(1): 13. Available online at: https://sloanreview.mit.edu/article/intuitive-decision-making/ Accessed 07.02.2022.
43. Simon (1997) op. cit., p. 136.
44. Simon (1997) op. cit.
45. Gore, J., & Sadler-Smith, E. (2011). Unpacking intuition: A process and outcome framework. *Review of General Psychology*, 15(4): 304–316.
46. Simon (1997) op. cit., p. 63.
47. Simon (1997) op. cit., p. 331.
48. Simon, H. A. (1986). Keieisha no yakuwa sai tozure (The functions of the executive revisited). Banado: Gendai shakai to soshiki mondai, pp. 3–17, p. 5)
49. Jung, C. G. (1923). *Psychological Types*. London: Kegan Paul
50. Simon, H. A. (1987). Making management decisions: The role of intuition and emotion. *Academy of Management Perspectives*, 1(1): 57–64, p. 63.
51. Simon (1997) op. cit., p. 354.
52. Simon (1997) op. cit., p. 137.
53. Epstein, S., Pacini, R., Denes-Raj, V., & Heier, H. (1996). Individual differences in intuitive-experiential and analytical-rational thinking styles. *Journal of Personality and Social Psychology*, 71(2): 390–405.
54. Barnard, CI (1938). *The Functions of the Executive*. Cambridge, MA: Harvard University Press, p. 306. Simon's seminal *Academy of Management Executive* article (1987) is entitled 'The role of emotion and intuition in managerial decisions', a critic might argue that the respective roles of intuition and emotion are treated somewhat separately with little analysis of intuitive affect.
55. Sadler-Smith, E. (2016). The role of intuition in entrepreneurship and business venturing decisions. *European Journal of Work and Organizational Psychology*, 25(2): 212–225.
56. Simon (1987), op. cit.
57. Dane, E., & Pratt, M. G. (2007). Exploring intuition and its role in managerial decision making. *Academy of Management Review*, 32(1): 33–54. Their article received the journal's Best Article award for 2007 and at the time of writing had been cited 1795 times (only four fewer than Simon's seminal 1987 article in the *Academy of Management Executive*).
58. Dane, E., & Pratt, M. G. (2007). Exploring intuition and its role in managerial decision making. *Academy of Management Review*, 32(1): 33–54, p. 40.
59. Sadler-Smith, E. (2008). *Inside Intuition*. Abingdon: Routledge.
60. Sadler-Smith, E. (2015). Wallas' four-stage model of the creative process: More than meets the eye? *Creativity Research Journal*, 27(4): 342–352.
61. Gendlin, E. T. (1969). Focusing. *Psychotherapy: Theory, Research & Practice*, 6(1): 4–15.
62. Translations are courtesy of Google Translate.
63. Gigerenzer, G. (2007). *Gut Feelings*. London: Penguin, p. 47
64. Bechara, A., Damasio, H., Tranel, D., & Damasio, A. R. (2005). The Iowa Gambling Task and the somatic marker hypothesis: Some questions and answers. *Trends in Cognitive Sciences*, 9(4): 159–162.

65. Sadler-Smith, E., & Shefy, E. (2004). The intuitive executive: Understanding and applying 'gut feel' in decision-making. *Academy of Management Perspectives*, 18(4): 76–91.
66. Sadler-Smith, E. (2016). 'What happens when you intuit?': Understanding human resource practitioners' subjective experience of intuition through a novel linguistic method. *Human Relations*, 69(5): 1069–1093.
67. Corbin, J. C., Reyna, V. F., Weldon, R. B., & Brainerd, C. J. (2015). How reasoning, judgment, and decision making are coloured by gist-based intuition: A fuzzy-trace theory approach. *Journal of Applied Research in Memory and Cognition*, 4(4): 344–355.
68. Sinclair, M., & Ashkanasy, N. M. (2005). Intuition: Myth or a decision-making tool? *Management Learning*, 36(3): 353–370, p. 362
69. Vaughan, F. (1979). *Awakening Intuition*. New York: Anchor Press, p. 78; see also: Sadler-Smith, E., & Héliot, Y. G. (2021). Searching for spiritual intuition in management. *Journal of Management, Spirituality & Religion*, 18(4): 332–354. A further departure from the conventional 'psychologizing' of intuition might also involve philosophizing intuition in business by reference to the works of Aristotle, Plato, Anselm, Ockham, Bacon, Descartes, Spinoza, Locke, Reid, Hume, Kant, Husserl, Bergson, Deleuze, Merleau-Ponty, and others; much work remains to be done in this area.
70. This paraphrases Karl Weick's 'people act their way into sense'. Weick, K. E. (2009). *Making sense of the organization, Volume 2: The impermanent organization*. Chichester: John Wiley & Sons, p. 130.
71. Weick, K. E. (1995). *Sensemaking in Organizations*. Thousand Oaks: SAGE.
72. Sonenshein, S. (2007). The role of construction, intuition, and justification in responding to ethical issues at work: The sensemaking-intuition model. *Academy of Management Review*, 32(4): 1022–1040.
73. Cunliffe, A., & Coupland, C. (2012). From hero to villain to hero: Making experience sensible through embodied narrative sensemaking. *Human Relations*, 65(1): 63–88.
74. 'Thrown' here is used in the sense of people finding themselves 'thrown into on-going situations and have to make do if they want to make sense of what is happening … You are thrown onto your intuitions and have to deal with whatever comes up as it come up'. Op. cit., p. 44.
75. Meziani, N., & Cabantous, L. (2020). Acting intuition into sense: How film crews make sense with embodied ways of knowing. *Journal of Management Studies*, 57(7): 1384–1419.
76. Weick, K. E. (2020). Sensemaking, organizing, and surpassing: A handoff. *Journal of Management Studies*, 57(7): 1420–1431, p. 1428.
77. Caralli, R. (2004). *The Critical Success Factor Method*. Pittsburgh: Carnegie Mellon SEI.
78. Coates, J. F. (2001). One point of view: Knowledge management is a person-to-person enterprise. *Research-Technology Management*, 44(3): 9–13.
79. Russell, R. K., & Tippett, D. D. (2008). Critical success factors for the fuzzy front end of innovation in the medical device industry. *Engineering Management Journal*, 20(3): 36–43.
80. Akinci, C., & Sadler-Smith, E. (2019). Collective intuition: Implications for improved decision-making and organizational learning. *British Journal of Management*, 30(3): 558–577.
81. Bingham, C. B., & Eisenhardt, K. M. (2011). Rational heuristics: the 'simple rules' that strategists learn from process experience. *Strategic Management Journal*, 32(13): 1437–1464.

82. Sadler-Smith, E. (2016). 'What happens when you intuit?': Understanding human resource practitioners' subjective experience of intuition through a novel linguistic method. *Human Relations*, 69(5): 1069–1093, p. 114 and p. 16
83. Isaacson, W. (2014). *Steve Jobs*. New York: Simon and Schuster, p.159.
84. Branson, R. (2005) *Losing my Virginity*. London: Virgin.
85. A lead article in *Inc.* magazine entitled 'Four Leaders Who Won by Following Their Instincts (Despite Being Told They Were Crazy)'. https://www.inc.com/sunny-bonnell/how-to-follow-your-instincts-in-business-even-when-people-say-youre-crazy.html Accessed 07.02.2022.
86. Ibid.
87. Hayashi, A. M. 2001. When to trust your gut. *Harvard Business Review*, 79(2): 59–65, p. 60.
88. Gigerenzer, G. (2007). *Gut Feelings*. London: Penguin, p. 17.
89. Kahneman, D. (2011). *Thinking, fast and slow*. London: Allen Lane, p. 12.
90. Kay, J. and King, M. (2020). *Radical Uncertainty*. New York: W.W. Norton & Company, p. 268.
91. Simon (1987) op. cit., p. 63.
92. Sadler-Smith & Shefy op. cit.
93. Klinger, S. (2002). *Intuition and Beyond*. London: Rider.
94. Schulz, M. L. (1999). *Awakening Intuition*. New York: Harmony.
95. Burke, L. A., & Miller, M. K. (1999). Taking the mystery out of intuitive decision making. *Academy of Management Perspectives*, 13(4): 91–99.
96. Sadler-Smith & Shefy op. cit.
97. Miller, C. C., & Ireland, R. D. (2005). Intuition in strategic decision making: Friend or foe in the fast-paced 21st century?. *Academy of Management Perspectives*, 19(1): 19–30.
98. Sadler-Smith, E. (2004). Cognitive style and the management of small and medium-sized enterprises. *Organization Studies*, 25(2): 155–181.
99. Khatri, N., & Ng, H. A. (2000). The role of intuition in strategic decision making. *Human Relations*, 53(1): 57–86.
100. Fenton-O'Creevy, M., Soane, E., Nicholson, N., & Willman, P. 2011. Thinking, feeling and deciding: The influence of emotions on the decision making and performance of traders. *Journal of Organizational Behaviour*, 32(8): 1044–1061.
101. Gawain, S. (2000). *Developing Intuition*. Novato, CA: New World Library.
102. Dane, E., & Pratt, M. G. (2007). Exploring intuition and its role in managerial decision making. *Academy of Management Review*, 32(1): 33–54.
103. Highhouse, S. (2008). Stubborn reliance on intuition and subjectivity in employee selection. *Industrial and Organizational Psychology*, 1(3): 333–342, p. 333.
104. Miles, A., & Sadler-Smith, E. (2014). 'With recruitment I always feel I need to listen to my gut': the role of intuition in employee selection. *Personnel Review*, 43(4): 606–627.
105. Derous, E., & Ryan, A. M. (2019). When your resume is (not) turning you down: Modelling ethnic bias in resume screening. *Human Resource Management Journal*, 29(2): 113–130.
106. Montoya, R. M., Horton, R. S., & Kirchner, J. (2008). Is actual similarity necessary for attraction? A meta-analysis of actual and perceived similarity. *Journal of Social and Personal Relationships*, 25(6): 889–922.

107. Greenwald, A. G., & Banaji, M. R. (1995). Implicit social cognition: Attitudes, self-esteem, and stereotypes. *Psychological Review*, 102(1): 4–27; Greenwald, A. G., & Krieger, L. H. (2006). Implicit bias: Scientific foundations. *California Law Review*, 94(4): 945–967.
108. Sadler-Smith, E., Akstinaite, V., & Akinci, C. (2021). Identifying the linguistic markers of intuition in human resource (HR) practice. *Human Resource Management Journal* (in press).
109. Klein, G. A. (2017). *Sources of Power: How People Make Decisions*. Cambridge, MA: MIT Press.
110. Bonabeau op. cit.
111. Kay, J., & King, M. (2020). *Radical Uncertainty*. New York: W.W. Norton & Company.
112. Meehl, P. E. (1954). *Clinical versus Statistical Prediction: A Theoretical Analysis and a Review of the Evidence*. University of Minnesota Press.
113. Liebowitz, J. (Ed.). (2014). *Bursting the Big Data Bubble: The Case for Intuition-Based Decision Making*. Boca Raton: CRC Press.
114. Sadler-Smith, E. (2014). Researching intuition: A curious passion. In Liebowitz, J. (Ed.). *Bursting the Big Data Bubble: The Case for Intuition-Based Decision Making*. Boca Raton: CRC Press, pp. 3–20.
115. Marr, B. (2019). 13 mind-blowing things artificial intelligence can already do today. *Forbes*. Available online at: https://www.forbes.com/sites/bernardmarr/2019/11/11/13-mind-blowing-things-artificial-intelligence-can-already-do-today/?sh=721c3a216502 Accessed 07.02.2022.
116. Du Sautoy, M. (2019). *The Creativity Code*. Cambridge, MA: Belknap Press.
117. Russell, S. (2020). *Living with artificial intelligence (1): 'The biggest event in human history'* The Reith Lectures. London: BBC. https://www.bbc.co.uk/programmes/m001216j Accessed 07.02.2022.
118. Overgoor, G., Chica, M., Rand, W., & Weishampel, A. (2019). Letting the computers take over: Using AI to solve marketing problems. *California Management Review*, 61(4): 156–185.
119. Huang, M. H., & Rust, R. T. (2021). Engaged to a robot? The role of AI in service. *Journal of Service Research*, 24(1): 30–41; D'Innocenzio A. (2016). Macy's has launched an in-store shopping assistant powered by IBM's Watson AI tech. *Insider*. Available online at: https://www.businessinsider.com/ap-macys-tests-artificial-intelligence-tool-to-improve-service-2016-7?r=US&IR=T Accessed 07.02.2022.
120. Gazit, M. (2020). The fourth generation of AI is here, and it's called 'Artificial Intuition'. *Neural*. Available online at: https://thenextweb.com/neural/2020/09/03/the-fourth-generation-of-ai-is-here-and-its-called-artificial-intuition/ Accessed 07.02.2022.
121. Softtek (2020). The fourth generation of AI arrives: Artificial intuition. Available online at: https://www.vectoritcgroup.com/en/tech-magazine-en/artificial-intelligence-en/fourth-generation-of-ai-arrives-artificial-intuition/ Accessed 07.02.2022.
122. Ma, L., & Sun, B. (2020). Machine learning and AI in marketing – Connecting computing power to human insights. *International Journal of Research in Marketing*, 37(3): 481–504.
123. Medway, R. (2018). Lexus Europe Creates World's Most Intuitive Car Ad with IBM Watson. *IBM Think Blog*. Available online at: https://www.ibm.com/blogs/think/2018/11/lexus-europe-creates-worlds-most-intuitive-car-ad-with-ibm-watson/ Accessed 07.02.2022.
124. Ibid.

125. Boran, M. (2017). Sorry, Domhnall Gleeson, I don't want to chat to you anymore. *The Irish Times*. Available online at: https://www.irishtimes.com/business/technology/sorry-domhnall-gleeson-i-don-t-want-to-chat-to-you-anymore-1.3265913
126. The Emotional Chatbots Are Here to Probe Our Feelings. *Wired*. 31 January 2018. Available online at: https://www.wired.com/story/replika-open-source/ Accessed 07.02.2022
127. Gobet, F., & Chassy, P. (2009). Expertise and intuition: A tale of three theories. *Minds and Machines*, 19(2): 151–180, p. 152
128. Susskind, R. E., & Susskind, D. (2015). *The Future of the Professions: How Technology Will Transform the Work of Human Experts*. New York: Oxford University Press.
129. Gigerenzer G. (2007). *Gut Feelings*. London: Penguin, p. 60
130. Susskind, D. (2020). *A World without Work: Technology, Automation and How We Should Respond*. London: Penguin.
131. Russell, S. (2020). *Living with artificial intelligence (1): 'The biggest event in human history'* The Reith Lectures. London: BBC. https://www.bbc.co.uk/programmes/m001216j Accessed 07.02.2022.
132. Harding, M., & Vasconcelos, G. F. (2022). Managers versus Machines: Do Algorithms Replicate Human Intuition in Credit Ratings?. arXiv preprint arXiv:2202.04218.
133. English Times (2022). 'Simple' AI can anticipate bank managers' loan decisions to over 95% accuracy. *English Times*. 20 February 2022. Available online at: https://englishtimes.uk/simple-ai-can-anticipate-bank-managers-loan-decisions-to-over-95-accuracy Accessed 22.02.2022.
134. Smith School of Business—Insight—Intuition in the Age of Big Data (queensu.ca).
135. https://frc.ri.cmu.edu/~hpm/book98/com.ch1/vinge.singularity.html
136. Myers, D. G. (2010). Intuition's powers and perils. *Psychological Inquiry*, 21(4): 371–377.

2
How Intuition Sometimes Gets It Wrong

Heuristics and Biases

Overview

The main idea of this chapter is that intuition can lead to inaccurate and biased judgements under particular sets of conditions as a result of the use of certain types of mental short cuts or 'heuristics'. The theory of 'heuristics and biases', which was the product of a seminal programme of research instigated by Daniel Kahneman and Amos Tversky, is centre stage. Two types of heuristics that have particular relevance for business decision-making are discussed: the 'representativeness' heuristic and the 'availability' heuristic. Heuristics are a reflection of the inherent computational limitations of the human mind. It is for this reason that the chapter begins with a discussion of a concept which is as important to intuition research as gravity is to physics, the concept of 'bounded rationality'.

Nobel and the Limits of Rationality

The Swedish chemist, engineer, inventor, businessman, and philanthropist Alfred Nobel (1833 to 1896) in his last will and testament gave the largest share of his fortune to the 'annual awarding of a series of prizes in physics, chemistry, physiology or medicine, literature and peace for contributions that have conferred the greatest benefit to humankind'. Amongst the physics laureates, for example, are Marie Curie (1903), Max Planck (1918), Albert Einstein (1921), and Niels Bohr (1922). Intuition researchers are fortunate to have amongst their ranks not one but two Nobel laureates in Herbert Simon and Daniel Kahneman, both of whom were awarded the prize for work based on two closely connected ideas that are as important to intuition research as gravity and energy are to physics: 'bounded rationality' and 'heuristics'. This chapter focuses on their works.

The first of these, Herbert Simon, contributed enduring insights regarding decision-making in general and intuition in particular. His discoveries were a product of his dissatisfaction with the inconsistencies he observed in economists' depiction of human decision processes, in particular their classical theories of 'utility maximization' (getting the highest level of satisfaction from an economic decision). Economic rationality is scrupulously logical and is based on rational actor assumptions. However, one of its drawbacks is that it inhabits an idealized world, and in his critique—encapsulated in his theory of 'bounded rationality'—Simon argued that actual decision-making behaviour in the real world falls short of perfect, economic rationality in a number of ways.[1]

Take the important decision of deciding whether or not to invest in a particular stock: this decision will be bounded by the constraints of time (a stock trader may have only seconds to decide whether to buy or not), the brain's computational capacity (trading a stock is likely to involve large numbers of complex and interacting variables), and imperfect information (one agent, the seller of the stock, may know more than the other agent, the buyer).[2] A human stock trader, as opposed to an algorithm, who acts within the constraints of time, information, and computational capacity is neither irrational nor fully rational, but only somewhat rational. A strategy that decision-makers often use to cope with these constraints, and in order to simplify decision-making, consciously or unconsciously, is to employ mental short cuts, also known as 'heuristics'. For example, consider a retail investor who is deciding whether or not to buy stocks in a company's IPO (initial public offering). If they decide to buy in the hope that its price will rise significantly based on recollections of previous IPOs that have been spectacularly successful, such as those of Apple or Amazon rather than on an exhaustive analysis of the prospects for a particular IPO, they would be using a mental short cut. The heuristic would be based on the ease of recall of previous IPO successes in the hope that history would repeat itself.[3] Only time would tell whether pinning one's hopes on history would be a wise choice.

Since its inception in the 1950s Simon's work not only won him the Nobel Prize (ironically in Economic Sciences) it also radically changed the face of decision research. Subsequent theories of human judgement and decision-making have been developed which further explain the imperfections and limits of human rationality and the practical consequences for decision-making. This chapter focuses on one such theory: the seminally important work of Amos Tversky and Nobel Laureate Daniel Kahneman who developed 'their own perspective on bounded rationality'.[4] Their work became known as the 'heuristics and biases' program of research.[5] It identified a number of sources of systematic errors that arise as a result of the use of intuitive short cuts in decision-making and problem-solving. In what follows the economic (classical) model of decision-making and Simon's critique of it are prequels to a discussion of Kahneman and Tversky's work. The focus is on the errors and biases that accrue from taking mental short cuts based on two heuristics in particular: 'representativeness' and 'availability'. Like Simon's decision-making research, heuristics and biases was important and impactful enough to warrant the awarding of the Nobel Prize in Economic Sciences (2002) to Daniel Kahneman.

Classical Rationality

If managers do not take decisions and make judgements in accordance with utility maximization and rational actor assumptions then a number of important questions arise: (1) how do they behave in taking real-world decisions; (2) what are the implications for the accuracy of judgements and decision-making if the processes used to arrive at them are substantial departures from rationality? Before answering these questions it is necessary to consider the classical model.

The economic model assumes actors are fully rational agents who not only seek but are capable, at least theoretically, of maximizing the 'utility' (i.e. satisfaction) they gain from a particular course of action. For example, in exercising a choice between two job offers a candidate might be well advised, according to the economic model, to perform a multi-attribute utility analysis (MAUA)[6] as follows: first, identify the attributes that are important in exercising the choice they are faced with (such as salary, promotion prospects, location, etc.); second, assign weights to these attributes reflective of their importance (i.e. value or utility) in terms of their current goals; third, subjectively rate each attribute, for example salary, for the two job offers systematically; fourth, perform a simple calculation of 'assigned weight' multiplied by 'subjective rating' for the two job offers to give a 'utility score' for each attribute; finally, sum of the utility scores for each attribute for both job offers in order to compare which choice is more likely to yield the maximum expected utility (the simple weighted sum of all the utilities is the 'utility function').

Solving this problem of choice using the rational model seems, on the face of it, to be straightforward and safe. It is simply a matter of specifying a comprehensive and coherent utility function that combines attributes and their respective weights to compute the best all-round alternative. In its simplest form this type of approach is known as 'Franklin's method' or Franklin's 'prudential algebra' (in the sense of being wise). It is named after Benjamin Franklin (1706 to 1790) who recommended it in the 1770s to his friend the English chemist Joseph Priestly as a reliable method for taking decisions as follows: 'my way [of taking a decision] is to divide half a Sheet of Paper by a Line into two Columns; writing over one *Pro* and over the other *Con*'. Then laboriously over three or four days' duration, Franklin would 'endeavour to estimate their respective Weights' and if he found 'a Reason pro equal to some two Reasons con' he would strike out all three, and if 'some two Reasons con equal to some three Reasons pro', all five would be struck out and 'thus proceeding [would] find at length where the Balance lies'. In so doing, Franklin would arrive at an objective determination of the wisest, or most prudential, thing to do.

The 29-year-old scrupulously logical Charles Darwin used a much-simplified version of the pro-versus-con approach to solve the conundrum of whether or not to pursue the project of getting married (marrying in general, with nobody in particular in mind at the time).[7] In his notebook of July 1838[8] Darwin listed the pros of marrying ('Children; Constant companion, (& friend in old age) who will feel interested in one; object to be beloved & played with; Home, & someone to take care of house; Charms of music & female chit-chat; These things good for one's health, but terrible loss of time') the cons of marrying ('Freedom to go where one liked; Conversation of clever men at clubs; Not forced to visit relatives, & to bend in every trifle; to have the expense & anxiety of children, perhaps quarrelling; Loss of time, cannot read in the Evenings, fatness & idleness; Anxiety & responsibility, less money for books etc.'). Notwithstanding the glaring and egregious gender bias in Darwin's analysis, the pros outweighed the cons and he scrawled 'Marry-Marry-Marry QED' in his notebook. Darwin searched for a suitable wife, and proposed to his cousin Emma Wedgwood, who accepted. They were married on 29 January 1839.[9]

In spite of its undoubted strengths as a systematic method for decision-making, the rational approach is time-consuming, cognitively demanding, and not necessarily objective or bias-free. For example, the selection and weighting of the various parameters involves subjective judgements. For these reasons it may not be the most practical or realistic method for taking decisions under conditions of uncertainty and time pressure.[10] In many real-world decisions, such as the on-the-spot decision of whether to buy a particular stock or the best way to fight a fire, listing the pros and cons would take up too much time in the volatile situations of stock trading and firefighting. Decision-making in the real world must be able to accommodate ambiguity, respond to rapidly changing conditions, attempt to quantify the unquantifiable, and work with vague and inaccurate estimates of future value.[11] There are unknowns, both known and unknown, that make many business decisions radically uncertain and more akin to sensing a solution to a problem than solving a clearly defined puzzle.[12] Whilst intuition cannot provide certainty, it can offer foresight for the experienced decision-maker.

Bounded Rationality

Some, and quite possibly many, people who have applied Franklin's pros-versus-cons method to their own consequential decisions will vouch for the fact that it works best when result accords with their prior gut feelings about what they feel should be the winning choice. If there is a discrepancy then certain adjustments (i.e. 'fudges') to the various attributes and their weights might be called for. Indeed, Simon himself was unsettled by multi-attribute methods because:

> First, I couldn't find in my own mind or and my friends' a consistent utility function—what we preferred depended it seemed to me terribly on what our attention happened to be on at any given moment; secondly, we never had full information or anything remotely compared to that about the consequences of choosing this or that—you could think of some consequences and miss other enormous ones; third, that when several people were involved we had no way of comparing their utilities.[13]

Simon's concept of 'bounded rationality', by contrast, takes into account the significant constraints (i.e. the bounds) under which decision-makers in the real world operate. Simon highlighted three limitations in particular: first, the decision-maker's limited knowledge of the available alternatives; second, their limited knowledge of the consequences that are likely to follow on from a particular choice; thirdly, the decision-maker's inadequate computational capacity. Simon concluded that in the real world decision-makers 'satisfice' rather than maximize. The word satisfice, combines 'satisfy' and 'suffice', and is intended to capture how decision-makers in the 'buzzing, blooming confusion that constitutes the real world'[14] look for a course of action that is 'good enough'.[15] Decision-makers satisfice because, in the words of Simon, 'they have not the wits [computational capacity] to maximize'.[16]

When we satisfice we do not examine all possible alternatives and consequences, instead we take decisions using 'relatively simple rules of thumb [heuristics] that do not make impossible demands upon [our] capacity for thought'.[17] For example, most of us satisfice by choosing a food item from a menu in a restaurant or a TV programme from a channel list that is good enough rather than labouring though all the alternatives and assessing their pros and cons. Following this line of reasoning, Simon was able to show how real-world decision-making and the thinking which underlies it can be formulated as a 'boundedly rational' process. The intuitive processes which are the workhorse of much day-to-day decision-making are boundedly rational because they operate by recognizing patterns and prototypes and match them with a behavioural response that has worked well under similar circumstances in the past. Such intuitive responses can lead to good or bad outcomes and do not require any 'veil of mystery'.[18]

Simon's verdict on the classical economic model of decision-making was that it is a 'very unsatisfactory [and] dubious way of describing human choice'.[19] The later generation of behavioural decision researchers who have stood metaphorically on Simon's shoulders classify the fully rational model as a normative theory of decision-making (i.e. it is a theory of how we *should* choose), which is an accurate description of how we actually *do* choose only some of the time and in certain situations. In our endeavours to be fully rational, we often end up being only somewhat rational because we are equipped with a computationally-compromised brain that evolved to be able to sense how to act.[20] Sometimes sensing is accurate, sometimes it is inaccurate, at other times it is good enough. Under certain circumstances, such as time-pressured situations or where there is limited information, sensing the right thing to do may be the only way to decide and take incisive action.

As we shall see shortly, particular types of intuitive thinking—based on a number of clearly identifiable mental short cuts—can lead to inaccurate and biased outcomes when solving certain types of problems. Such errors and biases are a consequence of human beings' natural inclination to rely on heuristics which reflect the operations of a brain that evolved to sense regularities in and make predictions about complex physical and social environments. Such heuristics do not conform to the rules of logic or probability but nonetheless, for most of our day-to-day decisions, they can be relied on habitually in preference to time-consuming, effortful analytical processing. It is for this reason that Tversky and Kahneman in 1971 concluded one of their earliest technical papers on 'erroneous intuitions' with the recommendation that decision-makers should treat their 'intuitions with proper suspicion and replace impression formation by computation whenever possible'.[21] More recently, Kahneman, along with colleagues Oliver Sibony and Cass Sunstein in their bestselling book *Noise: A Flaw in Human Judgement* (2021), concluded impartially that heuristics can sometimes be 'quite useful and yield adequate answers' but sometimes they lead to biases and 'systematic predictable errors of judgement'.[22]

Heuristics and Biases

Daniel Kahneman and Amos Tversky's work has demonstrated through a large body of evidence from studies in psychology laboratories how relying on intuition can result in biased and error-prone judgements and decisions. Their main focus has been on what happens when intuition gets it wrong and why it does so. Kahneman and Tversky established through various ingenious laboratory experiments that departures from rationality can be traced to errors embedded in the 'design of the machinery of [human] cognition'.[23] However Kahneman is keen to point out that the preoccupations of some psychologists with errors and biases is not meant to denigrate human intelligence, just as physicians' preoccupations with ill health does not denigrate good health[24].

The scientific partnership between Kahneman and Tversky was documented in Michael Lewis' 2016 book *The Undoing Project: A Friendship that Changed Our Minds*. In his reflection on their achievements, Kahneman highlights the significance of his partnership with Tversky and also acknowledges the role that luck played in their collaboration. In an interview with a British newspaper in 2014 he claimed that he would not have made any of the discoveries for which he was awarded the Nobel Prize in 2002 if it were not for a chance meeting with Tversky in a seminar at the psychology department of the Hebrew University of Jerusalem: 'It was sheer luck that I met him, that I liked him, that we worked together so well and that our method for doing so proved to be so influential'.[25] Kahneman described the work that they did together in their fourteen-year collaboration, and which comprises only a relatively small number of high-impact published articles, as 'the best either of us ever did'.[26]

Kahneman and Tversky reportedly had very different personalities and backgrounds. Kahneman has been described as having, 'a survivor's instinct, and a constant fear of the worst'[27] attributed to his harrowing childhood experiences during the Second World War in Nazi-occupied Europe. A former student described his 'defining emotion' as doubt.[28] Kahneman reputedly carried this worldview into his academic training as a psychologist and in his academic career moving 'from one idea to the next, never focusing' and distrustful of 'narrowness' in a world of specialism.[29] Tversky on the other hand was 'brilliant, voluble, and charismatic'; a hero solider in the Israeli army who was commended for bravery by General Moshe Dayan and generally considered as having 'genius-level intelligence' that frequently singled him out as 'the cleverest man in any room'. Their collaboration was described by Cass Sunstein and Richard Thaler (authors of the bestselling book *Nudge*) as the

'Lennon and McCartney' of social science, 'impossibly incongruous and yet perfectly complementary'.[30]

The scientific significance and academic impact of Kahneman and Tversky's work is hard to overestimate. Like Herbert Simon before him, Kahneman was awarded the Nobel Prize in Economic Sciences. The Nobel commendation of his work was for 'for having integrated insights from psychological research into economic science, especially concerning human judgment and decision-making under uncertainty'.[31] Tversky, very sadly, passed away in 1996, and the Prize cannot be awarded posthumously. Kahneman dedicated his 2011 two-million-copy bestselling book *Thinking, Fast and Slow* 'In memory of Amos Tversky'.

One reason their work resonates with non-scientists as much as with scientists is because of the way that Kahneman and Tversky presented and communicated the intuitive judgement 'puzzles' that were the cornerstone of their work. Puzzles in this sense are problems that have an unequivocally correct answer. They did not present them as abstract psychological tasks but as stimulating and thought-provoking problems which people were able to connect with and relate to easily and immediately. People not only felt suitably challenged by them but were also made all-too-aware of how their instinctive intuitive judgements could lead them seriously astray. The 'bat and ball' problem, to which according to Kahneman 'more than 50% of students at Harvard, MIT, and Princeton gave the intuitive—incorrect—answer', is a good example of the type of problem they used in their experiments: 'a bat and ball together cost $1.10. The bat costs one dollar more than the ball. How much does the ball cost?' It is recommended that you give the answer that occurs to you immediately, i.e. intuitively. The solution to the bat-and-ball problem is to be found in the footnote.[i] Are you part of the majority who give the intuitive but wrong answer?

Intuitive Judgement by Representativeness

The following judgement task—the 'Linda Problem'—is one of the most famous puzzles in all of psychology. It was first published in Tversky and Kahneman's landmark 1983 article in *Psychological Review* entitled 'Extensional versus intuitive reasoning: The conjunction fallacy in probability judgment' and has subsequently undergone a number of incarnations:

> Linda is 31-years old, single, outspoken and very bright. She majored in philosophy. As a student, she was deeply concerned with issues of discrimination and social justice, and also participated in anti-nuclear demonstrations.

The task is as follows.

> Based on this description, is Linda more likely to be: (1) a 'bank teller'; or (2) a 'bank teller who is active in the feminist movement'?

---

[i] The bat costs five cents and the ball costs a dollar and five cents.

Try it before you read on. Faced with these two choices a large majority of people (for example, 'about 85% to 90% of undergraduates at several elite US universities'[32]) judge that Linda is more likely to be a 'bank teller who is also active in the feminist movement' rather than merely a 'bank teller'. Consequently, most people choose Option 2 as the more likely. However, Option 1 is more likely than Option 2. Hence, Option 2 is the incorrect response. What was your answer; if you got the answer wrong why was this?

Kahneman and Tversky deliberately constructed the fictitious Linda's description to be representative of someone who is active in the 'feminist movement' and unrepresentative of a typical 'bank teller'. The vast majority of participants in the Linda experiment, which has been repeated many times, consistently violate a logical principle known as the 'conjunction rule' irrespective of whether they were 'naïve' or 'sophisticated' participants. The conjunction rule states that 'a conjunction (A and B) cannot be more probable than one of its constituents (A or B)', in other words the probability of being a bank teller (A) and being active in the feminist movement (B) cannot be greater than being a bank teller (A) alone, even though Option 2 (bank teller who is active in the feminist movement) intuitively 'feels', i.e. it is sensed, as though it is more likely to be true.

In probabilistic terms: $P(A\&B) \leq P(A)$ or $P(B)$.[33] By way of analogy, if the problem is presented as follows few people have difficulty in make the correct judgement: which is more likely that (A) you will get a puncture tomorrow whilst on the way to work, or (B) you will get a puncture tomorrow whilst on the way to work and a driver of a red car will stop and help you out?[34] For visually inclined problem-solvers, the conjunction can be imagined as a Venn diagram where the intersection of the two sets of bank tellers (A) and active feminists (B) is the conjunction (i.e. *both* a bank teller *and* active in the feminist movement) and is literally smaller than the two sets (A and B).[35]

Most people can understand the logic when it is explained to them verbally using the car example or visually using a Venn diagram. But nonetheless many people have difficulty accepting it because Linda as a bank teller who is active in the feminist movement simply feels more in keeping with their expectations and their sense of what Linda is actually like as a real person. Their response to the logical explanation is often 'Yes, but!'

Why do most people commit this logical error and why do so many of them remain steadfast in their conviction that Linda is more likely to be a bank teller who is active in the feminist movement rather than just a bank teller, even when an explanation is provided? More about that shortly. But if you remain unconvinced you are in good company because the eminent paleo-biologist Stephen J Gould remarked 'I know [the right answer], yet a little homunculus in my head continues to jump up and down shouting at me—"but she can't just be a bank teller; read the description!"'.[36]

The conjunction fallacy is the source of the error that lies behind what Kahneman and Tversky referred to as the 'representativeness heuristic'. In attempting to solve the Linda problem people typically evaluate the degree to which a thing 'x' (Linda in this case) feels as if it belongs to a class 'y' (bank tellers who are active in the feminist movement in this case). Linda (x) appears to be highly representative of bank tellers who are active in the feminist movement (y) and therefore the sense we have of Linda is that she is more likely to be a member of y, rather than of 'z' (the general category of bank tellers).[37]

The representativeness heuristic also makes us insensitive to the prior probability of outcomes by tempting us into ignoring 'base rates' (i.e. the prevalence of some item or occurrence) thus causing us to fall foul of making incorrect judgements and predictions.[38] This additional example, adapted from Kahneman's bestseller *Thinking, Fast and Slow*, illustrates how ignoring base rates can work to our disadvantage: if you see a person reading the *Financial Times* (*FT*) on the London Underground, which of the following is more likely: (1) this person has an MBA; (2) this person does not have a university degree? On the basis of the degree of similarity of the observed person (the *FT* reader) to the stereotype of someone with an MBA (for example, financially alert, aware and well-informed) we might be tempted to choose (1) ('I bet she's got an MBA'). However, given that there are many more non-graduates than MBAs using the London Underground, the simple likelihood that the *FT* reader is also an MBA is considerably lower than the probability that the *FT*-reading passenger does not have a university degree. Hence, (2) is more likely. This is called the 'base rate fallacy' because people tend to overlook prior probabilities and ignore the simple likely prevalence of an object. Instead they are swayed by the similarity of the object to a prototype or stereotype and the associated tendency to categorize people and things intuitively and sometimes imaginatively as well.

Conjunction errors (CE) and the base rate fallacy are a consequence of routine 'natural assessments' based on a computation of the similarity between the target (Linda and the London Underground *FT* reader) and an exemplar or prototype (of an 'active feminist' and 'MBA graduate'). This is because when we routinely and automatically adopt a heuristic mode of processing we are taking a low effort, mental short cut rather than thinking the problem through. As a result we arrive at a judgement not on the basis of logic or probability but on the basis of resemblance to concrete exemplars, stereotypes, or prototypes.[39] A corollary, however, is that if we habitually worked out every judgement from first principles using logic and probability we would be unable to function in the complex physical and social world that we inhabit; our time and cognitive resources would become exhausted very quickly. Fortunately for us, our brains evolved to sense similarities rather than solve probabilities. In so doing valuable cognitive capacity is freed up for other more demanding tasks. But the cost can be systematic errors.

The psychological mechanism that is at work here is 'attribute substitution'. In the case of the conjunction error attribution substitution leads to a harder probability-based question (whether Linda is more likely to be 'A' only or both 'A and B') being replaced in the subject's mind with a simpler similarity-based question which can be answered intuitively. An example from marketing would be: (1) Easier Question: 'Have I heard of this brand' (marketed by vividness / emotional content); Harder Question: 'What are my real needs and does this product meet them?' An example from employee selection would be: (1) Easier Question: 'Do I like this job candidate' (2) Harder Question: 'Does this person's aptitude, experience, and profile match requirements of the job?'

In each of these cases the simpler question can be solved effortlessly by sensing similarity to a stereotype. Kahneman likened this to activating a 'mental shotgun' which evokes 'answers to easier questions'.[40] Unfortunately, sometimes when we are required to make high-stakes probability-based judgements, 'shooting from the intuitive hip' can be a serious and costly mistake. For example, by only answering the question 'how impressive was the start-up entrepreneur's? pitch' (which is an easier question) rather than 'what is the most up-to-date evidence on the proportion of businesses that have failed in this sector of the market the past 12 months?' (a harder question) could prove costly to an inexperienced or overly-intuitive investor.

Problems with the Linda Problem

The judgement tasks used in the heuristics and biases research have attracted the criticism that they are 'mere laboratory curiosities' and simply demonstrate the fact that people find it hard to solve 'tricky' word problems and artificial puzzles.[41] For example, it might appear to subjects that the questioner in the Linda problem is trying to convey something 'extra' about the content and context of the fictitious Linda[42] over and above what is conveyed literally in the wording of the question. This may prompt them to make common-sense inferences. The eminent German psychologist Gerd Gigerenzer, whose alternative view on heuristics will be discussed in the next chapter, argued that the Linda problem is 'content blind' because it ignores the context and goals of our thinking in making, in this case, social judgements, and instead is concerned purely with mathematics and logic. Gigerenzer argues that it overlooks the intuitive intelligence that human beings need to operate in an ambiguous and uncertain world that requires them to 'go beyond the information given'.[43]

Other critics have argued that the intuitive error that most people make in the Linda problem could depend on the way the problem is formulated and presented. For example, people may be less inclined to give the incorrect response if the literal meaning is made explicit, for example by saying 'Linda is a bank teller (but we are not saying that she is only a bank teller and not also a feminist, we are leaving that option open)'. The critics' point is that the intuitive, but incorrect, answer to the original Linda problem may in fact reflect the useful intellectual skill of being able to infer (sometimes using our imagination) what a speaker is attempting to convey in a real-world interaction rather than what is semantically expressed in the literal formulation of the question in the artificial setting of the psychology laboratory.[44] It may in fact illustrate human beings' capacity for making sematic inferences intuitively, which can be a very useful but error prone sensing skill in many decision-making situations, especially in social judgements.[45] A corollary of this is that answering on the basis of similarity to a prototype (but which may lead to a wrong answer) may in fact be an intelligent inference based on an adaptive intellectual skill because it shows an intuitive awareness of what the speaker might have been attempting to say about Linda and her particular context.[46] Our intuitive mind is prepared to sense the situation and then take a 'bet' on what Linda is more likely to be on the basis of the description of Linda and her situation as presented in the question and as posed by the questioner.[47]

Representativeness in Business Venturing and Beyond

Entrepreneurship is an area of business which is rife with uncertainty. Decisions must often be taken under conditions of ambiguity and time pressure. In rational terms business venturing is risky and uncertain; it entails taking decisions without certain knowledge of outcomes and committing resources without a guarantee of a return.[48] In an unstable environment such as business venturing heuristics can certainly simplify and speed-up decision-making, but do they lead to suboptimal outcomes?

Between five and eight out of every ten new ventures fail within the first five years.[49] Nonetheless many would-be entrepreneurs believe their chances of success to be higher than those of the competition. They doggedly persist against very low odds of success. One reason they do so is that they overgeneralize from small, non-random samples often based on well-publicized stories of successful intuitive entrepreneurs whose all-or-nothing gambles paid off.[50] The problem is that small samples yield extreme results more often than large samples.[51] In the well-publicized small samples that people habitually tend to pay attention to, the entrepreneurial intuitive 'hits' tend to get lauded whilst the intuitive 'misses' of failed business venturers tend to get buried. This observation resonates with Former US President John F. Kennedy's remark that 'victory has a thousand fathers, but defeat is an orphan'.[52] By neglecting the base rates for failures, business venturers run the risk of overlooking the much larger number of business ventures that ended up collapsing under the weight of their own unwarranted optimism. As a result, business venturers who make intuitive judgements based on highly visible intuitive hits are more likely to arrive at significantly upwardly-biased estimates of their chances of success, oblivious of the actual base rates of success and the objective likelihood of failure.

Reliance on the representativeness heuristic, conscious or otherwise, leads many aspiring entrepreneurs to fail to appreciate that the odds against them are unreasonably high, to have undue confidence in early trends in their 'data' (the first few instances of comparable success that come to mind), and to be unduly self-assured in their ability to replicate others' successes. To compound matters, overly-intuitive entrepreneurs are capable of constructing a convincing explanation for discrepancies and outcomes that depart from their 'gut-felt' expectations or by attributing their intuitive miss to bad luck or other factors beyond their control.[53]

One such factor, and a close relative of 'unbridled intuition',[54] is hubris. Hubris is overconfidence, overambition, and disdain for advice and criticism. The ancient Greeks referred to it as 'thinking big'. Research in Finland into entrepreneurs' personal stories of business success and failure found strong evidence for hubristic overconfidence borne of unbridled intuition. Overly-optimistic entrepreneurs championed 'trendy' and 'novel' ways of conducting business, gained large sums of eager investors' capital along the way but lost sight of the everyday realities of starting up a business and of their chances of success. In the well-known Greek myth, Icarus's overconfidence in his newly acquired Godlike power of flight led to retribution and his demise. One failed entrepreneur in the Finnish study remarked that 'We should have learned how to walk before we tried to fly'.[55] In entrepreneurship 'intuitive myopia' is one consequence of the representativeness heuristic, it can lead to hubristic overconfidence and is a shortcoming to which inexperienced business venturers appear to be all too susceptible.

Is there something in the nature of the entrepreneurial mindset that differentiates them from other business people? Entrepreneurship researcher Lowell Busenitz found that whilst entrepreneurs do not appear to view themselves as preferring riskier ventures they seem to be more prone to making judgements on the basis of representativeness than managers in large organizations even after controlling for education, age, and risk propensity.[56] However, in the bigger picture every cloud has a silver lining, and the bias towards risk is not necessarily a bad thing for the economy overall, although it clearly is for those start-ups that fail. Busenitz argued that attitude towards risk amongst entrepreneurs may help to explain why a small subset of them are able to transform a novel idea into a growing and ultimately successful enterprise—they do so by forging ahead rather than laboriously calculating all the risks involved. Busenitz commented that if every new venture proceeded by a careful computation of risks and benefits in keeping with economic rationality then it is unlikely that many new and ultimately highly successful ventures would ever be started. Without intuitive judgement, with all its attendant biases and risks leading to extremely good as well as extremely bad outcomes, many entrepreneurial decisions would never be made.[57] A competitive advantage of an entrepreneurially-oriented mindset may be that it enables individuals to perceive and manage uncertainty differently, albeit riskily. Heuristic reasoning processes help bolder business venturers to sense and grasp those opportunities that their less intuitively biased counterparts are likely to shy away from. Ultimately entrepreneurial intuitions can lead to the radical transformation of entire industries in a Schumpeterian process of 'creative destruction' where foresight, intuition and the alertness of individuals are to the fore.[58]

However, intuitively sensed business opportunities can only contribute to economic and social development inclusively and fairly if they are translated into tangible business innovations in an impartial and equitable fashion.[59] Entrepreneurship researcher Scott Shane and colleagues' studied how university technology licensing officers in ninety-eight research universities in the United States made decisions about which academics' inventions should or should not be commercialized in new spin-off companies. Technology licensing officers favoured inventions that fitted the stereotype of a 'typical' inventor-entrepreneur, namely male, Chinese-named Asian inventors who have industry experience and are perceived as easy to work with. They found that randomly assigning a female faculty member to a team of inventors resulted in a lower likelihood that technology licensing officers would support the formation of a new spin-off company.[60] The results demonstrate powerfully how biases (conscious or non-conscious) as a result of the representativeness heuristic can create significant problems of access and equality of opportunity with serous negative consequences for diversity and inclusion. Prototypes are by their nature easy to recall and, moreover, ease of recall opens the door to another significant source of error and bias, the 'availability heuristic'.

Intuitive Judgement by Availability

The availability heuristic is a further example of our inclination to eschew exhaustive data analysis as a result of the tensions between our limited information processing capacities, the complexity of the social world we inhabit and the imperative to take action.[61] The availability heuristic helps us to understand how people make errors of judgements in situations where they are required to estimate the frequency of a given occurrence. This can be in contexts ranging from the trivial to the traumatic: anything from the number of words beginning with a given letter, the chances of winning on a lottery and divorce rates, right through to extreme events such as plane crashes, hurricanes and floods, nuclear accidents, and pandemics.

Death by firearm is one such extreme event. In the United States, examples of mass shootings are all too common and are, quite naturally, reported widely in the media. On 22 March 2021, a gunman inside a grocery store in Boulder, Colorado killed ten people, including the first police officer to arrive at the scene. On 16 March 2021, eight people, including six women of Asian descent, were killed at spas in the Atlanta area. On 3 August 2019, a gunman killed twenty-three people in a Walmart store in El Paso, Texas.[62] Informed by these objective data, consider the following question:

> Which of the following causes of death in the United States is more likely: (1) Assault by firearm (gun homicide); or (2) Self-harm by firearm (gun suicide)?

Most people judge that gun homicides are more common than gun suicides in the United States. However, the risk of death from shooting yourself is roughly twice as high as being shot dead by somebody else. Vivid, easy-to-imagine events are judged to have a higher probability of occurrence than hard-to-imagine events, especially when preceded by a vivid, recent, and hence easy-to-recall description.

When people make judgements of this type they tend to do so by relying on how easily relevant examples come to mind. Homicides by shooting in the United States make the news frequently—they are more 'available' for recall. Events such as homicide, extreme weather, terrorism, and plane crashes are also vivid and emotionally salient.[63] Emotional salience amplifies availability and allows such events to be brought to mind with little cognitive effort. Many people can recall with extraordinary clarity where they were on receiving news of a calamitous event such as the death of Diana Princess of Wales or the events of 9/11. Sensational media coverage makes gripping but relatively unlikely and unrepresentative events seem more likely than they actually are.[64] A familiar trope in the media industry is 'If it bleeds it leads' (so-called 'body bag journalism'[65]). People assess the chances of emotionally-charged happenings that are reported widely as having a much higher probability of occurring than is actually the case.

The cognitive mechanism is, by now, a familiar one to us: as with representativeness, an easier-to-answer question ('can I more easily recall instances of gun death by homicide versus gun deaths by suicide?') substitutes for answering a harder-to-answer question ('what are the actual death rates for gun homicides and gun suicides?'). It is the easy-to-answer question, rather than the hard-to-answer question, that informs judgement. Likewise, in the Linda problem an easy-to-arrive-at judgement which senses in terms of similarity is used instead of a hard-to-arrive-at judgement which would solve correctly in terms of probability.[66]

In psychological terms, the availability heuristic (also referred to as 'availability bias'[67]) is a simple form of associative thinking based on the operations of memory and which relies on ease of retrieval of information.[68] Moreover, the information on which the skewed judgement is arrived at is made on the basis of an already biased sample of information stored in long-term memory. This is especially true if the person making the judgement is drawn to reading salacious and sensationalized, or even fake, stories in the media or has personally experienced extreme events. Because of the way our intuitive mind works, narratives and personal experiences are much more effective in activating a heuristic response than are facts and figures. In such situations the person's 'intuitive mind' is keenly attuned to the risks of death from homicide, celebrity divorce rates, plane crashes and the like, and it responds accordingly. Addiction to salacious stories in the press and social media posts have enormous power to amplify this phenomenon.

The availability bias influences behaviour in a variety of ways. Richard Thaler and Cass Sunstein, the authors of the bestseller *Nudge*, point to the fact that in areas of the world susceptible to earthquakes, purchases of new earthquake insurance rocket in the aftermath of an earthquake but then rapidly recede once the vivid and emotionally charged reports decline and memories fade.[69] Daniel Kahneman also points out that people are like to be affected more strongly by ease of retrieval (hence more susceptible to availability bias) when they are engaged in an effortful task, are in a good mood, have a score low on a depression scale, have a high score on a faith in intuition scale, are novices as opposed to experts in the relevant area, and when they are, or are made to feel, powerful.[70] These are some of the early warning signs for situations that could create the conditions for judgements and decisions that could be skewed by availability.

Availability in Business

Whether an object or event is more or less available to recall, and therefore capable of influencing decision-making, depends on the object's or event's imaginability (for example, a shark attack is easy to imagine), vividness (a shark attack is a powerful image), and emotional salience (a shark attack is emotionally intense). Incidentally the chances of being killed by a shark, even in places such as Australia where such events are known to happen, are vanishingly small (the shark attack mortality rate is about one person per year[71]). Overweighting currently available information as a result of its imaginability, vividness, and emotional salience, rather than processing other potentially relevant information such as objectively identifiable risks or costs and benefits, has significant implications for decision-making in a number of areas of business.

In terms of the emotional salience aspect of availability it seems as though positive and negative emotions may have differential effects on decision-making, a so-called 'asymmetry effect' which results in a 'negativity bias'. For example, in online shopping, positive reviews are given less weight by prospective consumers than negative reviews; positive product attributes are perceived as less diagnostic of product quality, and positive reviews have a weaker effect on purchasing decisions.[72] In the travel business, negative traveller reviews have been found to outweigh price and pre-existing attitudes when choosing which trip to book. Travellers have been found to be willing to pay more to stay at a positively reviewed hotel consumers but will not select a negatively reviewed hotel at an equivalent discount.[73] It seems as though intuition itself is biased fundamentally towards being safe rather than sorry.

Consumers place greater weight on negative information than positive information. Negative information automatically evokes stronger cognitive and emotional responses which are then available to inform, and negatively bias, decision-making. This asymmetric effect of negative information suggests that people seek to avoid risks and automatically and intuitively assign more weight to losses than to gains. In prospect theory, another major contribution of Kahneman and Tversky, a loss causes a greater emotional impact on an individual than does an equivalent amount of gain. For example, the situation of gaining £50 should be valued the same as gaining £100 and then losing £50 because the end result is the same. However, most people view the single gain of £50 more favourably than the gain of £100 and the loss of £50. The negative feeling associated with the loss is greater than the positive feeling of pleasure associated with a gain. Consequently people tend to prefer avoiding a loss rather than securing a gain. More generally, feelings (i.e. affect), especially negatively-valenced ones, serve as a decision-making short cut in the form of an 'affect heuristic'. Human beings have evolved to have a natural aversion to losses.[74] As a result their intuitive judgements typically err on the side of caution. In evolutionary terms this makes sense because paying attention to negative information, for example in the form of a threat, is likely to be highly consequential for survival and therefore would be selected for.[75] It is better to instantly, but perhaps mistakenly, recoil from a snake-shaped stick than to ignore it or take the time to inspect it at close quarters.

The availability heuristic can exert a strong influence on perceptions of service quality. It does so as a result of the ease with which high quality and distinctive customer service can be brought to mind because of its imaginability and vividness. Service quality is an attribute that is valued highly not only by customers but also by investors. Hence the availability of information regarding the quality of service provided by a firm is likely to influence investment decisions. This would suggest that customer service announcements that are communicated vividly are likely to attract investors and have a positive effect of a firm's market value.[76] To test this assertion, researchers in the United States compared 113 retailers' advertising campaigns between 1995 and 2005 in order to evaluate the effect that a 'customer service emphasis' versus 'no customer service emphasis' in firms' advertisements had on their market value.[77] The researchers found that an announcement of an advertising campaign with a vivid customer service emphasis was followed by an abnormal return of 1.09 per cent on the market value compared to firms whose advertising campaign had no, or a banal, customer service emphasis. This equated to an average rise of $54million in the market value of the firms' studied. This was not simply a result of an advertising effect because similar results were not observed in firms that advertised but did not emphasize customer service.

An implication is that a retailer who promises a customer service experience that is vivid (for example, 'nice, friendly and knowledgeable staff') and easy to imagine (for example, 'simple, convenient, one-stop shopping experience') is more likely to create shareholder value. On the other hand, when a business promises to deliver more difficult to imagine customer service encounters and experiences, such as vague generalizations to 'customer service', these are less likely to be rewarded by investors. Easy-to-imagine, vivid, and emotionally salient customer service promises create greater value than harder-to-imagine, bland, and emotionally neutral promises through the operation of the availability heuristic.[78]

Behavioural finance researchers have argued that the availability heuristic might be a contributory factor to financial boom-and-bust cycles. A long series of widely publicized good outcomes could lead agents, such as investors and regulators, to overestimate bankers' capabilities and skills for managing risk. As a consequence, both banks and their investors underestimate the true risks associated with high-risk financial products (such as subprime mortgages) leading individuals and institutions to rush into invest in them resulting in a lending boom. Easy-to-recall memories of past occurrences of success result in risk itself being mispriced and bankers' risk-management abilities being overestimated. Increased market entry means more potential buyers of a bank's loans and this provides enhanced liquidity to the market for high-risk assets, attracting more institutions. The problem is compounded significantly when single assets, such as a mortgage loan, are used multiple times to create new trading opportunities. This was one of the problems in the credit crunch of 2008.[79] However, when investors eventually learn about the true risks associated with high-risk financial products intuitive judgements by nature seem to err on the side of caution. As a consequence creditors withdraw funding rapidly and sometimes overnight, and this run on the banks causes liquidity to dry up and a crisis commences.[80]

The availability heuristic has wider implications in business beyond marketing and finance. For example, it could be used to promote ethical behaviour in the workplace by raising the moral intensity of troublesome issues through emphasizing the vividness and salience of the potential outcomes (for example, the negative legal and personal consequences of unethical behaviour) and hence nudge employees towards being less likely to engage in such behaviours.[81] Likewise, the emotional salience of vivid images of extreme weather events could be used to influence pro-environmental behaviours via the availability heuristic. An effective approach for shifting mindsets and mobilizing action on climate change could be through appealing both to people's 'heads' via 'cold' rational processing and to their 'hearts' through a 'hot' intuitive processing. The hot route mobilizes the availability heuristic and the affect heuristic (see below). A classic example of vivid visual imagery being used to mobilize pro-environmental behaviour by appealing to people's intuitions was the influential documentary film *An Inconvenient Truth* (2006) which was part of the US Vice President Al Gore's attempt to educate people about the perils of global warming. Both the cold and the hot cognition routes are needed if climate change messaging is to be efficient and effective; the cold route can be activated by models and data whilst the hot route can be activated by metaphors (such as the James Lovelock's Gaia hypothesis), stories (such as homes being flooded or blown away as a result of extreme weather events), and visual images (for example, polar bears stranded on melting ice).

Why Heuristics Get It Wrong

Representativeness and availability are two of a number of systematic sources of errors and biases in judgement and decision-making which have been identified by heuristics and biases researchers. Others include the 'anchoring and adjustment heuristic', which explains phenomena such as bargaining in a bazaar or negotiating a deal in a house purchase where the trader or vendor comes in with an unreasonably high initial price and bidding proceeds downwards to a lower agreed price. The price is still over-inflated because it is fastened to and adjusted downward from a high initial anchor point. The 'affect heuristic', referred to briefly above, explains how information that is stored in long-term memory and can be accessed consciously or non-consciously is 'tagged' with affect in the form of a positively valenced feeling of 'goodness', or a negatively valenced feeling of 'badness'. This affective tag comes into play unconsciously and is used as a simpler and quicker way of arriving at a judgement in preference to weighing up pros and cons exhaustively or retrieving numerous examples from memory.

In classic study of the effect of the affect heuristic on judgement and decision-making, researchers found an inverse relationship between risk and benefits when people make judgements about nuclear power versus vaccinations: nuclear power is judged to be high on risks and low on benefits whilst vaccinations are perceived as being high on benefits and low on risks. These differential perceptions are a consequence of different feelings (i.e. the affective evaluation) towards nuclear power (negative, disliked) compared to vaccinations (positive, liked).[82] In presenting arguments in favour of things that are negative and disliked proponents may be tempted to amplify the benefits and downplay the risks accordingly in order to nudge behaviour in a particular direction.

Representativeness and availability are linked in that they operate according to the underlying principle of attribute substitution. The result is that by substituting an easier-to-answer question for a harder-to-answer question the possibility of error is introduced. Heuristics are part of a mental toolbox that evolved in *Homo sapiens'* ancestral environment and did so for good reasons that supported adaptation and survival. When human beings are confronted by a problem which their mind did not evolve to be able to solve (such as formal analyses of probabilities) they instead solve a seemingly similar or related problem that the human mind did evolve to be able to solve. For example, a person who is asked 'what proportion of business start-ups fail within five years?' is likely to answer as if they had been asked the question 'do any high-profile or personally familiar instances of start-ups that fail in the first five years come readily to mind?'[83] In this and in other examples of the representativeness and availability heuristics the decision-maker substitutes a 'heuristic (short-cut) attribute' (such as, recollections of vivid and salient examples of start-up failures) for the 'target attribute' (the mathematical probability of a start-up failing).[84]

Doing so is entirely natural and served us well in our ancestral environment. Even though the universe operates according to the laws of mathematics (including proportions, probabilities, and frequencies) this is not how the mind evolved through natural selection to work in its day-to-day functioning. Instead, the human mind operates by a different set of rules which lead us to abstract from a situation what we consider to be the essence of an entity (for example, by sensing and forming an impression) and then match this to a type or category, for example a stereotype of a feminist bank teller as in the Linda problem. Daniel Kahneman and Shane Frederick position these intuitive judgements as 'natural assessments' as being somewhere in between basic perception and complex reasoning. In practice they lead, for example to a perception, which may or may not be justified, of a stranger as being 'menacing', which is inseparable from a prediction of future harm.

David Myers, author of *Intuition, Its Powers and Perils*, described the link between perception and response as an ancient 'biological wisdom' which evolved out of the pressing need to be able to instantly assess the 'stranger in the forest' as friend or foe.[85] He calls this ability to form a lasting impression of someone within a few moments of meeting them as 'social intuition' (see Chapter 9). Myers argues that social intuition is adaptive because those amongst our ancestors who were able to read another person's motives and intentions accurately were more likely to survive and pass on their genes than those who were unable to do so. Differences between men and women in this regard are a perennially fascinating and potentially controversial topic. The psychologist Susan Blackmore observed that even though the notion of women's intuition 'is sometimes laughed at', she argues that women may be more intuitive because they generally have 'better verbal skills, are more interested in relationships, and gossip more than men do about social matters'.[86] Whether this is an accurate depiction of the differences between men and women is uncertain and the related question of whether women are more able than men to decode the non-verbal cues that are the basis of social intuition is open to debate. However Myers notes that even if evolutionary processes did select for women to have better social intuition than men, at the end of the day in human society it is culture also that sees or labels women as—and therefore brings them up and expects them to be—better non-verbal decoders than men. The danger is that the stereotype of female intuition, whether it is accurate or not, may feed into unhelpful and potentially dysfunctional gendered stereotypes. In my own research where we have observed gender differences in self-reported preferences for intuitive versus analytical thinking (see Chapter 11) those differences, even when they are statistically significant, tend to be quite small.

Heuristics and intuitive judgements, which can be accurate as well as error-prone, should be viewed not as the products of lazy and inattentive human beings who are by nature 'cognitive misers'.[87] Instead they are perhaps better seen as a way of arriving at judgements and taking decisions that served us well in the ancestral environment for the purposes of survival and passing-on of genetic material. Kahneman and Tversky's theory of heuristics and biases is an evolutionary account which recognizes that an organism's phylogeny[ii] yields 'noteworthy imperfections in function'. These imperfections presumably were tolerable in the ancestral environment and are so, at least to some extent, to this day.[88]

That said, the demands of *Homo sapiens*' ancestral environment have been superseded by the demands of our current social environment. Cultural evolution has outstripped biological evolution in the human organism. Consequently, judgement and decision-making in the modern world, and in business especially, requires analytical and computational processes, such as assessments of probability, as much as it requires intuitive and heuristics processes, such as pattern-matching to type. Although the human mind is capable of computation, its abilities in this regard are limited. Human inventions in counting and calculating technology, ranging from the abacus to the computer, have enabled tricky and arduous computations, which as cognitive misers we are inclined to shun, to be outsourced to machines—a trend which, in the information age, has accelerated rapidly.

Nonetheless, because human biological evolution lags behind human cultural evolution the human mind will always commit the blatant and habitual error-prone judgements in probability and frequency computation that the heuristics and biases research has exposed. This is because such errors are a natural and an inevitable product of human cognition. The fact that intuitions may be natural assessments does not excuse them from being wrong or leading to bad outcomes. Arriving at intuitive judgements purely on the basis of the perceived similarity of an entity (for example, a job candidate at interview) to a strongly-held prototype (which may be based on a negative stereotype) opens the door to bias (both conscious and non-conscious) and may lead to prejudice and discrimination. The natural assessment view offers neither an optimistic nor a pessimistic view of human nature, rather it is a view which recognizes the reasons *why* intuitive heuristics may have evolved in the first place. It also acknowledges that they can be both friend and foe when taking quick, low

---

[ii] The evolutionary development and diversification of a species or group of organisms.

effort judgements in ambiguous, fast-moving and socially complex environments, including business. Overcoming and debiasing our intuitive cognitions begins with an understanding of their nature. How to debias our judgements is discussed in Chapter 11 and as we shall discover in the next chapter, there are occasions when heuristic thinking that is 'fast' and 'frugal' can pay-off.

Summary

1. The main idea of this chapter has been that mental short cuts, for example representativeness and availability, can lead to incorrect judgements.
2. These errors of judgement occur in those situations when the human mind opts to sense a solution intuitively when it might have been better to solve the problem analytically.
3. One of the reasons this happens is because of attribute substitution whereby the human mind substitutes an easier-to-answer question for a harder-to-answer question.
4. Feelings also loom large and can bias our judgements of the risks and benefits depending on whether we happen to like or dislike something.
5. Mental short cuts such as the representativeness, availability and affect heuristics are natural assessments that are arrived at quickly and with cognitive economy.
6. These cognitive mechanisms likely served *Homo sapiens* well in its ancestral environment; they persist as an evolved, and therefore impossible to eradicate, feature of the human mind.
7. They are often ill-suited to the computational demands of modern decision-making environments and for this reason they sometimes get it wrong.
8. There are occasions when heuristic thinking that is 'fast' and 'frugal' can pay off.

Endnotes

1. Simon, H. A. (1997). *Administrative Behaviour*. New York: Free Press, pp. 93–94.
2. Spacey, J. (2019). 9 examples of bounded rationality. *Simplicable*. Available online at: https://simplicable.com/new/bounded-rationality Accessed 08.02.2022.
3. Corporate Finance Institute (no date). Heuristics. Available online at: https://corporatefinanceinstitute.com/resources/knowledge/other/heuristics/ Accessed 08.02.2022.
4. Gilovich, T., Griffin, D., & Kahneman, D. (Eds.). (2002). *Heuristics and Biases: The Psychology of Intuitive Judgment*. Cambridge: Cambridge University Press, p. 3.
5. Olsson, H. (2013). Heuristics and biases. *Oxford Bibliographies*. Available online at: https://www.oxfordbibliographies.com. Accessed 08.02.2022.

6. Klein, G. A., & Klinger, D. (1991). Naturalistic decision-making. *Human Systems IAC Gateway*, XI(3): 16–19.
7. Browne, J. E. (1996). *Charles Darwin: Voyaging*. Princeton: Princeton University Press.
8. Darwin Correspondence Project (no date). Darwin on marriage. Available online at: https://www.darwinproject.ac.uk/tags/about-darwin/family-life/darwin-marriage. Accessed 08.02.2022.
9. Rothman, J. (2019). The art of decision-making. *The New Yorker* 14 January 2019. Available online at: https://www.lapaul.org/papers/Rothmandecisionmaking.pdf Accessed 08.02.2022.
10. Hastie, R., & Dawes, R. M. (2001). *Rational Choice in an Uncertain World*. London: SAGE, p. 236.
11. Klein, G. A., & Klinger, D. (1991). Naturalistic decision-making. *Human Systems IAC Gateway*, XI(3): 16–19.
12. This is a reference to Donald Rumsfeld's remarks at a press briefing in February 2002 in which he pointed out the existence of 'known unknowns' (things we know that we don't know) and 'unknown unknowns' (this that we don't know that we don't know). See Kay and King (2020), op. cit. p. 7.
13. This quotation is transcribed from an interview with Simon available at: https://www.youtube.com/watch?v=ErnWbP_Wztk Accessed 24.03.2021.
14. Here Simon appears to be borrowing from William James' *Principles of Psychology* (1890). On page 93 of *Administrative Behaviour* (the fourth edition of 1997), Simon comments that most of the references he makes to psychology are from James' *Principles of Psychology* and John Dewey's *Human Nature and Conduct* (1930).
15. Simon, H. A. (1997). *Administrative Behaviour*. New York: Free Press, p. 119.
16. Ibid., p. 118.
17. Ibid., p. 119.
18. Simon, H. A. (1997). *Administrative Behaviour*. New York: Free Press, p. 331.
19. Interview with Simon available at: https://www.youtube.com/watch?v=ErnWbP_Wztk Accessed 24.03.2021.
20. Hastie, R., & Dawes, R. M. (2001). *Rational Choice in an Uncertain World*. London: SAGE, p. 224.
21. Tversky, A., & Kahneman, D. (1971). Belief in law of small numbers. *Psychological Bulletin*, 76(2): 105–110, p. 110.
22. Kahneman, D., Sibony, O., & Sunstein, C. R. (221). *Noise: A Flaw in Human Judgement*. London: William Collins, p. 161
23. Kahneman, D. (2011). *Thinking, Fast and Slow*. London: Allen Lane, p. 8.
24. Ibid., p. 4
25. Interview in the London *Evening Standard*, 18 March 2014.
26. Kahneman, D. (2011). *Thinking, Fast and Slow*. London: Allen Lane, p.6.
27. Adams, T. (2016). The Undoing Project review—'psychology's Lennon and McCartney'. *The Guardian*, 11 December 2016. Available online at: https://www.theguardian.com/books/2016/dec/11/undoing-project-michael-lewis-review-amos-tversky-daniel-kahneman-behavioural-psychology
28. Lewis, M. (2017). *The Undoing Project*. London: Penguin.
29. Adams, T. (2016). The Undoing Project review—'psychology's Lennon and McCartney'. *The Guardian*, 11 December 2016. Available online at: https://www.theguardian.

com/books/2016/dec/11/undoing-project-michael-lewis-review-amos-tversky-daniel-kahneman-behavioural-psychology
30. Sunstein, C. R., & Thaler, R. (2016). Two friends who changed how we think about how we think. *The New Yorker*, 7 December 2016. Available online at: https://www.newyorker.com/books/page-turner/the-two-friends-who-changed-how-we-think-about-how-we-think. Accessed 08.02.2022.
31. The Nobel Prize. *Daniel Kahneman, Facts*. Available online at: https://www.nobelprize.org/prizes/economic-sciences/2002/kahneman/facts/ Accessed 24.03.2021.
32. Kahneman, D. (2011). *Thinking, Fast and Slow*. London: Allen Lane, p. 158.
33. Tversky, A., & Kahneman, D. (1983). Extensional versus intuitive reasoning: the conjunction fallacy in probability judgment. *Psychological Review*, 90(4): 293–315.
34. Framed in this way it is patently obvious that B is less likely than A. Adapted from: https://www.psychologytoday.com/gb/blog/the-superhuman-mind/201611/linda-the-bank-teller-case-revisited
35. https://www.psychologytoday.com/gb/blog/talking-apes/201506/holy-heisenberg
36. Gould, S. J. (1991). *Bully for Brontosaurus*. London: Penguin, p. 469.
37. Kahneman, D. (2011). *Thinking, Fast and Slow*. London: Allen Lane, p. 420.
38. Ibid., p. 420.
39. Epstein, S., Denes-Raj, V., & Pacini, R. (1995). The Linda problem revisited from the perspective of cognitive-experiential self-theory. *Personality and Social Psychology Bulletin*, 21(11): 1124–1138.
40. Kahneman, D. (2011). *Thinking, Fast and Slow*. London: Allen Lane, pp. 149–150.
41. Gilovich, T., Griffin, D., & Kahneman, D. (Eds.). (2002). *Heuristics and Biases: The Psychology of Intuitive Judgment*. Cambridge: Cambridge University Press, p. 11.
42. Gigerenzer, G. (1996). On narrow norms and vague heuristics: A reply to Kahneman and Tversky (1996). *Psychological Review*, 103(3): 592–596.
43. Gigerenzer, G. (2007). *Gut Feelings*. London: Penguin, p. 95
44. Brogaard, B. (2016). 'Lind the bank teller' case revisited. Psychology Today. Available online at: https://www.psychologytoday.com/gb/blog/the-superhuman-mind/201611/linda-the-bank-teller-case-revisited Accessed 25.03.21.
45. Hertwig, R., & Gigerenzer, G. (1999). The 'conjunction fallacy' revisited: How intelligent inferences look like reasoning errors. *Journal of Behavioral Decision Making*, 12(4): 275–305.
46. Brogaard, B. (2016). 'Lind the bank teller' case revisited. Psychology Today. Available online at: https://www.psychologytoday.com/gb/blog/the-superhuman-mind/201611/linda-the-bank-teller-case-revisited Accessed 25.03.21.
47. Gigerenzer, G. (2007). *Gut Feelings*. London: Penguin, p. 43.
48. Miller, D. (2011). Miller (1983) revisited: A reflection on EO research and some suggestions for the future. *Entrepreneurship Theory and Practice*, 35(5): 873–894.
49. Wright-Whyte, K. (2018). Lacking Vision: 60% of small businesses fail within first five years, *Accounts and Legal*. Available online at: https://www.accountsandlegal.co.uk/small-business-advice/lacking-vision-60-of-small-businesses-fail-within-first-five-years Accessed 08.02.2022.
50. Kahneman, D., Slovic, P., & Tversky, A. (1982). *Judgment under Uncertainty: Heuristics and Biases*. New York: Cambridge University Press.
51. This is the 'law of small numbers', see: Kahneman, D. (2011). *Thinking, Fast and Slow*. London: Allen Lane, p. 111.

52. The American Presidency Project. (1961). The Presidents News Conference, 12 April 1961. Available online at: https://www.presidency.ucsb.edu/documents/the-presidents-news-conference-213 Accessed 08.02.2022.
53. Tversky, A., & Kahneman, D. (1971). Belief in the law of small numbers. *Psychological Bulletin*, 76(2): 105–110.
54. Claxton, G., Owen, D., & Sadler-Smith, E. (2015). Hubris in leadership: A peril of unbridled intuition?. *Leadership*, 11(1): 57–78.
55. Mantere, S., Aula, P., Schildt, H., & Vaara, E. (2013). Narrative attributions of entrepreneurial failure. *Journal of Business Venturing*, 28(4): 459–473, p. 465.
56. Busenitz, L. W. (1999). Entrepreneurial risk and strategic decision making: It's a matter of perspective. *The Journal of Applied Behavioral Science*, 35(3): 325–340.
57. Busenitz, L. W., & Barney, J. B. (1997). Differences between entrepreneurs and managers in large organizations: Biases and heuristics in strategic decision-making. *Journal of Business Venturing*, 12(1): 9–30.
58. Mosakowski, E. (1998). Entrepreneurial resources, organizational choices, and competitive outcomes. *Organization science*, 9(6), 625–643.
59. Ucbasaran, D., Westhead, P., & Wright, M. (2009). The extent and nature of opportunity identification by experienced entrepreneurs. *Journal of Business Venturing*, 24(2): 99–115.
60. Shane, S., Dolmans, S. A., Jankowski, J., Reymen, I. M., & Romme, A. G. L. (2015). Academic entrepreneurship: Which inventors do technology licensing officers prefer for spinoffs?. *The Journal of Technology Transfer*, 40(2): 273–292.
61. Hayibor, S., & Wasieleski, D. M. (2009). Effects of the use of the availability heuristic on ethical decision-making in organizations. *Journal of Business Ethics*, 84(1): 151–165.
62. *The New York Times* (2021). A list of recent mass shootings in the United States, 23 March 2021. Available online at: https://www.nytimes.com/2021/03/23/us/us-mass-shootings.html Accessed 08.02.2022.
63. Nisbett, R. E., & Ross, L. D. (1980). *Human Inference: Strategies and Shortcomings of Social Judgment*. Englewood Cliffs, NJ: Prentice Hall
64. Sunstein, C. R. (2002). *Risk and Reason: Safety, Law, and the Environment*. Cambridge: Cambridge University Press.
65. Randolph, E. (1989). Body bag journalism. *Chicago Tribune*, 5 November 1989. Available online at: https://www.chicagotribune.com/news/ct-xpm-1989-11-05-8901280504-story.html Accessed 08.02.2022.
66. Kahneman, D., Sibony, O., & Sunstein, C. R. (221). *Noise: A Flaw in Human Judgement*. London: William Collins, p. 166
67. Kahneman, D. (2011). *Thinking, Fast and Slow*. London: Allen Lane, p. 131.
68. Hastie, R., & Dawes, R. M. (2001). *Rational Choice in an Uncertain World*. London: SAGE p. 78.
69. Thaler, R. H., & Sunstein, C. R. (2008). *Nudge*. New Haven: Yale University Press, p. 25.
70. An intoxication with power (also referred to as 'hubris') crowds out leaders' rational decision-making processes and creates space for biased intuitive judgements to take centre stage. George W. Bush's inclinations to go with his gut instincts at the time of the Iraq invasion in 2003 has been cited as an example of a hubristically-inclined world leader's decisions becoming skewed significantly under conditions of complicit followership (a 'neoconservative' senior team) and a conducive context (post-9/11 and the 'war of terror'). See: Claxton et al. (2015) op. cit.

71. Mao, F. (2020). Is Australia really seeing more shark attacks? *BBC News*. Available online at: https://www.bbc.co.uk/news/world-australia-54112992 Accessed 02.04.2022.
72. Chen, Z., & Lurie, N. H. (2013). Temporal contiguity and negativity bias in the impact of online word of mouth. *Journal of Marketing Research*, 50(4): 463–476, p.464.
73. Nazlan, N. H., Tanford, S., & Montgomery, R. (2018). The effect of availability heuristics in online consumer reviews. *Journal of Consumer Behaviour*, 17(5): 449–460; Book, L. A., Tanford, S., & Chen, Y. (2016). Understanding the impact of negative and positive traveler reviews: Social influence and price anchoring effects. *Journal of Travel Research*, 55(8): 993–1007; Book, L. A., Tanford, S., Montgomery, R., & Love, C. (2018). Online traveler reviews as social influence: Price is no longer king. *Journal of Hospitality & Tourism Research*, 42(3): 445–475; Tanford, S., & Montgomery, R. (2015). The effects of social influence and cognitive dissonance on travel purchase decisions. *Journal of Travel Research*, 54(5): 596–610.
74. Griskevicius, V., & Kenrick, D. T. (2013). Fundamental motives: How evolutionary needs influence consumer behaviour. *Journal of Consumer Psychology*, 23(3): 372–386.
75. Baumeister, Roy F., Ellen Bratslavsky, Catrin Finkenauer, & Kathleen D. Vohs (2001), Bad is stronger than good. *Review of General Psychology*, 5(4): 323–70. Cited in Chen, Z. & Lurie, N. H. (2013). Temporal contiguity and negativity bias in the impact of online word of mouth. *Journal of Marketing Research*, 50(4): 463–476.
76. Wiles, M. A. (2007). The effect of customer service on retailers' shareholder wealth: the role of availability and reputation cues. *Journal of Retailing*, 83(1): 19–31.
77. Ibid.
78. Ibid.
79. Barber, L. (2020). *The Powerful and the Damned: Private Diaries in Turbulent Times*. London: W. H. Allen, p. 45.
80. Hayibor, S., & Wasieleski, D. M. (2009). Effects of the use of the availability heuristic on ethical decision-making in organizations. *Journal of Business Ethics*, 84(1): 151–165.
81. Ibid.
82. Finucane, M. L., Alhakami, A. L. I., Slovic, P., & Johnson, S. M. (2000). The affect heuristic in judgments of risks and benefits. *Journal of Behavioural Decision-Making*, 17: 1–17.
83. Adapted from: Kahneman, D., & Frederick, S. (2002). Representativeness revisited: Attribute substitution in intuitive judgment. In Gilovich, T., Griffin, D., & Kahneman, D. (Eds.). *Heuristics and Biases: The Psychology of Intuitive Judgment*. Cambridge: Cambridge University Press, pp. 49–81, p. 53.
84. Kahneman, D., & Frederick, S. (2002). Representativeness revisited: Attribute substitution in intuitive judgment. In Gilovich, T., Griffin, D., & Kahneman, D. (Eds.). (2002). *Heuristics and Biases: The Psychology of Intuitive Judgment*. Cambridge: Cambridge University Press, pp. 49–81, p. 53.
85. Myers, D. G. (2008). *Intuition, Its Powers and Perils*. New Haven: Yale University Press, p. 33
86. Blackmore, S. (2003). *Consciousness: An Introduction*. London: Hodder and Stoughton.
87. Fiske, S. T., & Taylor, S. E. (1991). *Social Cognition*. New York: McGraw-Hill Book Company.
88. Gilovich, T., Griffin, D., & Kahneman, D. (Eds.). (2002). *Heuristics and Biases: The Psychology of Intuitive Judgment*. Cambridge: Cambridge University Press, p. 10.

3
How Gut Feeling Sometimes Gets It Right
Fast and Frugal Heuristics

Overview

The two main ideas of this chapter are 'ecological rationality' and 'fast and frugal' heuristics. The work of the German psychologist Gerd Gigerenzer is centre-stage. Ecological rationality aims to understand how people can be effective decision-makers by using simple heuristics or 'rules of thumb' that fit well with the structure of their actual, as opposed to a lab-based, decision-making environment (hence 'ecological'). It has three principles: first, the metaphor of the mind as an 'adaptive toolbox'; second, the mind's 'evolved capacities' are the raw materials out of which heuristics are constructed; third, better decisions can be taken using less information—'less can be more'. Fast-and-fugal heuristics are simple, task-specific strategies for making judgements and taking decisions; they are one of the tools of bounded rationality. The theory of fast-and-frugal heuristics was developed by a team of researchers led by Gigerenzer whose view of intuition aligns with an evolutionary view of the mind as an adaptive toolbox.[i] Gigerenzer criticizes 'Linda-type' problems because they overlook the cognitive skills that enable human beings to go automatically beyond the information given to navigate an ambiguous and uncertain world. The chapter looks at three types of 'fast-and-frugals', the recognition-, social- and reason-based heuristics, and considers their relevance to and applications in business decision-making.

Less Can Be More

In 2009, BBC Radio 4 in its long-running programme about numbers and statistics 'More or Less' conducted a live experiment. It asked listeners in New York and London the following question: 'Which of the following US cities has the higher population: Detroit or Milwaukee?' The results were utterly counter-intuitive: 82 per cent of London listeners got the answer correct (Detroit) but only 65 per cent of New York

---

[i] One of Gigerenzer's most popular books on intuition is called *Gut Feelings*, hence the title of this chapter.

listeners answered correctly.[1] What could possibly explain why more Londoners than New Yorkers could give the correct answer to a question about American geography? The answer was that the New Yorkers knew too much whilst the Londoners had a beneficial degree of ignorance. As a result, Londoners could simply go with their gut. They had heard more about Detroit than about Milwaukee and therefore arrived intuitively at the not unreasonable conclusion, quickly and with cognitive economy, that Detroit was the larger of the two. A fast-and-frugal mental short cut led more Londoners than New Yorkers to the correct answer.

The view of intuition as a fast-and-frugal way of taking decisions presented in this chapter aligns with two fundamentals of human behaviour: bounded rationality with its origins in the work of Herbert Simon and human evolution with its origins in the work of Charles Darwin. These two themes coalesce in the work of Gerd Gigerenzer, Director of the Harding Centre for Risk Literacy in Potsdam and author of, amongst other works, *Gut Feelings: Short Cuts to Better Decision-Making* (2007). Gigerenzer is one of the originators and main proponents of 'fast-and-frugal heuristics' based on the principles of 'ecological rationality'. Fast-and-frugal heuristics are simple rules of thumb that can make us smarter in the real world. For example, the task of predicting the winner of a tennis Grand Slam tournament, such as Wimbledon, could be approached in at least two ways: first, by using the Association of Tennis Professionals rankings to predict that a higher-ranked player will win each game, or; second, take the mental short cut of predicting the winner based on the simple rule of thumb 'if you have heard of one player, but not the other, predict that the recognized player will win'. The rule of thumb is cognitively economical because there are only three rules: search (by retrieving recognition information from memory, 'have I heard of this player?'), stop (by stopping the search once a player is recognized, 'I have heard of this player, therefore stop searching'), and decide (by going with the recognized object, 'Conclude that this player is more likely to win').[2] Processes such as recognition are designed into the 'adaptive toolbox' of the human mind to be intuitive therefore there is 'no way round intuition' and in actual fact we 'could achieve little without it [intuition]'.[3] Gigerenzer's work presents an optimistic view of an unconscious mind that can be intuitively intelligent rather than dumb. His research gives us good reasons to trust our intuitions, sometimes.

Bounded and Ecological Rationality

There are some situations, including in business, where perfect (economic) rationality is not the best way to take a decision. Gigerenzer uses the term 'ecological rationality' to capture the idea that our thinking processes must match the requirements of a given decision-making environment. The concept of ecological rationality is based on two fundamental principles. First, the mind is an adaptive toolbox (this is a metaphor for the mind's repertoire of cognitive capacities) which contains tools in the form of rules of thumb (interchangeable in Gigerenzer's writings for heuristics) that help us to solve certain types of problems in the real world. The metaphor of a tool is intended to convey the idea that, for example, a screwdriver is useful for screwing-in a screw but useless for tightening a nut; for a that task a different tool, a spanner, is required. Second, far from being second-best to rationality, better decisions can be taken intuitively using less information—'less can be more'.[4]

Gigerenzer contrasts ecological rationality with one of the original precepts of the heuristics and biases research, namely that which mental short cuts were assumed to be second-best to effortful computational strategies, see Chapter 1. The aim of the classical approach is to maximize utility in keeping with the principles of economic rationality. But as we know, Herbert Simon considered the logical but idealized world of economic rationality as an unsettling, unsatisfactory, and ultimately dubious account of describing how humans actually make choices in the real world. In Gigerenzer's view the heuristics and biases approach emphasizes 'irrationality rather than rationality'[5], i.e. by focusing on when things go wrong, and can be considered to be 'non-ecological' in that 'it doesn't relate the mind to its [actual as opposed to artificial] environment'.[6]

Simon is a recurring figure in Gigerenzer's work and his theory of bounded rationality is a prequel to and forerunner of ecological rationality[7]. An intellectual thread is discernible from Gigerenzer (whose early work dates to the 1980s) back though Simon (1950s) and ultimately to Chester Barnard (1930s). Simon used a scissors analogy to emphasize the importance of the relationship between the mind and its environment in decision-making as follows: 'behaviour is shaped by a scissors whose two blades are the structure of task environments and the computational capabilities of the actor'.[8] Scissors only work when both blades are used. Hence, bounded rationality is defined both by the bounds (i.e. the limits) of actors' computational capabilities and their knowledge of alternatives and of consequences (the task environment). As was discussed in Chapter 2, human decision-makers 'satisfice' (make a choice that is good enough) because they do not, in Simon's words, have the 'wits' (i.e. the computational capacity based on the available information) to 'maximize' (make the 'best' choice in order to extract as much utility, or value, as possible from a decision). In line with Simon's scissors analogy, ecological rationality is defined by Gigerenzer as adaptive behaviours that arise out of the fit between mechanisms of the mind and the structure of the environment.[9] Based on this idea, Gigerenzer set out to understand: first, how various simple heuristics work; and second, in which environments it is intelligent to use them.

As far as the relationship between Gigerenzer's views and those of the heuristics and biases researchers on the simplifying operations of the human mind are concerned, Gigerenzer and his colleague Daniel Goldstein argued that it is misleading to think of heuristics and biases as being opposed to classical rationality because in their view they are actually on the same page. This is because a reasoning error in the heuristics and biases view is defined in terms of a discrepancy between logically and mathematically correct reasoning in the manner of classical rationality (for example, the logic of the conjunction principle or the mathematics of base rates) and the quick-and-dirty heuristics (such as representativeness or availability) that characterize actual reasoning.

Both classical rationality and heuristics and biases share normative assumptions about how decision-makers ought to choose (i.e. they prescribe a standard) based on the laws of mathematics, probability, and statistics. An implication, if one adopts a purist heuristics and biases stance, is that intuitions should be treated with suspicion and be replaced by computation whenever possible. As we know, the heuristics and biases research showed that humans are capable of departing seriously from the principles of economic rationality when they use their intuition and that this can have negative (for example, biased) consequences for judgement and decision-making.[10] The downside of intuition is laid bare. On the other hand, Gigerenzer's work presents an alternative, and more optimistic, view of intuition.

Rules of Thumb

A rule of thumb is a simple, quick and convenient means of estimation. Gigerenzer's work is concerned essentially with small set of rules of thumb or heuristics that can make us smarter in the real world. His 2001 book with Peter Todd was entitled *Simple Heuristics That Make Us Smart*. The heuristics that Gigerenzer and his co-researchers have studied are simple in that they are computationally fast and cognitively frugal ways of arriving at judgements and taking decisions. By 'fast' Gigerenzer is referring to mental short cuts that do not involve time-consuming computations and deliberations. By 'frugal' Gigerenzer is referring to mental short cuts that involve searching for and using only for some and not all of the available information, i.e. they are economical in terms of the mental resources required.

By way of example Gigerenzer and Todd describe a simple but critical heuristic used by physicians to make quick and accurate decisions in the critical care context of hospital emergency rooms. When victims of suspected heart attack are rushed into hospital emergency rooms doctors need to decide urgently if a patient is 'high risk' or 'low risk' and treat them accordingly. Rather than coming to a decision by combining a large number of relevant measures into an overall assessment (in the manner of 'maximization'), a much simpler approach can be adopted which consists of only three steps. Step one: classify as 'high risk' if the patient has a systolic blood pressure of less than 91, if not move to step two. Step two: classify as 'low risk' if the patient is less than 62.5 years old, if not move to step three. Step three, classify as 'high risk' if sinus tachycardia is present (i.e. a heart rate greater than 100 beats per minute). By using this heuristic to answer a maximum of three simple 'yes/no' questions a doctor can classify a patient's level of risk very quickly, give them priority and proceed to potentially lifesaving treatment.

Gigerenzer and Todd specify three reasons why this simple heuristic decision process is fast and frugal. First, it ignores a number of the available predictors. Second, it searches only for some of the available information. Third it uses simple 'yes/no' questions in a sequential step-by-step process. It has been found to be more accurate than other complex statistical methods, for example in classifying heart attack patients according to level of risk.[11] Even though such heuristics are executed habitually and intuitively by experienced and highly skilled practitioners, they are nonetheless deployed consciously and deliberately. An emergency room doctor would be able, if asked, to articulate the reasons behind the actions being taken. This contrasts with the view of intuition as 'knowing but without knowing how or why you know'.[12]

Gigerenzer positions fast-and-frugal heuristics as one of two categories of bounded rationality. The first is Simon's original form of bounded rationality in which the well-known mental short cut of satisficing works by setting an aspiration level that is good enough and terminating the search once a satisfactory alternative is found, as in the case of selecting an item of food from a restaurant menu. However, in Gigerenzer's view even this form of bounded rationality could end up being computationally unreasonable because it could leave the door open to extensive deliberation in order to set the appropriate aspiration level, for example by a diner laboriously and tediously going through every menu item and rating it on calories, nutritional value, cost, etc. Instead Gigerenzer whittles the process down further to a small number of mental short cuts that are highly efficient in terms of time, knowledge, and computation. In so doing Gigerenzer has sought to distil bounded rationality down into what he considers to be its 'purest form'.[13]

Fast-and-Frugal Heuristics

Gigerenzer and colleagues have identified four main classes of fast-and-frugal heuristics: (1) 'ignorance-based decision-making' (also referred to as the 'recognition heuristic'); (2) 'one reason decision-making' which relies on simple search and stopping rules (including the 'take the best', 'take the last', and 'minimalist' search rules); (3) 'elimination' (using cues to eliminate options until only one remains); and (4) in keeping with Simon's foundational thinking, 'satisficing'.[14] Additional heuristics include the 'gaze heuristic' and the '1/N' rule. Briefly, the gaze heuristic goes as follows: to catch a high ball in a sport, such as baseball or cricket, start running and adjust your running speed so that your angle of gaze remains constant. An example is of the 1/N heuristic goes as follows: to compile an investment portfolio that maximizes return and minimizes risk follow the 'wisdom of diversification by equal allocation', i.e. use the '1/N' rule for allocating resources equally between N alternatives (analogous to dividing your assets equally between your children).[15]

Gigerenzer proposes that fast-and-frugal heuristics are the 'tools' of bounded rationality and as such they are relevant to managerial decision-making in general and to managerial intuition in particular. Under the uncertain conditions that typify much of managerial work, complex strategies such as predicting job performance from applicant data, may be counterproductive in that they attempt to extract too much information from the data and can end up 'mistaking noise for signal'.[16] On the other hand, intuitive judgements based on fast-and-frugal heuristics present managers with strategies for cutting through a morass of data and making efficient and effective decisions on the basis of a few simple rules.[17] In what follows, several types of fast-and-frugal heuristics that are relevant to business decision-making will be discussed: recognition-based and social- and reason-based fast-and-frugal heuristics.

Recognition-based Fast-and-Frugal Heuristics

The recognition heuristic is perhaps best-illustrated using the simple problem that Gigerenzer and his co-researchers posed for two groups of students (Americans and Germans) in their early research and that the BBC replicated in its radio programme 'More or Less' (see above). The students were asked the following simple question on the very reasonable presumption that it would be easier for Americans and harder for Germans:

> Which of the following US cities has the higher population? Detroit or Milwaukee

The result surprised and momentarily wrong-footed Gigerenzer and his team. The Americans were divided; some opted for Detroit (60 per cent) while others opted for Milwaukee (40 per cent). Amongst the Germans however almost all of them (90 per cent) got it right (Detroit). The conundrum for the researchers was to try and understand why more people with a greater knowledge of American geography (Americans) made an incorrect judgement on the relative size of US cities while more people with less knowledge about American geography (Germans) made a correct judgement. The result seemed counter-intuitive: how could *more* knowledge be associated with *less* accurate judgements?

The explanation that Gigerenzer and colleagues offered was the simple, and intuitive, perceptual process of 'recognition'. The German students and the London radio listeners had little other than their intuition to go on rather than having well-informed reasons based on local knowledge. American students knew too much. They ended up being 'muddled in their judgement'.[18] The recognition heuristic is an example of 'ignorance-based' decision-making. It relies, as the name suggests, for its effectiveness on the principle of not knowing too much, that is of having a 'beneficial degree of ignorance'.[19] Gigerenzer and his colleagues reasoned that it was much more likely that the German students had heard of Detroit rather than Milwaukee. The lack of recognition of Milwaukee was indicative to them that Detroit, which they had heard of, had a larger population simply because it was known to them.

In general, for recognition to work there must be a substantial correlation between whether an entity is recognized or not and the criterion variable (in the above example, the criterion was population size). On the other hand, if the relationship between recognition and the criterion variable is random then the heuristic cannot work. For example, recognizing a city and judging its mean rainfall would not work because recognition and rainfall are not correlated. For a beneficial degree of ignorance to work the decision-maker's level of ignorance has to be correlated with the variable of interest and be beneficial in that it can yield a correct judgement. As a result, ignorant subjects are able to make beneficial, recognition-based inferences about a criterion variable based on knowledge that is not directly available to them. The Germans took, in this case, the sensible 'bet' that because they had heard of Detroit and not heard of Milwaukee it would not be unreasonable to infer that Detroit was the larger of the two. The correlation between recognition and the criterion variable (a feature of the environment) makes the relying on recognition (the relevant aspect of cognition) ecologically rational. Gigerenzer and his colleague Daniel Goldstein defined the recognition heuristic as follows:

> If one of two objects is recognized and the other is not, then infer that the recognized object has the higher value with respect to the criterion.[20]

The underlying psychological processes build on the human brain's evolved capacity for the efficient recognition of environmental cues and the use of recognition memory to make quick, low-effort judgements. It differs from Kahneman and Tversky's availability heuristic in two ways. First, Kahneman and Tversky's availability heuristic relies on recall as a result of imaginability, vividness and emotional salience (think of shark attacks) rather than a simple recognition (we can recognize things even though they may not be vivid and emotional). Second, Gigerenzer's recognition heuristic is 'binary' (involving a yes/no judgement between one of two objects) rather than being an evaluation of a situation based on imaginability, vividness and emotional salience. Gigerenzer and Goldstein characterize the recognition heuristic as 'non-compensatory' in that 'no other information about the unrecognized object is searched for and, therefore, no other information can reverse the choice determined by recognition'.[21]

The recognition heuristic has been studied as a predictor of outcomes in domains ranging from success in sports, to political elections and disease incidence rates.[22] For example, in a study of how laypeople make forecasts of the results of sports events, researchers asked groups with different degrees of knowledge (laypeople and experts, or 'soccer pundits') to forecast winners of the twenty-four first-round matches of the Euro 2004 soccer tournament and to indicate whether they had heard of the national soccer team for each participating country.[23] The researchers assessed the use of the recognition heuristic by looking at how often recognized teams were judged to be more likely to win when playing against an unrecognized team. Two outcomes of the research stood out. First, a recognized competitor was judged to be stronger than a non-recognized competitor in 90.5 per cent of lay persons' forecasts. Second, by using the recognition heuristic, lay participants were able to predict outcomes at well above chance levels (70 per cent accuracy). Fortunately for the official football body FIFA, the recognition heuristic's level of accuracy was below that of direct indicators of team strength such as FIFA rankings which predicted outcomes at around 85 per cent accuracy. Also encouragingly, soccer pundits outperformed lay participants on predicting the outcomes of the sixteen non-drawn matches (76.6 per cent versus 64.7 per cent respectively). When laypeople used the recognition heuristic in this study, they chose a recognized object in preference to an unrecognized one, regardless of other available information, and performed at levels above chance but below that of experts.

To test if and how people use available information in business, consumer behaviour researchers presented subjects with famous (easy-to-recognize) brands and less famous (less easy-to recognize) brands, for example, 'Dunlop' (heard of) and 'Gamma' (not heard of) in five product categories (for example, tennis racquets) along with positive, neutral or negative information about the brand (one- to five-star ratings).[24] The context was ecologically valid because subjects were presented with information in a simulated online shopping experience which was comparable to real-world online shopping which typically uses star-type recommendations. The results showed, unsurprisingly, that people rely substantially on recognition when choosing consumer products. The results also revealed three other findings that ought to be of interest to both marketers and consumers. First, recognized brands are preferred substantially preferred over unrecognized brands even if associated information about the recognized brand is clearly negative in comparison to the unrecognized brand. Secondly, positive star ratings had only a limited additional effect on the proportion of recognized brands chosen, compared to the neutral condition. Third, subjects took longer to choose when the recognized brand was accompanied by negative information, presumably because they were taking this information into account more carefully, for example by trying to make sense of 'why has this well-known brand got such a bad rating?' The results show that the recognition heuristic exerts a significant influence on consumer choice even when supplementary positive or negative information is available. Brand recognition appears to be one of the dominant influences on consumer choice. In practical terms, the recognition heuristic facilitates efficient decision-making when the choice set is large, as it often is especially in online purchasing environments. For the consumer, recognition makes life easier by reducing a larger choice set to a smaller consideration set.[25] It serves as an initial filtering mechanism which reduces the range of choices to a magnitude that our computationally compromised minds can cope with.

Gigerenzer illustrates various ways in which the mechanism of brand name recognition can work well or badly. Relying on brand name recognition is a reasonable heuristic to use when product quality is positively correlated with genuinely informative content about the product. The media play an important role in mediating between the recognition of an object and the quality (the criterion variable) for an object. Mere exposure makes recognition more likely. This gives the media enormous power, and this power is leveraged by the forces of advertising and marketing. If the amount of coverage in the media is warranted on the basis of, for example product quality (high product quality objects are mentioned more in the media than low quality products), this increases product recognition and influences consumer choice on reasonable grounds. However, the effect of the media works both ways. Recognition does not work well when it leads to relying on brand name recognition where recognition and quality are not correlated. The recognition heuristic may not be a sensible short cut if there is no correlation between quality and the information about the product in media, for example when spending on advertising simply increases brand recognition irrespective of brand quality.[26]

The recognition heuristic's strong claim is that when people make inferences about a recognized object they largely ignore other cues and arrive at their judgement largely on the basis of a binary of 'recognized' or 'unrecognized'.[27] This means that recognition is often used in a non-compensatory way, i.e. no other cues are used to reverse a judgement that is suggested by recognition.[28] Critics of this view—whilst not denying that recognition cues can often be valuable—argue that a balanced conclusion about the efficacy of recognition entails accepting that: first, heuristics such as recognition provide an adequate description of *some* decision-makers' behaviours *some* of the time; second, the evidence in support of the recognition heuristic is 'mixed'; third, that in coming to judgements people are likely to employ further information beyond mere recognition when discriminating between items, especially those which are expensive and involve consequential choices. This latter criticism has been supported by studies that show effects on judgement and decision-making of providing additional information.[29] New information about recognized brand objects (especially positive information) can affect choice. Hence, rather than being a purely non-compensatory strategy, it may be that recognition is processed in the mind in a compensatory way by being combined with other information in making purchases, for example product quality ratings but also additional information about a product's novel features or the firm's ethical, social, and environmental record.[30]

Gigerenzer and his team summarize the recognition heuristic as a smart and simple method for making inferences that is relied on consistently, and largely unconsciously, by people when it is ecologically rational to do so. They conclude that, as such, the recognition heuristic is an important adaptive tool and is the 'simplest realization of Herbert Simon's notion that boundedly rational decision making can arise from simple mental tools that are matched to the structure of the environment'.[31] The recognition-based heuristic is a general purpose tool that can be applied by novices in certain situations (for example, where they have a beneficial degree of ignorance) to yield decision outcomes that can be as good as the choices made through effortful and time-consuming analyses.[32]

However, the process may not be as clear-cut as presented. Recognition may assist in filtering the range of available options. Recognition gives decision-makers an initial sense for whether an object has a particular quality or an option is worth pursuing. This initial sense is triggered automatically and as such is a quick and cognitively economical way for making judgements and taking decisions. Acts of recognition are accomplished autonomously and largely unconsciously, i.e. they are intuitive. They make certain objects stand out and hence have the power to influence our decision-making even when we may not be aware that they are doing so[33]. That said, making doubly smart use of recognition sometimes entails pressing 'pause' and subjecting recognized objects to conscious scrutiny, for example by scratching the surface and enquiring into the environmental, social, and governance (ESG) track record of a recognized brand or business.[34]

Social and Reason-based Heuristics

In its simplest form the recognition heuristic is most successful when recognition is strongly correlated with the relevant criterion or outcome variable under conditions of a beneficial degree of ignorance. As we have seen it works, for example, when recognition of the name of a city correlates positively with its size (the criterion or outcome variable) and people do not know too much about the geography of the country concerned (as was the case in German students' knowledge of American geography). If recognition does not correlate with the criterion or outcome variable, if people are not sufficiently ignorant and when we are required to respond quickly to the behaviour of other people there are other ecologically rational fast-and-frugal short-cuts that Gigerenzer and his colleagues have identified. These involve searching actively for reasons or cues in the social or physical environment, and hence are referred to as social heuristics and reason-based heuristics.

Social-based Heuristics: An example of a social heuristic, which it is argued is based on human beings' unparalleled capacity for social learning and imitation,[35] is the 'Do-what-the-majority-do-heuristic: If you see the majority of your peers display a behaviour engage in the same behaviour'. Gigerenzer gives the example of 'get married when other people in one's social group do' as being the height of frugality since it involves little in the way of deliberation.[36] Such an approach comes with a strong health warning: simply following the crowd can create a herd mentality, is a high road to lazy thinking, and opens the door to unintended negative consequences such as groupthink, quashing of dissent, and other even more sinister outcomes.

The two basic forms of imitation identified by Gigerenzer are 'do what the majority of your peers do' and consistent with the idea of role modelling of behaviours, 'do what a successful person does'.[37] Whether imitation is appropriate or successful depends on the structure of the environment. Imitation can pay off in stable environments where what worked well in the past is judged as being likely to work well in the future. Imitation can also pay off where the consequences of a mistake are dangerous, for example a wise move might be to follow the crowd by not challenging a narcissistic CEO or an authoritarian president in a public arena. Imitation also results in the cultural transmission of information in wider society and in cultures of business organizations. In the cultures of business organizations, doing what the majority of our peers do satisfies our communal instincts and drives, creates conformity, and distinguishes the group from outsiders.[38] Moreover, creating a strong culture in a business that is difficult to imitate by a competitor is a rare and valuable source of competitive advantage.[39]

An efficient and sometimes effective social heuristic is to tap into the 'wisdom of crowds' by searching for and then averaging-out the actions of, or advice from, a number of different people or groups.[40] James Surowiecki, author of *The Wisdom of*

Crowds: Why the Many Are Smarter than the Few, noted that even though individually we may be hindered by limits to our rationality, it is possible, when collective judgements are aggregated in the right way, to reach a collectively 'wise' decision.[41] For example, in a study of investors' responses to acquisition announcements by a firm's management, it was found that investors do not draw blindly on management's perceptions of the anticipated synergies generated by an acquisition. They also draw on publicly available information in the form of stock market reactions to assess the management's claims. In so doing they are utilizing stock market sentiment astutely as a vicarious form of the wisdom of crowds.[42] 'Do-what-the majority-do' is one of a number of 'search-type heuristics'. It involves searching for and acting on cues from the observed behaviours of other people. Other search-type heuristics involve actively seeking reasons rather than passively responding to social cues such as observed behaviours.

Reason-based Heuristics: The recognition heuristic relies on the very simple cue of one of the options not being recognized. However, one of the obvious drawbacks of the recognition heuristic is when more than one of the available options is recognized or the decision does not lend itself to simple recognition. In such situations other strategies have to be mobilized. An alternative reason-based heuristic involving search employs the rule 'always choose the scenario where attribute "x" is best', where 'x' is one of a number of attributes. The validity of this heuristic has been tested in a medical context. It involved a study of the health consultation preferences of parents and guardians in the situation of their child becoming sick. Parents were presented with a scenario in which their child during the night is:

> Short of breath, wheezing and coughing and you decide to call a doctor ('general practitioner', GP). You have several options about the care you receive. These differ according to *who* your child sees, *where* they are seen, the *time* it takes between making the telephone call and receiving treatment, and whether the doctor seems to *listen* to what you have to say.[43]

Parents were offered the choice between two consultations (A and B) that varied in terms of: (1) where the consultation takes place; (2) whether the doctor is known to them; (3) time taken between making the call and treatment; and (4) whether the doctor seems to listen. A key factor in arriving at a decision was the relative importance that the parents attached to each of the four reasons for choosing a particular type of consultation. For the largest group of parents, the dominant reason was 'whether the doctors seems to listen to what you have to say'. The second most important reason was waiting time. The third most important reason was whether it was a doctor they knew. In fast-and-frugal terms the parents' decision-making in choosing between two different treatment scenarios involved a search-and-stop process as follows. Step 1: if the answer to the 'does the doctor listen question' is 'yes' for Consultation A and 'no' for Consultation 'B' then stop and choose Consultation A (and vice versa). Step 2: if the answer to the 'does the doctor listen question' is 'yes' for both Consultation A and B then proceed to the 'how long to wait' question, and if the answer is 20 minutes for Consultation A and 40 minutes for Consultation B then choose Consultation A. Step 3: if the waiting times are the same then proceed to the 'do you know the doctor' question, and if the answer is 'yes' for Consultation A, and 'no' for Consultation B then choose scenario A (and vice versa).

An example of the Take the Best heuristic in business would be a consumer choosing between different types of milk in the supermarket. The typical supermarket shelf is likely to contain dozens of different types, many of which are likely to be recognized. Supposing a consumer is keen to buy a low-fat skimmed milk, this is the first criterion which excludes immediately all the non-skimmed milks. Then suppose there are three which are skimmed, one is organic, one is not, and the other is lactose-free. If the consumer has a lactose intolerance the choice is made in favour of a low fat, lactose-free milk; this is the stopping rule; if not a different criterion needs to be mobilized until a stopping rule, such as price or locally sourced, is found which discriminates clearly between the options. In this process the three types of low-fat skimmed milk are not weighed-up concurrently according to a set of attributes, instead the most important criterion is taken first (low fat) and the process proceeds to the next most important criterion (for example lactose intolerance) and so forth until a decision can be made by taking the best. This is a cue-based heuristic that does not require the information about the different milks to be integrated, instead the consumer's choice is based on single cues at appropriate points in the process.

Gigerenzer describes this decision-making process as deploying the 'Take the Best' heuristic because it is a one-reason decision rule whereby a judgement is based on *one* good reason only at each step in the process. It is the 'best' one reason because it discriminates most effectively between the alternatives at a given point in the process rather than having to simultaneously and effortlessly consider multiple cues weight them and make an appraisal.[44] Decision-making using Take the Best entails using the cue that is the first to discriminate between the alternatives. The rule of thumb is 'take the best cue' and 'ignore the rest of the cues'.

The Take the Best heuristic has a simple 'lexicographic' structure meaning that it is a sequential process in which the ordering of alternatives is an important principle. Take the Best consists of three sequential 'building blocks'. First, a 'search rule' in which reasons are formulated in order of importance (in the example able they were in order: 'a listening doctor'; 'the waiting time'; and 'a known doctor'). Second, a 'stopping rule' in which searching stops as soon as the alternatives for one reason differ (in the example, they differed on 'a known doctor'). Third, a 'decision rule' in which the alternative is chosen on the basis of the differentiating reason (in the example, 'known' versus 'not known' doctor).

Burglary is a recognized career path for some professional criminals. The business of skilled burglary involves considerable knowledge and skill in choosing a target.[45] Gigerenzer studied how burglars incarcerated for their crimes in London prisons reported using the Take the Best heuristic in identifying which premises to break in to.[46] The most important cue was whether there was a burglar alarm or not. If one premises had an alarm and the other did not then the process is stopped and the non-alarmed premises was chosen for the break-in. If both or neither premises have an alarm then the burglars would proceed to the next question (for example, ground floor access) and so on until a differentiating cue (a reason to choose one over the other) is found. The police officers who hunted burglars also used Take the Best to get into the minds of their quarry, but their most important cue was whether or not a likely burglar could have access to the ground floor of the premises. Interestingly therefore, it seems as though the burglars and the police officers ranked the cues differently. This observation raises the intriguing question of how do burglars know how to rank the cues to achieve the best outcome, and similarly how do police officers arrive at their knowledge given that they do not perform break-ins? The answer seems to be that the burglars learn the best cue order from their direct experiences whereas the police offers learned about it indirectly and vicariously presumably from burglars they had arrested and interviewed who may or may not have been telling the truth.[47] Of course, a question is raised as to whether the really successful burglars who do not get caught and avoid ending up in prison, and hence are still out there performing break-ins, use a different Take the Best heuristic to the jailed, and presumably less successful, burglars.

In a very different and more legitimate business context Shenghua Luan, Jochen Reb, and Gigerenzer tested a variant of Take the Best, which they referred to as 'Δ-inference', in the context of personnel selection decisions. Personnel selection is rife with uncertainty and HR practitioners have a habit of showing a 'stubborn reliance' on intuition.[48] In this example, Take the Best decides which cues are valid and integrates them in a process of comparing differences (Δ, delta) between each valid cue to arrive at evaluation. In the Δ-inference heuristic the stopping rule is 'If the difference between a pair of options (for example, two job candidates) on a cue (for example, general mental ability) exceeds a threshold value Δ, then stop the search'. The decision rule is 'choose the option with the higher (better) cue value'.[49] In common with Take the Best, Δ-inference is sequential (cues are examined in order of importance), non-compensatory (the process stops if the difference for a cue exceeds a threshold), and frugal (the process is cognitively economical). Cues are ranked based on prior evidence or determination of their perceived importance. Luan and colleagues used the example of predicting future job performance (FJP) on the basis of general mental ability (GMA), conscientiousness (one of the personality 'big five', CON), and structured interview performance (SIP).

They illustrated the process with the case of two fictitious candidates who score as follows: Candidate A, GMA 116, CON 47, SIP 3.6; Candidate B, GMA 102, CON 55, SIP 3.9. On the basis of the three scores (GMA, CON, SIP) each candidate clearly has their pros and cons, GMA for A and CON and SIP for B. However, if GMA is ranked as the most important cue and the difference (Δ) between A and B is sufficiently large then Candidate A would be chosen without any need to reference CON or SIP, see Table 3.1. An alternative rational strategy would be to use logistic regression (a complex statistical weighting-and-adding strategy) with FJP as the dependent variable and GMA, CON, and SIP as the independent variables in the model and use this to solve the problem. However, this latter approach is likely to be resource intensive,

Table 3.1 Predictors of future job performance (Luan et al., 2019).

Predictors of Future Job Performance (FJP)	Candidate A	Candidate B
General Mental Ability (GMA)	116	102
Conscientiousness (CON)	47	55
Structured Interview Performance (SIP)	3.6	3.9

require specialist skills, and be time consuming and could therefore be potentially unrealistic.

Luan and colleagues compared a rational approach (logistic regression) with the heuristic approach (Δ-inference) using a real-world data set of 236 job applicants to an airline company. These were applicants who were eventually hired and had their on-job performance assessed by their supervisors three months later. The researchers ran several models which varied the sample size of observations on which predictions were based. Although future job performance (FJP) is notoriously difficult to predict, Δ-inference outperformed logistic regression with a prediction accuracy of around 0.63. The researchers interpreted this as evidence that a 'heuristic strategy [such as Δ-inference] can lead to more accurate predictions and decisions in a real-world personnel selection' and can perform better than complex strategies, albeit the differences are sometimes small.[50] The heuristic strategy had two distinct practical benefits: first, it involved only having to search around half of the cues to make a decision thus allowing for faster and less costly decisions; second, it avoided the temptations of analytical over-indulgence in situations where there is a surfeit of data.

Take the Best approaches (including Δ-inference) are sequential sampling strategies that terminate once evidence in favour of one alternative is found. Rational approaches also sequentially sample but they terminate only when all the available information has been sampled and assessed.[51] For boundedly rational human decision-makers operating in the real-world, sampling and evaluating all the available information can be an unreasonable and unmet expectation. The Take the Best approach is more ecologically rational than the classical rational approach because it better fits the constraints of time and resources under which real-world decisions—such as deciding which of two treatments for a sick child to select, which house to burgle, or which candidate to hire—are taken. The challenge for decision-makers in business is to be able to judge when a fast-and-frugal approach is likely to perform more accurately, will be quicker, and is less cognitively demanding than other approaches.

In a study of how managers in the creative industries took the decision of which innovation product to invest in (for example, 'which book to publish?', 'which film to produce?', 'what software to develop?', etc.) researchers found that the best results came from combining intuition (for example, having a hunch or gut feeling about a new design or product) with some very simple heuristics. These simple heuristics that managers relied on included tallying (the product with the highest number of favourable points), taking the best (the product they thought would be the best), experience (the one the most experienced person in the team wanted), majority (the one most people wanted), and recognition (the one that is most recognized). By relying on a combination of their gut feelings and these simple heuristics, managers were found to be able to take decisions at the fuzzy front end of new product development that were at least as accurate—and were definitely quicker—than when they relied on data and analytical processes alone to reach their decisions.[52]

Why Fast and Frugal Heuristics Get It Right, Sometimes

Gigerenzer defines an intuition as a judgement that appears rapidly in conscious awareness, whose underlying reasons we are not fully aware of and that is strong enough to warrant being acted upon. Intuitions are the products of evolved capacities of the brain that give rise to genetically, individually, and culturally created and transmitted rules of thumb that are the components of the human mind's adaptive toolbox. As such intuitions are short cuts and simplifications for making judgements and taking decisions which depend not only on the evolved cognitive capacities of the human brain but also on the characteristics of the environment in which judgements and decisions are taken.[53]

It is not unreasonable to assume that our understanding of heuristics would be aided greatly by knowing the purpose for which the capacity to take mental short cuts was designed and asking, 'why did it evolve?'. Presumably there are very good biological reasons why the brain acquired a capacity to make judgements and take decisions on the basis of a series of simple rules of thumb that turn out to be effective but which on the face of it appear to be contrary to the principles of classical rationality. The fast-and-frugal researchers speculate on some of the reasons why the capacity to deploy such heuristics might have evolved in the human organism. As an example, they cite the 'imitate the majority' heuristic referred to briefly above which would have served an adaptive function for promoting social behaviour, bonding, affiliation, and altruistic behaviour within and towards members of one's tribe. Similarly, to follow the wisdom of the crowd (or tribe in our evolutionary past) would likely be a safe and efficient bet.

Even though the capacity to make judgements and take decisions on the basis of mental short cuts evolved to solve a particular sets of adaptive challenges in *Homo sapiens*' physically and socially challenging ancestral environment they generalize to other tasks and can be used to solve a range of problems in our culturally created modern environment. For example, the adaptive challenge of hunting is met by the 'gaze heuristic' (automatically and accurately following the trajectory of an object in motion) and which is now applied successfully in sports in catching a ball, a purpose for which the underlying mechanism of 'maintaining constant angle of gaze' did not evolve. Likewise with the adaptive challenge of the allocation of scarce resources to achieve fairness in the apportionment of goods between offspring and friends (the $1/N$ heuristic). Gigerenzer and colleagues argue that $1/N$ can be applied successfully to dividing cash in an investment portfolio, a purpose for which the underlying cognitive mechanisms were not created. These modern applications are not equivalent to the purposes for which the underlying mechanism evolved but nonetheless the tools in the toolbox are practical and flexible can be adapted to suit other purposes.

Heuristics are comprised of building blocks that can be expressed as 'rules', for example 'search', 'stop', and 'decide' in the Take the Best heuristic, 'recognize' in the recognition heuristic and so forth. The raw materials for these building blocks are evolved capacities. An evolved capacity (such as recognizing, recalling, counting, etc.) is innate and prepared genetically by nature. It achieves its expression and application through experience and by nurture in the human organism's socio-cultural setting. Gigerenzer and colleagues give the example of cue ordering in Take the Best. Nature may have provided humans with cue-ordering capacity (for example, assess food edibility before food texture) whilst institutions require cue-ordering behaviour (for example, before turning right look for stop sign before assessing oncoming traffic). The practical challenge for us is identifying the class of situations in which any evolved capacity, as manifested in fast-and-frugal heuristics, is likely to be successful.

Gigerenzer and his colleague Ulrich Hoffrage argue that evolutionary explanations offer a plausible account for why the human mind is poorly attuned to making inferences on the basis of human creations such as probability theory or percentages that are only hundreds of years or at most millennia old. These are purposes for which the human mind could not possibly have evolved. On the other hand, the human mind did evolve to learn experientially, observationally, and socially. For most of our species' history we sampled and encoded information in the form of frequencies by processes such as simple tallying from encounters in the real world. Examples of tally sticks and tallying beads which could have been used to record frequencies have been found in archaeological sites that are tens of thousands of years old.[54]

The evolutionary psychologists Leda Cosmides and John Toobey argue that contrary to the judgement-under-uncertainty view (typified by the heuristics and biases approach), human beings evolved to be good intuitive statisticians of what they term the 'frequentist' school. Human beings are adapted for and skilled in using frequency information as both the input and the output for the assessment of likelihoods. Cosmides and Toobey develop their arguments via speculations on the example of hunting behaviour in the ancestral environment. The human brain did not evolve to compute a single-event probability that 'if we go to the north canyon today there is a 0.25 probability that the hunt will be successful'.[55] Instead, humans encountered the actual frequencies of experienced events, for example 'we were successful five out of the last 20 times we hunted in the north canyon'. They were therefore able to sense experientially that 'hunting in the north canyon today' would be a reasonable course of action. Moreover, it is much more likely that relevant information, such as 'how successful is the north canyon as a hunting ground?', was passed between individuals in the same social group and across generations through the use of narratives and images rather than as probabilities and statistics. Cosmides and Toobey refer to the 'rich flow of observable frequencies' that our ancestors were immersed in and which must have been 'used to improve decision-making'. It is this experiential mode, learning from, sensing of, and engaging with the world, to which our minds are adapted and attuned. Our inductive reasoning processes evolved to be alert to frequency information. They encode it automatically and effortlessly and then use it as the raw material for sensing situations of varying degrees of familiarity, making judgements and taking decisions intuitively.[56]

In support of this view, research suggests that framing a problem in naturalistic/frequentist terms rather than in mathematical/probabilistic terms appears to influence the way in which a problem is solved. For instance, the error of judgement associated with the conjunction fallacy which Kahneman and Tversky's Linda Problem so brilliantly exposed (see Chapter 2) was 'drastically reduced' when subjects were asked for *relative frequency* (that is, 'To how many out of 100 people do the Linda statements[ii] apply?') rather than *single event probability* (that is, 'Which of the following Linda statements are more likely?'). This subtle linguistic manipulation suggests that most people think it more probable that Linda is a bank teller and active in the feminist movement because of, at least in part, 'a common [but excusable] misunderstanding of the probability concept'.[57] Our evolved capacities for social judgement allow us to take a fair and reasonable bet that Linda is more likely to be 'bank teller who is active in the feminist movement' by inferring from the problem and its context. Those same evolved capacities also cause us to be perplexed when we are told that our intuitive but incorrect response to the Linda problem is flawed logically. It is worth reiterating that those same evolved capacities which can work well can also cause us to make social judgements that are biased, unfair, and discriminatory.

The nub question posed by Cosmides and Toobey is: 'If making accurate judgments under uncertainty is an important adaptive problem, why would natural selection have designed a mind that uses error-prone heuristics rather than an accurate calculus of probability?'[58] Another way of saying this is why would natural selection have designed the human mind to have a sensing system which automatically and intuitively makes quick, low effort judgements that can be systematically wrong? Cosmides and Toobey also note that although the evolved mechanisms on which our intuitions are based have been subjected to 'millions of years of field testing against a very rich and complexly structured environment' no system will be error-free even under natural conditions. In the modern world there are many real-world judgements that are not amenable to the alternative 'logic' of our intuitions. Consequently, intuition ends up being a hinderance because it evolved to solve a different set of problems under a different set of circumstances. Nonetheless we are stuck with it and fast-and-frugal heuristics are a psychological mechanism which helps to explain both the marvels and the flaws of intuitive judgement and decision-making.

Judgements and decisions that are not amenable to fully-fledged rational analysis abound in business management and evidence is beginning to accumulate for if and when fast-and-frugal heuristics perform well. A Take the Best approach based

---

[ii] Linda statements: 'Linda is a bank teller'; 'Linda is a bank teller and active in the feminist movement'

on ranked trustworthiness criteria (for example, 'conscientious and responsible') have been shown to outperform Franklin's pros and cons method in predicting HR selection decisions.[59] In a study of entrepreneurial decision-making it was found that entrepreneurs who based the decision of where to locate their businesses on a 'less-is-more' smaller and simpler consideration set distilled from a larger choice set enjoyed higher chances of meeting or exceeding their own expectations of success.[60] When retail investors make decisions about how much trust to place in a financial advisor it has been found that their level of trust depends on a simple heuristic based on the advisor's communication style. These 'honest signals'[61] that the financial adviser creates through their choice of words and tone, which are difficult to suppress and hence function as a reliable indicator, were more important to retail investors than standard metrics based on investment portfolios past performances.[62] These are the kinds of signals that our brains evolved to be alert to and make sense of intuitively.

In making consequential judgements in business, as well as other complex professional and personal domains, decision-makers should bear in mind that their brain did not evolve to solve sophisticated calculations, at least of the kind that the modern environment demands of us in our day-to-day living such as interest rates, exchange rates, the odds of success, etc. Instead, it evolved to make informed inferences under the constraints of information, time, and computation in uncertain, fast-moving, and potentially survival-compromising physical environments and social settings. The intelligent application of appropriate and effective fast-and-frugal heuristics offers managers a strategy for taking decisions under the different, but sometimes no less exacting, conditions and challenges of the modern environment.

Simplicity Is a Virtue

The human brain can only cope with so much information, as a consequence people often eschew complexity in favour of simplicity. Perhaps nowhere is this more true than in the area of consumer choice given the abundance of goods and services that the online environment has made available. Psychologists have sought to understand the relationship between consumer choice and satisfaction in order to answer the question: does more choice make for more satisfied consumers? For example, when potential consumers of gourmet jams were confronted by more (twenty-four) and fewer (six) flavours of gourmet jams, although more of them were attracted initially to the tasting booth with twenty-four jams, they were much more likely to purchase jam subsequently if they had encountered the display of only six jams. Likewise, even though people reported enjoying the process of choosing chocolate more when it was from a display of thirty rather than six different types, consumers ended-up more dissatisfied and regretful of the choices that were made from the thirty-chocolate display. In the extended choice situations consumers found the process of choosing to be more difficult and more frustrating than in the limited choice situation. The burden of making a good versus a bad decision made them discontented, and ultimately in the face of choice overload most opted for satisficing heuristic.[63] These findings support two of the main precepts behind fast-and-frugal heuristics: less can sometimes be more, and simplification can outperform complication.

Donald Sull of London Business School and Kathleen Eisenhardt of Stanford University in *Simple Rules: How to Thrive in a Complex World* used the simplification principle to devise strategies to help business decision-makers cut through noise in a world of too much choice and information overload and help managers to find their focus. The rules about simple rules are themselves simple, they should be: limited (i.e. we need only a handful of them); bespoke (i.e. no situation requires exactly the same rules as another); specific (i.e. focused on well-defined critical processes that cause bottlenecks); and clear (i.e. be guidelines that managers and employees can understand and act upon). For example, Airbnb stumbled around for two years trying to work out what they were about as a business until they de-complexified and reformulated their business strategy with a small number of simple rules that focused the business on recruiting hospitable hosts in desirable destination cities using a small number of clear and unambiguous rules for hosts: Rule 1, always use professional photos; Rule 2, always give the guests local tips; and finally, Rule 3, always have clean soap.[64]

Radu Atanasiu and his colleagues studied how these simple rules emerge in managerial work. They found that heuristics are improved by experience through a constant feedback loop of testing, adapting, refining, and reinforcing which then leads to their wider adoption in an organization through learning and imitation and may eventually end up as broader applications across entire industries. The ability to generate such heuristics is an important source of competitive advantage for a firm and they can become 'proverbs' that managers use on a daily basis, for example: 'don't hire for skills hire for attitude'; 'strike while the iron is hot/email back immediately'; 'a good expert with a big salary is worth more than three average employees with half the salary'; 'strategic projects need daily attention'; and 'asking myself as CEO "would I hire myself"'?[65]

As far as intuition is concerned, one of Sull and Eisenhardt's cardinal rules for developing simple rules is 'let data trump opinion'. In practice this means avoiding gut instincts if they end up seducing decision-makers into over-relying on recent events, prioritizing personal biases, and overlooking anomalous data points that do not fit with their preconceived notions.[66] But simple rules need not be antithetical to intuition; honing simple rules to the point at which they become habituated into automatic and effortless behaviours renders them essentially intuitive, for example: Warren Buffet's decree 'never invest in a business you cannot understand'; General Motors' head of human resources' simplification of a ten-page employee dress code into a two-word declaration 'dress appropriately'; and Netflix's boiling down of its complex expenses policy to the simple rule 'spend the company's money as if it were your own'.[67] In business decisions, and life more generally, simplicity can be a virtue.

Summary

1. The two main ideas of this chapter have been 'fast-and-frugal' heuristics' and 'ecological rationality'.
2. Fast-and-frugal heuristics distil bounded rationality down to a small number of mental short cuts that are highly efficient in terms of time, knowledge, and computational requirements.
3. 'If one of two objects is recognized and the other is not, then infer that the recognized object has the higher value with respect to the criterion' is the recognition heuristic.
4. The 'Take the Best' heuristic is a one-reason decision rule whereby a judgement is based on one good reason only at each step in a logical and sequentially ordered process.
5. Social fast-and-frugal heuristics include 'do what the majority do', 'imitate the successful', and 'tit-for-tat'.
6. When we take consequential judgements in business we should bear in mind that our brain did not evolve to solve sophisticated calculations that can now be outsourced to a machine.
7. The human brain evolved to make informed inferences under the constraints of information, time, and computation in uncertain, and sometimes threatening, fast-moving physical and social environments.
8. Ultimately, the speed and simplicity which fast-and-frugals embody are one way in which managers can take decisions in situations where time and information are at a premium and when optimal solutions are out of reach.

Endnotes

1. Gigerenzer, G., & Goldstein, D. G. (2011). The recognition heuristic: A decade of research. *Judgment and Decision Making*, 6(1): 100–121.
2. Raab, M., & Gigerenzer, G. (2015). The power of simplicity: a fast-and-frugal heuristics approach to performance science. *Frontiers in Psychology*, 6: 1672.
3. Gigerenzer, G. (2007). *Gut Feelings*. London: Penguin, p. 229.
4. Luan, S., Reb, J., & Gigerenzer, G. (2019). Ecological rationality: Fast-and-frugal heuristics for managerial decision making under uncertainty. *Academy of Management Journal*, 62(6): 1735–1759, p. 1735.
5. Gigerenzer, G. (2004). Fast and frugal heuristics: The tools of bounded rationality. In Koehler, D., & Harvey, N. (Eds.). *Blackwell Handbook of Judgment and Decision Making* (pp. 62–88). Oxford, UK: Blackwell, p. 65
6. Gigerenzer, G. (2013). Smart heuristics. In Brockman, J. (Ed.). *Thinking: The New Science of Decision-Making, Problem-Solving, and Prediction*. New York: Harper Collins, pp. 39–54, p. 48.
7. Gigerenzer draw attention in particular to: Simon, H. A. (1957). *Models of Man: Social and Rational*. New York: Wiley.

8. A Simon, H. A. (1990). Invariants of human behaviour. *Annual Review of Psychology*, 41(1): 1–20, p. 7
9. Gigerenzer, G., & Goldstein, D. G. (2011). The recognition heuristic: A decade of research. *Judgment and Decision Making*, 6(1): 100–121.
10. Gigerenzer, G., & Goldstein, D. G. (1996). Reasoning the fast and frugal way: Models of bounded rationality. *Psychological Review*, 103(4): 650–669.
11. Breiman, L., Friedman, J. H., Olshen, R. A., & Stone, C. J. (1993). *Classification and Regression Trees*. Chapman & Hall.
12. Sadler-Smith, E., & Shefy, E. (2004). The intuitive executive: Understanding and applying 'gut feel' in decision-making. *Academy of Management Perspectives*, 18(4): 76–91.
13. Todd, P. M., & Gigerenzer, G. (2000). Précis of simple heuristics that make us smart. *Behavioral and Brain Sciences*, 23(5): 727–741, p, 731.
14. Todd, P. M., & Gigerenzer, G. (2000). Précis of simple heuristics that make us smart. *Behavioral and Brain Sciences*, 23(5): 727–741.
15. Gigerenzer, G. (2007). *Gut Feelings*. London: Penguin, p. 27; Gigerenzer, G., & Todd, P. M. (1999). Fast and frugal heuristics: The adaptive toolbox. In Gigerenzer, G., & Todd, P. M. (Eds.). *Simple Heuristics that Make Us Smart* (pp. 3–34). Oxford: Oxford University Press.
16. Luan, S., Reb, J., & Gigerenzer, G. (2019). Ecological rationality: Fast-and-frugal heuristics for managerial decision making under uncertainty. *Academy of Management Journal*, 62(6): 1735–1759, p. 1736.
17. Luan, S., Reb, J., & Gigerenzer, G. (2019). Ecological rationality: Fast-and-frugal heuristics for managerial decision making under uncertainty. *Academy of Management Journal*, 62(6): 1735–1759.
18. Gigerenzer, G. (2007). *Gut Feelings*. London: Penguin, p. 8.
19. Ibid.
20. Gigerenzer, G., & Goldstein, D. G. (2011). The recognition heuristic: A decade of research. *Judgment and Decision Making*, 6(1): 100–121.
21. Goldstein, D. G., & Gigerenzer, G. (2002). Models of ecological rationality: the recognition heuristic. *Psychological Review*, 109(1): 75–90, p. 82.
22. Pachur, T., & Biele, G. (2007). Forecasting from ignorance: The use and usefulness of recognition in lay predictions of sports events. *Acta Psychologica*, 125(1): 99–116.
23. Ibid.
24. Thoma, V., & Williams, A. (2013). The devil you know: The effect of brand recognition and product ratings on consumer choice. *Judgement and Decision Making*, 8: 34–44.
25. Gigerenzer, G., & Goldstein, D. G. (2011). The recognition heuristic: A decade of research. *Judgment and Decision Making*, 6(1): 100–121.
26. Gigerenzer, G. (2007). *Gut Feelings*. London: Penguin, pp. 115 and 128.
27. Pachur, T., & Biele, G. (2007). Forecasting from ignorance: The use and usefulness of recognition in lay predictions of sports events. *Acta Psychologica*, 125(1): 99–116.
28. Pachur, T., Todd, P. M., Gigerenzer, G., Schooler, L., & Goldstein, D. G. (2011). The recognition heuristic: A review of theory and tests. *Frontiers in Psychology*, 2: 147.
29. Hilbig, B. E., Erdfelder, E., & Pohl, R. F. (2010). One-reason decision making unveiled: a measurement model of the recognition heuristic. *Journal of Experimental Psychology: Learning, Memory, and Cognition*, 36(1): 123–134; Hilbig, B. E., Scholl, S. G., & Pohl, R. F. (2010). Think or blink—is the recognition heuristic an 'intuitive' strategy? *Judgment and Decision Making*, 5(4): 300–309; Hilbig, B. E., & Pohl, R. F. (2008). Recognizing

users of the recognition heuristic. *Experimental Psychology*, 55(6): 394–401; Pachur, T., & Biele, G. (2007). Forecasting from ignorance: The use and usefulness of recognition in lay predictions of sports events. *Acta Psychologica*, 125(1): 99–116.
30. Oeusoonthornwattana, O., & Shanks, D. R. (2010). I like what I know: Is recognition a non-compensatory determiner of consumer choice? *Judgment and Decision Making*, 5(4): 310–325.
31. Pachur, T., Todd, P. M., Gigerenzer, G., Schooler, L., & Goldstein, D. G. (2011). The recognition heuristic: A review of theory and tests. *Frontiers in Psychology*, 2(147): p. 133.
32. Klein, G. A. (2015). A naturalistic decision making perspective on studying intuitive decision making. *Journal of Applied Research in Memory and Cognition*, 4(3): 164–168.
33. Gigerenzer, G. (2007). *Gut Feelings*. London: Penguin, p. 45.
34. Iacurci, G. (2021). Money invested in ESG funds more than doubles in a year. CNBC, 11 February 2021. Available online at: https://www.cnbc.com/2021/02/11/sustainable-investment-funds-more-than-doubled-in-2020-.html Accessed 15.02.2022.
35. Bandura, A., Ross, D., & Ross, S. A. (1961). Transmission of aggression through imitation of aggressive models. *The Journal of Abnormal and Social Psychology*, 63(3): 575–582.
36. Gigerenzer, G. (2004). Fast and frugal heuristics: The tools of bounded rationality. In Koehler, D., & Harvey, N. (Eds.). (2004). *Blackwell Handbook of Judgment and Decision Making* (pp. 62–88). Oxford, UK: Blackwell, p. 73.
37. Gigerenzer, G. (2007). *Gut Feelings*. London: Penguin, p. 217
38. Op. cit., p. 218.
39. Barney, J. B. (1986). Organizational culture: can it be a source of sustained competitive advantage? *Academy of Management Review*, 11(3): 656–665.
40. Hertwig, R., & Herzog, S. M. (2009). Fast and frugal heuristics: Tools of social rationality. *Social Cognition*, 27(5): 661–698.
41. Surowiecki, J. (2004). *The Wisdom of Crowds: Why the Many are Smarter than the Few*. New York: Doubleday.
42. Schijven, M., & Hitt, M. A. (2012). The vicarious wisdom of crowds: Toward a behavioral perspective on investor reactions to acquisition announcements. *Strategic Management Journal*, 33(11): 1247–1268.
43. Scott, A. (2002). Identifying and analysing dominant preferences in discrete choice experiments: an application in health care. *Journal of Economic Psychology*, 23(3): 383–398.
44. Gigerenzer, G., & Gaissmaier, W. (2011). Heuristic decision making. *Annual Review of Psychology*, 62(1): 451–482; Gigerenzer, G., & Goldstein, D. G. (1996). Reasoning the fast and frugal way: Models of bounded rationality. *Psychological Review*, 103: 650–669.
45. Piquero, A. R., Farrington, D. P., & Blumstein, A. (2003). The criminal career paradigm. *Crime and Justice*, 30: 359–506; Vaughn, M. G., DeLisi, M., Beaver, K. M., & Howard, M. O. (2008). Toward a quantitative typology of burglars: A latent profile analysis of career offenders. *Journal of Forensic Sciences*, 53(6): 1387–1392.
46. Garcia-Retamero, R., & Dhami, M. K. (2009). Take-the-best in expert-novice decision strategies for residential burglary. *Psychonomic Bulletin & Review*, 16(1): 163–169; Snook, B., Dhami, M. K., & Kavanagh, J. M. (2011). Simply criminal: Predicting burglars' occupancy decisions with a simple heuristic. *Law and Human Behavior*, 35(4): 316–326.
47. Gigerenzer, G. (2011). Take the best heuristic. Go Cognitive. Available online at: https://www.youtube.com/watch?v=s8hGSPRpCDY Accessed 15.02.2022.
48. Highhouse, S. (2008). Stubborn reliance on intuition and subjectivity in employee selection. *Industrial and Organizational Psychology*, 1(3): 333–342.

49. Luan, S., Reb, J., & Gigerenzer, G. (2019). Ecological rationality: Fast-and-frugal heuristics for managerial decision making under uncertainty. *Academy of Management Journal*, 62(6): 1735–1759, p. 1740.
50. Ibid.
51. Lee, M. D., & Cummins, T. D. (2004). Evidence accumulation in decision making: Unifying the 'take the best' and the 'rational' models. *Psychonomic Bulletin & Review*, 11(2): 343–352.
52. West, D. C., Acar, O. A., & Caruana, A. (2020). Choosing among alternative new product development projects: The role of heuristics. *Psychology & Marketing*, 37(11): 1511–1524.
53. Simon, H. A. (1956). Rational choice and the structure of environments. *Psychological Review*, 63: 129–138, p. 130. Cited in Hogarth, R. M., & Karelaia, N. (2007). Heuristic and linear models of judgment: matching rules and environments. *Psychological Review*, 114(3): 733–758.
54. Overmann, K. A., Wynn, T., & Coolidge, F. L. (2011). The prehistory of number concept. *Behavioral and Brain Sciences*, 34(3): 142–144.
55. Cosmides, L., & Tooby, J. (1996). Are humans good intuitive statisticians after all? Rethinking some conclusions from the literature on judgment under uncertainty. *Cognition*, 58(1): 1–73, p. 16.
56. Hasher, L., & Chromiak, W. (1977). The processing of frequency information: an automatic mechanism? *Journal of Verbal Learning and Verbal Behavior*, 16: 173–184; Hasher, L., & Zacks, R.T. (1979). Automatic and effortful processes in memory. *Journal of Experimental Psychology: General*, 108: 356–388. Cited in Cosmides, L., & Tooby, J. (1996). Are humans good intuitive statisticians after all? Rethinking some conclusions from the literature on judgment under uncertainty. *Cognition*, 58(1): 1–73, p. 20.
57. Fiedler, K. (1988). The dependence of the conjunction fallacy on subtle linguistic factors. *Psychological Research*, 50: 123–129, p. 123.
58. Cosmides, L., & Tooby, J. (1996). Are humans good intuitive statisticians after all? Rethinking some conclusions from the literature on judgment under uncertainty. *Cognition*, 58(1): 1–73, p. 11.
59. Hu, Z., & Wang, X. T. (2014). Trust or not: Heuristics for making trust-based choices in HR management. *Journal of Business Research*, 67(8): 1710–1716.
60. Berg, N. (2014). Success from satisficing and imitation: Entrepreneurs' location choice and implications of heuristics for local economic development. *Journal of Business Research*, 67(8): 1700–1709.
61. Pentland, A. (2010). *Honest Signals: How They Shape our World*. Cambridge, MA: MIT Press.
62. Monti, M., Pelligra, V., Martignon, L., & Berg, N. (2014). Retail investors and financial advisors: New evidence on trust and advice taking heuristics. *Journal of Business Research*, 67(8): 1749–1757.
63. Iyengar, S. S., & Lepper, M. R. (2000). When choice is demotivating: Can one desire too much of a good thing? *Journal of Personality and Social Psychology*, 79(6): 995–1006.
64. Hellman, M. (2017) Book review: Simple Rules: How to Thrive in a Complex World. Available online at: https://www.marketingjournal.org/book-review-simple-rules-how-to-thrive-in-a-complex-world-by-donald-sull-and-kathleen-m-eisenhardt/ Accessed 15.02.2022; Weisul, K. (no date). How to radically simplify the management of your start-up. *Inc*. Available online at: https://www.inc.com/kimberly-weisul/how-to-simplify-management-startup.html. Accessed 15.02.2022.

65. Atanasiu, R., Ruotsalainen, R., & Khapova, S. (2022). A simple rule is born: How CEOs distil heuristics. *Journal of Management Studies* (in press). Available at: https://doi.org/10.1111/joms.12808 Accessed 04.04.2022.
66. Sull, D. & Eisenhardt, K. (2016) *Simple Rules: How to Thrive in a Complex World*. New York: Harper Business, p. 138.
67. Weisul, K. (no date). How to radically simplify the management of your startup. *Inc.* Available online at: https://www.inc.com/kimberly-weisul/how-to-simplify-management-startup.html. Accessed 15.02.2022.

4
Why Intuition Often Gets It Right
Recognition-Primed Decision-Making

Overview

The main idea of this chapter is that experienced decision-makers are able to make fast, accurate judgements and take effective decisions through the intuitive processes of pattern recognition and pattern matching. The model of how this works is called the 'recognition-primed decision (RPD) model'. It is one of the cornerstones of the field of 'naturalistic decision-making' (NDM) research. The work of the applied psychologist Gary Klein is centre stage. In common with fast-and-frugal heuristics, and unlike heuristics and biases, RPD is based on the idea that intuition can be a source of decision-making power when exercised by the right person, the right way, under the right circumstances. By emphasizing pattern recognition and pattern matching the RPD model resonates with Herbert Simon's definition of intuitions as analyses frozen into habit and the capacity for rapid response through recognition. RPD's applications in business are discussed and a potential new variant of it, 'intuition-based inquiry', is presented.

Naturalistic Decision-Making

Business decision-making is complex and riven with uncertainties and time pressures. The most difficult decisions that managers have to make are those where the stakes are high and speed is of the essence. In many situations where decisive action is required it is not possible postpone decisions or wait for more information be available. When time is of the essence and information is incomplete, leaders and managers have to take bold decisions; watching and waiting is not an option.[1] This is especially true in high-impact and low-probability, so-called black swan, events. For example, in the credit crunch, when the global financial system was on the verge of a death spiral, the then UK Prime Minister Gordon Brown led the world in his bold action of taking a massive public stake in the failing banks to the tune of £37 billion of taxpayers' money.[2] When the coronavirus pandemic broke out in 2020, the New Zealand government under Jacinda Ardern's leadership acted hard and fast by shutting the country's borders. Similarly, in the world of business, Apple acted decisively by closing down most of it stores globally.[3] To understand how leaders

Intuition in Business. Eugene Sadler-Smith, Oxford University Press. © Eugene Sadler-Smith (2023).
DOI: 10.1093/oso/9780198871569.003.0004

and managers take incisive action in such circumstances it is not possible to reduce problems to isolated variables that can be manipulated and studied at leisure in the controlled environment of a psychology laboratory. Sometimes it is necessary to step outdoors and into the managers' natural environment of the field to see and feel at first hand what is going on.

The heuristics and biases (Chapter 2) and fast-and-frugal (Chapter 3) researchers tend to study decision-making in laboratory settings under tightly controlled conditions using naïve participants on artificially constructed tasks such as the Linda and Detroit/Milwaukee problems[4] Naturalistic Decision-Making (NDM), on the other hand, aims to understand and improve decision-making by studying it in field, rather than laboratory, settings. NDM researchers study how experienced participants, such as firefighters, nurses, and managers, take decisions under conditions of time pressure, high stakes, inadequate information, and dynamic conditions.[5] And whilst the heuristics and biases research tends to focus on intuition's downside, NDM and the recognition-primed decision model (RPD) in particular, like Gigerenzer's fast-and-frugal heuristics, focuses on intuition's upside.

The origins of the recognition-primed decision model (RPD) can be traced to studies of one of the most extreme decision environments in terms of uncertainty, time pressure, high stakes, and unstable conditions that any human being is likely to face[6]—firefighting. Since its discovery in the 1980s, the RPD model has been applied to other types of high-stakes, consequential decision-making in areas such as medical care, military operations, and business management. The originator of the theory, Gary Klein, is senior scientist at the research and consulting firm Macro Cognition LLC. In common with Gigerenzer's theory of fast-and-frugal heuristics—and in contrast to Kahneman and Tversky's theory of heuristics and biases—Klein's model aims to understand the benefits of intuition, rather than its shortcomings. The RPD model seeks ultimately to help professionals in areas a diverse as firefighting and finance to take better decisions by leveraging intuition as a source of power.[7]

The origins of the recognition-primed decision model can be traced to various separate research projects undertaken in in the 1980s, a number of which were commissioned by the US military.[8] The US armed forces were interested in decision-making for two main reasons. First, they wanted to gain a better understanding of military commanders' cognitive processes such as attention, perception, memory, judgement, and problem-solving under conditions of time pressure and uncertainty. Second, they needed to find ways to help military commanders take more effective decisions in the field. Even though the different groups of researchers worked separately, they arrived at similar conclusions about how people take high-stakes decisions under conditions of instability, uncertainty, and time pressure.[9]

Cognitive Continuum Theory

Notable amongst these early projects was Kenneth Hammond and his colleagues' study commissioned by the United States Office of Naval Research of how expert highway engineers took consequential decisions, which was published in 1984. Hammond and his team, based at the University of Colorado at Boulder, discovered that whether highway engineers take decisions intuitively or analytically depends on their levels of experience and the type of task they are performing.[10] Hammond found that 'low certainty' tasks that required the processing of large amounts of information in a short time tended to be dealt with intuitively, for example judging the aesthetic quality of a road. On the other hand, 'high certainty' tasks that require large amounts of information to be processed sequentially tended to be dealt with analytically, for example estimating the amount of traffic for a highway. Their discovery was considered quite radical because of the pre-eminence at the time of the rational decision model. This was in spite of it having two significant shortcomings: first, the rational approach is vulnerable to substantive failures such as insufficient information, incorrect information, and insufficient time; second, it is also vulnerable to procedural failures such as incorrect assignment of values in the decision-making model, using the wrong model, and computational errors.

Hammond identified two fundamentally different types of thinking: intuitive thinking is rapid, low in cognitive control, and low in conscious awareness; analytical thinking is slow, high on cognitive control, and high in conscious awareness.[11] The parallels with Chester Barnard's distinction between logical and non-logical processes are clear (see Chapter 1). Hammond did not consider intuition and analysis to be a straightforward dichotomy, instead he placed them at opposite ends of a 'cognitive continuum' ranging from analytical through 'quasi-rational' to intuitive. The theory became known as 'cognitive continuum theory'. As well as managers' thinking processes, the tasks themselves could also be more or less analytical or intuitive on a 'task continuum'. Highway engineers' judgements were found to be most accurate when their cognitive processes matched the demands of the task. Hammond called this the 'correspondence-accuracy principle', i.e. whether a decision was accurate or not depended on whether it corresponded to the demands of the task. It seems obvious now, but it was not at the time.

Another thing that Hammond and this team discovered was that experienced engineers could 'switch cognitive gears' when their predominant mode of thinking failed, for example when a 'snap' intuitive judgement failed they would switch to careful analysis and vice versa.[12] Hammond was at pains to point out that most real-world decisions are neither purely analytical nor purely intuitive. Instead most real world decisions are complex and multifaceted, containing a mix of intuitive and analytical problem-solving and decision-making challenges. Cognitive continuum theory shows that taking effective decisions in the real-world entails using a mixture of both analysis and intuition, i.e. decision-making is rarely a question of *either* intuition *or* analysis, but much more likely to be a question of *both* intuition *and* analysis. Hammond also claimed that because people cannot simultaneously deploy intuition and analysis in parallel, they 'oscillate' up and down the continuum between the intuitive and analytical modes of thinking.[13] Hammond and colleagues surmised that with the right person under the under right circumstances, intuitive and quasi-rational cognition can perform at least as well as analytical cognition.

Hammond later speculated on the evolutionary origins of intuitive and analytical cognition. He argued that the natural environment of hunter-gatherers in prehistoric times must have induced and selected for cognitive activity that was 'very near the intuitive pole of the continuum'.[14] Subsequently, other intuition researchers have suggested that the 'intuitive mind' is older in evolutionary terms than the 'analytical mind'; for this reason some psychologists have even gone as far as to refer to them as 'old mind' and 'new mind' respectively.[15] The environment for modern decision-makers is much more diverse than that faced by our hunter-gatherer forebears, varying greatly from situations that are 'highly intuition-inducing' (such as the social skill of reading someone's motives and intentions) to those that are 'highly analysis-inducing' (such as the systematic task of compiling a spread sheet). Modern decision environments often require decision-makers to iterate between intuition and analysis and integrate them into an overall assessment based on both modes of thinking rather than either/or.[16]

Hammond's cognitive continuum theory is in keeping with Herbert Simon's theory of bounded rationality. It suggests that most real-world decisions are made in a 'quasi-rational' mode because the majority of task environments induce elements of 'both intuition and analysis'.[17] That said, Hammond's term of 'quasi-rational' privileged the rational pole of the continuum (i.e. it is not 'quasi-intuitive'). Nonetheless, his research was pioneering in that it was one of the first field-based studies to shed light on the crucial question of 'is it better to be analytical or intuitive?' when taking consequential decisions in real-world contexts. The answer, not surprisingly, is that 'it depends'. It depends on two critical factors. The first is the decision-maker's level of expertise: a high level of experience is a prerequisite for effective intuitive judgement and decision-making. The second factor is the type and context of the decision: intuition works best with experienced participants in conditions of complexity, time pressure, and uncertainty where observable cues are related to outcomes.

It is worth reiterating that at the time, the early 1980s, Hammond's empirical evidence and the conclusions that were drawn from it would have been surprising and unsettling given the strong allegiance and attachment to the rational model of decision-making in management and business schools at that time. The mainstream management research literature was largely silent on the issue of intuition, even though Barnard and Simon penned some of their most profound thoughts on the subject several decades earlier. With the benefit of hindsight, this lag is understandable given that management research draws on fundamental developments in its base disciplines such as psychology. In psychology it was not until the late 1970s that psychologists themselves were beginning to study 'automatic-versus-controlled' information processing, 'unconscious cognition', and so-called dual-process or dual-system theories of thinking and reasoning (see Chapter 5).[18] For these reasons Hammond's work on highway engineers' decision-making is significant and prescient. It also makes Barnard's insights from the 1930s all the more remarkable (see Chapter 1).

Intuitive Decision-Making on the Fire Ground

A further and even more significant breakthrough in intuition research outside of the laboratory occurred in the late 1980s. Gary Klein and his colleagues Roberta Calderwood and Anne Clinton-Cirocco set out to discover how highly proficient and experienced urban fire ground commanders (FGCs) took decisions under conditions of extreme time pressure and instability in situations where there could be significant consequences for both life and property. The research was written up as a technical report entitled 'Rapid Decision Making on the Fire Ground' for the US Army Research Institute for the Behavioural and Social Sciences (November 1985). It was not published in any scientific journal until almost a quarter of a century later in the *Journal of Cognitive Engineering and Decision Making*. This was because Klein was 'not aware of any [academic] journal [at the time] that would consider it'.[19] The novelty of the research and the low status accorded by social scientists to intuition was such that when Klein presented his work at conferences he deliberately avoided using the term 'intuition'.

Klein and his colleagues' research was conducted with twenty-six experienced firefighters (their mean experience was twenty-three years) in the Ohio and Indianapolis fire departments. Data were gathered using in-depth interviews. The interviews probed so-called critical incidents that were non-routine and that demanded FGCs' exercise their expertise. The interviews homed in on three critical issues: the options identified; the option(s) selected; and the reasons for the option chosen. Klein and his team hypothesized that FGCs would not be able to identify multiple options and deliberate over them in line with the classical model of decision-making because of the time pressures they were under and the need to take incisive action in what were often life-or-death situations. Instead they came up with what was for the time a radical hypothesis: FGCs would identify only two options, rather than several as suggested by the classical decision-making model, and then choose between these two. The original report described thirty-two non-routine incidents in vivid detail, including a fire in a tanker truck containing a full load of jet fuel and complicated by the presence of another tanker fifty feet behind, an overpass rescue in which a woman was lying semi-conscious over the superstructure holding up a sign over a busy highway interstate, and a fatal house fire involving the attempted rescue of two children, sadly both of whom died.

In line with the researchers' expectations, the conventional several-options hypothesis was not confirmed but—and this was one of the most striking features of Klein's research—neither was the two-options hypothesis. The researchers were astonished and nonplussed when they discovered that even their seemingly daring two-options hypothesis turned out to be 'conservative'. This was because the FGCs were, in fact, not comparing *any* options at all. One of them remarked to Klein's startled team that 'I don't make decisions. I don't remember when I've ever made a decision'.[20] It was not that there were not any options (for example, 'stay in burning building and fight fire' or 'evacuate burning building and regroup'), it was simply that in most situations it was obvious intuitively to an experienced FGC what needed to be done. Where an intuitively-generated option was imagined to be unworkable via a process of 'mental simulation' they moved to the next best and so on until a viable option was found. FGCs used their experience in a three-step process. First, to identify without deliberation, i.e. intuitively, whether or not the current situation is typical of a 'prototype situation'. Second, to identify a viable course of action and mentally simulate its likelihood of success. Third, to implement the course of action that is most likely to be successful for that situation.

Out of a total of 134 decision points identified in the thirty-two incidents studied by Klein and his team, zero were categorized as '[multiple] option selection', ten were categorized as 'deliberation' (7.5 per cent) and 114 were categorized as 'prototype' (85 per cent).[21] In other words, there were only a few situations where experienced FGCs had to go through a process of deliberation. The vast majority of FGCs' decisions were made on the basis of matching a current situation intuitively to general prototypes that were held in long-term memory and formed from merging together of numerous prior experiences. In Klein's words:

> The FGCs encounter a decision point; they recognize a match to a prototype, and the prototypical scenario guided by experience tells them how to proceed. In this way, they implement a course of action without ever considering any of the other options at the decision point. In our interviews, we probed this very carefully, and the FGCs were clear that [at that point] they were not aware of other options. That is why they did not feel that they were making decisions.[22]

How the FGC's knew what to do is as important as *what* they actually chose to do. The 'how' was intuition. Klein described intuition as a process that 'depends on the use of experience to recognize key patterns that indicate the dynamics of the situation'.[23] He defined intuition as 'the way we translate our experiences into action'.[24] For example, in 'Apartment Floor Collapse' (Incident #4) the FGC was in command of the fire in the first-floor apartment of a two-storey residence. The flames were found to be located in a room adjoining the smoke-filled living room. The FGC in this incident sometimes had the habit of leaving the ear flaps on his mask open, which meant on this occasion that he could not only feel but also hear that the room was unusually hot and unusually quiet. It was fortunate that he did so. His team hit the visible flames with water but to no avail, in the words of the FGC: 'It was different ... it didn't react normally. If you cool something down [with water], it becomes cool and this didn't. The *quietness* got me. There was something wrong'. Then, for reasons that were inexplicable at the time but which became apparent later, the FGC ordered his team to evacuate the room where the flames were located. Seconds after he did so the floor of the room that they had just evacuated collapsed. It turned out that the main fire was not in the room itself but in the basement underneath. It was this that accounted for the unusual quietness and heat. The FGC's intuition sensed that something about the situation made it not 'feel right'. This sense turned out to be correct, and it saved his own life and those of his team. If they had have stayed put, they would have plunged into the main fire which was raging in the space beneath them.

86 Why Intuition Often Gets It Right

Another incident in which the 'feel' of the fire was vital involved a blaze in a plastics factory. The firefighters were on the roof of the building. When it was hit with water the fire did not behave as they anticipated; their expectations were violated. The perplexed firefighters reported that the roof somehow felt 'spongy'. The FGC went up to investigate:

> He found that the roof indeed had a spongy feel and ordered his men off of it. He concluded that the fire was larger than he had thought and was probably burning directly below them. There is no way to describe what a spongy roof feels like. This recognition comes only with experience of walking on roofs that are solid and roofs that are spongy and learning to discriminate between them.[25]

The cues that were felt viscerally in his body caused the experienced FGC to sense things were not as they first seemed or how they ought to be. His intuition communicated to him the unsettling message that the situation did not tally with his experiences and were out of kilter with his expectations for such fires. The intuitive unease came to him as 'strange feelings'. On this occasion this particular FGC came to the conclusion that he might even have extrasensory perception (ESP).

Intuitive Expertise, Not Intuitive ESP

It is not only intuitive firefighters who can end up believing they are psychics. In his 1999 book *Sources of Power* Klein related the case of an anti-air warfare officer on a Royal Navy warship in the 1992 Persian Gulf War. The ship, HMS Gloucester, was stationed to protect the aircraft carrier USS Missouri. The Gloucester found itself being approached by a fast-moving potentially hostile radar contact. The dilemma was that the radar contact could have been an Iraqi Silkworm missile (about the size of a single decker bus and capable of sinking a warship), or it could have been an American A-6 warplane returning to its carrier from a bombing run on the mainland. The anti-air warfare officer, Lieutenant Commander Michael Riley, on the face of it had no way of knowing whether the blip on the screen was friend or foe. But he had to act quickly. His intuition told him the contact was hostile and it had to be intercepted. He was convinced that it was a Silkworm. Riley gave the order for it to be shot down.

The outcome for Riley and HMS Gloucester was positive. The blip was indeed an Iraqi Silkworm and headed straight for them. Colleagues who later looked at the recordings remarked that, based on what Riley saw on his instruments, there was no way to distinguish between a Silkworm and an A-6 airplane. The entire life-threatening incident took around ninety seconds. Riley could not pin his assessment down to objective data such as altitude, velocity, and acceleration. Maybe Riley just got lucky. He confessed to the researchers that the only way he could come to terms with what happened was that he must have had ESP. However, ESP was not the explanation: subsequent scrupulous forensic analysis by experts revealed subtle cues in the data which confirmed Riley's intuition, like that of the FGC in the previous incident, as being psychological not psychical. But Riley himself still could not say how he 'knew that he knew'. He knew without knowing why or how he knew.

The real reason that experienced firefighters, military personnel, and others who have to take decisions in similarly pressing circumstances are able to respond intuitively and effectively to a wide range non-routine incidents has nothing to do with paranormal prediction. It has everything to do with acute perception and subtle pattern recognition that is the product of extensive learning and high-quality experience. In spite of the exhortations of the many professional 'intuitive psychics' who claim to be able to predict intuitively what will 'come to pass',[26] a simpler and more plausible explanation for the firefighting and warship cases is 'intuitive expertise', not intuitive ESP.

Intuition is one of the hallmarks of expert performance; effortful deliberation on the other hand is a characteristic of novice performance. This is not to imply that experts do not deliberate, they do in certain circumstances. But all newcomers, who are to begin with 'unconsciously incompetent' (they do not know what they need to know), need to experience and analyse a wide array of situations in order to become competent. Through the processes of learning from experience, preferably under the guidance of a more experienced colleague, they get to better understand what they do not know. As a result, they become 'consciously incompetent' and are able to move beyond their comfort zone. As novices build up their expertise over thousands of hours of deliberate and focused (i.e. high-quality) practice, their analyses eventually become frozen into habits and the capacity for rapid response through recognition.[27] They ultimately transition through a state of 'conscious competence' to 'unconscious competence' in which they 'know' but do not always know 'how or why they know'.[28]

The Recognition-Primed Decision (RPD) Model

The decisions studied by naturalistic decision-making (NDM) researchers contrast markedly with the decisions studied in laboratory-based decision research. Laboratory-based decisions have well-defined goals using highly structured artificial tasks. The decisions themselves are often taken by inexperienced participants, such as psychology undergraduates, under stable conditions with a lack of time pressure and low stakes and inconsequential tasks. Gigerenzer referred disparagingly to these kinds of tasks as 'toy problems'.[29] Naturalistic decisions on the other hand are most certainly not toy problems. They have goals and tasks that are ill-defined and loosely structured. They are performed under dynamic conditions with time pressure and high stakes, have action feedback loops and typically involve experienced and multiple participants. Conditions are such that the time nor the available information are conducive to identifying a comprehensive set of options, debating and deliberating over the relevant attributes, evaluating each option in terms of these attributes, and systematically deriving an overall utility score. As an approach this would be dubious to say the least and ineffectual at worst.[30] Instead a very different and much more economical and ecologically rational evaluation strategy has to be followed.

In his book *Sources of Power* (1999) Klein used the incident of an 'Overpass Rescue' to illustrate the evaluation strategy used by an experienced FGC in taking a high-stakes life-or-death decision under a very demanding set of conditions.[31] A woman, possibly drunk or on drugs, had either fallen or jumped from a highway overpass and was draped over the superstructure that held up one of the signs. The rescuers had to decide how to pull the woman to safety. The first option that occurred to the FGC was to use a snap-on rescue harness; he rejected this as it required the person to be in a sitting or face-up position. He moved to a second option: use the harness but from the back, but this was rejected because of the risk of putting too much pressure on the victim's back. He moved to a third option: use a rescue strap rather than a snap-on harness; this was rejected for the same reasons as the harness. His final option was the improvised use of a ladder belt which is used ordinarily to secure firefighters to the top rung of a ladder to prevent them from falling. He imagined how using the ladder strap would work, liked the idea, and went ahead with it. Klein calls this latter part of the process 'mental simulation'. This incident, as well as having a happy ending, illustrates the three essential features of the RPD model: speed, singular evaluation, and mental simulation.[32]

Speed: In coming up with the various options the FGC's thinking was fast and automatic, taking 'only about a minute'—about as long it takes to read the above account aloud. Klein commented that this might seem to be only a very short time but 'if you imagine going through it in your mind, a minute is about right'. The human brain operates with extraordinary speed when it engages the intuitive mode and in laboratory studies has been found to be capable of above-chance judgements of coherence within a couple of seconds.[33]

Singular evaluation: Klein referred to the strategy of evaluating each option in turn before turning to the next one as 'singular evaluation'. He contrasted this with the 'comparative evaluation' of traditional pros-versus-cons decision analysis. Klein described comparative evaluation as being analogous to ordering food from a menu: all the options are on the table, so to speak, and are compared before the best alternative is selected. Singular evaluation, on the other hand, is analogous to driving through an unfamiliar neighbourhood and noticing that your vehicle is getting low on fuel. In this situation the rational thing to do is to search for a service station and stop at the first 'reasonable' one that you come across rather than searching for the 'best service station in town'.[34] Singular evaluation works not by searching through all of the available options to come up with the best (i.e. maximizing in economists' terms), but instead choosing the first option that works (i.e. satisficing in Simon's boundedly rational terms). Klein's analogy is not only illuminating, it also shows the close affiliation between RPD and Simon's theory of bounded rationality and the concept of satisficing (Chapter 1). The singular evaluation strategy is an example of satisficing, and RPD can be thought of as another model of bounded rationality (alongside 'heuristics and biases' and 'fast-and-frugal' heuristics).

Mental simulation: in the example of the overpass rescue the FGC evaluated each of the singular options as they occurred to him by imagining them being carried out. He did so in in his mind's eye and metaphorically fast-forwarded a 'video' in his head to mentally simulate what he anticipated would be the likely sequence of events and the consequences if the provisional option were to be taken. The script, so to speak, for the action in the video-in-the-head is based on mental models of how such a rescue would work out, built up from numerous prior experiences of similar rescues.

The example of the overpass rescue illustrates the two principal sources of decision-making power in RPD: 'intuitive pattern recognition' and 'analytical mental simulation'. The role of mental simulation, as well as being in itself a vital part of the model, also highlights an important, but sometimes overlooked aspect of the RPD model: RPD is not simply a model of intuitive pattern matching; RPD is a model of *both* intuition (the intuitive pattern matching part of the process) *and* analysis (the deliberative mental simulation part of the process).[35] In revisiting their original work in 2010 a quarter of a century after they conducted their original fieldwork, Klein and his colleagues expressed some regret that they had not made the point more forcefully in the 1988 write-up that 'the RPD model is not simply about intuition but is a blend of intuition (the prototype matches) and analysis (the mental simulation)'.[36] In this respect RPD is a 'dual' model of decision-making (see Chapter 5).

In the original research, Klein and colleagues presented three variants of the RPD model ('simple match', 'diagnose situation', and 'evaluate course of action').[37] In his later book *Intuition at Work* (2003), Klein condensed these various permutations into a simple step-by-step model that explains succinctly how the intuitive power of intuition and the analytical power of mental simulation work in tandem to help experienced decision-makers take fast, accurate decisions under conditions of time pressure, ill-defined goals, and dynamic conditions. It shows why, for most of the time, experienced decision-makers do not need to undertake exhaustive, deliberative analyses or work out how to resolve every situation from first principles. When experienced participants take decisions under these conditions, intuitive pattern recognition occurs by default in a majority of cases and is followed by the intervention of analytical mental simulation only where necessary.

Intuitive pattern recognition: The power of intuition derives from a pattern-recognition process which works as follows. The situation generates cues that enable the experienced decision-maker to recognize patterns instantaneously. These patterns automatically activate 'action scripts' which are then deployed to affect the situation without any further deliberation.[38] In the original research, Klein and his team documented the simple matching-to-prototype process in around 80 per cent of cases. Klein makes an important distinction between action scripts and an ordinary 'routine'. An action script is not a prescribed sequence of steps that anybody could carry out, analogous to a recipe for making and baking a cake, which is more like a simple routine that can be written down and followed even by a novice. An action script is different. It is a general course of action that experienced participants use to accomplish incisive decisions in the light of the complexity of the situation and which takes account of the dynamics of the situation.[39] In essence, actions scripts are strategies for taking action based on experienced decision-makers' skills in making sense of and responding to events as they are perceived *and* as they unfold over time. The key features of the process are that: first, the pattern tells a decision-maker *what* needs to be done (for example, to conduct a search and rescue in an apartment building); second, the action script tells the decision-maker *how* to do it (for example, conducting the right type of search and rescue in the light of the size, type, and layout of the building, the nature of the fire, and the skills and experience of the crew).[40]

Analytical mental simulation: Pattern recognition is the first and most intuitive part of the process. It is used to identify an acceptable option quickly and effortlessly. Mental simulation is the second and more analytical part of the process. It is used to evaluate the action script by imagining in the mind's eye the results of implementing the script. Experienced participants can accurately mentally simulate whether or not an action script is likely to work because they have 'complex domain-relevant mental models' (schemas)[41] of their professional domain which grow and become richer as a result of implicit and explicit learning, experience, and feedback. Firefighters, for example, have mental models of the way fires spread, the way different types of buildings will withstand exposure to flames, the way a fire reacts when a hole is chopped in a roof, etc. They are essentially experience-based beliefs about how the world works and as such are theories of action which help us to describe, explain, and predict the world.[42]

As noted, and contrary to first impressions, recognition-primed decision-making is not a purely intuitive model of decision-making. It involves mental models and mental simulation as well as intuitive pattern recognition. Recognition-primed decision-making is a two-stage process in which two complementary systems of thought—intuition (pattern matching) and analysis (mental simulation based on mental models)—are used by experienced participants to take fast, accurate, and sometimes life-saving decisions under the most challenging of conditions. Seen in this way, RPD echoes many of the principles of dual-process or dual-systems models of cognition, and Daniel Kahneman's well-known distinction between System 1 processing ('thinking fast') and System 2 processing ('thinking slow') (see Chapter 5).[43]

More recent research, again with firefighters, has investigated how experts discriminate between subtle information cues through the processes of cue discrimination and information filtering.[44] Cue discrimination works by 'situation assessment' which involves gleaning salient information from passers-by and victims (for example, 'you could ask people around for information about a particular location if you are unsure') and noticing cues that relate directly to the fire such as smoke colour and texture, fire intensity, cracking of walls, etc. (for example, 'When the smoke is white/light then the fire is not dangerous. But when you see the smoke deep and dark, it means the fire is dangerous'). Information filtering is the ability to discriminate between relevant and irrelevant cues under time pressure. The filtering process reduces the chances of working memory becoming overloaded and being detrimental to performance. Examples of principal cues include the colour of the smoke, the type of material involved, intensity of the blaze, the type of building, the likely cause, cracks and layout in the building, and the presence and mental state of potential trapped victims. This pre-screened information is then used to decide on a course of action.

In the research study referred to above, the vast majority of incidents were dealt with by firefighters trusting their instincts and acting instantaneously, i.e. within 60 seconds (104 out of 134 decisions) points, a much smaller number, i.e. 27 decision points, were dealt with by validating intuitions before acting, and a tiny minority (three out of 134) involved deliberation, for example by consulting fire manuals.[45] Effective performance on the fire ground depends on the decision-maker's ability to scan, recall, and filter relevant information quickly both from internal sources (for example, patterns held in long-term memory) and external sources (for example, relevant cues from a multiple sources of information). Intuitive expertise enables decision-makers not only to notice cues but also to sense which of them are the most relevant.

RPD in Business Decisions

RPD applies to business decision-making. Imagine, for example, an experienced marketing manager who is required to choose between three options being proposed by an advertising agency for an ad campaign to launch a new product. The three options are: advertising on social media; email marketing; and search engine marketing (SEM).[46] The manager recognizes intuitively that the email marketing option being proposed has a number of features (these are the principal cues) that are just like those that were used in a very successful email marketing campaign for a new product launch in her previous role at a different organization (this is pattern recognition). The manager can sense intuitively how email marketing could be applied with some modifications to the launch of the new product (this is the action script). This is the situation generating cues that lets the manager recognize patterns that activate an action script. This is the intuitive pattern recognition part of RPD.

However, the marketing manager must also assess whether the email marketing option will work for this particular product launch in her organization. The manager quickly builds in her mind an outline structure for an email marketing campaign in terms of how new leads would be acquired, how the list of leads would be built, how incentives to reply could be used, by whom, and how the content would be generated, etc. (this is the mental model). She then imagines how this kind of email advertising campaign would work in her current organization (this is the mental simulation). While running the simulation in her head she realizes that unlike before there will be an issue around regulatory compliance of email marketing that was not a problem in her previous organization. She judges that the email advertising campaign will not work on this occasion and moves to the next best option, that of social media advertising and imagines how this might work out in practice. By running a 'video-in-the-head' she is able to evaluate how this second option might work and so on through the various options. This is the manager using her experience-based mental model to run a mental simulation to assess the action script. The marketing manager is able to run the simulation because she, like Klein's experienced firefighters, has the necessary expertise: firstly, to recognize the similarities between the current situation and patterns and prototypes held in long-term memory—this process is accomplished intuitively; secondly, her mental model of email advertising is sufficiently complex and domain-relevant to enable her to run a valid and reliable mental simulation—this process is accomplished analytically and requires imagining the consequences of one's actions. In combining intuitive pattern recognition with analytical mental simulation, she is able to arrive at an expert judgement which rules out the email campaign in favour of a second more viable option.[47] Moreover, she is not simply moving from one routine to the next, but is making subtle and nuanced judgements based on her experience.

Intuition-based Inquiry

Rail travellers in the UK will be familiar with the following public safety announcement: 'If you see something that doesn't look right, speak to staff or text British Transport Police. We'll sort it. See it, say it, sorted.' As well as pattern-matching, our intuitions also work by pattern mismatching, that is by detecting inconsistencies, incongruities, and irregularities—when 'something doesn't look right'. Things did not 'feel' right for the firefighters in Klein's research for whom the blaze was too quiet or for whom the roof of the burning building felt too spongy. Experienced decision-makers are particularly adept at sniffing out situations that do not stack up by intuiting anomalies and aberrations that indicate a deviation from a familiar pattern or are out of sync with their expectations.[48]

In RPD terms, when this happens there is no matching to a prototype, therefore no action script can be activated. Hence there is no course of action that can be evaluated by mental simulation. The decision-maker ends up in a state of perplexity for reasons that are not immediately apparent. Their puzzlement is in itself intuitive because they *feel* that something is not right but they do not know *why*. Their intuition, which gate crashes their consciousness and offers its voice involuntarily, causes them to be confounded. Unlike in singular evaluation based on pattern-matching, there is no next option to turn to for how to resolve the situation immediately. In such situations intuitive judgements manifest as feelings of unease,[49] which evoke curiosity. The decision-maker, faced with an intuitive felt-sense that things are not as they should be, has the challenge of deciding how to respond. They end up have to make sense of an incongruous situation.

Police officers, like firefighters, are required to take decisions under conditions of time pressure, dynamism, and uncertainty, added to which the very nature of police officers' work compels them to take decisive action in order to resolve situations so as to protect life and property. Consequently, many of the decisions that police officers take on a day-to-day basis have to be accomplished—often out of sheer necessity—intuitively. For example, they may have to undertake life-saving acts whilst waiting for other emergency services to arrive, decide on the spur of the moment whether to perform a vehicle stop, or be able to distinguish between truth and lies.[50] Such decisions are amongst the most difficult and demanding aspects of a police officer's role.[51] Moreover, exercising judgement and taking decisions on the basis of intuition can have significant consequences for personal and public safety especially when it involves potentially controversial actions such as stop-and-search. Getting such decisions wrong can impact significantly on the public's trust in and society's attitudes towards policing.[52]

Police work provides researchers with a unique setting in which to study what happens when a situation generates cues, but rather than those cues comprising a pattern that *can* be matched to a prototype and hence activate an action script, the pattern *cannot* be matched because it is aberrant or anomalous. My colleague Cinla Akinci and I were intrigued as to what experienced peak-performing police officers do in such situations. We discovered that when something does not 'look or feel right' experienced officers 'go find out why'.[53] In other words they engage in sense-making.

We conducted in-depth interviews with twenty-seven officers who were amongst the very best at what they do. They were 'peak-performing knowledgeable agents', i.e. expert police officers, who knew what they were trying to achieve, spoke convincingly about their experiences, and were able to explain their thoughts, actions, and intentions. We asked them to tell us about occasions in which they used their intuition in first-response situations. The stories they told us covered everything from suspected breaking and entering, through vehicle stops and domestic incidents, to searching for missing persons. Through detailed analyses of many thousands of words of interview transcripts we discovered that in such situations police officers use their intuition in two ways.

The first way in which police officers used their intuitions came as no surprise to us. A typical example was a 'river rescue' in which a member of the public had fallen into a fast-flowing river at night and was being carried towards a weir:

> He's screaming for help, he needs to be saved, so, you know, there's no intuition at this stage, there's common sense—that bloke needs saving—what is available to me? So, I call up on the radio: how long for the lifeguards, how long for the fire brigade with their boats. Both of them were 30 minutes plus, okay? Common sense says that guy's not going to hang on for 30 minutes. Right. Is there any other access to him? No. I'm at the closest point on the riverbank. So, then I'm stuck—I've got two decisions, haven't I? I try and get him, or I watch him die—that's what it comes down to. I'm going in the River {redacted} at two o'clock in the morning in the pitch black in a wooden boat with one oar to save someone who's on the edge of a weir.

In this situation the officer intuitively made sense of the context, mentally simulated the option of calling for help, foresaw that it was not viable, and discounted that

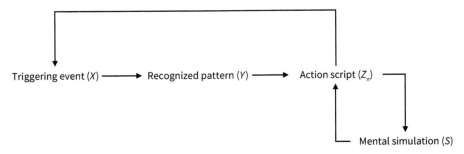

Figure 4.1 Recognition-based intuition

option. Then he came up with a second option of carrying out an improvised rescue himself, using a wooden boat with only one oar that happened to be available, he mentally evaluated this option as viable and executed a successful rescue. All of this happened very quickly. The river rescue was a situation that generated cues that allowed the officer to recognize a pattern (a person in a river at night being carried towards a weir) that activated an action script (call the specialist emergency services), which was evaluated by mental simulation as not viable (they would not arrive in time), this activated the next best option and its action script (the use of a boat that happened to be nearby), which was evaluated by mental simulation as viable and thereby executed to affect the situation (a successful rescue).

This is RPD in action and in this context we called it 'recognition-based intuition', the general form of which is: a triggering event 'X' occurs, a general pattern 'Y' is recognized, and an action script 'Z_1' suggests itself which is mentally simulated (S) and either executed to affect the situation (X) or rejected in favour of the next available option 'Z_2', and so on until a viable action script is found and executed in order to resolve the situation, see Figure 4.1.

The second way in which police officers used their intuitions in first-response was markedly different, as illustrated by this example where an officer attended an incident at a house in which there turned out to be more to the incident than met the eye:

> It [the complaint seemingly] was [about] somebody banging on somebody's door, and they'd left before we got there, and really there wasn't much for me to do. But something just didn't seem right about the situation, and it just felt as though something was… there was more going on than they'd said. If it wasn't for the fact that I'd had that feeling that something wasn't right there would have been no necessity for me to ask extra questions. Everything I needed to do was done, so I could have just gone on my way. But just something didn't quite seem right. I asked a few more questions as to why this is happening, and it seemed a little bit odd to me. I'm going to have to find out what it is. But there was nothing from the information I'd been given—and we act on information—that would lead me to think something else had occurred. It was just something wasn't right, and that's all I could think of. They weren't saying anything to me that would make me think,

oh, there's more to this, or there's something else that's gone on. They were quite calm about it. They just said, we don't want to do anything else. We know who it is. We're not worried about it. And that was it really. But it just didn't seem right to me. There was something that was… the back of my head going, there's something else here, and I don't know what it is yet. It's kind of just that I couldn't move on from the fact that there was something else. It was just a case of this needs to be… I need to do something more with this.

The 'something else' that the officer sensed was metaphorically lurking in the shadows turned out to be an allegation of a serious sexual assault. The situation generated cues that led the officer to intuit that the complainant's pattern of behaviour did not match a prototype of a typical domestic complaint; there was no action script that could be used to resolve the situation. The officer was dogged by feelings of unrest and unease and was puzzled and perplexed as to how to proceed. Instead of mobilizing an action script, the cues led the officer to recognize intuitively that this was a situation that warranted further investigation. The decision-maker felt compelled to go beyond the available information. This prompted further inquiry which would confirm whether or not the officers' disquiet was legitimate.

We called this type of intuition-based first-response 'intuition-based inquiry', the general form of which is: a triggering event 'A' occurs, intuitive affect 'B' is evoked, but no action script suggests itself, hence further investigation and analysis 'C' is warranted. This helps the decision-maker to make sense of their initial intuitive response (D) and ultimately, having made sense of it, take an action to affect the situation (E), see Figure 4.2.

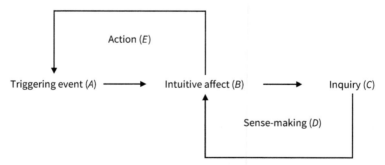

Figure 4.2 Intuition-based inquiry

Through intuition-based inquiry, decision-makers seek to reduce uncertainty and resolve ambiguities by means of an analytical inquiry rather than the activation of an action script. The inquiry is intuition-based in that it is a response to an intuitive felt-sense that a situation necessitates further detailed investigation in order to be made sense of and resolved satisfactorily. If there is a generic action script as such then it is 'conduct further inquiries'. The officers we interviewed described other instances of this phenomenon:

You think well, this isn't quite right, and then you might pick up a little, a couple of little things, and then you tend to sort of say, oh, I think I'll just check on this, just check on that, and just in case there's some more to this than meets the eye.

I'll say, no, that's not right; I don't think that's right, there's more to it than this. Or there's something else going on here, let's dig a bit... you know, and, sure enough, most of the time I am right, something else has happened.

If you see something that doesn't look right, go and find out why it doesn't look right, because nine out of ten times, there'll be something wrong.

Recognition-based intuition (RBI) and intuition-based inquiry (IBI) are two ways in which experienced police officers take intuitive decisions under conditions of time pressure, inadequate information, and dynamic conditions. They both involve intuition, but they lead to the triggering situations being resolved in quite different ways.

Intuition-based Inquiry in Business

Intuition-based inquiry also is observed in business decision-making in situations where a triggering event evokes the sense that further investigation is warranted. One area in which this is observed commonly is in hiring decisions. A view that is widely shared amongst industrial and organizational psychologists is that 'analysis outperforms intuition' in the prediction of human performance and hence is the preferred approach in employee selection decisions.[54] Managers on the other hand often place more faith in their intuitive ability to 'read people' when taking employee selection decisions.[55] For example, a survey of over 600 business leaders from twelve countries found that over two-thirds of business decision-makers think that intuition is important and should be used in the hiring and promotion of staff.[56] But why do managers seem to cling to the idea of selecting people on the basis of intuition when the research suggests that relying on objective data in selection decisions outperforms intuitive judgement?[57]

In a qualitative study of the use of intuition in selection decisions, human resources (HR) manager Andrew Miles and I found that intuitive pattern matching was used in HR decisions for a variety of purposes including as a predictor of a potential employees' personality ('sense you've got of the person and their character') and their performance (both positive 'a really good feeling about her, and she was hired, and she is brilliant' and negative 'A salesperson should electrify you... so if you haven't got that in a conversation, they're not a salesperson, don't waste your time'). The managers we interviewed used intuition to predict how someone might respond under pressure, for example 'You have a gut feeling for people and how they react under pressure'. They also used mental simulation to back up their gut feelings for whether or not they should hire a candidate, for example 'You can almost imagine what they are going to be like in front of a customer'.

However, we also discovered that one of the biggest selection decision challenges faced by managers is where a candidate meets or exceeds the necessary criteria (for example, resumés, test scores, etc.) but for whom something simply does not look or feel 'right', usually based on the hiring manager's reading of how the candidate comes across or answers questions in the interview. The following quotes capture how managers described such situations: 'I thought there was something funny, I thought the answer was all right but, there was something odd there', '[intuition is] like a little tripwire in my head', and 'I just got this feeling that he was going to really, really struggle'. Depending on their intensity, sensations such as these can make interviewers distinctly uneasy about some candidates, and although the source of their disquiet often cannot be identified they are left with the judgement that to hire the person could be a serious mistake. When a hiring manager 'senses that something doesn't stack up' should they consign their intuitions to the closet or should they trust their gut? The answer is neither. Confining intuitions to the closet is a bad idea. They simply fester and can come back to haunt a manager at a later date (e.g. 'I wish I'd listen to my intuition, it somehow knew'). In such situations intuitions should at least be put on the table. There are good professional and legal reasons why only going with your gut and eschewing hard data in recruitment and selection decisions is ill-advised. Intuition is an acknowledged source of unconscious bias. We intuitively look for data that confirm our preconceived opinions, and beliefs. Going unreservedly with your gut can lead to discriminatory selection decisions and have negative effects on diversity and inclusion.[58] In the case of the business angels in Chapter 1, objective business viability data was used in combination with subjective person perception to give an overall assessment. Likewise in hiring decisions, the best results are likely to come from a blend of analytical solving and intuitive sensing.

Combining Intuition and Analysis

The ability to intuitively sense anomalies and inconsistencies is a product of learning and experience and is a valuable source of soft data which is risky to ignore. The sense of something not stacking up is not unique to HR decisions in business. Other management dilemmas such as the business venturing opportunity that seems 'too good to be true' or the balance sheet that somehow does not seem to 'add up' even though all the figures appear to be in order are situations where intuitions can sound an alarm. When analytical thinking gives a positive assessment but the intuitive assessment is negative the sensible course of action is to check out the analysis, for example by re-running the analysis or getting more data. Conversely, when the intuitive thinking gives a positive assessment but the analytical assessment is negative a sensible course of action is to challenge the intuition, for example by being your own devil's advocate or co-opting someone else into this role. A useful metaphor is that of a traffic light. When intuition *and* analysis say 'yes', the signal is 'green'. When intuition *and* analysis say 'no', the signal is 'red'. When intuition says 'yes', but analysis says 'no' the signal is 'amber': you should check out your intuition. When analysis

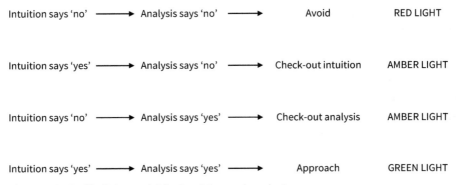

Figure 4.3 Traffic light model for intuition and analysis

says 'yes', but intuition says 'no' the signal is also an amber light: you should check out your analysis.[59] This method of 'integrating and iterating' is explored in more detail in Chapter 11, see Figure 4.3.

The key to effective decision-making in policing, management, and many other areas of professional practice is recognizing when intuition can be a help and when it can be a hindrance. Intuition-based inquiry offers managers a way out of this dilemma. It does so by combining both intuition and analysis. Intuition should be listened to but not followed unreservedly and indiscriminately. When intuition sounds an alarm, especially in high-stakes business decisions such as strategy, hiring, and venturing, it may be alerting the decision-maker to some aspect of a complex situation that their rational mind has been unable to process explicitly. In these circumstances, intuition's legitimacy is amplified if the decision-maker has been in similar situations in the past, if they are an expert in the area, and if other people share the same intuitive response.[60]

Summary

1. The main idea of this chapter is that intuition can be a source of decision-making power when it is exercised by the right person under the right circumstances.
2. Under dynamic and uncertain conditions, experienced decision-makers' intuition works in a process of recognition-primed decision-making (situation, cues, pattern recognition, action script, mental simulation).
3. In recognition-primed decision-making a triggering event occurs, a general pattern is recognized, and an action script is identified, mentally simulated, and either executed to affect the situation or rejected in favour of the next available option; the process continues until a viable action script is found and executed.
4. In intuition-based inquiry a triggering event occurs, intuitive affect is evoked, but no strategy suggests itself, therefore further investigation is warranted until

a solution is found which resolves and makes sense of the intuitive affect so as to be able to then take action.
5. Implicit and explicit learning as a result of extensive, high-quality experience are vital in building decision-makers' capabilities (based on complex domain-relevant schemas) to exercise effective intuitive judgements under dynamic and uncertain conditions.
6. Intuition-based inquiry is a variant of recognition-primed decision making in which the decision-maker makes sense analytically of their initial (partially-formed) intuition before taking action.
7. Taking effective real world decisions is likely to involve both intuitive and analytical thinking processes as complementary sensing and solving components in a dual-system of decision-making.

Endnotes

1. Alexander, A., De Smet, A., & Weiss, L. (2020). Decision-making in uncertain times. McKinsey and Company. Available online at: https://www.mckinsey.com/business-functions/people-and-organizational-performance/our-insights/decision-making-in-uncertain-times Accessed 11.02.2022.
2. Rawnsley, A. (2010). The weekend Gordon Brown saved the banks from the abyss. *The Guardian*, 21 February 2010. Available online at: https://www.theguardian.com/politics/2010/feb/21/gordon-brown-saved-banks Accessed 11.02.2022.
3. Alexander, A., De Smet, A., & Weiss, L. (2020). Decision-making in uncertain times. McKinsey and Company. Available online at: https://www.mckinsey.com/business-functions/people-and-organizational-performance/our-insights/decision-making-in-uncertain-times Accessed 11.02.2022.
4. Macrocognition (no date). The macrocognition perspective. Available online at: http://www.macrocognition.com/perpsective/overview.html Accessed 11.02.2022.
5. Klein, G. A. (1999). *Sources of Power: How People Make Decisions*. Cambridge, MA: MIT Press, p. 4
6. Klein, G. (2008). Naturalistic decision-making. *Human Factors*, 50(3): 456–460.
7. The book in which Gary Klein presents the RPD model is called *Sources of Power: How People Make Decisions* (Cambridge, MA: MIT Press).
8. Hammond, K. R., Hamm, R. M., Grassia, J., & Pearson, T. (1984). *Report No. 252: The relative efficacy of intuitive and analytical cognition: A second direct comparison*. Boulder: University of Colorado; Klein, G. A., Calderwood, R., & Clinton-Cirocco, A. (1988). *Technical Report 796: Rapid decision making on the fire ground*. US Army Research Institute for the Behavioural Sciences, June 1988.
9. Lipshitz R. (1993). Converging themes in the study of decision-making in realistic settings. In Klein, G. A., Orasanu, J., Calderwood, R., & Zsambok, C. E. (Eds.). *Decision-making in Action; Models and Methods*. Norwood: Ablex Publishing, pp. 103–137.
10. Ibid.
11. Hammond, K. E. (1993). Naturalistic decision-making from a Brunswickian viewpoint. In Klein, G. A., Orasanu, J., Calderwood, R., & Zsambok, C. E. (Eds.). *Decision-making in Action; Models and Methods*. Norwood: Ablex Publishing, pp. 205–227, p. 216.

12. Lipshitz R. (1993). Converging themes in the study of decision-making in realistic settings. In Klein, G. A., Orasanu, J., Calderwood, R., & Zsambok, C. E. (Eds.). *Decision-making in Action; Models and Methods*. Norwood: Ablex Publishing, pp. 103–137, p. 124.
13. Hammond, K.E. (1993). Naturalistic decision-making from a Brunswickian viewpoint. In Klein, G. A., Orasanu, J., Calderwood, R., & Zsambok, C. E. (Eds.). *Decision-making in Action; Models and Methods*. Norwood: Ablex Publishing, pp. 205–227, p. 218.
14. Hammond, K.E. (1993). Naturalistic decision-making from a Brunswickian viewpoint. In Klein, G. A., Orasanu, J., Calderwood, R., & Zsambok, C. E. (Eds.). *Decision-making in Action; Models and Methods*. Norwood: Ablex Publishing, pp. 205–227, p. 219.
15. Evans, J. S. B. (2014). Two minds rationality. *Thinking & Reasoning*, 20(2): 129–146.
16. Hammond, K. E. (1993). Naturalistic decision-making from a Brunswickian viewpoint. In Klein, G. A., Orasanu, J., Calderwood, R., & Zsambok, C. E. (Eds.). *Decision-making in Action; Models and Methods*. Norwood: Ablex Publishing, pp. 205–227, p. 220
17. Ibid. (original italics).
18. Walter Schneider and Richard Shiffrin's work on controlled versus automatic information processing appeared in *Psychological Review* in 1977, see: Schneider, W., & Shiffrin, R. M. (1977). Controlled and automatic human information processing: I. Detection, search, and attention. *Psychological Review*, 84(1): 1–66; Shiffrin, R. M., & Schneider, W. (1977). Controlled and automatic human information processing: II. Perceptual learning, automatic attending and a general theory. *Psychological Review*, 84(2): 127–190.
19. Klein, G., Calderwood, R., & Clinton-Cirocco, A. (2010). Rapid decision making on the fire ground: The original study plus a postscript. *Journal of Cognitive Engineering and Decision Making*, 4(3): 186–209, p. 207
20. Klein, G. A. (1999). *Sources of Power: How People Make Decisions*. Cambridge, MA: MIT Press, p. 11.
21. Klein, G. A., Calderwood, R., & Clinton-Cirocco, A. (2010). Rapid decision making on the fire ground: The original study plus a postscript. *Journal of Cognitive Engineering and Decision Making*, 4(3): 186–209.
22. Klein, G. A., Calderwood, R., & Clinton-Cirocco, A. (1988). *Technical Report 796: Rapid decision making on the fire ground*. US Army Research Institute for the Behavioural Sciences, June 1988, p. 12.
23. Klein, G. A. (1999). *Sources of Power: How People Make Decisions*. Cambridge, MA: MIT Press, p. 31.
24. Klein, G. A. (2003). *Intuition at Work*. New York: Doubleday, p. xvi.
25. Klein, G. A., Calderwood, R., & Clinton-Cirocco, A. (1988). *Technical Report 796: Rapid Decision Making on the Fire Ground*. US Army Research Institute for the Behavioural Sciences, June 1988, p. 23.
26. Barnum, M. (2014). *Psychic Abilities for Beginners: Awaken Your Intuitive Senses*. Woodbury, Minnesota: Llewellyn Worldwide, p. 4.
27. Klein, G. A. (1999). *Sources of Power: How People Make Decisions*. Cambridge, MA: MIT Press, p. 29.
28. https://www.gordontraining.com/free-workplace-articles/learning-a-new-skill-is-easier-said-than-done/ Accessed 08.07.2022.
29. Gigerenzer, G. (2019). Expert Intuition Is Not Rational Choice. *The American Journal of Psychology*, 132(4): 475–480, p. 475.

30. 'Dubious' is the word Simon used to describe the economic model of rational choice; see Chapter 1.
31. This is 'Incident #9' in the original report: Klein, G. A., Calderwood, R., & Clinton-Cirocco, A. (1988). *Technical Report 796: Rapid Decision Making on the Fire Ground*. US Army Research Institute for the Behavioural Sciences, June 1988.
32. Klein, G. A. (1999). *Sources of Power: How People Make Decisions*. Cambridge, MA: MIT Press, pp. 18–19.
33. Bolte, A., & Goschke, T. (2005). On the speed of intuition: Intuitive judgments of semantic coherence under different response deadlines. *Memory & Cognition*, 33(7): 1248–1255.
34. Klein, G. A. (1999). *Sources of Power: How People Make Decisions*. Cambridge, MA: MIT Press, p. 20.
35. Klein, G. A., Calderwood, R., & Clinton-Cirocco, A. (2010). Rapid decision making on the fire ground: The original study plus a postscript. *Journal of Cognitive Engineering and Decision Making*, 4(3): 186–209, p. 207.
36. Klein, G. A., Calderwood, R., & Clinton-Cirocco, A. (2010). Rapid decision making on the fire ground: The original study plus a postscript. *Journal of Cognitive Engineering and Decision Making*, 4(3): 186–209, p. 207.
37. Klein, G. A. (1999). *Sources of Power: How People Make Decisions*. Cambridge, MA: MIT Press, p. 25.
38. Klein, G. A. (2003). *Intuition at Work*. New York: Doubleday, p. 16.
39. Ibid., p. 15.
40. Ibid., p. 280.
41. Dane, E., & Pratt, M. G. (2007). Exploring intuition and its role in managerial decision making. *Academy of Management Review*, 32(1), 33–54.
42. Klein, G. A. (2003). *Intuition at Work*. New York: Doubleday p. 17–18.
43. Kahneman, D. (2011). *Thinking, Fast and Slow*. London: Allen Lane.
44. Okoli, J. O., Watt, J., & Weller, G. (2022). A naturalistic decision-making approach to managing non-routine fire incidents: evidence from expert firefighters. *Journal of Risk Research*, 25(2): 198–217.
45. Ibid.
46. https://www.cyberclick.net/advertising/advertising-campaign
47. This example is an elaboration of the process described in: Klein, G. A. (2003). *Intuition at Work*. New York: Doubleday, p. 17.
48. Klein, G. A. (1999). *Sources of Power: How People Make Decisions*. Cambridge, MA: MIT Press, p. 35.
49. Dane, E., & Pratt, M. G. (2007). Exploring intuition and its role in managerial decision making. *Academy of Management Review*, 32(1): 33–54.
50. Elmqvist, C., Brunt, D., Fridlund, B., & Ekebergh, M. (2010). Being first on the scene of an accident. *Scandinavian Journal of Caring Sciences*, 24: 266–273; Mann, S., Vrij, A., & Bull, R. (2004). Detecting true lies: police officers' ability to detect suspects' lies. *Journal of Applied Psychology*, 89: 137–149; Williams, B. N., & Stahl, M. (2008). An analysis of police traffic stops and searches in Kentucky: a mixed methods approach offering heuristic and practical implications. *Policy Sciences*, 41: 221–243.
51. Hails, J., & Borum, R. (2003). Police training and specialized approaches to respond to people with mental illnesses. *Crime & Delinquency*, 49(1): 52–61.

52. Correll, J., Park, B., Judd, C. M., Wittenbrink, B., Sadler, M. S., & Keesee, T. (2007). Across the thin blue line: Police officers and racial bias in the decision to shoot. *Journal of Personality and Social Psychology*, 92(6): 1006–1023.
53. Akinci, C., & Sadler-Smith, E. (2020). 'If something doesn't look right, go find out why': How intuitive decision making is accomplished in police first-response. *European Journal of Work and Organizational Psychology*, 29(1): 78–92.
54. Highhouse, S. (2008). Stubborn reliance on intuition and subjectivity in employee selection. *Industrial and Organizational Psychology*, 1(3): 333–342, p. 336
55. Myers, D. (2002). *Intuition, Its Powers and Perils*. New Haven: Yale University Press, p. 189.
56. Signium (2018). Signium Intuition Index. Available online at: https://www.signium.com/news/intuition-index/#:~:text=Signium%20is%20pleased%20to%20share%20our%20Intuition%20Index.&text=We%20spoke%20to%20more%20than,value%20of%20intuition%20in%20practice Accessed 11.02.2022.
57. Gino, F. (2014). How data beats intuition at making selection decisions. *Scientific American*. Available online at: https://www.scientificamerican.com/article/how-data-beats-intuition-at-making-selection-decisions/ Accessed 11.02.2022; Kuncel, N. R., Klieger, D. M., Connelly, B. S., & Ones, D. S. (2013). Mechanical versus clinical data combination in selection and admissions decisions: a meta-analysis. *Journal of Applied Psychology*, 98(6): 1060.
58. Biagini, C. (2019). When it comes to hiring, don't trust your gut. *Forbes*, 22 July 2019. Available online at: https://www.forbes.com/sites/forbeslacouncil/2019/07/22/when-it-comes-to-hiring-dont-trust-your-intuition/?sh=32780239716c Accessed 11.02.2022.
59. Sadler-Smith, E. (2008). *Inside Intuition*. Abingdon: Routledge.
60. Insurance Business America (2016). Balancing data and gut instincts in hiring decisions. Available online at: https://www.insurancebusinessmag.com/us/business-strategy/balancing-data-and-gut-instincts-in-hiring-decisions-39387.aspx Accessed 11.02.2022.

5
The 'Two-Minds' Model

Overview

The main idea of this chapter is that human cognition is accomplished in two contrasting ways, one which is fast, automatic, and unconscious (known as 'Type 1 processing) and another which is slow, deliberate, and conscious ('Type 2'). Human beings have, metaphorically speaking, 'two minds in one brain'. This general cognitive architecture is known as 'dual-process theory'. Various labels have been applied to these contrasting ways of thinking such as 'System 1' (the intuitive system) and 'System 2' (the analytical system), 'old mind' and 'new mind' (which reflects their evolutionary origins, etc.). Conflict and cooperation between the two systems is discussed and debated. One dual-process theory in particular, regarded by some as a landmark contribution, is singled out for attention: Seymour Epstein's 'Cognitive-Experiential Theory' (CET). The applications of dual-processing in business are discussed. The chapter concludes with the debate about when should intuitive (System 1) processing be trusted. Guidelines for when to go with your gut are provided based on a distinction between 'kind learning structures'/'high-validity environments' which build good intuitions and 'wicked learning structures'/'low-validity environments' which do not.

Two Minds in One Brain

The idea of two contrasting ways of thinking, one quick, emotionally hot, automatic, effortless, holistic, and intuitive and the other slow, emotionally cold, deliberative, effortful, analytical, and rational, has a long history in psychology and human culture more generally. Philosophers, poets, and scientists from classical, through renaissance to modern times have contemplated the tensions between 'reason' and 'passion', 'head' and the 'heart', and the 'conscious' and 'unconscious'. Aristotle is reputed to have remarked that 'educating the mind without educating the heart is no education at all'; Galileo observed that 'where the senses fail us, reason must step in'; in *Titus Andronicus* Shakespeare penned 'My heart suspects more than mine eye can see'; and Pascal wrote that 'the heart has reasons of which the head knows nothing'.[1]

The separation of conscious thinking from unconscious thinking gained significant traction in psychology and psychiatry in the late nineteenth and early twentieth centuries. The contents of the unconscious mind as a reservoir of feelings, thoughts, urges, and memories—as well as a source of mental disorders—figured prominently in Freud's psychoanalysis and Jung's analytical psychology. At the turn of the nineteenth century[2] William James, one of the founders of modern psychology, described in his *Principles of Psychology* (1890) a 'secondary consciousness … cut off from the primary or normal [consciousness], but susceptible to being tapped [into] and made to testify its existence in various odd ways'.[3] In *The Varieties of Religious Experience* (1902) James went further and argued that the unconscious mind could explain many important psychological phenomena, including intuitions, which are formed unconsciously but subsequently become available to conscious awareness.

The idea of two minds in one brain,[4] one that is slow, effortful, and deliberative and adept at solving (System 2, rational and analytical) and the other that is fast, effortless, automatic, and adept at sensing (System 1, experiential and intuitive), is a helpful metaphor for thinking about the different types of processes involved in decision-making. The two-minds model works well as a descriptive tool, and came to wider attention in Nobel laureate Daniel Kahneman's book *Thinking, Fast and Slow*.[5] The idea has impacted on policy and practice in organizations, for example the World Bank in its *World Development Report 2015: Mind, Society, and Behaviour* recognized that 'When making decisions, we cannot manage without the automatic system, and it can produce remarkably well-adapted choices at a trivial cost of effort in decision-making'.[6]

The long-standing idea that cognitive processes can be divided into two main 'families' was embraced widely in the latter half of the twentieth century.[7] Under the generic label of 'dual-process theories' psychologists proposed a grand 'cognitive architecture' which framed human thinking and reasoning in terms of a fast, effortless, and intuitive processing mode and a slow, deliberative, and analytical mode. Debates continue in the behavioural and brain sciences as to the precise nature and the effectiveness of these two systems of thought (for example, when is the slow, analytical mode of thinking better than the fast, intuitive mode?) and how they interact (for example, are they activated simultaneously, or is intuition the brain's 'default mode' and is the switch made to analytical thinking only as and when required?).[8] As far as business management is concerned, the ever-insightful Herbert Simon argued that the effective manager 'does not have the luxury of choosing between "analytic" and "intuitive" approaches'[9] in problem-solving and decision-making. To be effective the mind of the manager must be ambidextrous. In our preoccupation with intuition, it is easy to overlook the fact that intuition is, literally, only half the picture. To be able to explain how the intuitive mind functions in business we need to understand its relationship with its counterpart, the analytical mind.[10]

Dual-Process Theory

The two-minds model is more correctly referred to as 'dual-process theory'. The origins of modern dual-process theories can be traced to simultaneous developments over half a century ago in new and vibrant subfields of psychology such as 'implicit learning', 'social cognition', 'behavioural decision theory' as well as in the psychology of thinking and reasoning more generally. Fundamental to dual-process models of the mind (sometimes referred to as 'dual-system' models) is a distinction between cognition which is fast, automatic, and unconscious and therefore impervious to introspection (sometimes referred to as 'Type 1' processing) and cognition which is slow, deliberate, and conscious and hence available to introspection (sometimes referred to as 'Type 2' processing). Human beings have, speaking metaphorically, 'two minds in one brain'.[11]

Many of the key developments in this field can be traced back to research that took place in the 1960s, 1970s, and 1980s.[12] For example, research in the 1960s revealed two kinds of learning, one which is conscious and 'explicit' and the other which is unconscious and 'tacit'. The most well-known example of tacit knowledge is how to ride a bicycle: people who can ride a bicycle will be unable to say which way to turn the handlebars to prevent falling off, but since staying upright is essential to riding a bicycle, anyone who can ride one must know which way to turn the handlebars to avoid a fall. Bicyclists know, but they cannot put what they know into words; in this respect their knowledge of how to ride a bicycle is tacit.[13] Implicit learning is the process by which knowledge is acquired independently of conscious attempts to learn. Implicit learning, usually acquired by doing rather than being told, produces knowledge that is tacit and intuitive.[14]

The 1970s witnessed further important developments in behavioural decision theory (BDT) in the work of Kahneman, Tversky, and others (see Chapter 2) which discovered that many of the systematic sources of error in human judgement can be attributed to the operation of intuitive, i.e. Type 1, processing which results in mental short cuts or heuristics such as judging someone on the basis of how closely they resemble a prototype or stereotype (as in the Linda Problem discussed in Chapter 2). In the 1980s researchers demonstrated: how people could hold both explicit and implicit (i.e. tacit or unspoken) beliefs and attitudes towards objects and people; that individuals can be unaware of their implicit attitudes and the effects they have on behaviour; and that the explicit and implicit need not correspond.[15] For example, someone might say that they believe that men and women are equally good at intuition, but it is possible that they associate intuition more strongly with women, i.e. they implicitly hold a stereotype of 'female therefore more intuitive', without being explicitly aware of it.[16]

The term 'cognitive unconscious' is thought to have been first coined by the cognitive psychologist Arthur Reber in the 1960s.[17] Reber was particularly interested in how human beings are able to learn complex skills unconsciously and effortlessly. He described 'implicit learning' as an inductive process through which knowledge about complex environments is acquired and used largely independently of any awareness both of the processes and products of that learning.[18] Implicit learning is a *process* of knowledge acquisition whereas tacit knowledge (captured in Michael Polanyi's famous phrase 'we know more than we can tell'[19]) refers to the *products* of implicit and other learning processes.

Classic experiments by Reber and colleagues demonstrated the existence and power of implicit learning using so-called 'artificial grammar' (AG) tasks. AG research established something quite remarkable about human cognition: people could reliably discriminate between letter strings created by an artificial grammar algorithm which possessed a subtle internal statistical structure but in themselves were meaningless (for example the grammatical string VXSSSV) and genuinely random strings (for example, the non-grammatical string VXRRS).[20] However, even though people could distinguish the grammatical strings from random strings, they were unable to articulate the actual structure underlying the grammatical letter strings.[21] They intuited that some underlying rule was at work. They could identify if a string corresponded to the rule. But could not say how or why the rule and the grammatical structure worked.

In business, implicit learning by observation, imitation, and role modelling leads to the acquisition of complex mental models which are the basis for accurate intuitive judgements.[22] For example, when researchers conducted experiments to compare different ways for learning business negotiation skills (for example, observation, direct instruction, etc.) they found that an observational learning group who simply watched a re-enactment of a negotiation conducted by skilled negotiators learned the most despite that fact that no formal concepts or strategies were mentioned or formally taught as such. As with the artificial grammar (AG) grammar learners, even though the informal observational learners showed the greatest improvement in skill level compared to those who were given formal textbook instruction of how to negotiate, they were unable to articulate what it was that had helped them to improve.[23]

Implicit learning is far from being a dumbed-down version of explicit learning. Implicit learning is a cognitively sophisticated covert information processing system. It is thought that it is based on neurophysiological structures that are evolutionarily ancient and to which conscious cognitive processing was added at a later stage in *Homo sapiens*' evolution.[24] Reber cites the processes of socialization and acculturation as prime examples of complex processes of knowledge acquisition that take place implicitly. Implicit learning is instrumental in not only developing essential social skills but also in acquiring cultural prejudices which are obtained implicitly and which may lead to pernicious outcomes. Reber points to learning our natural language as another example of where we have a 'rich set of intuitions' about how language works that are acquired naturally during childhood without conscious attempts to do so. The conscious awareness that an individual has about the knowledge they have acquired implicitly is only the tip of the iceberg of the total knowledge that is used to guide behaviour, which includes complex decision-making tasks such as those faced by the firefighters, police officers, and managers discussed in Chapter 4.[25]

Subsequently variations on the theme of unconscious/implicit versus conscious/explicit processing resulted in the development of other dual-process models. For example, in the field of social cognition, Shelly Chaiken and colleagues developed a dual 'heuristic-systematic' model of persuasion which proposed two contrasting modes of social thinking. 'Heuristic processing' involves focusing on salient and easily comprehended cues (such as a person's physical appearance) which activate previously-learned judgemental short cuts (heuristics) and enable quick, automatic, low-effort judgements. 'Systematic processing', on the other hand, involves careful attention to available information and includes higher-level thinking and reasoning processes which support slower, more deliberative, effortful judgements about another person.[26] In Chaiken's model heuristic processing is assumed to be the default mode whilst systematic processing is initiated only when people have the cognitive capacity, time, and motivation to expend the additional mental effort required. Heuristic processing is first out of the blocks, providing a mental short cut to a judgement or decision, whilst systematic processing is mobilized if and when additional confirmatory evidence is required. Systematic processing supplements heuristic processing up to the point at which a person's confidence in their overall judgement (based on both heuristic and systematic processing) reaches a sufficiency threshold.[27]

Marketers have long-understood the role of mental short cuts based on heuristic processing of the kind Chaiken and others have identified and have used it with great commercial success. For example, in the 1930s psychologists worked with major tobacco companies to actually promote smoking by associating smoking with success, accomplishment, social acceptance, and confidence.[28] Less controversially, the use of animals in advertising is a common tactic in marketing campaigns. Famous examples include MGM's lion, Duracell's 'bunny', and Coca Cola's polar bears. The use of animal imagery exploits evolutionarily ingrained animal–human bonds and the positive effects that attachments to animals can have on a person's social identity, self-perception, and physical and psychological well-being.[29] Researchers found that the use of pets such as dogs and cats in advertisements not only inspired positive feelings about the product or brand through heuristic processing,[30] it also suppressed systematic processing. In the case of animal ads, if people like animals they are more likely to make the mental short cut of liking the product or brand as well: 'love the dog, love the ad, love the product'. The heuristic system automatically substitutes the question of whether one likes the animal (which for animal lovers is easy to answer) for the question of whether or not one likes the product (which may require more effortful processing). The heuristic processes which drive such behaviours are intuitive and operate below the level of conscious awareness.

Aside from applications in advertising and branding, Chaiken's heuristic-systematic model has proven to be a powerful tool for bringing about positive change in policy areas such as health awareness, public safety, environmental issues.[31] It can be used deliberately to 'nudge' people's behaviour in ways that are considered best for themselves and their families, wider society and the natural environment.[32] Nobel Prize–winning behavioural decision scientist Richard Thaler and law professor Cass Sunstein in their bestselling book *Nudge* (2008) proposed 'nudging' as an evidence-based approach for designing decision-making environments that influence and shape behaviours on a large scale. A nudge is an intervention that softly steers or politely prods individual's behaviours in a desired direction without them necessarily being consciously aware. The UK government under Prime Minister David Cameron set up a Behavioural Insights Team (BIT), commonly referred to as the 'Nudge Unit', in 2010 with the aim of applying behavioural science to the creation of 'choice architectures' that support public policy aims and initiatives. Thaler's research from the 1980s, distinguished between having myopic (short-sighted doing, interested only in immediate gratification) versus forward-looking (long-term planning, interested in the future effects of one's choices) time-based considerations. One of the most significant and far-reaching applications of the nudge in the UK was the introduction of a forward-looking automatic enrolment for pensions policy, which has resulted in an extra 10 million people now being signed up for a pension as a result.[33] Employees can opt out, but they have to make a conscious decision to do so. The 'nudgees' (i.e. employees) have had their gratification deferred for them by the 'nudgers' (i.e. the UK government). It is seen as a subtle way to get people to act in their own long-term best interests.

The objective of the nudge is to prod individuals' behaviours in predetermined directions. In doing so it utilizes some of the well-known properties of the heuristic system. For example, anchors, as in the anchoring and adjustment heuristic (see Chapter 2), can serve as nudges as in the following example. Charities often ask for donations of £10, £50, £100, or 'other', with the aim of anchoring and adjusting up from a base level of £10 rather than a lower anchor of £5. The heuristic system is subtly and surreptitiously offered a starting point for its decision of how much to donate.[34] As a further example, in the wake of the pandemic, people are able to easily think of examples of the negative consequences of infectious diseases. Post-pandemic, by leveraging the power of the availability heuristic, advertisers have been able to nudge people into buying greater quantities of everyday household cleaning products to the extent that 'cleaning products are now part of consumers' survival strategy because, in the era of the pandemic, lax germ management can lead to negative health consequences'. This has nudged the status of mundane products, such as wipes and sprays, into 'lifestyle products' when in fact a much cheaper bottle of bleach would do the job just as well.[35]

Dual Attitudes

Dual-process theories of social psychology reveal how individuals can hold dual—and sometimes conflicting—attitudes concurrently. Timothy Wilson and colleagues proposed a 'dual-attitude model' to explain how it is possible for people to hold simultaneously implicit and explicit attitudes towards the same object or person which differ substantially.[36] Moreover, implicit attitudes can sometimes offer better predictions of behaviour than explicit attitudes and habitual responses for two reasons. First, people might lack the ability to introspect correctly about an unconscious intuitive process such as their attitudes to particular social groups. Second, they might be reluctant to reveal negative and discriminatory attitudes, such as racism or sexism, which influence their behaviour.[37]

Psychologists have devised ingenious computer-based techniques based on reaction times to test implicit attitudes. The Implicit Association Test (IAT) measures the strength of association between a concept (for example, a person's skin colour, or sexual preference) and the evaluations of that concept (good or bad). The IAT is based on the principle that making a response via a computer keyboard is easier, i.e. quicker, when items are more closely related in one's mind. For example, an implicit preference for straight people relative to gay people would result in a faster response to a task when 'straight and good' or 'gay and bad' are paired than when 'gay and good' or 'straight and bad' are paired. People are unable to consciously control their responses because the test runs at a fast pace. You can test your implicit attitudes towards a range of issues including disability, religion, sexuality, skin tone, and weapons by visiting Harvard's Project Implicit website.[38]

The IAT shows that prejudice can be both explicit and implicit. People can believe sincerely that they are not prejudiced but nonetheless possess negative implicit attitudes which may then unconsciously, i.e. intuitively, affect their behaviours.[39] For example, a test of implicit associations between concepts (for example, 'family' and 'career') and evaluations (for example, 'male' and 'female') might reveal a strong intuitive association between 'male and career' and between 'female and family'. Similarly, a white, middle-class male might, with apparent sincerity, report unambivalent positive feelings towards a person who is not like him in an explicit test of attitude. However a more subtle and nuanced implicit test, such as the IAT, might reveal negative attitudes emanating from non-conscious stereotypes and associations. These may then prevail, albeit unconsciously, over espoused attitudes in actual decision-making and result in biased and prejudiced decisions in areas such as employee selection or promotion. The IAT has been found to predict discrimination in hiring, healthcare, education, and law enforcement.[40] The extent to which the explicit or the implicit attitude prevails in determining how one behaves depends on whether an individual has the requisite metacognitive awareness (i.e. the extent to which they are able to introspect on or think about, and ultimately control, their own thinking processes), cognitive capacity, and motivation. Overcoming implicit attitudes requires firstly being able to access or retrieve an explicit non-discriminatory attitude, and secondly being able to deploy an explicit attitude to override a discriminatory implicit attitude.

In the study of ethical consumption researchers have found that dual attitudes help to explain the gap between positive attitudes towards ethical consumption on the one hand and unethical consumption practices on the other.[41] One study found that whilst 30 per cent of consumers reported caring about ethical consumption, only 3 per cent of purchases actually reflected ethical consumption practices.[42] The so-called '30:3 phenomenon' reveals an attitude–behaviour gap in which consumers are clearly not 'walking the ethical talk'. This is likely due to disconnects and dissociations between implicit (what one actually believes and therefore how one behaves) and explicit (what one says one believes and how one claims one behaves) cognitive processes.[43] The decoupling of attitudes and practices in a mind that is divided by unconscious/implicit and conscious/explicit processes may help to explain why many people say one thing about climate change (for example, they agree that it presents a crisis) but actually do another (for example, make little or no effort to reduce their carbon footprint).[44]

System 1 and System 2

Conscious-versus-unconscious cognition and heuristic-versus-systematic processing are two examples from an abundance of dual-process and dual-system theories that have been proposed, developed, and tested over the past fifty years. It is estimated that there are in excess of twenty different models of dual-thinking processes including: 'associative versus rule-based'; 'heuristic versus systematic'; 'recognition-primed versus rational choice'; 'implicit cognition versus explicit cognition'; 'experiential versus rational'; and 'intuitive versus analytical'.[45] In order to make sense of a potentially confusing array of concepts, models, and theories the psychologist Keith Stanovich, in his 1999 book *Who Is Rational?* coined the generic terms 'System 1' and 'System 2' to refer to the two underlying cognitive systems which are the ultimate sources of Type 1 processes such as intuition and Type 2 processes such as rationality.[46] Stanovich brought together many of the properties that had been assigned previously to a variety of qualitatively different processing types, such as intuitive and rational or heuristic and systematic, into two general groupings. These were based on shared 'family resemblances', for example 'associative', 'non-conscious', and 'intuitive' are some of the family likenesses in the System 1 family of processes.[47]

Stanovich is also keen to point out that the term 'system' does not imply that there are two underlying and distinct information processing or brain systems that are the biological bases of dual-processing. As we shall discover in Chapter 6, System 1 and System 2 rely on a variety of interlinked cognitive and neural systems and processes.[48] For example, System 1's processes are associated with a number of brain regions such as the limbic system (linked with emotional processing) whilst System 2's processes are associated with higher brain regions such as the prefrontal cortex (associated with goal-directed, planning and conscious decision-making behaviours).[49]

The System 1 / System 2 split does not correspond to left–right hemispheric differences within the human brain. Any claims that intuition is in the 'right brain' are an oversimplification; more on this in Chapter 6.[50] A further misconception, in some dual-process theories at least, is the inference is that intuition is simply error-prone, lazy thinking, and is always the source of biased judgement and decision-making or, by the same token, that System 2 always outperforms System 1.[51] Intuition and analysis are qualitatively different types of thinking, both can lead to bad as well as good outcomes. To focus only on the fallibility of System 1 overlooks its adaptive value in areas such as expert judgement and decision-making under time pressure, moral and social judgements, and creativity.[52]

In general terms, the overall cognitive architecture of the two systems can be summarized as follows: *System 1*: holistic, automatic, cognitively undemanding, comparatively fast, acquired experientially, high-capacity, parallel processing, intuitive, implicit, unconscious, independent of general intelligence, and evolutionarily old; *System 2*: analytic, controlled, cognitively demanding, comparatively slow, acquired formally, low-capacity, sequential processing, reflective, explicit, conscious, linked to general intelligence, and evolutionarily recent.[53] Although lists of properties such as these could be taken to imply that the attributes for System 1 always perfectly line up, for example that intuition is independent of general intelligence, this is not necessarily the case. The best that can be said is that the features for each system are more likely to be broadly related, like the members of an extended family, rather than aligned exactly.[54]

One of the defining attributes of System 1 is that it is evolved to be automatic. As a consequence, intuitions are executed instinctively whenever relevant triggering conditions are encountered. This means that intuitions typically 'just happen' in response to an eliciting situation, for example a job candidate's presentation or an entrepreneur's pitch, without our consciously bidding them to do so. In theory the outputs of System 1 are monitored by System 2 which intervenes if it judges that the System 1 response might lead to a suboptimal outcome that is contrary to the decision-maker's goals.[55] For example, by analysis intervening in a high-value purchasing decision in which intuition, driven by hopes and desires, has been in the driving seat. This does not always work out, and sometimes intuition retains the upper hand and the 'heart rules the head'.

A further difference between the two systems is that System 1 automatically contextualizes problems by considering the overall situation (System 1 is contextual and 'big-picture' conscious) whilst System 2 works by decontextualizing them, thus enabling it to solve complex, abstract, intellectual problems (System 2 is decontextual and detail-focused).[56] System 1 therefore works better with concrete experiences, narratives, and images whilst System 2 works better with generalizations and abstract information.

System 1 is thought to have evolved relatively early in human evolution and may not be unique to our species, whereas System 2 is thought to have evolved only relatively recently and is uniquely human.[57] Psychologist Jonathan Evans,[58] a long-time proponent of the dual-processing concept, acknowledged this evolutionary aspect of dual-processing by referring to System 1 as 'old mind' and System 2 as 'new mind'. It was he who posited the presence of two minds in one brain.[59] *Homo sapiens*' old mind is evolutionarily ancient and shared with other animals, whilst our new mind is 'a uniquely human and recently acquired addition plug-in [or download] that does a great deal less than we generally assume'.[60] Evidence for the development of a new mind overlain on top of an old mind is to be found in profound and abrupt changes in the archaeological record circa 40,000 years ago. It was around this time that representational art appeared suddenly in cave paintings, there were rapid advancements in the design of tools, weapons, and other artefacts, and some evidence of a 'theory of mind' has been found (see Chapter 9).[61] From about 300,000 until about 40,000 years ago Neanderthals (*Homo neanderthalensis*) were the dominant hominids in Europe.[62]

Fast-versus-Slow Thinking

Dual-process theory was brought to the attention of a wider public beyond the scientific community with the publication of Daniel Kahneman's bestselling 2011 book *Thinking, Fast and Slow*. Its impact on the popular understanding of the two-minds model and its relevance to business is considerable, so much so that other psychologists have described dual-process theories as having become 'wildly popular' as a result of the reception of Kahneman's book by a general readership.[63] *Thinking, Fast and Slow* was a summary account for a non-specialist audience of several decades of important scientific work stretching back to the 1970s, not least the collaboration between Kahneman and Amos Tversky (see Chapter 2). In the early 2000s, in association with Shane Frederick, Kahneman adopted Stanovich's generic labels System 1 and System 2[64] to signify: an automatic, effortless, associative, rapid, parallel, process, opaque 'intuitive' System 1; a controlled, effortful, deductive, slow, serial, self-aware 'reflective' System 2.

The term 'system' is used by Kahneman for a collection of interrelated processes that are distinguished in terms of their automaticity, content, and speed, for example System 1 is effortless, associative, and fast. Kahneman and Frederick also make two important observations about the System 1/System 2 distinction. First, although System 1 is more primitive than System 2, it is not necessarily less capable. Second, complex cognitive operations, such as the analyses of specific situations and experiences, eventually migrate from System 2 to System 1, which aligns with Herbert Simon's definition of intuitions as 'analyses frozen into habit and the capacity for rapid response through recognition'. In terms of sequencing, because System 1 is fast, it proposes an intuitive response quickly. By way of analogy the 'fast horse' (intuition) beats the 'slow horse' (analysis) in a race to cross the finishing line.[65] The System 1 response may then be either accepted unquestioningly (as in the Linda problem) or quality controlled by System 2 and either endorsed, corrected, or rejected (in a 'stewards' enquiry', to extend the horse-racing analogy). A not dissimilar process can be found in Gary Klein's recognition-primed decision (RPD) model (see Chapter 4) in which the viability of an action script is assessed by mental simulation and either accepted or modified or rejected in favour of the next best option that intuitively comes to mind.

In *Thinking, Fast and Slow* Kahneman portrays the two systems as agents with their own abilities, functions, and limitations. He summarizes their operation and interaction as follows. Both systems are active when we are awake. System 1 runs automatically and cannot be turned off, whilst System 2 idles in a low-effort mode using a fraction of its capacity. System 1 continually generates inputs for System 2 in the form of impressions, intuitions, intentions, and feelings. The labour is divided between the two systems in such a way as to be highly efficient, which means being driven by System 1 for most of the time. When System 1 tries to solve problems for which it did not evolve and to which it is not suited, such as logical and statistical tasks, it often produces systematic errors and biased responses. System 1 is impulsive and incessant, it likes to provide an answer, but in doing so often it will frequently give its response to an easier-to-answer question rather than a harder-to-answer question. System 2 may be mobilized when System 1 runs into difficulties, cannot find an appropriate response or is surprised and discombobulated, as in the case of intuition-based inquiry (see Chapter 4).

System 1 judgements are often acted on without System 2 stepping in, for example when we choose the job candidate we happen to like rather than the best person for the job, or invest in the pitcher with the best presentation rather than the best project. Doing so can result in biased decisions and expensive mistakes. When this happens, both System 1 and System 2 are, metaphorically speaking, 'culpable': System 1 for making the incorrect suggestion in the first place; and System 2 for failing to step in and thus allowing System 1's choice to be actioned unchallenged.[66] Kahneman described System 2 as being like a 'lazy policeman' who has the authority but often lacks the will to intervene. To compound the issue, System 2 also may be guilty of self-deception as follows. Consciousness (System 2) has a putative executive (i.e. higher-order) control function which may, paradoxically, have led it to the illusory belief that it is in charge. But in reality, the unconscious (System 1) may be in the driving seat for most of the journey.[67] System 2 more generally has been likened to the Chief Executive of an organization who sits in her penthouse C-suite office thinking mistakenly she is calling the shots when in fact System 1, comprising the 'minions' on the lower floors, is actually running the show.[68]

Dynamics of the Two-Minds Model

For the two-minds model to be useful in business it is necessary but not sufficient to simply enumerate lists of oppositely aligned attributes for the two systems, as in the above account. If we are to understand how intuition is accomplished in managerial work, we also need to specify what the relationship is between intuitive (System 1) and analytical (System 2) processing. A long-time proponent of dual-process theory, Jonathan Evans, offered a number of possibilities for how the relationship between the intuitive and the analytical minds might work in practice. The first of these is referred to by Evans as the 'default-interventionist (DI)' mode. When we make judgements or take decisions in the DI mode, our intuitive (System 1) processes generate habitual responses, and these are acted on unless there is intervention by analytical (System 2) processes. In the DI mode, System 2 involvement is optional, not guaranteed; decision-makers in this situation can be thought of as 'cognitive misers'.[69] The second way in which the two systems might work together is referred to by Evans as the 'parallel-competitive (PC)' mode. In the PC mode, intuitive and analytical processes operate interactively and work together jointly in generating a response 'each having their say with conflict resolved if necessary'.[70]

An example of the DI mode is when consumers recognize and respond effortlessly and intuitively with minimal conscious thought to the purchase of everyday low-value items, such as a detergent or a soft drink. Brand recognition for Fairy Liquid or Coca Cola works by System 1 either reactively recognizing them as familiar brands (when they are seen on a supermarket shelf) or by proactively bringing them to mind first (when we need to wash the dishes or have a soft drink). In either case the familiar brand's emotional resonance is likely to evoke a good feeling (a 'positively valenced affective response') which signals 'approach' behaviours, i.e. to purchase the said item. Because purchasing such a low-value item is relatively inconsequential there is for the most part no requirement for System 2 to intervene and approve or amend System 1's intuitive response. For many people it is not necessary to weigh up the pros and cons or go to the internet to get the latest customer star ratings of an established brand such as Fairy Liquid or Coca Cola in order to decide whether it is worth switching to another less well-known brand of detergent or soft drink. The System 1 button is an easy one for marketers to press by building familiarity, creating positive emotional resonances, and making consumer choice a quick, low-effort cognitive process.[71]

System 1's responses in the supermarket aisle can be manipulated with surprising ease by a skilled marketer. In a study of how to influence wine buyers' behaviours, four French and four German wines matched for price and dryness/sweetness were displayed in the drinks aisle of a supermarket.[72] From the shelf above them, French accordion and German Bierkeller music were played on alternate days. French wine outsold German wine when French music was played. German wine outsold French wine when German music was played. In a sample of buyers who were subsequently questioned, only around 10 per cent of them admitted that the type of music being played had influenced their choice consciously. For the unwitting majority, the music's powerful effect on their buying behaviours was not something that consumers were aware of.

It is possible to explicitly link the design features of an advertisement to the attributes of System 1 processing, for example speed and emotionality, in order to consciously try to change buyers' behaviours. The brand consultancy Brandspeak measures the 'System 1 strength' of an advertisement in terms of 'spontaneous visual awareness' (which leverages the recognition and availability heuristics) and 'emotional resonance' (which leverages the affect heuristic). On the other hand, a product's System 2 attributes do not need any sophisticated analysis because objective properties such as price and quality are easily identified and measured. The brand consultancy 'System 1' (named after the psychological System 1) suggests that System 1 processes can be leveraged effectively by an approach to branding that uses three factors adopted directly from dual-process theory: first, 'fame' (which makes a brand come to mind based on the availability heuristic); second, 'feeling' (which gives a brand a feel-good factor based on the affect heuristic); third, 'fluency' (which makes the brand recognizable based on a processing fluency heuristic). By activating spontaneous awareness, emotional arousal, visual recognition, and association, consumers' intuitive System 1 processes and responses can exert a powerful influence on their buying behaviour.[73] On the downside, a negative experience of a product or service can also emotionally 'tag' a brand with negative feelings, so that next time the brand is encountered, System 1's affect heuristic (see Chapter 2) is mobilized and the benefits of purchasing the brand are intuitively outweighed by the risks. Intuitive impressions, like first impressions, count, and these affective tags tend to be 'sticky' and may prove hard to dislodge once experienced.

With high-value items the outcome is consequential, hence a purchasing decision is more likely to be passed over to System 2 for closer scrutiny. In this situation brands that rely superficially and heavily on visual recognition and emotional resonance to gain attention will be at a disadvantage if they do not stand up subsequently to a detailed System 2 scrutiny.[74] In the case of expensive and emotionally salient brands such as Apple, choosing them may be a no-brainer for fans and devotees, however for other consumers who are less committed emotionally, Apple's products need to simultaneously appeal intuitively to System 1 and intellectually to System 2. When faced with a choice between high-value items that have dual appeal, System 1 and System 2 are activated in parallel and may compete for which of them has the final say. In this situation, consumers would typically marshal additional data, for example internet product and service reviews and ratings, in addition to simple affect-as-information to supplement their decision-making.

An example of the parallel competitive (PC) mode in consumer choice would be the decision of choosing between two high-value items that have both emotional resonance which appeals to System 1 and objective attributes that will satisfy the analytical scrutiny of System 2. For example, choosing between a BMW and a Mercedes is a high-value, consequential purchase. Both brands have an emotional resonance that will appeal to potential buyers' System 1. Both brands also meet stringent criteria for performance, quality, etc. that a System 2 analysis would demand. The choice between them then becomes a toing-and-froing between System 1 and System 2. In this situation the two systems operate in parallel and act jointly to determine the outcome. For low-value items such as a bottle of detergent or a can of soft drink, marketers may be content to take the risk of putting all their eggs in the System 1 basket because for much of the time the DI mode works perfectly well. However, for high-value items it is worth the marketer's while to recognize that human cognition is both a dual-system process (intuitive and analytical) and that the relationship between the two systems can operate in quite different ways, DI (intuitive-then-analytical) and PC (intuitive-and-analytical). In branding and product advertising, especially for high-value items, both System 1 and System 2 need to be activated. Consumers themselves would be well advised to press pause before they go with their gut in a high-value purchase.[75]

Empirical evidence from a study by Ioannis Thanos of strategic decision-making in over one hundred of the leading service firms in Greece suggests that the combined use of analysis and intuition leads to good-quality strategic decisions and is superior to intuition or analysis alone. The research also discovered that using analysis and intuition in combination leads to more successful decisions, especially in dynamic business settings. In terms of the sequencing, the research found evidence both for analysis-then-intuition and for intuition-then-analysis. In the case of the analysis-then-intuition sequence, managers analysed the pros and cons of all potential markets, which resulted in large amounts of data; but at some point they 'got lost with all this information' and so they restricted the decision process about which market to enter to the most experienced managers, who made the final decision on the basis both of the evidence and by drawing on their experience-based intuitions. In the case of the intuition-then-analysis sequence, managers made the decision to expand abroad after a feeling that the local market had matured; based on their 'knowledge, past experiences, and instincts' about international markets, they shortlisted two and then proceeded to an in-depth analysis based on the countries' economic prospects, legislative systems, political stability, consumer attitudes to foreign firms, and the local competition.[76]

Other research by Giulia Calabretta and colleagues on the dynamics of analysis and intuition in innovation projects found that one of the keys to successful outcomes in new product development was paradoxical thinking. Paradoxes imply contradiction between the so-called 'focal elements' of the paradox, for example 'exploitation and exploration', 'collaborate or compete', or 'intuition and analysis'. These contradictions and the tensions between them can be managed and turned to advantage by paradoxical thinking: essentially, and in the simplest terms, this means adopting a 'both/and' mindset rather than an 'either/or' mindset.[77] They offered the example of an innovation project in which the analysis–intuition tension was not eliminated but was rather worked with by: firstly, structuring available information in a way responds to the need for clear and comprehensive information sources as a basis for analysis; secondly, making connections on the basis of patterns, association, and connections which may be latent or implicit but which can only be intuited from the data and which ultimately lead to innovative solutions. As one of the managers they interviewed remarked: 'It's like a structure emerging. It's not that I get all the information and then I try to make sense of it. It's something that emerges by going back and forth, talking [with the client]'. The outcome is based partly on the data and partly on qualitative, intangible, feeling-related criteria such as 'likeability', 'feels good', and 'fits the lifestyle of customers'. These affective evaluations enabled managers to move forward from the fixed baseline of prior sales data to a more forward thinking, and foresighted, perspective which leads to more innovative outcomes by iterating between and integrating both analysis and intuition. The synthesis of analysis and intuition arrived at by adopting a paradox mindset can lead to an outcome which is greater than either intuition or analysis alone.[78]

The two-way relationship between System 1 and System 2 assumes that a monitoring mechanism operates in determining why some problems receive more attention from System 2 than others. Valerie Thomson and her colleagues have proposed that a metacognitive judgement in the form of a 'Feeling of Rightness' (FoR) accompanies the output from System 1 and that this determines the extent of System 2's engagement.[79] Metacognitive in this context means 'thinking about thinking', and metacognition involves an awareness and understanding of one's own thinking (cognitive) processes. Intuitions have been defined as affectively charged judgements,[80] and the Feelings of Rightness which accompany intuitions vary in their intensity. We should not lose sight of the fact that certainty (which is an extreme Feeling of Rightness) is no guarantee of correctness. The intuitive mind can sometimes be seduced by positive affect, i.e. good vibes, (technically a 'positively-valenced intuitive affect') about a particular choice, but simply feeling good about an alternative should not necessarily be conflated with the accuracy of the judgement.[81] Wishful thinking or the desirability bias, for example the soon-to-be bride and groom who have an intuition that the sun will shine on their wedding day but have no control over the outcome, can fuel unwarranted over-optimism.[82] Such optimism is more likely to be justified in situations where the decision-maker has the requisite expertise and can exercise some control over events.

The Experiential Mind

This section focuses on a detailed account of one particular two-minds models, namely, Cognitive-Experiential Theory (CET). CET is a dual-process theory which explains why and how the combined influence of *both* experiential-intuitive thinking (System 1) *and* analytical-rational thinking (System 2) is essential for effective judgement and decision-making in real-world situations.[83] CET is a parallel-competitive (PC) dual-process theory. It is singled out here because it presents intuition and analysis as joint processes, for the attention it gives to intuition as an 'experiential' process, and because of its keen uptake by management researchers even though CET was not developed as a theory of intuition in business as such.

CET was developed by Seymour Epstein (1924–2016), Professor of Psychology at University of Massachusetts at Amherst. Epstein refers to System 1 intuitive processing as 'intuitive-experiential'[84], and refers to System 2 analytical processing as 'analytical-rational'.[85] Epstein first presented his theory in 1973 roughly contemporaneous with Kahneman and Tversky's early work on heuristics and biases in an article with the somewhat arcane title of 'The self-concept revisited or a theory of a theory'. He later elaborated on CET in his *American Psychologist* citation classic 'Integration of the cognitive and the psychodynamic unconscious' (1994). Later still, he encapsulated the theory in his magnum opus *Cognitive-Experiential Theory: An Integrative Theory of Personality* published two years before Epstein passed away in 2016 at the age of 91.[86] Epstein's CET has been described by the eminent dual-process researcher Jonathan Evans and his colleague and philosopher of mind, Keith Frankish, as a 'landmark development' in the history of dual-process theory.[87]

Epstein's theory is significant for intuition in business for three reasons. First, CET switches attention away from psychologists' preoccupation with the negative, maladaptive manifestations of the intuitive system (for example, the fixation on intuition's well-established fallibility in computational and logical tasks carried out in laboratory settings) and away from clinical psychoanalysts' preoccupation with the emotionally and personally dysfunctional and detrimental aspects of unconscious thoughts.[88] Second, 'affect' in the form of gut feelings, hunches, and vibes (i.e. intuition) plays a critically important role in CET. Third, CET switches attention towards the adaptive, and hence beneficial, functions of intuitive-experiential and analytical-rational processing separately and in combination. In so doing, it offers insights into decision-making in the complex social environment of business organizations. In practical terms, CET can help mangers to understand if, when, and how to go with their gut feelings.

Epstein's theory is eclectic. It integrates various aspects of self-theory, learning theory, cognitive science, psychoanalytical theory, and theories of emotions. Its roots penetrate into Sigmund Freud's psychoanalytical theory, C. J. Jung's analytical psychology, Alfred Adler's individual psychology, Abraham Maslow's hierarchy of needs, and Carl Rogers' personality theory. At the end of his long and productive career, Epstein recollected that CET came to him in an insightful 'light-bulb' moment when he realized that the self-concept (i.e. the image we have of ourselves) is not simply a 'conscious [explicit] concept of the self'[89] as the humanistic psychologist Carl Rogers had believed but is instead an implicit, i.e. unconscious, and organized concept with three attributes. First, it is automatically acquired from a person's lived experience. Second, it consciously and unconsciously directs a person's adaptive and maladaptive behaviours in everyday life. Third, it develops though interactions with the 'data' of experience and hence has growth properties across the lifespan.[90]

Epstein proposed that the implicit beliefs that an individual derives automatically from the data of experience are organized into a dynamic structure—the 'experiential system'—which exerts a strong and profound influence over a person's feelings, thoughts, and behaviours. In particular, narratives and images appeal to the experiential system because they are emotionally engaging and represent events and objects in a way that corresponds to how they are experienced in real life, for example stories often involve characters and physical appearances in specific places and at particular times.[91] In business, advertising appeals directly to the experiential system through emotionally-charged narratives and vivid imagery. In CET the self has the ability to control actions and change over time—it has both 'agentic' (control) and 'growth' (change) properties[92].

As well as having deep roots, Epstein's theory is a broad canvas. Our focus of interest—intuition—is only a 'subset' of experiential processing and of CET. The intuition aspect of CET does not include many of the things within the broader remit of Epstein's concept of experiential processing more generally such as irrational fears, religious beliefs, superstitions, and psychomotor coordination. For this reason, only a limited aspect of CET is considered here, namely intuition as the operation of the experiential system as it applies to the processes of judgement and decision-making. Epstein argued that almost everything that has been attributed to intuition can be explained by the operation of the experiential system. He also designed and validated a questionnaire called the 'Rational Experiential Inventory' (REI) for the assessment of individual differences in preferences for intuitive-experiential and analytic-rational processing, sometimes referred to as cognitive style or thinking style (see Chapter 11).[93]

In common with other dual-process theories, CET's fundamental assumption is that humans navigate and interact with the world using to two information processing systems, an 'experiential system' (broadly equivalent to System 1, also referred to by Epstein as the experiential-intuitive system) and a 'rational system' (broadly equivalent to System 2).[94] Epstein summarized the attributes of these two systems as follows.

Experiential system: is oriented to what feels good; operates on the basis of implicit beliefs encoded in cognitive-affective (thinking-feeling) networks of associative relationships; operates holistically by reacting to things in their entirety; behaviour influenced mainly by feelings often associated with past experiences; encodes reality concretely (for example, in visual images, metaphors, and narratives); faster processing oriented towards more immediate and impulsive action; slower to learn and more resistant to change; produces outcomes that are self-evidently valid. An example of the operation of the experiential system in business is the by now familiar one of preferring a job candidate because they give off a positive vibe.

Rational system: is oriented to what is accurate and logical; operates on the basis of explicit beliefs encoded in affect-free, cognitive networks of cause-and-effect relationships; operates analytically by breaking things down into their component parts; behaviour influenced mainly by conscious appraisal of events; encodes reality in abstract symbols (for example, words, and numbers); slower processing oriented towards more delayed and deliberative action; faster to learn and less resistant to change; produces outcomes that are justifiable by logic and evidence.[95] An example of the operation of the rational system in business is preferring a job candidate because they excel across a battery of objective tests.

Associative Learning and the Hedonic Principle

CET does not succumb to the 'System-2-is-good'/'System-1-is-bad' fallacy that bedevils a number of other dual-process theories.[96] In CET, experiential-intuitive and rational-analytic processing are qualitatively rather than quantitatively different. If they were quantitatively different then more of one, for example rational processing, would always and everywhere be good, whilst more of the other, for example experiential processing would be bad. This is not the case. The experiential system is adaptive in that it evolved to automatically learn from experience, involves thought without analysis, has a feeling of certainty, is fast and effortless, operates by means of pattern recognition, is capable of generating skilled responses, can outperform analysis, and is a sensible voice worthy of heeding in certain situations. In CET, intuition's distinguishing features are that it is associative and affective. These two attributes reflect the two 'master motives'[97] by which the experiential system operates, namely an 'associative learning principle' and a 'hedonic principle'.

Associative learning principle: Epstein explained the experiential system's associative learning principle in terms of an automatic associative learning mechanism that operates in two ways. First, learning occurs by 'conditioning' as a result of directly experiencing an association between a stimulus and an outcome (as in Palov's dogs associating the sound of a bell with the presence of food) or experiencing an association between an outcome that follows directly from a response (as in a rat pressing a lever to obtain food). Second, learning occurs vicariously by 'observational learning', i.e. as a result of observing another person's behaviour for example in the case of a person emulating the behaviours of a role model.[98] Through the processes of conditioning and observational learning human beings construct a working mental model of their world which enables them to navigate and adapt successfully to their environment; much of the time this navigability is achieved through intuition. Hence, a manager's working model of their world is constructed experientially, shaped by social interaction with bosses, peers, and subordinates, and developed and adjusted by observations of role model behaviours within the cultural milieu of their organization. This working model of the world then demarcates and determines how the manager navigates their world. The majority of their behaviours are executed largely without conscious deliberation. If it were otherwise, getting by on a day-to-day basis would be excessively laboured and arduous and the process of managing would be inefficient, ineffective, and more or less impossible.

Hedonic principle: The hedonic principle explains the role of 'affect' (that is, involving experiences of feelings[99] such as gut feelings, hunches, and vibes) in experiential processing. The hedonic principle, from the Greek *hēdonikos* meaning 'pleasure', is an important influence on behaviour because pleasure (or its contrastive, pain[100]) motivates behaviour and 'affects almost everything a person does' since, self-evidently, people 'want to feel good' rather than to feel bad.[101] In terms of how intuitive judgement works, the hedonic (i.e. affective) principle means that people will approach or be disposed towards situations that elicit a positively valenced ('feel-good') affect and avoid or be disposed against situations that elicit a negatively valenced ('feel-bad') affect. The experiential system, via intuition, provides an affectively charged signal which motivates and directs behaviour away from certain courses of action (i.e. avoidance) and towards other courses of action (i.e. approach).

By way of example: in Klein's research, the experienced fire ground commander's negatively valenced intuition that the roof felt spongy in an unexpected and hard-to-define way gave him a bad sense and motivated his behaviour to order the evacuation of the building (an 'avoid' behaviour). Likewise, a potential investor's bad 'vibe' about an entrepreneur's pitch that sounds too good to be true is a signal to avoid rather than approach a business venturing opportunity. Intuition's 'affective charge' varies in terms of intensity as well as valence (that is, positive/approach versus negative/avoid). A gut feeling may be so slight as to be barely detectable by the intuitor but nonetheless exert an influence on their behaviours. At other times it may be intensely felt, as in Starbucks boss Howard Schulz's reported intense (and positive) visceral gut reaction to Italian coffee culture and which inspired him to try to bring the same ethos and ambience to the streets of the United States in establishing Starbucks. The conscious and non-conscious influences that these affective processes can have on judgement and decision-making are visceral to the extent that they have identifiable biological and neural bases (see Chapter 6).

Consider the experienced marketing manager who recognizes that an email marketing strategy has a number of attributes that are comparable to those that were used in a previously highly successful email marketing campaign. In terms of Cognitive-Experiential Self-Theory (CET) her experiential system senses intuitively that such a strategy is likely to work. Her experiential system signals 'approach'. The same manager recognizes intuitively that the social media advertising strategy that was being proposed has attributes that are similar to those she has seen fail badly in the past. Consequently, her experiential system senses that the social media advertising proposal would not work and it signals 'avoid'. A positive gut feel emanating automatically and quickly from her experiential system motivates approach behaviours towards the email marketing option. A negative gut feel emanating from the same source motivates avoid behaviours away from the social media advertising option. The marketing manager's experiential system has learned empirically from experience, whilst her tacitly held knowledge allowed her to generalize rapidly, automatically, and effortlessly to new situations without the need to undergo lengthy, deliberative, and effortful evaluations, thus obviating any need to solve each situation analytically from first principles. Objective signals perceived from the environment through the five senses are processed (from outside to inside) and generate an intuitive felt-sense which serves as a signal from within which is then used to affect the situation (from inside to outside).

CET's hedonic/affective principle also means that feelings can be a 'mixed blessing'[102] in that they can lead to bad as well as good outcomes. The affective principle has a biasing effect on rational processing when, for example, an inexperienced entrepreneur has positive gut feelings about his first business venture that he feels will be a 'sure fire' success but which leads to a reckless start-up decision. This is the desirability bias in action, and it emanates from intuition and the workings of the underlying experiential system (System 1) processes. Similarly, the hedonic/affective principle has a biasing effect when a white, male, middle-class hiring manager has a good vibe about a candidate who happens to be like him and a bad vibe about a job candidate who does not happen to be like him and is unlike people that he happens to like. The result would be a discriminatory hiring decision. This is the confirmation bias in action, and it emanates from intuition.

The interaction between the two systems is bi-directional; it is analogous in Epstein's words to a 'dance'[103] between experientiality (System 1) and rationality (System 2). For most of the time the interactions between them may be seamless, to the extent that to the thinker it appears as a single uninterrupted process. On other occasions, experientiality and rationality compete for control. For example, when a customer cannot decide between two makes of mobile phone because one is more functional and less expensive (as evaluated by System 2) whereas the other is more fun to use (as evaluated by System 1) but is more expensive to buy and run (as evaluated by System 2). Both have products their appeal, and there is a dilemma of which to choose. The customer experiences a state of conflict between the experiential system, which prefers the fun-to-use but expensive phone, and the rational system, which prefers the cheaper, more functional product. In this 'reciprocal chain'[104] of interactions, the experiential system can draw on the rational system to support its inferences and judgements, which may turn out to be erroneous and biased. It does so in a process of post-hoc rationalization of an earlier-to-arrive intuitive judgement. For example, this would happen if a hiring manager skewed the interpretation of data by downplaying the negatives and emphasizing the positives to support the job application of a candidate that he happens to like. Likewise, the rational system can co-opt the experiential system to justify or pursue its own ends, for example by deliberately using vivid imagery or convincing rhetoric to convey a message based on analytics and logic, thus influencing behaviour more convincingly than could be achieved using data and a rational argument unaided.[105] Advertisers and charismatic politicians use these techniques as a matter of course to convince consumers about their products or potential supporters whose votes they seek to procure.

When brand recognition leverages instant recognition and emotional salience, it bypasses the rational system, using the experiential system's hedonic principle. The highest value item that most people will purchase in their lifetimes is their home. Estate agents are not unaware, albeit implicitly, of the fact that the experiential system can be influenced forcefully by emotionally salient words and pictures. To influence potential buyers' behaviours, they use positively connoted and ornate language such as 'bijou' or 'charming' when the property is in fact small, 'original features' for a property that is need of modernization, 'deceptively spacious' when it is not that spacious at all.[106] Accompanying such descriptions with flattering visual imagery and by viewing the property's best features first and last only serves to amplify and reinforce the overall impact of positive features and images on the buyer's experiential system. On the other hand, estate agents do not offer potential buyers an objective list of 'reasons-to-buy' versus 'reasons-not-to-buy' in order to appeal directly and unemotionally to the buyer's rational system.

In dual-processing, speed of decision-making is also of the essence, especially when it comes to choosing between different brands. The experiential-intuitive system is primed to take instinctive decisions and the rational-analytical system can be something of a laggard. The brand that succeeds in coming to and lodging in the mind of the consumer first may end up being, almost literally, the no-brainer choice. Advertisements which elicit and evoke positive emotions, instant visual recognition, and desirable associations literally have a head start in consumer choice.[107] Knowledge of the potency of the experiential system is making inroads into advertising metrics and AI applications, for example, by making predictions about the effectiveness of advertisements based on an advertisement's 'star' (emotional response), 'spike' (speed of brand recognition and emotional intensity created), and 'fluency' ratings (the strength of brand presence in the ad, which is essentially whether consumers recognize the brand in the ad).[108] The brand consultancy 'System 1' has developed innovative AI-based 'FaceTrace'" technology to monitor how people feel in terms of positive and negative primary emotions such as disgust or happiness when watching an advertisement. These metrics can then be used to improve advertisements by making them more attuned to potential consumers' experiential systems.[109] Whilst this is not artificial intuition as such, it is an example of an application of the of 'affective computing' technology.[110]

When Should System 1 Be Trusted?

Some dual-process theories draw a qualitative distinction between a System 1 that is depicted as unequivocally 'bad' because it generates error-prone and systematically biased judgements and a System 2 that is depicted as unambiguously 'good' because it is seen as generating rational and more accurate judgements.[111] Many psychologists, including prominent dual-process researchers themselves, lament the perpetuation of this good-versus-bad fallacy.[112] System 1's intuitions result in both good and bad outcomes, as do System 2's analyses. This begs the question of when should System 1 be trusted?

The heuristics and biases research programme initiated by Kahneman and his colleague Amos Tversky in the 1970s sought to answer the questions 'what errors and biases does System 1 create', 'what are the features of System 1 that lead to such errors and biases', and 'why are such errors and biases not corrected by System 2?' Several factors are important in answering these questions: 'attribute substitution', which is concerned with cognitive processes; 'complex domain relevant schemas', which are concerned with the cognitive substrates of decision-making; and the linked concepts of the 'validity of the environment' and 'learning structures', which are concerned with the context in which intuitive judgements are acquired and exercised.

Attribute Substitution: As was discovered in Chapter 2, one of the reasons for systematic errors and biases in judgement and decision-making is that human beings have an in-built proclivity to substitute an easier-to-answer question for a harder-to-answer question. The actual mechanisms by which attribute substitution occurs vary. It can happen by means of the availability heuristic, for example where the question of 'what proportion of CEOs are implicated in ethical scandals?' would be answered as if the question were 'which instances of unethical CEO behaviour spring immediately to mind?'. Substitution can also happen by means of the representativeness heuristic, for example where the question of 'would this candidate be able to do the job competently' would be answered as if the question were 'how impressive was the candidate's PowerPoint presentation?' Attribute substitution can be a source of biased and inaccurate intuitive judgements and decisions.

Complex Domain-Relevant Schemas: On the upside, as a result of lengthy and intense periods of exposure to complex and challenging scenarios and situations, decision-makers' mental models evolve into highly sophisticated domain-specific representations (i.e. mental models) of the world and how it works. These mental models are sometimes referred to as 'complex domain-relevant schemas' (CDRS).[113] CDRSs are the raw materials for the skilled intuitive judgements that distinguish experts from novices.[114] Without CDRSs there can be no skilled intuitions or intuitive expertise. Their 'domain-specificity' means that intuitive expertise in one field, such as firefighting, does not transfer to a dissimilar domain, such as management.

CDRSs develop though the processes of exposure, experiential learning, and feedback. This creates domain-specific knowledge of relationships between cues, behaviours, and results. In recognition-primed decision-making for example, associations are learned between the cues that a particular situation generates (these include, in the case of firefighting, the colour, smell, and sound of the flames), that enable an experienced decision-maker to recognize a patterns in the cues intuitively (for example, recognizing a certain sort of flame as characteristic of a particular type of fire) which then activate action scripts for how to respond (for example, how to tackle a such a situation). Knowledge created through effortful System 1 processing transitions over an extended period of time through the processes of experience and feedback from System 2 to System 1, where it becomes embedded as rational analyses frozen into habitual intuitions.[115] It is this knowledge that gives experienced decision-makers the capacity for rapid, skilled response though pattern recognition.

Validity of the Environment: Whether an intuitive judgement is likely to be accurate or not depends on the existence of stable and predictable relationships between cues, behaviours, and outcomes. Heuristics and biases researcher Daniel Kahneman and recognition-primed decision researcher Gary Klein, whose approaches to intuition are often viewed as conflicting, used the term 'validity' to describe the structure of the environment in which the decision-maker is operating.[116] In a notable 'failure to disagree' (which was the subtitle of their influential 2009 article in *American Psychologist*), Kahneman and Klein used the examples of firefighting and the trading of shares to illustrate the differences between 'high-validity environments' and 'low-validity environments'.

In the case of firefighting there are likely to be principal cues in the environment (sometimes available to all five senses of sight, smell, sound, taste, and touch), which can be substantiated by learning and experience, that indicate that a particular type of burning building is about to collapse. This is a high-validity environment in which the firefighter's intuitive judgements are quite likely, but not guaranteed, to be accurate. However, in the case of stock market trading, there is unlikely to be publicly available information that could be used to predict how a particular stock likely to perform. Moreover, if such valid information existed the price of the stock would already reflect it.[117] This is a low-validity environment in which any intuitive 'predictions' about the future value of particular individual company stocks are not likely to be accurate. Hence, System 1 is more likely to be wrong when it is used to make intuitive predictions in low-validity environments. System 1's judgements are also likely to be unreliable when there is a poor match between the current situation and seemingly similar situations that have been encountered in the past, and when the decision-maker lacks sufficient experience.[118]

Kind-versus-Wicked Learning Structures: In high-validity environments the chances of making accurate intuitive judgements are increased greatly by experiential learning processes which incorporate feedback of results so that the decision-maker learns the 'right lessons' from experience.[119] For example, doctors who treat patients on accident and emergency wards may not always get feedback on how well they treated a patient if the patient is moved on within the hospital, moves out into community care, or is simply discharged. In this situation, the doctor is put at a learning disadvantage compared to a doctor who sees a patient through from first presenting to being discharged. Robin Hogarth, author of *Educating Intuition*, describes a 'kind learning structure' (or kind learning environment) as one in where the availability of accurate feedback increases the likelihood of—whilst not guaranteeing—a positive outcome. High-validity environments are kind learning structures. They enable the development of good intuitions. But it is not simply a matter of experience, even in high-validity environments. More experience is not necessarily better. Quality of experience also matters, and the quality of experiential learning processes can be enhanced substantially by feedback and coaching (see Chapter 11).

By contrast, a 'wicked' learning structure' (or wicked learning environment) is one in which feedback is absent or the feedback that is available is misleading.[120] Low-validity environments are wicked learning structures. They constrain the development of good intuitions. An example of a kind learning structure in business would be a manager who is co-opted onto an interview panel as an independent panellist, uses her intuitive judgement, and gets to find out how well the newly hired appointee performs in their job. Conversely, not making such feedback available to the cop-opted manager would make the environment a wicked learning structure because the manager would not get to find out how accurate their intuitions about the candidate were. Wicked learning structures are a good way to build bad intuitions.

Experience itself has its downside and intuitive expertise can be a double-edged sword. Experience and intuition can be liabilities when they become frozen into an institutionalized practice which goes unchallenged and is oblivious to changes in the business context. When this happens, managers can become overly dependent on outdated or inappropriate mental models. As a result, they may fail to notice changes in their environment until it is too late. A study by Gerard Hodgkinson of UK real estate agents' perceptions of their competitive space (for example, the image they had of who their rivals are and what the market conditions were) found that estate agents became overly dependent on a prevailing and overly optimistic shared mental model of a buoyant market which had become out of step with a significant downturn in the marketplace. Their expertise congealed into a 'cognitive inertia' such that responses to the market situation were intuitive but formulaic. Rather than taking time to reflect and reconsider, they became impervious to the fact that their competitive strategies had become outmoded. This had disastrous consequences for a number of the big players in an ailing but once boisterous marketplace.[121] Likewise, Kodak's missing out on the digital photography revolution has also been attributed to the dysfunctional mix of managers' cognitive inertia combined with a bureaucratic organizational structure. The failure of Kodak to respond to digitization, in spite of the fact that it invented the first digital camera in 1975, has been referred to as a classic case of 'corporate hubris'.[122] In the face of a disruptive technology entering their competitive space the company chose to be wilfully blind, as typified in this response from a Kodak executive at the time '[filmless photography was] cute—but don't tell anyone about it'.[123]

Critical Voices

Although the two-minds model has achieved almost paradigmatic status in some quarters and its proponents lauded, there are dissenting voices which have become louder and more incessant in recent years. Prominent amongst these are Gerd Gigerenzer (whose work on fast-and-frugal heuristics we met in Chapter 3) and others. One of the main points of disagreement is with regard to the role that rules play in the proposed differences between System 1 and System 2, for example another name for System 2 is 'rule-based' whereas System 1 is 'associative'.[124] Some critics argue that it is fallacious to refer to System 2 processes as rule-based with the implication that System 1 is rule-free. Their argument is that judgements that are commonly referred to as intuitive and deliberative (i.e. analytical) are rule-based and that the same rules can underlie both types of processing. By rules they mean if–then relationships between cues and judgements. So for example, by learning, conditioning, social development, experience, and acculturation, an expectancy is set up that a given cue will likely be followed by some event (for example, in firefighting the appearance of a certain type blaze is likely to be associated with particular outcomes). The rule describes the association between the cue and outcome and the behaviour that emanates from this rule, for example making a prediction can be exercise deliberately or intuitively. Gigerenzer argues that heuristics, such as the recognition heuristic (see Chapter 3), are based on the same set of core capacities (such as perception of cues, memory of prior instances, association between cues and outcomes, and recall, etc.) regardless of whether they are executed consciously (i.e. analytically) or unconscious (i.e. intuitively).

The key idea here seems to be the process of habituation leading eventually to automatization of things that were effortful initially. Through the routinization of rules prior analyses become intuitive, for example in sports and musical performance, what once was effortful, with sufficient quantity and quality of practice, becomes effortless. This is apparent in the transition from rigid rule-following novice behaviour to fluid, context-sensitive expert performance. Paradoxically, in some sports it appears that being required to focus on a well-honed skill can causes anxieties which disrupt skilled performance; for example a number of professional golfers report experiencing a sudden loss of the ability to execute an automated skill such as putting. This phenomenon is known colloquially as having 'the yips'. Indeed, it is worth recalling Herbert Simon's definition of intuitions as 'analyses [which includes rules] frozen into habit' which give an expert the capacity for rapid response through matching a cue to an anticipated outcome based on previous experiences of that cue–outcome relationship. The critics of the dual-model offer a 'uni-model' (i.e. single system) as an alternative to the dual-process paradigm in which analytical and intuitive reasoning processes are both rule-based, with one of the main differences being in how the rules are executed.[125] In repost to this criticism, Jonathan Evans and Keith Stanovich, two major proponents of dual-process theories, argued that by labelling what goes on under the auspices of both systems, rule-based is a 'semantic device' to encourage the view that System 1 and System 2 can be collapsed into a single entity.[126]

Perhaps the key is whether or not any reasoning behind an intuitive judgement can be articulated or not; knowing what to do without explicitly knowing the rule that guides behaviour, or at least being able to articulate it easily, is one of the hallmarks of intuition.

Summary

1. The main idea of this chapter is that human beings can be thought of as having 'two minds in one brain', The two minds are: (a) an intuitive mind (related terms are 'System 1' and 'Type 1 processing'); and (b) an analytical mind (related terms are 'System 2' and 'Type 2 processing').
2. System 1 is holistic, automatic, cognitively undemanding, comparatively fast, acquired experientially, high-capacity, a parallel processor, intuitive, implicit, unconscious, and evolutionarily old.
3. System 2, is analytic, controlled, cognitively demanding, comparatively slow, acquired formally, low-capacity, a sequential processor, reflective, explicit, conscious, and evolutionarily recent.
4. It is a fallacy to think of System 2 as 'good' and System 1 as 'bad' for decision-making; System 1 processes, such as intuition, can lead to good outcomes when exercised by the right person under the right circumstances.
5. Intuitions can lead to good outcomes when they have been built up in kind learning structures (i.e. with timely, accurate and diagnostic feedback) and are exercised in high-validity environments (i.e. where there are stable and reliable relationships between cues and outcomes).
6. Critics argue that dual-system models can be collapsed into a single rule-based 'uni-model' system.
7. This dual-system, whether metaphorical or real, does not correspond to left brain and right brain hemispheric differences, and any claim that intuition is in the right brain is best treated as a 'neuromyth'.

Endnotes

1. Pennycook, G. (2018). A perspective on the theoretical foundation of dual-process models. In De Neys, W. (Ed.). *Dual Process Theory 2.0*, (pp. 5–27). Abingdon: Routledge, p. 6.
2. James predated Freud and Jung: Freud's *The Interpretation of Dreams* was published in 1900, and Jung's *Psychology of the Unconscious* was published in 1916.
3. Weinberger, J. (2000). William James and the unconscious: Redressing a century-old misunderstanding. *Psychological Science*, 11(6): 439–445, p. 442.
4. This phrase (and the title of this chapter) is co-opted from Evans, J. S. B. (2010). *Thinking Twice: Two Minds in One Brain*. Oxford: Oxford University Press.
5. Melnikoff, D. E., & Bargh, J. A. (2018). The mythical number two. *Trends in Cognitive Sciences*, 22(4), 280–293.

6. The World bank (2015). *World Development Report 2015: Mind, Society, and Behaviour*. Washington, DC: The World Bank. Available online at: https://www.worldbank.org/en/publication/wdr2015 Accessed 21.02.2022.
7. Kahneman, D., & Frederick, S. (2002). Representativeness revisited: Attribute substitution in intuitive judgment. In Gilovich, T., Griffin, D., & Kahneman, D. (Eds.). *Heuristics and Biases: The Psychology of Intuitive Judgment*. Cambridge: Cambridge University Press, pp. 49–81, p. 51.
8. De Neys, W. (Ed.). (2018). *Dual Process Theory 2.0*. Abingdon: Routledge, pp. 5–27.
9. Simon, H. A. (1987). Making management decisions: The role of intuition and emotion. *Academy of Management Perspectives*, 1(1): 57–64, p. 63.
10. Sadler-Smith, E. (2010). *The Intuitive Mind: Profiting from the Power of Your Sixth Sense*. Chichester: John Wiley and Sons.
11. Evans, J. S. B. (2003). In two minds: dual-process accounts of reasoning. *Trends in Cognitive Sciences*, 7(10): 454–459.
12. Einhorn, H. J., & Hogarth, R. M. (1981). Behavioral decision theory: Processes of judgement and choice. *Annual Review of Psychology*, 32(1): 53–88.
13. Cook, S. D., & Brown, J. S. (1999). Bridging epistemologies: The generative dance between organizational knowledge and organizational knowing. *Organization Science*, 10(4): 381–400.
14. Reber, A. S. (1989). Implicit learning and tacit knowledge. *Journal of Experimental Psychology: General*, 118(3): 219–235.
15. Evans, J. S. B. (2010). *Thinking Twice: Two Minds in One Brain*. Oxford: Oxford University Press, pp. v–vi.
16. Based on an example from the Frequently Asked Questions page from Harvard University's Project Implicit web page. Available online at: https://implicit.harvard.edu/implicit/faqs.html#faq1 Accessed 14.02.2022.
17. Frankish, K., & Evans, J. S. B. (2009) The duality of mind: An historical perspective. In Evans, J., & Frankish, K. (Eds.). *In Two Minds: Dual Processes and Beyond*. Oxford University Press, pp. 1–29, p. 14.
18. Sadler-Smith, E. (2008). *Inside Intuition*. Abingdon: Routledge, p. 128.
19. Polanyi, M. (1966) *The Tacit Dimension*. Gloucester, MA: Peter Smith/Doubleday (reprinted. 1983), p. 4.
20. Redington, M., & Chater, N. (1996). Transfer in artificial grammar learning: A re-evaluation. *Journal of Experimental Psychology: General*, 125(2): 123–138.
21. Patterson, R. E., Pierce, B. J., Bell, H. H., & Klein, G. (2010). Implicit learning, tacit knowledge, expertise development, and naturalistic decision making. *Journal of Cognitive Engineering and Decision Making*, 4(4): 289–303.
22. Dane, E., Rockmann, K. W., & Pratt, M. G. (2012). When should I trust my gut? Linking domain expertise to intuitive decision-making effectiveness. *Organizational Behaviour and Human Decision Processes*, 119(2): 187–194.
23. Nadler, J., Thompson, L., & Boven, L. V. (2003). Learning negotiation skills: Four models of knowledge creation and transfer. *Management Science*, 49(4): 529–540.
24. Reber, A. S. (1992). An evolutionary context for the cognitive unconscious. *Philosophical Psychology*, 5(1): 33–51.
25. Ibid.

26. Chaiken, S. (1980). Heuristic versus systematic information processing and the use of source versus message cues in persuasion. *Journal of Personality and Social Psychology*, 39: 752–66.
27. Smith, E. R., & Collins, E. C. (2009). Dual-process modes: A psychological perspective. In Evans, J., & Frankish, K. (Eds.). *In Two Minds: Dual Processes and Beyond*. Oxford University Press, pp. 197–216.
28. Beattie, G., & McGuire, L. (2016). Consumption and climate change: Why we say one thing but do another in the face of our greatest threat. *Semiotica*, 213: 493–538.
29. Hirschman, E. C. (1994). Consumers and their animal companions. *Journal of Consumer Research*, 20(4): 616–632.
30. Lancendorfer, K. M., Atkin, J. L., & Reece, B. B. (2008). Animals in advertising: Love dogs? Love the ad! *Journal of Business Research*, 61(5): 384–391.
31. Chaiken, S., Ledgerwood, A. (2012). A theory of heuristic and systemic processing. In Van Lange, P. A., Kruglanski, A. W., & Higgins, E. T. (Eds.). *Handbook of Theories of Social Psychology*. London: SAGE, pp. 246–266.
32. Thaler, R. H., & Sunstein, C. R. (2008). *Nudge: Improving Decisions about Health, Wealth and Happiness*. New Haven: Yale University Press.
33. Institute for Government (2020). Nudge unit. Available online at: https://www.instituteforgovernment.org.uk/explainers/nudge-unit Accessed 21.02.2022.
34. Thaler, R. H., & Sunstein, C. R. (2008). *Nudge: Decisions about Health, Wealth and Happiness*. New Haven: Yale University Press, p. 24.
35. Rosenberg, J. (2020). Covid-19 creates permanent changes in homecare. Mintel. Available online at: https://www.mintel.com/blog/household-market-news/covid-19-creates-permanent-changes-in-homecare Accessed 21.02.2022.
36. Wilson, T. D., Lindsey, S., & Schooler, T. Y. (2000). A model of dual attitudes. *Psychological Review*, 107(1): 101–126.
37. Messner, C., & Vosgerau, J. (2010). Cognitive inertia and the implicit association test. *Journal of Marketing Research*, 47(2): 374–386.
38. Project Implicit: Learn More Harvard University. Available online at: https://implicit.harvard.edu/implicit/faqs.html Accessed 21.02.2022.
39. Wilson, T.D. (2002). *Strangers to ourselves: Discovering the adaptive unconscious*. Cambridge, MA: Belknap Press, pp. 133 and 191.
40. Project Implicit: Learn More Harvard University. Available online at: https://implicit.harvard.edu/implicit/faqs.html Accessed 21.02.2022.
41. Govind, R., Singh, J. J., Garg, N., & D'Silva, S. (2019). Not walking the walk: How dual attitudes influence behavioral outcomes in ethical consumption. *Journal of Business Ethics*, 155(4): 1195–1214.
42. Cowe, R., & Williams, S. (2000). *Who Are the Ethical Consumers? Ethical Consumerism Report*. London: Co-operative Bank.
43. Govind, R., Singh, J. J., Garg, N., & D'Silva, S. (2019). Not Walking the Walk: How Dual Attitudes Influence Behavioral Outcomes in Ethical Consumption. *Journal of Business Ethics*, 155(4): 1195–1214.
44. Beattie, G., & McGuire, L. (2016). Consumption and climate change: Why we say one thing but do another in the face of our greatest threat. *Semiotica*, 213: 493–538.
45. Sadler-Smith, E. (2008) *Inside Intuition*. Abingdon: Routledge, p. 193

46. Stanovich later withdrew from the 'system' nomenclature, preferring instead to use the labels of 'Type 1' and 'Type 2' processing. In this book the system nomenclature will be used as this appears to have become common usage.
47. Stanovich, K. E. (2009). Distinguishing the reflective, algorithmic, and autonomous minds: Is it time for a tri-process theory? In Evans, J. S. B. T., & Frankish, K. (Eds.). *In Two Minds: Dual Processes and Beyond* (pp. 55–88). Oxford University Press.
48. Thompson, V. A. (2014). What intuitions are… and are not. In *Psychology of Learning and Motivation* (Vol. 60, pp. 35–75). Academic Press.
49. Lieberman, M. D. (2007). Social cognitive neuroscience: a review of core processes. *Annual Review of Psychology*, 58: 259–289.
50. Pink, D. (2006). *Why Right-Brainers Will Rule the Future*. London: Marshall Cavendish.
51. Evans J. S. B., & Stanovich K. E. (2013). Dual-process theories of higher cognition: Advancing the debate. *Perspectives in Psychological Science*, 8: 223–241.
52. Kaufman, S. B., & Singer, J. L. (2012). The creativity of dual process 'System 1' thinking. *Scientific American*, 17 January 2012. Available online at: https://blogs.scientificamerican.com/guest-blog/the-creativity-of-dual-process-system-1-thinking/ Accessed 21.02.2022.
53. Stanovich, K. E., & Toplak, M. E. (2012). Defining features versus incidental correlates of Type 1 and Type 2 processing. *Mind & Society*, 11(1): 3–13, p. 5
54. Melnikoff, D. E., & Bargh, J. A. (2018). The mythical number two. *Trends in Cognitive Sciences*, 22(4): 280–293, p. 283
55. Stanovich, K. E., & Toplak, M. E. (2012). Defining features versus incidental correlates of Type 1 and Type 2 processing. *Mind & Society*, 11(1): 3–13, p. 5; Thompson, V. A. (2014). What intuitions are… and are not. In *Psychology of Learning and Motivation* (Vol. 60, pp. 35–75). Academic Press, p. 44.
56. Hodgkinson, G. P., & Clarke, I. (2007). Conceptual note: Exploring the cognitive significance of organizational strategizing. *Human Relations*, 60(1): 243–255, p. 246.
57. During the Late Pleistocene (129,000–11,700 BP).
58. Evan has been referred as the 'godfather' of the standard dual-process model, see: De Neys, W. (Ed.). (2018). *Dual Process Theory 2.0*. Abingdon: Routledge.
59. Evans, J. S. B. (2003). In two minds: dual-process accounts of reasoning. *Trends in Cognitive Sciences*, 7(10): 454–459, p. 458.
60. Frankish, K., & Evans, J. S. B. (2009) The duality of mind: An historical perspective. In Evans, J., & Frankish, K. (Eds.). *In Two Minds: Dual Processes and Beyond*. Oxford University Press, pp. 1–29, p. 18.
61. Baron-Cohen, S. (1999). An evolutionary theory of mind. In Corballis, M., & Lea, S. (Eds.). *The Descent of Mind: Psychological Perspectives on Hominid Evolution*. Oxford: Oxford University Press.
62. Evans, J. S. B. (2003). In two minds: dual-process accounts of reasoning. *Trends in Cognitive Sciences*, 7(10): 454–459; Bressan, D. (2018). Climate change may have contributed to the extinction of the Neanderthals. *Forbes*, 1 September 2018. Available online at: https://www.forbes.com/sites/davidbressan/2018/09/01/climate-change-may-have-contributed-to-the-extinction-of-neanderthals-and-rise-of-modern-humans/?sh=2fbaa3bf652f Accessed 21.02.2022.
63. Melnikoff, D. E., & Bargh, J. A. (2018). The mythical number two. *Trends in Cognitive Sciences*, 22(4): 280–293, p. 283.
64. Adopted from: Stanovich, K. E., & West, R. F. (2000). Individual differences in reasoning: Implications for the rationality debate? *Behavioral and Brain Sciences*, 23(5): 645–665.

65. Evans, J. S. B. (2007). On the resolution of conflict in dual process theories of reasoning. *Thinking & Reasoning*, 13(4): 321–339.
66. Kahneman, D. (2011). *Thinking, Fast and Slow*, London: Allen Lane, pp. 152–153.
67. Frankish, K., & Evans, J. S. B. (2009). The duality of mind: An historical perspective. In Evans, J., & Frankish, K. (Eds.). *In Two Minds: Dual Processes and Beyond*. Oxford University Press, pp. 1–29.
68. Evans, J. S. B. T. (2003). *Thinking Twice: Two Minds in One Brain*. Oxford: Oxford University Press, pp. 5–6; Kahneman, D. (2011). *Thinking, Fast and Slow*, London: Allen Lane, pp. 21, 24–25.
69. De Neys, W. (Ed.). (2018). *Dual Process Theory 2.0*. Abingdon: Routledge.
70. Evans, J. S. B., & Stanovich, K. E. (2013). Dual-process theories of higher cognition: Advancing the debate. *Perspectives on Psychological Science*, 8(3): 223–241, p. 227
71. System 1 Book, p. 40.
72. North, A. C., Hargreaves, D. J. & J. McKendrick, D. J. (1999). 'The influence of in-store music on wine selections', *Journal of Applied Psychology*, 84(2): 271–276.
73. Available online at: https://www.brandspeak.co.uk/blog/articles/system-1-versus-system-2-start-your-brand-thinking-the-way-your-customers-think/; https://www.smartinsights.com/digital-marketing-strategy/its-time-for-marketers-to-tap-into-system-1-thinking/ Accessed 21.02.2022.
74. Available online at: https://www.brandspeak.co.uk/blog/articles/system-1-versus-system-2-start-your-brand-thinking-the-way-your-customers-think/ Accessed 21.02.2022.
75. Ibid.
76. Thanos, I. C. (2022). The complementary effects of rationality and intuition on strategic decision quality. *European Management Journal* (in press). Available online at: https://doi.org/10.1016/j.emj.2022.03.003
77. Keller, J., & Sadler-Smith, E. (2019). Paradoxes and dual processes: A review and synthesis. *International Journal of Management Reviews*, 21(2): 162–184.
78. Calabretta, G., Gemser, G., & Wijnberg, N. M. (2017). The interplay between intuition and rationality in strategic decision making: A paradox perspective. *Organization Studies*, 38(3–4): 365–401.
79. Thompson, V. A., Turner, J. A. P., & Pennycook, G. (2011). Intuition, reason, and metacognition. *Cognitive Psychology*, 63(3): 107–140.
80. Dane, E., & Pratt, M. G. 2007. Exploring intuition and its role in managerial decision making. *Academy of Management Review*, 32(1): 33–54.
81. Ibid., p. 39
82. Krizan, Z., & Windschitl, P. D. (2009). Wishful thinking about the future: Does desire impact optimism? *Social and Personality Psychology Compass*, 3(3): 227–243.
83. Cognitive-Experiential Theory (CET) was formerly referred to as Cognitive-Experiential Self-Theory (CEST).
84. Epstein, S. (2011) The influence of valence and intensity of affect on intuitive processing. In Sinclair, M. (Ed.). *Handbook of Intuition Research*. Cheltenham: Edward Elgar, pp. 37–51, p. 37.
85. Evans, J. S. B. (2007). On the resolution of conflict in dual process theories of reasoning. *Thinking and Reasoning*, 13: 321–339.; Hodgkinson, G. P., & Sadler-Smith, E. 2018. The dynamics of intuition and analysis in managerial and organizational decision making. *Academy of Management Perspectives*, 32(4): 473–492.

86. University of Massachusetts Amherst (2016) Obituary: Seymour Epstein. Available online at: https://www.pbs.umass.edu/news/obituary-seymour-epstein-professor-emeritus-psychology Accessed 21.02.2022.
87. Frankish, K., & Evans, J. S. B. (2009) The duality of mind: An historical perspective. In Evans, J., & Frankish, K. (Eds.). *In Two Minds: Dual Processes and Beyond*. Oxford University Press, pp. 1–29, p. 19.
88. Kaufman, S. B. (2016). An ode to Seymour Epstein, originator of modern dual-process theory (1925–2016). *Scientific American* Blog, 27 May 2016. Available online at: An Ode to Seymour Epstein, Originator of Modern Dual-Process Theory (1925–2016)—Scientific American Blog Network Accessed 21.02.2022.
89. Epstein, S. (2014). *Cognitive-Experiential Theory: An Integrative Theory of Personality*. Oxford: Oxford University Press, p. 10.
90. Ibid., p. 111.
91. Epstein, S. (1994). Integration of the cognitive and the psychodynamic unconscious. *American Psychologist*, 49(8): 709–724.
92. Epstein, S. (2014). *Cognitive-Experiential Theory: An Integrative Theory of Personality*. Oxford: Oxford University Press, p. xiii.
93. Epstein, S., Pacini, R., Denes-Raj, V., & Heier, H. (1996). Individual differences in intuitive-experiential and analytical-rational thinking styles. *Journal of Personality and Social Psychology*, 71(2): 390–405.
94. Epstein, S. (2011). The influence of valence and intensity of affect on intuitive processing. In Sinclair, M. (Ed.). *Handbook of Intuition Research*. Cheltenham: Edward Elgar, pp. 37–51.
95. Epstein, S. (2011). The influence of valence and intensity of affect on intuitive processing. In Sinclair, M. (Ed.). *Handbook of Intuition Research*. Cheltenham: Edward Elgar, pp. 37–51, p. 39.
96. Pennycook, G., De Neys, W., Evans, J. S. B., Stanovich, K. E., & Thompson, V. A. (2018). The mythical dual-process typology. *Trends in Cognitive Sciences*, 22(8): 667–668.
97. Epstein, S. (2014). *Cognitive-Experiential Theory: An Integrative Theory of Personality*. Oxford: Oxford University Press, p. 14.
98. Ibid., pp. 104–105.
99. *APA Dictionary of Psychology*. Available online at: https://dictionary.apa.org/affect Accessed 21.02.2022.
100. Stanford Encyclopaedia of Philosophy (2013). Hedonism. Available online at: https://plato.stanford.edu/entries/hedonism/ Accessed 21.02.2022.
101. Epstein, S. (2014). *Cognitive-Experiential Theory: An Integrative Theory of Personality*. Oxford: Oxford University Press, p. 15.
102. Ibid.
103. Ibid., p. 87.
104. Ibid.
105. Epstein, S. (2014). *Cognitive-Experiential Theory: An Integrative Theory of Personality*. Oxford: Oxford University Press.
106. Lunn, E. (2009). Don't be swayed by estate agent jargon. Love money. Available online at: https://www.lovemoney.com/news/1775/dont-be-swayed-by-estate-agent-jargon Accessed 21.02.2022.

107. System 1 vs System 2: Think like your customers. Brandspeak. https://www.brandspeak.co.uk/blog/articles/system-1-versus-system-2-start-your-brand-thinking-the-way-your-customers-think/ Accessed 21.02.2022.
108. System 1 (no date) Empowering every marketer to create great advertising. Available online at: https://testyourad.system1group.com/ Accessed 21.02.2022.
109. Ibid.
110. Picard, R. W. (2003). Affective computing: challenges. *International Journal of Human-Computer Studies*, 59(1–2): 55–64.
111. Melnikoff, D. E., & Bargh, J. A. (2018). The mythical number two. *Trends in Cognitive Sciences*, 22(4): 280–293.
112. Evans, J. S. B., & Stanovich, K. E. (2013). Dual-process theories of higher cognition: Advancing the debate. *Perspectives on Psychological Science*, 8(3): 223–241.
113. Dane, E., & Pratt, M. G. (2007). Exploring intuition and its role in managerial decision making. *Academy of Management Review*, 32(1): 33–54; Dreyfus, H. L., & Dreyfus, S. E. 2005. Peripheral vision: Expertise in real world contexts. *Organization Studies*, 26(5): 779–792.
114. Ibid.
115. Simon, H. A. (1987). Making management decisions: The role of intuition and emotion. *Academy of Management Perspectives*, 1(1): 57–64.
116. Kahneman, D., & Klein, G. (2009). Conditions for intuitive expertise: a failure to disagree. *American Psychologist*, 64(6): 515–526.
117. Ibid., p. 520
118. Epstein, S. (2014). *Cognitive-Experiential Theory: An Integrative Theory of Personality*. Oxford: Oxford University Press, p. 306.
119. Hogarth, R.M. (2001). *Educating Intuition*. Chicago: Chicago University Press, p. 87.
120. Ibid., pp. 89–90.
121. Hodgkinson, G. P. (1997). Cognitive inertia in a turbulent market: The case of UK residential estate agents. *Journal of Management Studies*, 34(6): 921–945.
122. Lucas Jr, H. C., & Goh, J. M. (2009). Disruptive technology: How Kodak missed the digital photography revolution. *The Journal of Strategic Information Systems*, 18(1): 46–55.
123. Mui, C. (2012). How Kodak failed. *Forbes*, 18 January 2012. Available online at: https://www.forbes.com/sites/chunkamui/2012/01/18/how-kodak-failed/?sh=67700a26f27a Accessed 21.02.2022.
124. Sloman, S. A. (1996). The empirical case for two systems of reasoning. *Psychological Bulletin*, 119(1): 3–22.
125. Gigerenzer, G., & Regier. T. (1996). How do we tell an association from a rule? Comment on Sloman (1996). *Psychological Bulletin*, 119: 23–26.; Keren, G., & Schul. Y. (2009). Two is not always better than one: A critical evaluation of two-system theories. *Perspectives on Psychological Science*, 4(6): 533–550.; Kruglanski, A. W., & Gigerenzer, G. (2011). Intuitive and deliberative judgments are based on common principles. *Psychological Review* 118: 97–109; Mugg, J. (2016). The dual-process turn: How recent defences of dual-process theories of reasoning fail. *Philosophical Psychology*, 29 (2): 300–309.
126. Evans, J. S. B., & Stanovich, K. E. (2013). Dual-process theories of higher cognition: Advancing the debate. *Perspectives on Psychological Science*, 8(3): 223–241.

6
Core Processes of Intuition

Overview

The main idea of this chapter is that there are multiple brain systems and 'associated core processes' which are the neural bases for intuitive cognition. Two minds in one brain can be thought of as a metaphor for two different types of thinking. There is no one part of the brain where System 1 (including intuition) is located exclusively, and the idea that intuition is in the right brain is considered a neuromyth. The limitations of the traditional methods used by business researchers are acknowledged and the methods of neuroscience are discussed as an alternative way to 'capture' the biological bases of intuition. Five of the core processes of intuition that have been identified and studied using the methods of neuroscience are proposed. These core processes are: 'perceptions of coherence'; 'pattern recognition'; 'somatic markers'; 'interoception'; and the 'mirror mechanism'. The neural correlates of these core processes are discussed. The relevance of these five core processes of intuition for problem-solving and decision-making is business is explored.

Is Intuition in the Right Brain?

The human brain is estimated to consist of over 100 billion neurons with 100 trillion connections. This complexity and connectivity prompted one of the discoverers of the DNA double helix, the Nobel Laureate James Watson, to comment that, 'The brain is the last and grandest biological frontier, the most complex thing we have yet discovered in our universe. The brain boggles the mind'.[1] At a more macro level it has long been known that the human brain, in common with that of other mammals, is split into two separate hemispheres connected together by a dense bundle of nerve fibres called the corpus callosum. In the 1960s, psychobiologist and Nobel Laureate Roger W. Sperry (1913–1994) showed in experiments with cats and later with epileptic patients that if the two hemispheres of the brain are separated by severing the corpus callosum, information cannot be transferred between the hemispheres; in effect the individual is left with two brains, each doing different jobs, inside one skull. These experiments also demonstrated that each hemisphere has its own specialized functions, for example, the left hemisphere specializes in language, logic, critical thinking, number, and reasoning, whilst the right hemisphere specializes in functions such as facial recognition and spatial comprehension. Daniel Pink, author of the bestselling *A Whole New Mind: Why Right-Brainers Will Rule the Future*, commented that the contrasts between how the two hemispheres operate is a powerful metaphor for how we navigate the world.[2]

The localization of language and serial processing in the left hemisphere became equated with a linear, analytical thinking style, and the localization of non-verbal and simultaneous processing became equated with a non-linear, holistic thinking style.[3] Popular interpretations of the psychology of hemispheric dominance went as far as branding people as intuitive 'right-brain types' or analytical 'left-brain types'. A small step blurred the line between fact and conjecture, leading to the giant leap that 'intuition is in the right brain'. As far back as 1977 an article in *Harvard Business Review* described intuitive hunches as an 'effective right-hemispheric process', and forty years later an article in the popular business magazine *Forbes* claimed that 'intuition operates through the entire right side of our brain'. But there were naysayers and sceptics from the start: as early as 1987, one writer claimed that these simple dichotomies of the brain function have 'as much relation to the known facts about hemisphere functioning as astrology does to astronomy'.[4] As far as intuition is concerned, the idea of intuition in the right brain and analysis in the left is probably best thought of as a metaphor for two contrasting ways of thinking rather than a literal representation of how and where intuition and analysis operate.[5]

Metaphors can be useful when psychologists try to translate technical ideas, such as dual-processing theory, into a language that non-specialist audiences can understand. The idea of System 2 as the 'lazy policeman' or 'the deluded CEO who thinks she's in charge' and even the 'two minds in one brain' idea itself (which was the main idea of Chapter 5) are examples of how metaphors can be used to get ideas across to non-specialist audiences. In his bestselling 2011 book *Thinking, Fast and Slow* Nobel Laureate Daniel Kahneman left readers in no doubt that System 1 and System 2 are 'fictitious characters' to the extent that they are not discrete entities with interacting parts, nor is there 'one part of the brain that either system would call home'.[6] Contrasts between two modes of thinking processing—fast, automatic, and effortless; and slow, deliberative, and effortful—may be two distinct 'systems' of the mind only in a metaphorical sense. If the idea of intuition being the right brain is a metaphor, what do we actually know about intuition and the brain—and how can we capture its workings?

Capturing Intuitions

Capturing intuition is an exacting research challenge. Given intuition's transient and seemingly insubstantial nature, trying to capture it may even sound like an oxymoron. But this has not deterred neuroscientists, behavioural scientists, and management researchers from trying to get a grip on this once hard-to-define and often hard-to-pin down phenomenon. Much of the knowledge that has been built up over the past couple of decades about intuition in business has been gleaned from self-report surveys that typically ask managers how much they think they rely on their intuition (for example, using questionnaires such as Seymour Epstein's Rational-Experiential Inventory, see Chapter 5)[7] or from interviews in which managers are asked to recollect and recount incidents of intuitive decision-making (for example, asking them about their intuitive 'hits' and 'misses').[8]

One of the earliest studies of this type was by business intuition pioneer Weston H. Agor, who conducted a survey in the mid-1980s of over 2,000 managers in the US from a wide variety and levels of businesses and followed this up with an extensive set of interviews. One of Agor's most important findings, which has been replicated several times, is that managers at the top of organizations score higher on use of intuition in decision-making than middle- or lower-level managers.[9] Because it was cross-sectional, Agor's survey did not tell us why this was so. For example, did senior managers' greater experience make them more intuitive, or could they 'go with their gut' because they had more power and discretion to do so? Agor did not fall into the common trap of only studying intuitive hits; in the interviews he also asked executives to describe instances where they followed their intuition and it missed. Amongst the reported reasons for intuitive failures were self-deception, pretence and wishful thinking (desirability bias), attachment to a thing or person, executive ego, and the emotional pressures and stresses that come with being a boss. Agor's research was published in one of the first business books on the subject, *Intuition in Organizations: Leading and Managing Productively* (1989).

In 1994, the Indian management scholar and practitioner Jagdish Parikh published the results of his ambitious International Survey of Intuition of over 1,300 managers in several countries across the globe. Parikh and his colleagues found that: intuition was rated as most relevant in strategy/planning and human resources work (over 75 per cent of respondents); less than 10 per cent described intuitions as a sixth sense; there was overall agreement that the majority of managers use intuition and that intuition contributes to business success.[10]

A decade after the publication of Agor's pioneering work, Lisa Burke and Monica Miller conducted in-depth interviews with sixty experienced professionals in senior positions in major organizations in the US to get a better picture of how and why managers used intuition in business decision-making. In what has become a landmark study, Burke and Miller found that the situations that are likely to benefit from the use of intuition include when time is of the essence, when explicit guidelines are lacking, when the environment is uncertain, and when data and quantitative analyses require a check and balance. Interestingly, nobody in the sample viewed intuition as a personality trait or a paranormal power, and over 90 per cent reported that they had used intuition in workplace decisions by combining it with rational analysis.[11]

Whilst contributing much, this type of research can only take us so far because the methods used (questionnaire and interviews) suffer from a number of drawbacks, including interviewer bias (for example, the interviewers' expectations interfering with their objectivity), time-lapse considerations (for example, a lag between the event being studied and the collection of data), selective recall (for example, interviewees not remembering some events or omitting them), and social desirability (for example, respondents giving what they believe to be socially acceptable responses).

Whilst this type of research represents an important step forward in building a basic understanding of intuition in business,[12] its focus tends to be on individuals' perceptions and recollections of how they think they use, or have used, intuition not how they actually use it in practice.[13]

Fortunately, subjective accounts of experiences of intuition can be supplemented by more objective data from a number of sources, including laboratory experiments (which has been a mainstay of intuition research in psychology) and more recently the methods of the brain sciences. Amongst the techniques for looking at the interior workings of the intuitive mind are electro-physiological (for example, electro-encephalography, EEG, which measures the electrical signals produced in the brain) and neuroimaging (for example, functional magnetic resonance imaging, fMRI, which measures dynamic regulation of blood flow in the brain) procedures. Combining experimental psychology with neuroscience makes the functional neuroimaging of behaviour a reality and provides biological insights into what actually happens inside someone's brain when they intuit.

The idea that the left hemisphere of the brain would control only logic, analysis, sequential processing, and language, while the right hemisphere would control only spatial and simultaneous perception, imagination, and intuition has been described as 'misleading'.[14] Neuroscience has identified a number of systems and subsystems in the human brain that are good candidates for being the neural bases of intuitive processing. These areas are distributed from back to front, top to bottom, and left to right. There is no direct mapping of these brain areas onto two general systems. Functional neuroimaging studies do not support the 'neuromyth'[15] that intuition is in the right brain. Cognitive neuroscience is a fast-moving and highly technical field. From the perspective of intuition in business we need only concern ourselves with a number of core processes for which neuroscience has identified a variety of neural substrates. These five core processes are: 'perceptions of coherence'; 'pattern recognition'; 'somatic markers'; 'interoception'; and the 'mirror mechanism'.

Perceptions of Coherence

It would be adaptive and advantageous for an organism if it were able, without effort or deliberation, to continuously monitor and make sense of the constant stream of sensations that impinge on its five senses. Intuition is a psychological process that helps us to interpret and make sense of the 'buzzing, blooming confusion'[16] that we find ourselves immersed in throughout the whole of our waking lives. It does so by sensing, and one way in which this capability works is through a preliminary, non-conscious perception of the coherence between cues or objects in the environment. The interpretation of these preliminary perceptions, sometimes referred to as the 'gist' of an object or situation, is then used to guide conscious thoughts and behavioural responses.[17] The outcome (intuition) and the processes leading to that outcome (intuiting) are separated in terms of their proximity to consciousness such that the subject (the intuitor) has the sense of knowing (the outcome, intuition, is

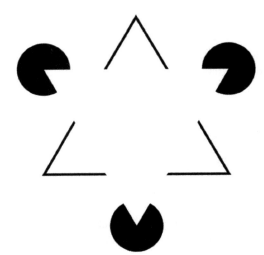

Figure 6.1 Kanizsa triangle illusion.

tangible) without knowing how or why they know (the process, intuiting, is intangible). For example in the case of visual perception, when seeing an ambiguous arrangement of visual elements, the human brain intuitively fills in the blanks to construct a recognizable pattern, as in the famous example of the Kanizsa triangle illusion, see Figure 6.1. Subjective contours are supplied automatically and effortlessly by the visual system.[18] These Gestalt (i.e. pattern or configurational) principles of visual perception, also known as principles of closure, are a feature of a brain that has evolved to see structures and patterns by default as a means of quickly making sense of the world in order to perceive, think, and act.[19]

In business the designers of the logos for NBC (the six-feathered peacock) and Federal Express (a bold white arrow concealed between the letters 'E' and 'x' in FedEx) used this Gestalt principle of closure to produce a striking visual image that creates immediate brand recognition. As well as filling in the blanks, as in the NBC and FedEx logos, the brain also makes inferences on very limited information, resulting in a sense that the parts of a visual image are coherent without necessarily being able to say what the pattern represents. People are able to judge if something is coherent without necessarily being able to say what the elements cohere into.[20] The end result, whether an object is recognized or not, is an immediate impression of coherence. For example, in Figure 6.2 the arrangement of visual elements on the left cohere into a meaningful object, whilst those on the right do not, even though they are exactly the same elements.[i] The brain's capacity for visual inference has helped to shed light on the brain areas involved in the ability to intuitively sense perceptions of coherence.

A promising candidate for the neural substrate of the brain's system for sensing patterns of coherence in visual cues is the orbitofrontal cortex (OFC). The OFC is part of the prefrontal cortex (PFC) and is positioned immediately above the eye

---

[i] The image is that of a camel.

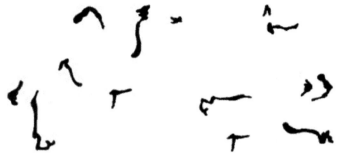

Figure 6.2 Gestalt closure task: meaningful (left) and non-meaningful (right) arrangements of the same visual elements.
Source: Reprinted from Bowers, K. S., Regehr, G., Balthazard, C., & Parker, K. (1990). Intuition in the context of discovery. *Cognitive Psychology*, 22(1): 72–110 with permission of Elsevier.

sockets (i.e. the orbits, hence the name), see Figure 6.3. The PFC itself makes up a substantial proportion of the brain, is much larger in humans than in other primates,[21] and includes dorsolateral PFC, dorsomedial PFC, ventrolateral PFC, ventromedial PFC (the VMPFC), as well as the OFC.[22] Interactions between these various subregions of the PFC,[ii] and their communications with other brain regions, are associated with important executive control functions, including goal-directed behaviour, planning, decision-making, and problem-solving.[23] Executive control functions, such as decision-making and planning, can be impaired significantly in patients who have sustained damage to the PFC through injury or disease.[24]

In order to test the OFC's role in intuitive perceptions of coherence, researchers at the Max Planck Institute for Cognitive and Brain Sciences in Germany used a visual recognition task (a Gestalt Closure Task) in which participants were presented with fragmented black and white line drawings in two conditions, 'object condition' and 'non-object condition'.[25] In the object condition, participants were presented with a fragmented but nameable image of a familiar object, for example, a violin, cat, etc., based on the principles illustrated in Figure 6.2. In the non-object condition, participants were presented with a meaningless fragmented black and white image using exactly the same visual elements as in the object condition. Participants were presented with the visual stimuli for 400 milliseconds and required to indicate whether they felt the line drawing depicted a coherent representation of a meaningful object without necessarily being required to name the object. Whilst they were working on this task their brains were scanned using fMRI.

The researchers, Kirsten Volz and Yves von Cramon, found that the OFC was activated when participants judged an image to be coherent. These activations, which occurred across networks of visual associations in the OFC, created a gist for the

---

[ii] In terms of neuroanatomy: 'lateral' means towards the edge of the brain; 'medial', towards the middle; 'dorsal', towards the top; 'ventral' towards the bottom.

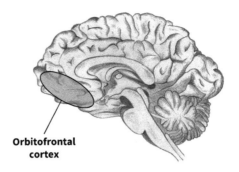

Figure 6.3 Approximate location of orbitofrontal cortex; associated with perceptions of coherence.
Source: Brain image drawn by Sarah Sadler-Smith, based on an image by Vasilisa Tsoy/Shutterstock.com

entity. This gist, or essence, enabled participants to sense intuitively whether or not the image was a coherent representation of an identifiable object. Similar research conducted at Harvard Medical School found that blurred images of everyday objects (for example, blurred or filtered images of an umbrella) elicited early recognition activation in the left OFC which preceded by 50 milliseconds full recognition of the object (for example, as an umbrella) in the fusiform gyrus (the brain region on the basal surface of the temporal and occipital lobes[iii] which are responsible for high-level visual processing).[26]

Taken together, these findings indicate that when there is insufficient visual information for full recognition, for example because the image is fuzzy or there is only a partial representation of an object, automatic activation takes place in brain systems that are capable of sensing coherences. The sense of coherence occurs in advance of being able to name the object itself. It is an intuitive visual perception of coherence. These findings suggest that the OFC is part of the brain's system for sensing intuitively whether an incomplete stimulus has a gist which is potentially meaningful. The fact that preliminary recognition of the object is taking place suggests that it must be based on the observer's existing but implicit knowledge of the object based on prior instances of it.

As an evolved capacity of the human brain, this ability to sense coherences is adaptive in that it determines whether an object is worthy of further attention. Intuition takes a rough first cut at deciding if the object is meaningful on the basis of the incomplete visual stimuli being initially processed in the sensory areas of the occipital lobe. This information is then passed on to the OFC, where further processing gives rise to a coarse representation of the gist of the object if it judged as is meaningful. This information then goes for further, more detailed processing to other areas of the brain. At the subjective level, OFC processing is perceived by the subject as a preliminary hunch or gut feeling, experienced without being able necessarily to name the object but which may be used to influence decision-making downstream of the initial visual processing.[27]

[iii] These are two of the four major lobes of the brain. The 'temporal lobe' is on the side of the brain. The 'occipital lobe' is at the back of the brain. The other lobes are the 'frontal lobe' and the 'parietal lobe'.

To sum up: in situations where there is insufficient information or insufficient time, the brain's 'gist' detection system identifies a most likely interpretation for the input information that has been received.[28] Volz and Von Cramon propose that the OFC uses critical aspects of the input (i.e. its gist) in order to detect potential content or meaning in the available information. This is then further processed by downstream areas in the brain. This visual sense-making system may have wider implications for how intuitive processing works.

Perceptions of coherence allow us to experience and integrate hunches, gut feelings, and initial guesses based on information from a variety of sources into a holistic perception and overall judgement. This sense of coherence can be a precursor to an insight whereby the object becomes tangible and identifiable. Once identified it is then available to conscious awareness for further analytical processing. Perceptions of coherence help to explain how intuitions (for example, as 'feelings of knowing' and 'tip of the tongue' phenomena[29]) precede insights (for example, as in 'Eureka' moments). An insight is the moment in which we 'connect the dots' but a perception of coherence tells us in the first place whether there are dots that might be connectable.

Whilst not directly related to the perception of patterns of visual coherence, the brain is also adept at joining to dots to make coherent, and sometimes novel, patterns in other ways. For example, in business, successful entrepreneurs are adept in sensing patterns and coherences that others do not see. This capability helps them to identify new business opportunities by filling in gaps and connecting the dots. Entrepreneurship researcher Robert Baron described business opportunity recognition as a cognitive process than involves the perception of coherence in an overall pattern of technological, economic, political, social, and demographic cues in the business environment. The elements of the overall pattern can sometimes be from diverse and seemingly unconnected areas. This diversity can result in the much sought-after quality of novelty. For example, Henry Ford made the connection between a meat packing dis-assembly line in Chicago (in which the animal carcasses moved past the meat cutters to be disassembled) and motor car manufacture to develop the idea of the assembly line in which the cars came to the worker to be assembled rather than the other way round.[30]

Baron gives the example of Chester Carlson, who is credited with inventing the modern photocopying machine in 1938. Carlson had a diverse background in that he held both a law degree and a technical degree. He was actively engaged in searching for a solution to the pressing need for improved methods for copying and was helped in his efforts by the fact that he could both understand the necessary technical processes and also appreciate the professional need for a copying technology. He used his prior knowledge to sense a potential solution to the problem of making multiple, dry permanent copies of documents. He innovated the use of 'electrophotography' based on the principle that some materials become better conductors of electricity when exposed to light.[31] Once the elements came together in his mind into a coherent pattern, the process seemed intuitively obvious, so much so that he was worried that some other inventor could easily replicate his breakthrough. Carlson took immediate steps to prevent anyone else stealing a march on his invention.[32]

Diversity of knowledge and experience is invaluable for sensing unrealized connections between previously and seemingly unconnected domains. Another example of the entrepreneurial mindset's ability to sense coherences is the founding of Expedia. In this case, the dots that were connected included increased personal computer ownership, development of flight tracking software, computer systems that could provide information on tens of thousands of hotels across the globe, and techniques for conducting secure online financial transactions. Expedia's founders did not make the leap in a single 'Eureka' moment, rather they sensed an emerging pattern that was suggestive of a valuable new business opportunity. Their discovery was more of a slow burn in making sense of the coherences that were latent in the business environment rather than a single light-bulb moment event. An initial sense (for example, as a glimmer, intimation, or intuitive hunch) becomes a developed sense (for example, as an illumination or insight leading to a scientific discovery or technical invention).[33]

Whether the brain activations that are involved in such real-world perceptions of coherence are the same as those observed in laboratory studies of visual coherence is a question for future research. It seems likely that a wider network of systems and processes will be involved, but nonetheless this research demonstrates the brain's remarkable capacity to intuit coherences automatically and non-consciously. New methods of brain imaging such as functional near infrared spectroscopy (fNIRS), a non-invasive neuroimaging technique which can be used to constantly monitor brain activity during free movement activities such as sports, driving a vehicle, or simply moving,[34] is a promising method for the study of intuitive processing in business contexts.

Pattern Recognition

Patterns figure prominently in intuition in two ways. Firstly, patterns which have in them a coherence which may contain the germ, gist, or glimmer of an important idea or breakthrough, as in the above examples of the invention of the photocopier and the founding of Expedia. Secondly, patterns are important for the ways in which, in the hands or the heads of experts, they expedite decision-making to the point at which it becomes automatic and intuitive.

Board games are often used a proxies for problem-solving and decision-making. They allow scientists to study in a controlled way through the use of brain imaging and related techniques how the intuitive mind functions and how its underlying brain processes operate. As this tends to be impractical in the study of decision-making in the workplace, proxies such as chess and other board games tend to be used. The origins of a systematic, scientific programme of research into how intuition-as-pattern-recognition works are to be found in studies of chess players by Adriaan de Groot, William Chase, and Herbert Simon in the 1960s and 1970s. De Groot was both a psychologist and chess master, and his research showed that chess experts did not necessarily think further ahead than novices, but they did have a striking ability to make sense of the gist and structure to be found in complex and non-random chess patterns of pieces (see also Chapter 7). Chess experts, moreover, are able to decide quickly and automatically via their intuitions as to the likely best next-move based on prior experiences and learning.[35]

Inspired by de Groot's work, Chase and Simon in the 1970s found that when chess pieces were arranged on the board meaningfully, experts had significantly superior recall compared to novices. However, when the chess pieces were scrambled randomly on the board the experts' advantage over the novices disappeared. This gave Chase and Simon the clue they were looking for about how experts play chess intuitively; the answer was that chess experts recognized patterns. In the chess experts' minds, particular patterns become associated with successful moves, and this relationship is encoded and stored in long-term memory. Chase and Simon concluded that chess experts are able to recognize and respond rapidly because they possess, and hence can draw on, tens of thousands of patterns stored in long-term memory acquired through playing over many years.[36] Chess masters, through the non-conscious process of pattern matching, sense the best next-move and play chess, and sometimes multiple games, quickly, intuitively, and successfully. This is one of the reasons why Simon referred to intuition as prior analyses that have been frozen into habits, and it is this which gives experts the capacity for rapid response through recognition.[37]

When these groundbreaking studies were first conducted it was not possible to map the neural mechanisms which are the basis of expertise in chess. However, half a century later, researchers have turned to the methods of neuroscience in order to identify the precise neural correlates of experts' ability to unconsciously process patterns and respond quickly, automatically, and accurately in another complex board game, the Japanese variant of chess, Shogi (the 'Game of Generals'). Shogi is a two-player strategy game played on a nine-by-nine board with an average game length of 110 moves and 10^{220} possible moves. This compares with an eight-by-eight board, an average game length of 80 moves, and 10^{120} possible moves for chess. The cognitive and computational challenges posed by shogi are formidable to say the least, added to which is the complicating factor of the 'drop rule' which allows for the re-entrance of captured pieces. The IBM computer 'Deep Blue' defeated chess grand master Garry Kasparov in 1997, but it took until 2012 for a computer to beat a shogi professional.[38] Expert shogi players, in common with chess masters, often report that their best next-move often comes to mind intuitively rather than through deliberative and exhaustive analysis. Being able to highlight the brain regions involved in playing shogi would be a significant step forward in identifying the brain regions that are involved when experts intuitively recognize patterns.

A group of researchers led by Keiji Tanaka at the Riken Brain Science Institute in Japan conducted an fMRI experiment to study the brain regions involved in the perception of patterns by expert shogi players. They found two activations that were specific to shogi experts. One was an activation in the precuneus (part of brain's

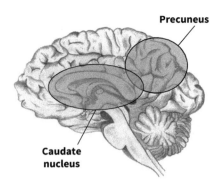

Figure 6.4 Approximate locations of precuneus associated with pattern recognition and caudate nucleus associated with generation of best next-move.
Source: Brain image drawn by Sarah Sadler-Smith, based on an image by Vasilisa Tsoy/Shutterstock.com

parietal lobe) which occurred during the perception of coherent and realistic shogi board patterns (compared to scrambled shogi or other unrelated visual patterns such as scenes and faces). The other was in the caudate nucleus of the basal ganglia (a group of structures found deep inside the brain) which occurred during the intuitive generation of the best next-move. The levels of activations in these two brain regions varied in step (i.e. they co-varied), thus indicating a pairing of pattern recognition with best-next move generation, see Figure 6.4. This suggests that recognition and response are underlain by an integrated neural circuitry across a number of inter-linked brain regions and systems.

The precuneus is a part of the parietal lobe of the brain. The parietal lobe is located between the frontal lobe and the occipital lobe at the rear of the head. The precuneus plays an important role in a variety of complex functions including recollection and memory, episodic memory retrieval, visuospatial processing, and reactivity to cues in the environment.[39] The two caudate nuclei are paired C-shaped structures that lie near the thalamus deep inside the brain. They are part of the basal ganglia (the older more primitive part of the brain) and play an important role in procedural and associative learning as well as habit formation.[40] The precuneus–caudate circuit enables quick and automatic perception of board patterns and supports best next-move generation in board game experts. Clearly, this neural circuitry did not evolve to facilitate shogi or chess playing, but nonetheless this capacity which evolved in *Homo sapiens'* ancestral environment now extends to pattern recognition in our species' current environment.

In a separate study, researchers at the Riken Institute trained novices to play a simplified version of the shogi ('mini-shogi') to a near-expert level within several months. During this training process, novices transitioned from consciously generating a series of moves and evaluating their consequences to a quick, automatic, and unconscious generation of best next-moves. Interestingly, the participants found it difficult to explain or justify how they identified best next-moves. They knew tacitly, without knowing how or why they knew, whether or not a particular move was likely to be successful. As a consequence of training, both the response time and their performance were found to be negatively correlated, i.e. superior performance was associated with faster moves. This indicated that the generation of best next-moves depended on quick, low-effort intuitive processing rather than slow, effortful deliberations. Over a relatively short time period the shogi novices' deliberative analyses became frozen into intuitive habits.[41]

The fMRI analysis also revealed that the caudate nucleus (the more 'primitive' brain region) was associated with moves taken in the short response times (one second or less), whilst cortical activations (the higher brain region) were associated with longer response times (between one and eight seconds). Novices' responses to problems were confined to the higher cerebral cortex. Because of their lack of expertise, their brains were unable to outsource the analysis of the best next-move to their intuition. Instead they had to effortfully process what the best next-move would be. The researchers also speculated that the caudate nucleus may be implicated in an 'inhibition-of-inhibition' process which supports the quick selection of one response from the many available options. Also, the rich supply of dopamine[iv] neurons in this brain region is thought to support reinforcement learning though the pairing of experience and rewards.

As a result of rigorous daily training and feedback, typically over many years, fully automatic processing by the precuneus–caudate nucleus circuit may be accomplished. This enables experts in general, not only in board games, to take decisions quickly, accurately, with little conscious effort. High-quality practice combined with timely and accurate feedback builds the neural connections that are the substrate of expert judgement. The neuroscience findings also suggests that: first, different brain systems are activated in the brains of experts compared to those of novices; second, the expert's brain 'shunts' tasks that can be performed intuitively from the cerebral cortex to the more primitive basal ganglia; third, this frees up capacity in the higher levels of the cortex for those tasks that cannot be performed intuitively.[42]

The phenomenon of switching processing between different subsystems is an efficient way for the brain to operate and has implications for decision-making in business. For example, by discriminating between tasks that can be outsourced to intuition (for example, performing routine responses to familiar problems) versus those that can only be performed successfully by analysis (for example, justifying the budget for a new project), it is possible to train employees so that they can do two things: first, perform certain tasks automatically and intuitively; secondly, know when a task requires intuitive or analytical processing, and use the most appropriate type of processing accordingly. Metacognition ('thinking about thinking') helps decision-makers to consciously monitor and control their cognitive process. This switching of 'cognitive gears'[43] allows intuitive and analytical thinking processes to operate as efficiently and effectively as possible, for example by consciously evaluating initial intuitions based on gist and feeling of rightness and actively mobilizing analytical processing if and when it is necessary.[44] Effortful processing can be reserved

---

[iv] Dopamine is a 'feel good' neurotransmitter and is associated with reward.

Somatic Markers

Neuroscience and psychology provide compelling evidence that human beings have an evolved capacity to sense complex patterns unconsciously and to make judgements and take decisions accordingly. Intuition is embrained and embodied. If neuroscience has provided promising evidence for the biological bases of intuitive cognition, what does it have to say about the bodily phenomenon of gut feelings? The presence of bodily markers which provide signals and guide judgement and decision-making have been detected objectively using physiological measures such as micro-sweating (measured by means of 'skin conductance responses'). Moreover, these signals have been shown to occur *before* the person is able to identify the change in their bodily state consciously. It seems that our bodies can intuitively 'know' things that our conscious mind has not caught up with. This can influence our behaviours before we ourselves, or perhaps more accurately our analytical mind, knows what is going on. The most famous experiment which demonstrated this phenomenon is the so-called Iowa Gambling Task (IGT). It was first conducted in the 1990s by a team of researchers at the University of Iowa led by Antonio Damasio and including Antoine Bechara and Hannah Damasio.

In the IGT experiments participants are presented with four decks of cards (A, B, C, and D). Participants, the 'players', are required to choose one card at a time from any of the four decks. Each time they pick a card they either win or lose money. Players start with a pot of $2,000 in 'play money' (but looking like the real thing). The aim of the game is to maximize monetary gain and minimize loss. The game lasts for one hundred trials, but this is not known to the player at the outset. The player is told that turning each card is likely to earn them a sum of money (i.e. they make a gain) but that every now and then turning a card will result in them having to pay a sum of money to the experimenter (i.e. they will incur a loss). Players know what their aggregate performance is in terms of money gained or lost but are unable to keep a precise tally for gains and losses associated with each deck. Instead they have to rely on a general sense for how things are going. What is not known to the players is that the decks are loaded: decks A and B are a gambling minefield; they yield either a $100 gain or sudden high payment losses (up to $1,250). Decks C and D on the other hand are quite tame; they yield either a $50 gain or the occasional modest loss (typically less than $100). In order to do well at the IGT the player needs to figure out which decks are good (C and D) and which are bad (A and B).

Most people start out by sampling the four decks randomly. They get lured early on by $100 successes and tend to go initially for the bad decks A and B. But gradually, having had a few sudden large losses which start to outweigh the $100 gains, they switch preferences to the good decks C and D which give modest gains ($50) and the occasional modest loss. As a result of implicit learning they develop a sense that

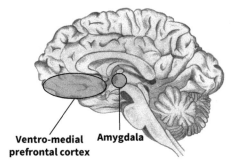

Figure 6.5 Approximate location of ventro-medial prefrontal cortex and amygdala; associated with somatic markers.

Source: Brain image drawn by Sarah Sadler-Smith, based on an image by Vasilisa Tsoy/Shutterstock.com

decks A and B are more dangerous. This sways them away from these bad decks and towards more sensible choices from the good decks C and D. This intuitive strategy usually pays off resulting in modest overall gain at the end of the game.

The lead researcher, Antonio Damasio, is a clinical neurologist and treats patients with a variety of neurological disorders including those who have incurred damage, either through injury or disease, to the ventro-medial (i.e. bottom-middle) region of the prefrontal cortex, (the VMPFC), see Figure 6.5. The researchers compared the behaviours of the VMPFC patients with those of the normal participants (i.e. those without damage to the VMPFC). The behaviour of the ventro-medial patients was in marked contrast to participants with intact VMPFCs. Ventro-medial patients consistently turned more cards in the bad $100-paying decks (A and B) and fewer cards in the good $50-paying decks (C and D). Over the course of the game they ended up choosing disastrously, so much so that they sometimes ran out of money part-way through and had to take out an extra loan from the experimenter. One of Damasio's patients, Elliott, described himself as a low-risk person; he was fully engaged in the task and clearly wanted to win but nonetheless performed disastrously. Damasio's other patients who had non-PFC brain lesions played the gambling game in the same way as the normal participants.

In order to try and figure out what was going on, Hannah Damasio came up with the idea of monitoring the participants' bodily reactions by recording their skin conductance responses (a measurement of micro-sweating on the players' fingertips). These physiological measures revealed remarkable differences between the normal participants and the ventro-medial patients. As the normal participants eased into the game they generated a skin conductance response prior to choosing from the bad decks. The magnitude of their skin conductance response increased as the game progressed and as they started to incur significant losses. This happened at about turn ten, well before they realized what was going on, which was at about turn fifty. It seems as though the normal participants unconsciously figured out which were the bad decks and their bodies signalled intuitively that the bad decks should be avoided. They then started to behave in a more risk-averse way. Somatic markers (from the Greek *soma* meaning 'body') helped normal participants predict future negative outcomes. Ventro-medial patients on the other hand failed to learn from experience. They showed 'no anticipatory skin conductance responses whatsoever' as the game progressed and were unable to make optimal decisions.[45] Another group of patients, those with bilateral damage to the amygdala (part of the limbic system, found in the temporal lobe, and linked to the processing of emotions) were also unable to generate anticipatory skin conductance responses when selecting from the bad decks. The amygdala patients also chose disadvantageously.[46]

These findings suggest that the VMPFC and the amygdala support a general pattern of behaviour for normal participants which enables them to assess risk effectively by testing out all four decks. They learn implicitly that decks A and B give high gains but also carry a significant risk of high losses. They then switch, again implicitly, to choosing from decks C and D because these decks are less punitive in terms of losses even though they generate only modest gains. By about turn fifty normal participants have worked out that A and B are the bad decks. By about turn eighty they can explain fully, i.e. explicitly, what is going on. But their bodies knew by about turn ten. Damasio and his colleagues explained this remarkable finding as follows. Normal participants benefited from the generation of bodily (somatic) markers—gut feelings—which helped them to learn to avoid the bad decks (A and B) and to approach the good decks (C and D).[47]

In general, somatic markers aid decision-making by steering us away from behaviours with negative expected returns and towards behaviours with positive expected returns. This process operates without us being aware consciously, at least initially, of the reasons for our approach or avoid behaviours. It may also be the case that even amongst normal individuals some people are more attuned to their bodily signals. This may help them to avoid the bad situations and approach good situations earlier than others who are less attuned to their bodily signals. Generalizing from the IGT laboratory experiments to decision-making more widely, the VMPFC is involved in representing and regulating somatic markers which are probably the closest thing that has been identified by science to a gut feeling (albeit not in the 'gut' per se).[48] It means that individuals in whom the relevant brain systems are intact are able to sense intuitively which choices are good and which are bad. Having this sensing capacity paves the way for prudent choices, which result in good outcomes overall.

These findings reflect real life. Ventro-medial patients tend to exhibit impulsiveness, have an inability to inhibit responses or delay gratification and make disadvantageous choices in personal and professional life. Without somatic markers they are bereft of the gut feelings which are generated in anticipation of future events and which intuitively signal good or bad outcomes before 'we', i.e. in our analytical mind, become aware. Moral psychologist Jonathan Haidt points out that in VMPFC patients the absence of gut feelings makes every option feel as good as every other, so the only way to decide is through consciously weighting the pros and cons which if taken to extremes can lead to paralysis by analysis.[49] One of Damasio's patients, Elliott, confirmed this when he succumbed to analysis paralysis by laboriously analysing for over 20 minutes the trivial choice of when his next appointment would be.

In VMPFC patients the ability to analyse costs and benefits in a 'cold' way is maintained, but they are bereft of the lift that comes from the feeling that allow us to mark things as good, bad, or indifferent literally 'in the flesh'.[50] Haidt likens it to making a choice about a boring item for which you have few feelings; for example when buying a washing machine, weighing up the pros and cons between different makes and models becomes cognitively demanding and mentally exhausting because for most people the passion required to tip the balance one way or the other is absent. This is one reason why branding, which creates strong emotional resonances with consumers via System 1, can be a potent influence on decision-making even on something as mundane as the purchase of a kitchen appliance. Moving to the less mundane, for some people, just seeing a prestige car brand's badge can tip the balance in favour of an expensive choice. Many other kinds of real-world decisions, such as which house to buy, which job to take, etc., depend on the presence of gut feelings to give a decision the necessary 'lift'. The gut feeling, hunch, or vibe is the somatic marker which gives us a bodily signal as to what we should do next in such situations.[51]

The somatic marker hypothesis (SMH) is a neural theory of decision-making which explains the steps which take place unconsciously in the brain and the body prior to a choice being exercised.[52] Our bodies may know before we do and tell us how to behave, for example 'beware of danger ahead'.[53] The SMH highlights the important role that affect plays in decision-making by providing knowledge in the form of gut feelings that help us to take decisions under conditions of risk and uncertainty. SMH research has yet to be extended outside the laboratory in order to understand how gut feelings as somatic markers enable or constrain effective decision-making in business. However, from what is already known about intuition and expertise it would seem reasonable to suppose that when the gut feelings of experts are negatively valenced (i.e. the give a bad 'vibe') they tacitly guide them *away* from a particular course of action. When they are positively valenced (i.e. a good 'vibe') they are likely to guide them *towards* a particular course of action. The bodily sensations experienced by experts in situations that demand approach or avoid behaviours are likely to be a more reliable guide than those of novices.

A case in point is that of Starbuck's Howard Schulz's reaction to the novelty of Italian espresso bars ('The vision was so overwhelming, I began shaking') which gave him the idea of bringing the 'ritual and romance' of Italian coffee culture to the American high street.[54] As well as compelling a particular choice, somatic markers can also help decision-makers to prioritize and be used as a first rough cut to sift through available options reducing an unmanageably large choice set to a smaller and more manageable consideration set. This makes the deliberating over the costs and benefits of a shortlist of items (the consideration set) less laborious and more efficient by the screening out of options that are not worth analysing. At the fuzzy front end of new product development, gut feelings can be an efficient method for reducing a range of choices worth pursuing down to a more manageable number.[55]

Somatic markers can also influence decision-makers' anticipation of outcomes.[56] Researchers at Stanford Business School identified specific neural circuits associated with risk-seeking choices (such as gambling at a casino) and risk-averse behaviours (such as buying insurance). They found that activating the neural circuitry in the nucleus accumbens (located near the font and bottom of the brain and part of the reward system[57]) may shift behaviours towards risk-seeking. On the other hand, activating the circuitry in the anterior insula (an area of the brain buried deeply within the cerebral cortex and thought to be involved in our present-moment awareness and representing body states[58]) may shift behaviours towards risk avoidance. The release of dopamine (the feel-good neurotransmitter) in the nucleus accumbens is essential for the normal functioning of this part of the brain's circuitry.[59] The researchers commented that this may be one reason why casinos deliberately surround guests with anticipation-of-reward cues such as food, liquor, and gifts in order to excite their nucleus accumbens, whilst insurance companies draw potential customers' attention to the anticipation of losses in order to excite their risk-averse behaviours via the insula.

Interoception

Intuition, as a mode of perception, is intimately related to the internal state of the body. The body is the 'theatre' in which the drama of intuition takes place.[60] When the outcomes of intuiting are conscious, they are experienced as a change in the bodily felt-sense,[61] described metaphorically as a subtle shift in the perceived shape of the contours of the internal body landscape.[62] The ability to sense intuition as change in the internal state of the body and as a bodily signal is important both in understanding the biological bases of intuition and also in improving intuitive awareness. Improving one's abilities to 'hear' and 'listen' to gut feelings is one way to make more informed use of intuition in personal and professional life. In our own research, Erella Shefy and I tested various methods of developing intuitive awareness such as 'mindfulness', 'listening to the body', and 'journaling' with a group of executive MBA students.[63] We identified beneficial outcomes in areas such as metacognition, sense of perspective (seeing the relative importance of workplace problems and decisions more objectively and not being overwhelmed by them), and intra- and interpersonal sensitivity (for example, by cultivating the stance of being neutral observers of their own and others' body language and behaviours).

The term 'interoception' refers to sensations concerning the internal state of the body and the detection of bodily signals, including the extra-cerebral signals such as gut feelings which influence thought and behaviour. Interoception is distinguished from exteroception, which is the perception of the external environment, and from proprioception, which is sensing the position of the body in space.[64] Interoceptive signals are associated with bodily (somatic) feelings such as increased heart rate, breathlessness, abdominal sensations, and thermal stress. Interoceptive attentiveness is an individuals' focused attention to a particular interoceptive signal, such as breathing, temperature, or heart rate. A research method that is commonly used to determine how sensitive an individual is to their internal bodily state is heartbeat detection (cardioception[65]). This involves comparing the number of heartbeats an individual is able to count with the actual number of beats, as measured using ECG.

This gives an error score the inverse of which is a measure of interoceptive accuracy.[66] People with high interoceptive awareness have enhanced subjective sensitivity to more general internal bodily signals, as measured by the Body Consciousness Questionnaire scale (for example, 'I am sensitive to internal bodily tensions').

On the basis that individuals display variability in their ability to perceive cardiac signals, a team of researchers led by Natalie Werner at the Ludwig-Maximilians-University in Munich compared individuals with good versus poor cardiac perception on decision-making performance as measured using the Iowa Gambling Task. They found that participants with good cardiac perception made significantly fewer choices from the bad decks and significantly more from the good decks. Their findings may help to explain why roughly a third of normal participants in the IGT fail to improve their performance during the game; perhaps such individuals are less well attuned to the internal state of the body and unable to 'hear' or could not 'listen' to what their gut was trying to tell them. Differences between people in their ability to tune in to somatic markers may mean that some individuals are better able than others to improve their intuitive decision-making skills by being able to attend to their body's reposnses to risk.

In a subsequent fMRI study, the same team of researchers found a relationship between interoceptive (heart rate) awareness and activity in the right anterior insula[v] in advance of disadvantageous decisions, see Figure 6.6. This is consistent with other research which found that activity in the anterior insula may help to shift behaviours towards risk avoidance.[67] The insula has been described as the 'primary hub for interoception'.[68] More specifically, the right anterior insula is the brain region in which visceral responses appear to be processed and become accessible to conscious awareness, thus providing a felt-sense that influences subsequent behaviours.

Interoceptive awareness can be a double-edged sword. Barnaby Dunn and colleagues studied the relationship between the strength of interoceptive awareness and cognitive and affective processes.[69] When individuals were able to tune in to bodily signals which favoured advantageous choices, this helped them to make good choices. However, when the bodily signals they tuned in to favoured disadvantageous

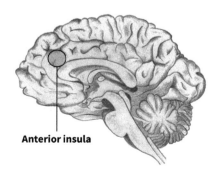

Figure 6.6 Approximate location of anterior insula; associated with interoceptive awareness.

Source: Brain image drawn by Sarah Sadler-Smith, based on an image by Vasilisa Tsoy/Shutterstock.com

---

[v] The insula is tucked away inside a fissure (the lateral sulcus) that separates the frontal and parietal lobes from the temporal lobe.

choices, this hampered good decisions. Being able to tune in to intuition is a mixed blessing: it can be beneficial for decision-making when the gut feelings are associated with good choices but can be deleterious for decision-making when the gut feeling is for a bad choice.

Studies of individual differences in interoceptive awareness have tended to be conducted in laboratory settings on non-consequential decisions. This begs the question 'do the conclusions about the role of the internal sense of the body and its potential neural correlates (such as the insula) extend to decision-making in the world of business?' A team of researchers based at Addenbrooke's Hospital at the University of Cambridge explored whether hedge fund traders in the City of London with higher interoceptive awareness made more money.[70] The eighteen traders (all male) were involved in high-frequency trading, meaning that they held their trading position usually for seconds or for minutes at most. The traders had to assimilate and process large volumes of quantitative data in order to recognize price patterns and make split-second, high-risk decisions intuitively. The situation at the time of the research for these traders was especially demanding because it was in a highly uncertain period at the end of the European sovereign debt crisis in 2010. Overall, the traders had significantly higher interoceptive awareness scores (measured using a heartbeat detection task) than a control group of university students.

The researchers analysed the relationship between interoceptive awareness and trading performance by looking at whether heartbeat detection scores predicted traders' average daily profit-and-loss (P&L) over the previous year. Interoceptive awareness was not only positively associated with P&L, it was also associated with the number of years that traders survived in what was one of the most challenging of financial markets. Junior traders had similar levels of interoceptive awareness to the control group, whilst experienced traders had much higher levels of interoceptive awareness than junior traders. These results were interpreted as suggesting that the market selects for traders with high interoceptive awareness (described as 'good gut feelings'). The causality is not clear because on the other hand high-intensity trading might hone a trader's bodily awareness. The researchers concluded that the importance that is given to gut feelings for choosing profitable trades in the financial sector is more than a mere 'mythical entity of financial folklore'.[71] It suggests that sensitivity to bodily changes provides traders with useful cues that can help them to select, under conditions of extreme uncertainty, high-stakes and time pressure, the trade that feels right. More generally, this research offers promising evidence that gut feelings, via the process of interoception of somatic markers, can exert a significant influence on financially consequential decision-making behaviours.[72]

If interoceptive awareness is advantageous for decision-making, is it possible to train individuals to become more interoceptively aware? Biofeedback techniques in which participants are given correct or incorrect feedback on their performance in a heartbeat discrimination task have been shown to enhance interoceptive accuracy.[73] Other non-biophysiological methods are also effective in enhancing interoceptive awareness. Mindfulness (moment-to-moment awareness), meditation, and related techniques entail paying attention in the present moment in a manner that is open, non-reactive, and non-judgemental. This was one of the techniques Erella Shefy and I used in our study of intuitive awareness amongst MBA students (see above).[74] Neuroimaging studies of experienced meditation practitioners have revealed structural alterations in the insula.[75] It appears as though the practice of mindfully attending to bodily sensations may strengthen connectivity within the insula and the broader interoceptive network. Enhanced interoceptive awareness, which can be developed as a result of meditation practices,[76] may enhance the capability to sense subtle changes in bodily states in response to external stimuli.[77] Bodily awareness is important because an intuition is not experienced with the same intensity as a primary emotion such as anger, fear, or joy, rather it is a more subtle sense of the total body situation which brings many associations together and out of which an emotion may or may not be produced.[78] It is a sense that can be sharpened by the right kinds of practices (see Chapter 11).

The Mirror Mechanism

In highly social species, such as primates and amongst whom *Homo sapiens* is the most social, the behaviours of others of the same species provide a constant stream of visual and auditory information which has to be interpreted and acted upon. This information is potentially useful in a wide variety of social situations and processes such as inferring others' feelings and their motives and intentions and in social learning through imitation and role modelling. Our 'social intuitions' produce spontaneous inferences about the traits and behaviours of others. When they work well they can oil the wheels of social organization and functioning. When they work badly they can result in inaccurate and biased interpretations and inferences.

In the early 1990s a group of Italian neuroscientists led by Giacomo Rizzolatti of the University of Parma made an extraordinary discovery about the motor system of macaque monkeys. They were studying the properties and function of a specific area of the ventral motor cortex[vi] called 'F5'. They were astonished to find a type of neuron that fired in the F5 area of the monkey's brain not only when it grasped a piece of food, such as a peanut, with its own hand but also when it observed another monkey or a human experimenter or performing this action. The monkey's brain constructed a representation of a physical act even though it was not performing the action itself.

They named this type of neuron a 'mirror neuron'. The main property of these mirror neurons was a matching process which enabled the observing individual (for example, the monkey) to achieve an automatic understanding of another individual's (for example, the experimenter) goal-directed motor acts. This discovery is potentially significant, especially if extended to humans, because the mirroring mechanism could have a number of complementary functions including how one individual understands intuitively the meaning, purpose, and consequences of another's observed action.[79] At the risk of oversimplifying: I observe your action and

---

[vi] The motor cortex is involved in the planning, control, and execution of voluntary movements.

my mirror neurons put me in the same state of mind that produced your action, thus enabling me to infer your feelings and intentions. The two brains 'communicate' even though they are physically detached. Some neuroscientists argue that mirror neurons are involved in 'theory of mind', i.e. one human being's ability to attribute internal states including thought and motions to another human being (see Chapter 9). On the other hand some critics have commented that this 'sounds a lot like telepathy'.[80]

The eminent cognitive neuroscientist V. S. Ramachandran of University of California San Diego speculated that mirror neurons will do for psychology what DNA did for biology 'provide a unifying framework and help explain a host of mental abilities that have hitherto remained mysterious and inaccessible to experiments'.[81] Mirror neurons have been hailed by their proponents as one of the keys to understanding social cognition.[82] Critics have dismissed mirror neurons as 'the most hyped concept in neuroscience'.[83] Anecdotally, when Rizzolatti's original research paper was sent to the prestigious journal *Nature* to be considered for publication, it was rejected because it was deemed 'very interesting for physiologists but has no broad interest for the public'.[84] Fortunately, the paper was accepted by another journal and has since been cited several thousand times. The work of Rizzolatti and his team has been acclaimed as providing a potential explanation for a number of important social and psychological phenomena that previously did not appear to have any clear neurological basis.

The original research focused on mirror neurons in the minds of monkeys, but later research has shown that mirror neurons also exist in the corresponding areas of the human brain, see Figure 6.7. In humans the system may have evolved the ability to interpret more complex actions than the simple grasping of a peanut.[85] Rizzolatti translated the process to humans with the fictional vignette of John and Mary:

> John watches Mary, who is grasping a flower. John knows what Mary doing—she is picking the flower—and he also knows why she is doing it. Mary smiles at John, and he guesses that she will give him the flower as a present.[86]

The scene lasts for only a few seconds, but John, with speed and fluency and without any need to consciously deliberate, infers and extrapolates Mary's actions, motives, and intentions.

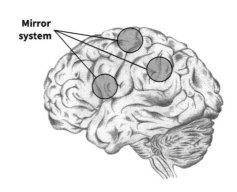

Figure 6.7 Approximate locations of mirror neurons; associated with mirror mechanism.

Source: Brain image drawn by Sarah Sadler-Smith, based on an image by Vasilisa Tsoy/Shutterstock.com

Mirror neurons are the neuronal substrate in which an action performed by one person activates the same motor pathways responsible for performing the action in another person's brain. As a result, the observer understands viscerally the doer's actions because the mirroring mechanism allows them to experience it vicariously in their own mind. Additionally, in humans it has been observed that certain neurons that are activated in response to pain are also activated when someone else is seen to be in pain. The possibility is raised that a mirroring process is involved in emotional, and in particular, empathetic responses in humans.[87] The expression 'I feel your pain' could have some literal truth to it.[88]

Human beings also have an intuitive tendency to align their behaviour with others during social interaction. The social cognitive neuroscientist Matthew Lieberman refers to this as 'a complex reciprocal non-verbal "dance" that occurs between interaction partners'.[89] Supportive evidence is to be found in research showing that people with autism have a lack of mirror neuron activity in several regions of the brain involved in the processing of social information, including the inferior frontal gyrus. This deficit may help to account for some of the chief diagnostic signs of autism, including absence of empathy.[90] Researchers have concluded that it is reasonable to conclude that empathy involves the simulation of the mental states of other people and that the mirror neuron system may be part of the human brain's larger-scale network for empathy.[91]

In evolutionary terms, mirror neurons may have been selected for because they provided the adaptive advantage of 'intersubjectivity', a term coined originally by the philosopher Edmund Husserl to refer to the intuitive exchange of thoughts, feelings, and intentions between two persons.[92] Mirroring could have been something that developed late in primate evolution which may be why it is more well-developed and extensive in humans than in other monkeys and apes. If primitive human communication began with non-verbal gestures, then mirror neurons could have played a pivotal role in the evolution of more complex verbal language.[93]

As alluded to already, mirror neurons are not uncontroversial. An alternative hypothesis is that mirror neurons are the product of an associative learning process analogous to Pavlovian conditioning. According to this line of thinking, motor neurons become mirror neurons if the individual has experiences in which the observation of an action and its execution are close together in time and space. For example, in a synchronous activity such as training for a physical action as in sports or dancing in which actions are observed, imitated, and with practice and feedback, become largely intuitive.[94]

The mirroring process in workplaces may provide the brain-based substrate for the intuitive exchange of thoughts, feelings, and intentions between persons which then gets honed and augmented through experiential learning processes and higher-level reasoning.[95] Daniel Goleman, author of the bestselling book *Emotional Intelligence*, and his colleague Richard Boyatzis argue that mirror neurons are important in organizations because leaders' emotions and actions prompt followers, via the mirroring mechanism, to resonate with or imitate their leaders unconsciously. This process can have potent effects on how people feel and act.[96] For example, good-natured negative feedback (delivered with nods and smiles) can have a more productive effect than ill-natured positive feedback (delivered with grimaces and frowns).[97] Leaders' displays of emotion can also have a collective effect which is mirrored unconsciously by the group thereby affecting the overall team emotional climate.[98] Whilst leader behaviours can be sources of positive or negative emotionality, there is some research to suggest that negative leader emotionality has greater potency than positive emotionality. If this is correct, then leaders may need to be cautious about being a role model and a literal and metaphorical mirror for maladaptive and unproductive behaviours.[99] Charismatic leaders are particularly adept at influencing followers to mirror their moods and behaviours, but over the longer term this can have negative consequences if leaders become overconfident and comtemptuous and fall prey to hubris.[100]

Summary

1. The main idea of this chapter is that there are multiple brain systems and 'core processes' which are the neural bases for intuitive cognition.
2. The five core processes of intuition discussed in this chapter are 'perceptions of coherence'; 'pattern recognition'; 'somatic markers'; 'interoception'; and the 'mirror mechanism'.
3. Perceptions of coherence in a pattern of cues give decision-makers an initial sense or 'gist' of a situation (Chapter 10).
4. Pattern recognition expedites decision-making to the point at which it becomes automatic and intuitive and sheds light on how expert (problem-solving) intuition works (Chapter 7).
5. Somatic markers help to explain how our bodies may be able to know before we do.
6. Interoceptive awareness helps us to tune into the intuitive felt-sense and hear the 'voice' of intuition.
7. Spontaneous inferences about the behaviours, motives, and intentions based on the mirror mechanism help to explain how we are able to 'read' other people's feelings, motives and intentions through the processes of social intuition (Chapter 9).
8. These core processes also support the idea that intuition is not unitary, i.e. there is more than one type of intuition (see Chapters 7, 8, 9 and 10).

Endnotes

1. Ackerman S. (1992). *Discovering the Brain*. Washington (DC): National Academies Press (US); 1992. Foreword. Available from: https://www.ncbi.nlm.nih.gov/books/NBK234155/ Accessed 05.04.2022.
2. Pink, D. (2008). *A Whole New Mind*. London: Marshall Cavendish, p. 26.

3. Vance, C. M., Groves, K. S., Paik, Y., & Kindler, H. (2007). Understanding and measuring linear–nonlinear thinking style for enhanced management education and professional practice. *Academy of Management Learning & Education*, 6(2): 167–185.
4. Hines, T. (1987). Left brain/right brain mythology and implications for management and training. *Academy of Management Review*, 12: 600–606.
5. Hodgkinson, G. P., Sadler-Smith, E., Burke, L. A., Claxton, G., & Sparrow, P. R. (2009). Intuition in organizations: Implications for strategic management. *Long Range Planning*, 42(3): 277–297.
6. Kahneman, D. (2011). *Thinking, Fast and Slow*, London: Allen Lane, p. 29.
7. Epstein, S., Pacini, R., Denes-Raj, V., & Heier, H. (1996). Individual differences in intuitive–experiential and analytical–rational thinking styles. *Journal of Personality and Social Psychology*, 71(2): 390–405.
8. Akinci, C., & Sadler-Smith, E. (2020). 'If something doesn't look right, go find out why': how intuitive decision making is accomplished in police first-response. *European Journal of Work and Organizational Psychology*, 29(1): 78–92; Akinci, C., & Sadler-Smith, E. (2019). Collective intuition: Implications for improved decision making and organizational learning. *British Journal of Management*, 30(3): 558–577.
9. Hodgkinson, G. P., & Sadler-Smith, E. (2003). Complex or unitary? A critique and empirical re-assessment of the Allinson-Hayes Cognitive Style Index. *Journal of Occupational and Organizational Psychology*, 76(2): 243–268.
10. Parikh, J., Neubauer, F. F., & Lank, A. (1994). *Intuition: The New Frontier of Management*. Oxford: Blackwell.
11. It is interesting to note that amongst the earliest post-Agor publications on the subject were in the prestigious journal *Academy of Management Executive* (now renamed *Academy of Management Perspectives*) which, as the name suggested, had the mission of bringing management research to a professional business audience: Burke, L. A., & Miller, M. K. (1999). Taking the mystery out of intuitive decision making. *Academy of Management Perspectives*, 13(4): 91–99; Sadler-Smith, E., & Shefy, E. 2004. The intuitive executive: Understanding and applying 'gut feel' in decision-making. *Academy of Management Perspectives*, 18(4): 76–91; Miller, C. C., & Ireland, R. D. (2005). Intuition in strategic decision making: Friend or foe in the fast-paced 21st century?. *Academy of Management Perspectives*, 19(1): 19–30. This journal has continued this tradition with the more recent publication of: Hodgkinson, G. P., & Sadler-Smith, E. (2018). The dynamics of intuition and analysis in managerial and organizational decision making. *Academy of Management Perspectives*, 32(4): 473–492.
12. See: Akinci, C., & Sadler-Smith, E. (2020). 'If something doesn't look right, go find out why': How intuitive decision making is accomplished in police first-response. *European Journal of Work and Organizational Psychology*, 29(1): 78–92; Calabretta, G., Gemser, G., & Wijnberg, N. M. (2017). The interplay between intuition and rationality in strategic decision making: A paradox perspective. *Organization Studies*, 38(3–4): 365–401.; Meziani, N., & Cabantous, L. (2020). Acting intuition into sense: How film crews make sense with embodied ways of knowing. *Journal of Management Studies*, 57(7): 1384–1419.
13. Lufityanto, G., Donkin, C., & Pearson, J. (2016). Measuring intuition: nonconscious emotional information boosts decision accuracy and confidence. *Psychological science*, 27(5): 622–634.

14. Massaro, S. (2016). Neuroscientific methods for strategic management. In Dagnino, G. B., & Cinici, M. C. (Eds.). *Research Methods for Strategic Management* (pp. 253–282). Abingdon: Routledge, p. 254.
15. Dekker, S., Lee, N. C., Howard-Jones, P., & Jolles, J. (2012). Neuromyths in education: Prevalence and predictors of misconceptions among teachers. *Frontiers in Psychology*, 3(429): 1–8.
16. James, W. (1890). *The Principles of Psychology* (Volumes I and II). New York: Holt.
17. Volz, K. G., & von Cramon, D. Y. (2006). What neuroscience can tell about intuitive processes in the context of perceptual discovery. *Journal of Cognitive Neuroscience*, 18(12): 2077–2087, p. 2077.
18. Kanizsa, G. (1976). Subjective contours. *Scientific American*, 234(4): 48–53.
19. User Testing (2019). & Gestalt principles of visual perception. Available online at: 7 Gestalt Principles of Visual Perception: Cognitive Psychology for UX | UserTesting Blog Accessed 21.02.2022.
20. Bowers, K. S., Regehr, G., Balthazard, C., & Parker, K. (1990). Intuition in the context of discovery. *Cognitive Psychology*, 22(1): 72–110.
21. Teffer, K., & Semendeferi, K. (2012). Human prefrontal cortex: Evolution, development, and pathology. *Progress in Brain Research*, 195: 191–218.
22. Neuroscientifically Challenged (2015). Know your brain: Orbitofrontal Cortex. Available online at: https://www.neuroscientificallychallenged.com/blog/know-your-brain-orbitofrontal-cortex Accessed 21.02.2022.
23. Stalnaker, T. A., Cooch, N. K., & Schoenbaum, G. (2015). What the orbitofrontal cortex does not do. *Nature Neuroscience*, 18(5): 620–627.
24. Bechara, A., Damasio, H., Damasio, A. R., & Lee, G. P. (1999). Different contributions of the human amygdala and ventromedial prefrontal cortex to decision-making. *Journal of Neuroscience*, 19(13): 5473–5481.
25. Volz, K. G., & von Cramon, D. Y. (2006). What neuroscience can tell about intuitive processes in the context of perceptual discovery. *Journal of Cognitive Neuroscience*, 18(12): 2077–2087.
26. Bar, M., Kassam, K. S., Ghuman, A. S., Boshyan, J., Schmid, A. M., Dale, A. M., …, & Halgren, E. (2006). Top-down facilitation of visual recognition. *Proceedings of the National Academy of Sciences*, 103(2): 449–454.
27. Horr, N. K., Braun, C., & Volz, K. G. (2014). Feeling before knowing why: The role of the orbitofrontal cortex in intuitive judgments—an MEG study. *Cognitive, Affective, & Behavioral Neuroscience*, 14(4): 1271–1285.
28. Volz, K. G., & von Cramon, D. Y. (2006). What neuroscience can tell about intuitive processes in the context of perceptual discovery. *Journal of Cognitive Neuroscience*, 18(12): 2077–2087, p. 2083.
29. Koriat, A., & Levy-Sadot, R. (2001). The combined contributions of the cue-familiarity and accessibility heuristics to feelings of knowing. *Journal of Experimental Psychology: Learning, Memory, and Cognition*, 27(1): 34–53.
30. Johnson, C. (2019). How connecting the dots sparks brilliant innovation. LinkedIn. Available online at: https://www.linkedin.com/pulse/how-connecting-dots-sparks-brilliant-innovation-carla-johnson Accessed 05.04.2022.
31. Xerox Corporation (no date). Chester Carlson and xerography. Available online at: https://www.xerox.com/en-us/innovation/insights/chester-carlson-xerography Accessed 21.02.2022.

32. Owen, D. (2008). *Copies in Seconds: How a Lone Inventor and an Unknown Company Created the Biggest Communication Breakthrough Since Gutenberg—Chester Carlson and the Birth of the Xerox Machine*. New York Simon and Schuster.
33. Meziani, N., & Cabantous, L. 2020. Acting intuition into sense: How film crews make sense with embodied ways of knowing. *Journal of Management Studies*, 57(7): 1384–1419, p. 1405.
34. See for example Cortivision: https://www.cortivision.com/. Accessed 14.03.2022.
35. De Groot, A. D., Gobet, F., & Jongman, R. W. (1996). *Perception and Memory in Chess: Studies in the Heuristics of the Professional Eye*. Assen: Van Gorcum & Co.
36. Chase, W. G., & Simon, H. A. (1973a). Perception in chess. *Cognitive Psychology*, 4: 55–81.
37. Simon, H. A. (1987). Making management decisions: The role of intuition and emotion. *Academy of Management Perspectives*, 1(1): 57–64.
38. Steger, I. (2017). Artifical intelligence has brought 'doubt and suspicion' to the ancient world of Japanese chess. Quartz. Available online at: https://qz.com/906447/artificial-intelligence-has-brought-doubt-and-suspicion-to-the-ancient-world-of-shogi-or-japanese-chess/ Accessed 21.02.2022.
39. Science Direct (2015). Precuneus (extract from article). Available online at: https://www.sciencedirect.com/topics/neuroscience/precuneus Accessed 21.02.2022.
40. Yin, H. H., & Knowlton, B. J. (2006). The role of the basal ganglia in habit formation. *Nature Reviews Neuroscience*, 7(6): 464–476.
41. Wan, X., Nakatani, H., Ueno, K., Asamizuya, T., Cheng, K., & Tanaka, K. The neural basis of intuitive best next-move generation in board game experts. *Science* 331: 341–346 (2011).
42. Asia Research News (2011). Revealing how experts' minds tick. Available online at: https://www.asiaresearchnews.com/html/article.php/aid/6065/cid/2/research/science/riken/revealing_how_experts%E2%80%99_minds_tick.html Accessed 21.02.2022.
43. Louis, M. R., & Sutton, R. I. (1991). Switching cognitive gears: From habits of mind to active thinking. *Human Relations*, 44(1): 55–76.
44. Thompson, V. A., Turner, J. A. P., & Pennycook, G. (2011). Intuition, reason, and metacognition. *Cognitive Psychology*, 63(3): 107–140.
45. Damasio, A. R. (1994). *Descartes' Error: Emotion, Rationality and the Human Brain*. New York: Putnam, p. 221.
46. Bechara, A., Damasio, H., Damasio, A. R., & Lee, G. P. (1999). Different contributions of the human amygdala and ventromedial prefrontal cortex to decision-making. *Journal of Neuroscience*, 19(13): 5473–5481.
47. Werner, N. S., Duschek, S., & Schandry, R. (2009). Relationships between affective states and decision-making. *International Journal of Psychophysiology*, 74(3): 259–265.
48. Werner, N. S., Duschek, S., & Schandry, R. (2009). Relationships between affective states and decision-making. *International Journal of Psychophysiology*, 74(3): 259–265.
49. Haidt, J. 2012, *The Righteous Mind*. London: Allen Lane, p. 33–34.
50. Baer, D. (2013). The neuroscience of trusting your gut. *Fast Company*, 12 June 2013. Available online at: https://www.fastcompany.com/3,022,954/the-neuroscience-of-trusting-your-gut Accessed 21.02.2022.
51. Ibid.
52. Reimann, M., & Bechara, A. (2010). The somatic marker framework as a neurological theory of decision-making: Review, conceptual comparisons, and future neuroeconomics research. *Journal of Economic Psychology*, 31(5): 767–776, p. 768.

53. Damasio, A. R. (1994). *Descartes' Error: Emotion, Rationality and the Human Brain*. New York: Putnam, p. 123.
54. Sadler-Smith, E. (2008). *Inside Intuition*. Abingdon: Routledge, p. 230.
55. https://www.kantar.com/expertise/innovation/offer-development/idea-development-and-screening
56. Kuhnen, C. M., & Knutson, B. (2005). The neural basis of financial risk taking. *Neuron*, 47: 763–770; Reimann, M., & Bechara, A. (2010). The somatic marker framework as a neurological theory of decision-making: Review, conceptual comparisons, and future neuroeconomics research. *Journal of Economic Psychology*, 31(5): 767–776.
57. Neuroscientifically Challenged (2015). Know your brain: Nucleus accumbens. Available online at: https://www.neuroscientificallychallenged.com/blog/2014/6/11/know-your-brain-nucleus-accumbens Accessed 21.02.2022.
58. Neuroscientifically Challenged (2015). Know your brain: What is insula? Available online at: https://www.neuroscientificallychallenged.com/blog/2013/05/what-is-insula Accessed 21.02.2022.
59. Nicola, S.M., Taha, S. A., Kim, S. W., & Fields, H. L. (2005). Nucleus accumbens dopamine release is necessary and sufficient to promote the behavioral response to reward-predictive cues. *Neuroscience*. 135(4): 1025–1033.
60. Damasio, A. (1999). *The Feeling of What Happens: Body, Emotion and the Making of Consciousness*. San Diego, CA: Harcourt Brace and Co, Inc., p. 51.
61. Gendlin, E. (1978). *Focusing*. New York: Bantam.
62. Damasio, A. R. (1994). *Descartes' Error: Emotion, Rationality and the Human Brain*. New York: Putnam, p. 154.
63. Sadler-Smith, E., & Shefy, E. (2007). Developing intuitive awareness in management education. *Academy of Management Learning & Education*, 6(2): 186–205.
64. Garfinkel, S. N., Seth, A. K., Barrett, A. B., Suzuki, K., & Critchley, H. D. (2015). Knowing your own heart: distinguishing interoceptive accuracy from interoceptive awareness. *Biological Psychology*, 104: 65–74.
65. Schulz, S. M. (2016). Neural correlates of heart-focused interoception: a functional magnetic resonance imaging meta-analysis. *Philosophical Transactions of the Royal Society B: Biological Sciences*, 371(1708): 20160018.
66. Schandry, R. (1981). Heart beat perception and emotional experience. *Psychophysiology*, 18(4): 483–488.
67. Werner, N. S., Duschek, S., & Schandry, R. (2009). Relationships between affective states and decision-making. *International Journal of Psychophysiology*, 74(3): 259–265.
68. Gibson, J. (2019). Mindfulness, interoception, and the body: A contemporary perspective. *Frontiers in Psychology*, 10: 2012–2012.
69. Dunn, B. D., Galton, H. C., Morgan, R., Evans, D., Oliver, C., Meyer, M., …, & Dalgleish, T. (2010). Listening to your heart: How interoception shapes emotion experience and intuitive decision making. *Psychological Science*, 21(12): 1835–1844.
70. Kandasamy, N., Garfinkel, S. N., Page, L., Hardy, B., Critchley, H. D., Gurnell, M., & Coates, J. M. (2016). Interoceptive ability predicts survival on a London trading floor. *Scientific Reports*, 6(1): 1–7.
71. Op. cit., p. 5.
72. Holzer, P. (2017). Interoception and gut feelings: Unconscious body signals' impact on brain function, behaviour and belief processes. In Angel, H. L., et al. (Eds.). *Processes of*

Believing: The Acquisition, Maintenance, and Change in Creditions (pp. 435–442). Cham: Springer.
73. Garfinkel, S. N., Tiley, C., O'Keeffe, S., Harrison, N. A., Seth, A. K., & Critchley, H. D. (2016). Discrepancies between dimensions of interoception in autism: Implications for emotion and anxiety. *Biological Psychology*, 114: 117–126.
74. Sadler-Smith, E., & Shefy, E. (2007). Developing intuitive awareness in management education. *Academy of Management Learning & Education*, 6(2): 186–205.
75. Fox, K. C. R., Nijeboer, S., Dixon, M. L., Floman, J. L., Ellamil, M., Rumak, S. P., ... Christoff, K. (2014). Is meditation associated with altered brain structure? A systematic review and meta-analysis of morphometric neuroimaging in meditation practitioners. *Neuroscience & Biobehavioral Reviews*, 43: 48–73.
76. Fox, K. C. R, & Cahn, B. R. (2017). *Meditation and the Brain in Health and Disease*. University of Stanford School of Medicine, unpublished manuscript.
77. Gibson, J. (2019). Mindfulness, interoception, and the body: A contemporary perspective. *Frontiers in Psychology*, 10: 2012–2012.
78. Gendlin, E. T. (1982). *Focusing*. New York: Bantam.
79. Gallese, V., Fadiga, L., Fogassi, L., & Rizzolatti, G. (1996). Action recognition in the premotor cortex. *Brain*, 119(2): 593–609, p. 606.
80. Heyes, C. (2010). Mesmerising mirror neurons. *Neuroimage*, 51(2): 789–791.
81. Ramachandran, V.S. (no date). Mirror neurons and imitation learning as the driving force behind the great leap forward in human evolution. Unpublished manuscript for Third Culture: http://www.edge.org/3rd_culture/ Accessed 21.02.2022.
82. Heyes, C. (2010). Mesmerising mirror neurons. *Neuroimage*, 51(2): 789–791.
83. Jarrett, C.B. (2012). Mirror neurons: the most hyped concept in Neuroscience? *Psychology Today*; Heyes, C., & Catmur, C. (2021). What happened to mirror neurons? *Perspectives On Psychological Science*, [1745691621990638]. https://doi.org/10.1177/2F174569162199063
84. Go Cognitive: Education Tools for Cognitive Neuroscience (2011). *Giacomo Rizzolatti—Mirror neurons: From Monkey to Human*. Available online at: https://www.youtube.com/watch?v=yKPTuCoop8c Accessed 21.02.2022.
85. Ramachandran, V. S., & Oberman, L. M. (2006). Broken mirrors. *Scientific American*, 295(5): 62–69, p. 65.
86. Rizzolatti, G., Fogassi, L., & Gallese, V. (2006). Mirrors in the mind. *Scientific American*, 295(5): 54–61, p. 54.
87. Ramachandran, V. S., & Oberman, L. M. (2006). Broken mirrors. *Scientific American*, 295(5): 62–69, p. 65.
88. Rizzolatti, G., Fogassi, L., & Gallese, V. (2006). Mirrors in the mind. *Scientific American*, 295(5): 54–61, p. 59.
89. Sadler-Smith, E. (2008). *Inside Intuition*. Abingdon: Routledge, p. 280.
90. Williams, J. H. (2008). Self–other relations in social development and autism: multiple roles for mirror neurons and other brain bases. *Autism Research*, 1(2): 73–90.
91. Iacoboni, M. (2009). Imitation, empathy, and mirror neurons. *Annual Review of Psychology*, 60: 653–670.
92. Cooper-White P. (2014) Intersubjectivity. In: Leeming, D. A. (Ed.). *Encyclopaedia of Psychology and Religion*. Boston, MA: Springer. https://doi.org/10.1007/978-1-4614-6086-2_9182

93. Rizzolatti, G., Fogassi, L., & Gallese, V. (2006). Mirrors in the mind. *Scientific American*, 295(5): 54–61; Fogassi, L., & Ferrari, P. F. (2007). Mirror neurons and the evolution of embodied language. *Current Directions in Psychological Science*, 16(3): 136–141.
94. Heyes, C. (2010). Mesmerising mirror neurons. *Neuroimage*, 51(2): 789–791.
95. Green, C. (2012). Nursing intuition: A valid form of knowledge. *Nursing Philosophy*, 13(2): 98–111.
96. Goleman, D., & Boyatzis, R. (2008). Social intelligence and the biology of leadership. *Harvard Business Review*, 86(9): 74–81.
97. Dasborough, M. T. (2006). Cognitive asymmetry in employee emotional reactions to leadership behaviors. *The Leadership Quarterly*, 17(2): 163–178.
98. Dasborough, M. T., Ashkanasy, N. M., Tee, E. Y., & Herman, H. M. (2009). What goes around comes around: How meso-level negative emotional contagion can ultimately determine organizational attitudes toward leaders. *The Leadership Quarterly*, 20(4): 571–585.
99. Dasborough, M. T. (2006). Cognitive asymmetry in employee emotional reactions to leadership behaviours. *The Leadership Quarterly*, 17(2): 163–178.
100. Ghadiri, A., Habermacher, A., & Peters, T. (2012). Neuroscience for business. In Argang Ghadiri, A., Habermacher, A., & Peters, T. (Eds.). *Neuroleadership* (pp. 17–53). Berlin, Heidelberg: Springer; Sadler-Smith, E. (2019). *Hubristic Leadership*. London: SAGE.

7
The Expert Sense

Overview

The main idea of this chapter is that expert intuition (the 'expert sense') is developed through a lengthy process of skill acquisition. The origins of research into expert intuition are to be found in studies of chess masters. The principles of pattern recognition in chess have been extrapolated to management. Both the amount (notionally '10,000' hours) and the quality (deliberate with expert coaching and feedback) of practice are important in the development of intuitive expertise and the expert sense. Skill acquisition proceeds though a number of stages from 'novice' through to 'expert'. Dreyfus's 'Skill Acquisition Model' (SAM) is centre stage. Novices simply follow rules without taking the subtleties of the context into account, whereas expert performance is situational, holistic, and intuitive. On rare occasions experts are able to achieve a high-level state of 'flow'. Parallels between expert intuition in the professional fields of nursing and management are discussed. Collective intuition, built by learning, dialogue, and feedback between experts, is proposed as a valuable, rare, and difficult-to-imitate source of competitive advantage for an organization. For expert intuitions to be integrated and institutionalized into an organization, they must first be articulated and interpreted.

Expertise in Chess

Why begin a chapter on expertise in a practical field such as business with a discussion of the game of chess? The reason is that the origins of modern scientific thought and many of the most enduring insights about how intuition works are to be found in research conducted over half a century ago in which chess was used as a proxy for complex problem-solving and decision-making. We have met chess and its Eastern counterpart Shogi already, albeit briefly in Chapter 6. To this day chess is one of the domains which provides much of the experimental data about the fundamentals of intuition.[1] The general models and theories which came out of the chess and intuition research are the building blocks of more recent models of expert performance such as the recognition-primed decision (RPD) model (see Chapter 5). The origins of this work can be traced back to Herbert Simon's groundbreaking work which was preceded by influential work on thinking in chess by the Dutch psychologist and chess master Adriaan de Groot.

Intuition in Business. Eugene Sadler-Smith, Oxford University Press. © Eugene Sadler-Smith (2023).
DOI: 10.1093/oso/9780198871569.003.0007

People are often surprised that intuition and chess are linked given that, on the face of it, chess with its working out of best next-moves and countermoves appears to be the epitome of logic and analysis.[2] But like management, chess problems are based on incomplete information (one player cannot know the other player's mind), time is important (chess tournaments have time constraints within which to conduct the requisite number of moves), and decisions may have to be changed in mid-stream (because one player does not know what the other player will do next).[3] Chess decisions involve solving complex problems in the moment by imagining how a move is likely to play out based on the lessons of learning and experience. Like management, decision-making in chess does not provide any certainties it can only provide the likelihood that the moves which are made, if they are based on informed choices and not just random guesses, are more likely to lead to a good outcome.[4] Like chess players, managers have to make decisions in-the-moment using their best judgements, mental simulations and forward projections and be ready to use and trust their experience-based intuitions.[5]

Adriaan de Groot and Thought in Chess

The story of intuition in chess begins with the work of Dutch chess master and psychologist Adriaan de Groot (1914 to 2006). De Groot has been described as 'the most influential Dutch psychologist of the [twentieth] century'. The Swedish psychologist K Anders Ericsson (the expert on expertise and originator of the '10,000 hour' rule, see below and Chapter 9) described de Groot as the 'founding father of empirical work on beginners and experts'. De Groot was a polymath: he studied mathematics, philosophy and psychology at the University of Amsterdam and was influenced by the works of the psychoanalyst CG Jung and psychotherapist Alfred Adler.[6]

De Groot's work on chess masters was to some extent autobiographical; he was a chess master himself and member of the Dutch national team in the 1930s. De Groot's magnum opus (as far as this aspect of his work is concerned) is *Thought and Choice in Chess* (1965). The book is a highly technical analysis of how chess players think. De Groot got into the minds of chess experts by using think-aloud protocols, for example by presenting them with a chess position and asking them to think out-loud while finding the best next-move. In *Thought and Choice in Chess* he described how chess masters treat the interpretation of chess problems not as an immediate isolated move to be solved rationally but as a holistic perception of and response to a given problem which uses 'nuances of intuitive and emotional preference' based on experience and which give rise to 'vague insight'[7]. These vague insights–what might be termed 'hints' or 'intimations' as to the best next-move–lead intuitively to what de Groot referred as 'favourite [move] forming'[8]. But the favoured move is arrived at a result of the scanning and sensing of possibilities rather than a 'completely pure comparative examination' of potential moves.

De Groot referred to intuition a lot in *Thought and Chess*. He believed intuition to be 'an important method of chess thinking'[9] and declared the intuitive moment as being 'extremely important in chess.'[10] He described intuition in chess as 'a player's feeling for a position' which gives rise to 'anticipations'[11] and manifests as 'an intuitive faith in a particular possibility'.[12] These intuitively arrived at possibilities—which he called 'favourites' —and their associated anticipations (which render them hypothetical best next-moves[13]) can be tested analytically by a sample calculations (by computing the moves ahead). But De Groot's view was that most of the time the experts' intuitive appraisal is reasonably accurate such that 'spurious verification cannot do much harm' to the initial assessment of the best next-move, i.e. it does not change it much but merely serves to confirm. This means that, in common with the firefighters studied by Klein (see Chapter 4), the chess players' intuitively generated best next-move is often left largely intact even when analysis is given the opportunity to have its say.[14] When the expert is confronted by a choice between two moves a feeling, impression or hunch–in other words an intuitive felt-sense–tips the balance in favour of a particular move. De Groot described this as the 'intuitive completion of the argumentation'.[15] He was also keen to point out that the completion of the argument is rarely a eureka-type phenomenon where the player experiences 'wait a minute!' or 'aha!' moment.[16]

De Groot's analysis was very much at odds with prevailing thought in chess and in psychology. It attracted critical attention because intuition was something that the 'rigid theory of *Denkpsychologie* [psychology of thought] does not take into account'.[17] De Groot assigned intuition (along with the other I's of 'insight', 'inspiration', and 'illumination') to a general class of ideas 'which tend to have a blinding halo: a halo which keeps both protagonists [for intuition] and antagonists [against intuition] from thinking clearly over the idea in question out of devotion and scorn, respectively'.[18]

As far as chess masters' learning is concerned, de Groot considered expertise in chess to be acquired only partially by 'book learning'. He described formal learning as the substructure on which the master builds a superstructure of 'unconsciously applied' and 'not readily specifiable' intuitive methods.[19] Formally acquired explicit knowledge and experientially acquired tacit knowledge are mutually interwoven elements of expertise in chess. They differ in that formal knowledge can be verbalized (i.e. it is explicit), is retrievable from memory and is the smaller part of chess expertise, whereas intuitive knowledge cannot be verbalized (i.e. it is tacit) and can only be actualized by situations in which it can be used. In de Groot's analysis intuition is the larger part of chess expertise.[20]

From Chess to Business

Following de Groot in the 1970s Herbert Simon and William Chase at Carnegie Mellon University sought to isolate the perceptual processes and mental structures that chess masters use in performing instinctively and intuitively. One the findings from de Groot's research which particularly resonated with Chase and Simon was experts' remarkable ability to reconstruct a meaningful chess position almost perfectly after viewing it for only five seconds—a skill that was notable by its absence in novices and which disappeared in experts when the pieces were arranged randomly. The fact that a chess master could recall the location of 20 or more pieces even though human short term memory has a capacity of around seven items[21] was attributed to a process of 'chunking'. In the process of chunking experts perceive and remember chunks, i.e. small assemblages, of information each composed of four or five chess pieces arranged into a meaningful sub-configuration on the overall board rather than remembering and recalling the position of the individual pieces. The ability of chess masters to play intuitively and instinctively was attributed by Chase and Simon to the existence of an elaborate cognitive apparatus stored in experts' long-term memory made up of meaningful chunks of information amassed through many years of learning, practice, experience and feedback. Simon estimated there may be as many as 50,000 patterns lodged in the long-term memory a chess master and that these patterns take around ten years of intensive study and practice to be acquired and retained.[22]

De Groot, Chase and Simon all concurred that a good move in chess often comes to the expert's mind quickly. The remainder of the time taken to execute the move is spent in verifying whether or not the intuitively generated move is both plausible and without any apparent weaknesses. Fast, unconscious processing allows the expert to sense what will be a good move straightaway.[23] In dual-process or two minds terms, System 1 (the intuitive mind) identifies a plausible move and System 2 (the analytical mind) is mobilized where necessary to verify System 1's intuition. Novice chess players on the other hand, determine the right move by a slow, conscious, deliberative reasoning process. Their System 2 is working overtime and System 1 has little or no contribution to make, other than the possibility of making an ill-informed guess because it does not have the requisite amount of prior experience to quickly and automatically draw on. However, in repeatedly going through this analytical process the novice is adding to their mental library of possible moves on the long road towards mastery and expertise.

Simon's thinking is important not least because he extrapolated from de Groot's foundational work, and the experiments that he himself conducted with Bill Chase, to management. Simon remarked that the 'intuitive skills of managers depend on the same kinds of mechanisms as the intuitive skills of chess masters' and that 'it would be surprising if it were otherwise.'[24] Also, as with chess, Simon points out that intuition in management does not operate independently of analysis for a number of reasons. First, intuitions are analyses that have been frozen into habit and the capacity for rapid response through recognition, so intuition and analysis have an almost symbiotic relationship in which intuition feeds-off prior analyses. Second, intuition and analysis are essential, complementary and, when used in the right way, mutually reinforcing components of effective decision-making. Third, decision-making is likely to entail a close combination of intuitive skills and analytical skills, the precise mix being determined by the type of decision that is being taken. A further and recurrent theme in expertise in chess, management and many other complex practical and professional domains is the essential role that practice plays in elevating human achievement from the 'swampy lowlands'[25] of novice performance the lofty heights of expertise.

10,000 Hours

Expert performers in sports, arts science, and business possess levels of skill that enable them to make fast, fluent, accurate decisions. The acknowledged 'expert on experts' was the Swedish psychologist K. Anders Ericsson (1947–2020). It was Ericsson who carried out the original research in the 1990s behind the so-called '10,000-hours rule' popularized by the bestselling author Malcolm Gladwell in his book *Outliers* (2008). It stands to reason that it takes a long time to become an expert, but the 10,000-hours rule research quantified this common-sense observation. Ericsson found that even the most gifted performers need a minimum of ten years (or roughly 10,000 hours) of intense training and deliberate practice to become an expert. The figures of ten years and 10,000 hours are rough-and-ready rules of thumb rather than precise formulations. It is not so much 'practice, practice, practice' as both *quality* of practice and *quantity* of practice. Deliberate practice through specific and sustained efforts, especially under expert guidance and with accurate and timely feedback, enhances skill levels and enables people to achieve remarkable things in their personal and professional lives.[26] For example, the tennis champion Rafael Nadal was training five times a week, every week, for an hour-and-a-half by the age of seven. Under the strict coaching regime of his uncle Toni he could play tennis equally well with his left or right hand, played groundstrokes double-handed on both sides, and was eventually coached to play left-handed, even though he eats, throws, plays golf, basketball, and darts right-handed.[27]

The celebrated 10,000-hours rule originates from a study by Ericsson and colleagues of violinists at the Music Academy of West Berlin (Hochschule der Kuenste). The study was published originally in 1993, and its findings have been replicated and extended, but also critiqued (see below). Professors at the Hochschule were asked to nominate three groups of ten of young violinists (mean age 23 years) on the basis of their level of skill on the instrument as follows: 'best violinists': these had potential for careers as international soloists; 'good violinists': these were good but not outstanding players; 'music teachers': these were reasonably proficient on the instrument and would probably become music teachers themselves. Ericsson and his team also gathered additional data from ten violinists (mean age 51 years) at the Berlin Philharmonic Orchestra and the Radio Symphony Orchestra of Berlin, two of the world's leading orchestras. The Hochschule violinists were asked to make retrospective estimates by answering the question: 'over the course of your entire career, even since you first picked up the violin, how many hours have you practised?' These estimates were multiplied by the number of weeks in a year and summed across years to give accumulated practice estimates. By the age of 20 years, the music teachers had accumulated just over 4,000 hours, the good violinists accumulated just short of 8,000 hours, and the best violinists and the orchestra members had accumulated over 10,000 hours of deliberate practice. Hence the 10,000-hours rule, which translates into 1,000 hours per year for ten years or around three hours per day for ten years. Incidentally, in their studies of expertise in chess, Bill Chase and Herbert Simon estimated that a chess master has 'spent perhaps 10,000 to 50,000 hours staring at chess positions'.[28] This discovery led Ericsson and colleagues to conclude that 'there is complete correspondence between skill level of the groups [of violinists] and their average accumulation of practice'.[29] That said, the original study has been criticized for playing down the role of natural talent by attributing differences in musical ability to how much the musicians practised.

The 10,000-hours rule was the centre piece of Malcolm Gladwell's bestselling book *Outliers*. In it, Gladwell claimed that the 10,000-hours rule reminds us that the closer psychologists look at the careers of the gifted, two things emerge: the smaller the role innate talent seems to play; and the bigger the role preparation seems to play.[30] Gladwell offered the 10,000-hours rule as an explanation for the remarkable achievements of, amongst others, the Beatles, attributing their ability to the accumulated practice they gained in the nightclubs of Hamburg playing hundreds of shows for many hours per night. Some people appeared to mis-read Gladwell's assertions as the claim that with enough practice anyone can become really good at anything. But this is not what he meant and he has gone on record as saying so. However, the critics rounded on him. For example, in an article in *Time* magazine one critic wrote that 'best-selling author Malcolm Gladwell popularized the idea that 10,000 hours of appropriately guided practice was "the magic number of greatness", regardless of a person's natural aptitude'.

Like any numerical rule of thumb, 10,000 hours is best treated as an average. For example, other research in chess has found that master status can be attained in as little as 3,000 hours, whereas it took some players in excess of 50,000 hours.[31] In actual fact, Gladwell also pointed out two important issues: first, no one succeeds at the highest level without some degree of ability or innate talent; second, in cognitively demanding fields such as medicine or management, there are no 'naturals' who can walk straight out of medical school or an MBA classroom to become a world-class surgeon or CEO; third, everybody can benefit from a little bit of help in the form of lucky breaks or privileges.[32]

An attempt at a replication of Ericsson's original study at the Cleveland Institute of Music in 2019 gave somewhat mixed results. In the Cleveland study both the best and the good violinists had accumulated around 11,000 hours of deliberate practice with little to separate them, whilst the merely accomplished (equivalent to the music teachers in the original study) accumulated around 6,000 hours.[33] Something other than accumulated practice seemed to be at work. The researchers, Brooke Macnamara and Megha Maitra, believe that practice is less of a driver at the very highest levels that the original Berlin study made out: 'Once you get to the highly skilled groups, practice stops accounting for the difference. Everyone has practised a lot and other factors, such as ability, context and luck, are at play in determining who goes on to that super-elite level'.[34] Whilst deliberate practice is undoubtedly important and helps to distinguish the good performer from the mediocre performer, it may not be the prime factor that some readers of the 10,000-hours rule have understood it to be.

Practice Makes Perfect?

At the highest levels there appears to be a difference that makes the difference between the good performer and the elite performer. This 'X-factor' will vary according to the domain, but age and genetics are likely to play a role. In chess it could be a combination of intelligence, working memory, and speed of processing. In athletics it could be a combination of musculature and skeletal and metabolic factors. Age and genetic factors in general impose an upper limit on the power of practice. Aside from the unavoidable determinants of time and genes, social factors are also important. Being in the right place at the right time can create once-in-a-lifetime opportunities and also give access to the right social networks. Take entrepreneurial alertness for instance: this predisposes some individuals to being able to spot where unexploited opportunities exist and move incisively to take advantage of such discoveries.[35] The beginnings of eBay can be traced to a group of entrepreneurs being alert to the opportunity to connect people through launching a virtual 'flea market'. But they did so at a point in time when technology had made it possible to meet the consumers' unmet need to connect buyers and sellers directly, hence cutting out the person in the middle.[36] It was not simply a question of any innate alertness they may have possessed, it was a question of right idea, right place, and right time.

Deliberate practice is an important factor in elevating performance to the highest levels, but when it is treated as the sole factor 10,000 hours may become an unhelpful generalization.[37] 10,000 hours is an average (half of the Berlin Hochschule expert violinists spent less than 10,000 hours while half spent more), also some skills take much longer to reach expert level whilst others take much less time. As noted above, the 10,000-hours rule should not be interpreted as 'with enough practice anyone can become an expert in anything'. Any such claim flies in the face of both common sense and science. Moreover, the requisite 10,000 hours could be compressed by simply doing more intense practice (eight hours a day would compress ten years into about three-and-a-half years). But it is the quality of practice, for example by working outside of one's comfort zone and getting timely and accurate feedback, which is vitally important. Simply adding more low-level procedural tools to one's toolbox will not help with the development of high-level expertise, nor will doing the same low-level task over and over again elevate performance to the next level.[38]

Becoming an expert involves a shift in mindset from procedure-following to problem-solving.[39] Ericsson wrote that 'living in a cave doesn't make you a geologist', by which he meant simply staring at rocks does not extend and deepen your knowledge and appreciation of them, something extra is needed.[40] Simply practising what you are already good at, hoping for the best through hit-and-miss experiences or only learning by making mistakes does not raise your game. On the other hand, deliberate practice combined with timely, accurate and relevant feedback makes a significant difference.[41]

Perhaps deliberate practice needs to be treated more seriously in business. In an article for *Harvard Business Review*, Ericsson bemoaned the fact that unlike elite performers in chess or sports, senior business leaders do not appear to take on board the idea of deliberate practice. For example, setting aside a couple of hours each day, even if it was in four half-hour blocks, for deliberately practising a new skill could, over the course of a year, add up to 700 hours a year or about 7,000 hours in a decade, which is not too far short of 10,000.[42] Defining deliberate practice in business and management is more difficult than in regimented and well-defined domains such as chess, tennis, or classical music where the rules do not change.[43] But essential and unchanging managerial skills such as listening, delegating, prioritizing, motivating, and communicating can all be identified and deliberately practised. If a manager's aim is to become more intuitive then common sense tells us that deliberate practice allied to feedback from bosses, colleagues, coaches, and mentors on how accurate their intuitive judgements and decisions are will help to build good intuitions. On the other hand, lack of feedback, poor feedback, or untimely feedback is probably one of the best ways for a manager to build bad intuitions.[44]

Experts performers are able to perform at a very high level in complex domains including sports, medicine, arts, and management consistently. Expertise is acquired through the acquisition of domain-specific knowledge as a result of prolonged periods of experience, focused deliberate practice, and feedback.[45] People who perform at the highest levels work with a coach or teacher so as to intentionally improving aspects of their performance over an extended time period through deliberate practice. The concept of deliberate practice belies the romantic myth of born geniuses, infant prodigies, and of people suddenly discovering that they are outstandingly good at something. Some people do undoubtedly have hidden talents and some are born prodigies, but such hidden and prodigious talents need nurturing. For this to happen a person needs to be in the right place at the right time. The opportunity that is available to all of us is the potential to create, through the right type and regimen of training and practice, levels of skill that we would not otherwise possess. In doing so we take advantage of the prodigious adaptability of the human brain and body to develop complex skills to the point at which they become intuitive.[46] The liberating potential of Ericsson's big idea is that anyone, by dint of determination and discipline, can put this gift to work and elevate performance to exceptional levels and at the same time build intuitive 'muscle power'.[47]

One of the most dramatic illustrations of how intuitive muscle power can save lives was the 'Miracle on the Hudson' when US Airways pilot Chesney 'Sully' Sullenberger had to land his Airbus A320 on the Hudson River in New York following a rare double bird strike that put both of his engines out of action. He had no option but to try to perform a textbook emergency landing in which he had to ensure the undercarriage was up; slow down the aircraft; fly into the wind; fully extend the wing flaps; get rid of as much fuel as possible; slow down enough but not too much as to stall; make sure the wings were perfectly level; lower the tail; keep the nose at an angle of 12 degrees; and finally gently skim the water until the 68-tonne plane came to a halt. Sullenberger was well equipped to do all this based on over forty years of flying experience: he got his first pilot's licence at 14; was a former USAF fighter pilot; served as a flight instructor; had served on numerous flight accident investigations; and, appropriately for this manoeuvre, was a certified glider pilot. The miracle on the Hudson was not a miracle: it was a classic example of the power of intuition at work.[48]

On Becoming an Expert

Whether geniuses or infant prodigies, such as Mozart (who happened to be the son of a musician and also had a sister who was a musical prodigy) or Picasso (the son of a highly skilled painter), are born or made is a perennially fascinating and unresolved question. Experts, on the other hand, such as expert doctors, nurses, or managers it is reasonably safe to say, are made rather than born (nobody is born an expert manager). But how does someone become an 'expert'? The Dreyfus brothers Hubert and Stuart, both professors at University of California Berkeley in philosophy and engineering respectively, developed the 'Skill Acquisition Model' (SAM), which describes how people progress systematically through various stages from novice through to expert in professional fields such as medicine and management.

Perhaps unsurprisingly, one of the Dreyfuses main ideas is that intuition is a distinguishing feature of expert performance. The origin of their Skill Acquisition Model was a project supported by the United States Air Force Office of Scientific Research (AFSC) that was designed to study McDonnell Douglas F-15 fighter pilots' performance in emergency situations. The research aimed to uncover the stages through which high-level skilled performance in the complex domain of air-to-air combat develops. They interviewed pilots in-depth. Their aim was to improve the design and implementation of training programmes for fighter pilots and in military training more generally. Their research report was published in February 1980. Incidentally, Gary Klein, the originator of the recognition-primed decision (RPD) model (see Chapter 5) played a small role in the development of the Dreyfus Skill Acquisition Model. Klein was a research psychologist at the Air Forces' Human Resources Laboratory in the mid-seventies and he recommended that the air force look into the work of the Dreyfus brothers, out of which grew the F-15 study and the Skill Acquisition Model.[49]

The Skill Acquisition Model specifies five stages of skill development: novice; advanced beginner; competent; proficient; expert. In the first stage, novices follow rules; they do not, and need not, feel any responsibility other than for following the rules; they monitor and bring their behaviour into conformity with the rules; and they learn skills without taking the subtleties of the context into account. The Dreyfuses give the example of a novice pilot who knows the basic skills of how to read cockpit instruments and manipulate controls in response to instrument readings and make sense of context-free visual cues such as the angular displacement of the horizon. Similarly, intuition researcher Gary Klein cited the example of novice police officer cadets: they cannot yet cope with complex decision-making, instead they have to be taught to master basic routines, for example, how to flag down a vehicle or direct traffic around an accident. Once these basic routines are mastered, so that they become more-or-less automatic, the brain's attentional capacity is freed up and can be used to handle more complicated situations.[50] Likewise in management, junior managers for example have to learn to master the basic skills of constructing and interpreting a spreadsheet before they can move onto the more complex task of financial planning. Having mastered these basic skills, attentional capacity is freed up for other higher-level skills, such as appreciating the bigger financial picture that a spreadsheet, when read in context, communicates.

Over time novices pass through the subsequent stages of 'advanced beginner', 'competent', and 'proficient' and eventually reach the levels of 'expert'. Expert performers have a repertoire of experienced situations and associated responses that is broad and deep enough so that each new situation evokes an 'intuitively appropriate' action. Experts' responses are non-analytical in the sense that they do not require extensive deliberation; they are able to act seemingly without needing to think. For example, the expert pilots whom the Dreyfuses interviewed reported that their performance was so intuitive that 'rather than being aware that they are flying an airplane, they have the experience that *they* are flying'. The expert pilots were 'in the zone' to the extent that when they suddenly reflected on what they were actually doing there was a degradation of performance and 'the disconcerting realization that rather than simply flying, [the pilot] is controlling a complicated mechanism'.[51]

An expert's performance is situation-specific, contextualized, holistic, and intuitive. By comparison a novice's performance is non-situation specific, decontextualized, decomposed, and analytical. In rare and precious moments, even experts sometimes surpass themselves when they experience instances of intense absorption in which they transcend their own high standards. On such occasions they become master performers who cease paying conscious attention to their performance and allow mental energy previously used for monitoring to go into producing masterful actions. The level of mastery is analogous to the state of 'flow' identified by the Hungarian-American psychologist Mihaly Csikszentmihalyi (1934 to 2021). In flow there is a 'one-pointedness' of mind where there is a close match between challenges and skills (a fine line is trodden between boredom and anxiety), distractions (such as health or financial concerns) are excluded from consciousness, and there is no anxiety about failure (performers are too absorbed to be concerned by it). Self-consciousness disappears (performers are too involved to care about protecting the ego), sense of time becomes distorted (hours may pass in what seems like minutes or time may slow down), and the activity becomes 'autotelic' (performed as an end in itself, as opposed to 'exotelic', performed only to achieve another end).[52] With this level of mastery comes a quieting of the analytical mind. By being relieved of the monitoring role of analysis in both producing and evaluating performance, the master performer becomes intuitively absorbed in and becomes at one with the act of performing.[53]

In the Skill Acquisition Model, intuitive mastery is the ultimate destination. In practice it manifests as the capability to make refined, nuanced discretionary judgements in real time, under conditions of limited information, time pressure, and dynamism. The Skill Acquisition Model does not claim that there are no principles or rules for experts, on the contrary, expert performance rests on a solid foundation of formal learning and previously learned rules. Formal rules are the basis for the highest levels of skilled performance. For example, in art the skill of painting is based on the rules of drawing; the British artist David Hockney observed that by learning rigorously how to draw proficiently artists learn how to *look*. This is important in art because there can be no painting *of* the world without looking *at* the world. However, at the expert level there is no need for rigid rule-following or using rules as a defence mechanism or a screen.[54] The development of expertise entails a moving towards greater reliance on intuition, which means that experts are in the hallowed position of being able to discard or break old rules and make new ones as befits the situation. The cultural integration and institutionalizing of experts' intuitions may even end up changing the rules of a domain. For example Pablo Picasso, along with Georges Braque, created new rules about painting with the invention of cubism. As a result, the rules of painting changed forever in the turbulent and volatile years of the early twentieth century. Over the longer-term, the integration and institutionalization of experts' intuitions into accepted practices results in the transmission of new rules from experts to other practitioners, and in this way professional practice progresses.

Expertise, mastery, and flow can also be a source of happiness in professional life. Csikszentmihalyi points out that just as a violinist gets paid for playing her instrument as well as getting intrinsic enjoyment from doing so, likewise a CEO gets status and good money for leading a business and should also get intrinsic rewards and enjoyment from it. According to Csikszentmihalyi one of the secrets of a happy life is to learn how to get flow from as many things that we do as possible. Given that work takes up the vast majority of most people's waking lives, achieving mastery of one's profession and being privileged to experience rare and valuable moments of flow paves the way for a happier and more rewarding working life and career. But being able to achieve a state of flow requires mastery of one's chosen domain, and mastery is only be arrived at after a long journey along the road of skill acquisition from novice, through to expertise, and eventually mastery. If, through expertise and mastery, work becomes an end in itself, then, in Csikszentmihalyi's idealized world 'nothing is wasted in life, and everything we do is worth doing for its own sake'.[55]

Whether skill acquisition falls neatly and discretely into the five stages documented by the Dreyfus brothers has been debated. But even if there are not five distinct stages, the developmental process that the Skill Acquisition Model describes makes sense to Gary Klein, who recommends treating the Dreyfus stages as 'snapshots of progress' rather than identifying them as separate stages of professional development[56]. The developmental process that the Skill Acquisition Model captures makes a great deal of sense as model of how, as a result of learning and experience, we are able to transition towards a greater reliance on intuition.

This reliance on intuition is not confined to extreme occupations such as firefighting and flying fighter jets. For example, intuitions play a crucial role and may even be necessary when judges make decisions in difficult legal cases, and expecting or obliging judges and jurors to rely completely on deliberate calculations and probabilities seems to be less than promising.[57] The use of intuition is becoming more widespread across occupations. Educational researchers Christian Harteis and Stephen Billet argue that intuition is a relevant and important attribute of most if not all jobs that require fast decision-making, whether this is a taxi driver deciding on the fastest route to take, to the problem-solving strategy of a car mechanic. They also make the point that more and more jobs are requiring employees to take faster and more consequential decisions as a result of decision-making responsibilities being delegated and distributed across the workforce, rather than being concentrated in the hands of senior managers.[58] Developing intuitive expertise is becoming a priority for many more workers in modern organizations. Likewise in military operations, Norwegian researchers Bjørn Bakken and Thorvald Haerem found that the demands placed on officers is not necessarily a clear-cut distinction of analytical (lower ranks) or intuitive (higher ranks). In the NATO Manual they found that higher-level commanders such as Generals should have 'experience, creativity, decisiveness and understanding', whilst lower-level commanders should combine both an instinctive grasp of the situation (a *Fingerspitzengefühl*, 'fingertips' feeling) and an attention to detail. Modern workplaces demand experienced and cognitively flexible employees who are capable of handling unfamiliar as well as familiar problems and situations using both intuition and analysis.[59]

Intuitive Expertise in Nursing

The most well-known application of the Dreyfus Skill Acquisition Model is in the field of nursing. Patricia Benner of the University of California San Francisco is one of a small number of recipients of the 'Living Legends of the American Academy of Nursing' (2011) awarded in recognition of her contribution to the nursing profession and the provision of healthcare services in the United States and across the world. Her magnum opus in the field of expertise and intuition is *From Novice to Expert: Excellence and Power in Clinical Nursing Practice* (1982). The book, which was one of the products of federally funded research carried out in the San Francisco Bay Area, was based on practising nurses' experience-based narratives of their working lives (in effect their 'stories'). Its essence is that expertise in nursing develops and grows through experience and implicit and informal learning and that as a consequence expert performance cannot be completely codified, objectified, and formalized. This is because, in Benner's own words, expert nursing practices are more than a collection of techniques; in each new situation they have to be 'worked out anew in particular relationships in real time'.[60] In common with others who possess complex skills that have been learned experientially, expert nurses know more than they can tell.

Experience is a requisite for expertise in nursing, and as in any other professional field including management. Expertise melds formally acquired technical-scientific, rational-analytic ways of knowing with an intuitively and experientially acquired 'practical wisdom'. Using the terms set out by Aristotle over two millennia ago, professional practice requires both *techné* (i.e. practical knowledge) and *phronēsis* (i.e. practical rationality), Benner's words:

> *Techné* can be captured by procedural and scientific knowledge, knowledge that can be made formal, explicit, and certain, except for the necessary timing and adjustments made for particular patients. *Phronēsis*, in contrast to techné, is the kind of practical reasoning engaged in by an excellent practitioner lodged in a community of practitioners, a practitioner who, through experiential learning and for the sake of good practice, continually lives out and improves practice.[61]

In this regard there is an ethical dimension to expertise: practical wisdom, *phronēsis*, is socially situated, which means that inevitably it involves taking decisions with a concern for doing what is good and right in the community of others (for example, a work team or any wider social group) where 'human concerns' are to the fore and guide professionals' actions.[62] Ultimately, *phronēsis* should contribute to the 'happiness' or 'living well' (*eudaimonia*) in the community of other human beings. As a counter example, in the financial crash of 2008 the CFOs and CEOs of the major banks failed to exercise *phronēsis* because they knowingly lent money beyond people's ability to pay.[63] According to the Nobel economics' laureate Joseph Stiglitz, they unwisely misjudged the risks;[64] the unintended negative consequences of their hubristic incompetence reverberated well beyond the banks themselves.[65]

At its time of publication in the 1980s, Benner's *From Novice to Expert* was seen in some quarters as a threat to some of the nursing profession's deeply-held beliefs and assumptions because it presented a challenge to rational models of decision-making and professional practice. It made some educators uncomfortable by giving recognition and credence to the 'perceptual sensibilities' that are the touchstone of expert nursing practice, for example 'gut feelings', 'a sense of uneasiness', and 'the feeling that things are not quite right'. But, in Benner's own words, 'in all cases definitive evaluation of a patient's condition requires more than vague hunches', and by virtue of their experience expert nurses allow their intuitive perceptions to lead them to confirming evidence.[66] This process is similar to the 'intuition-based inquiry' that Cinla Akinci and I discovered from our analysis of the stories that peak-performing police officers told us about their experiences of handling first-response (see Chapter 4).[67] It also underscores the idea that in most situations intuition cannot be understood, or indeed practised, separately from analysis.[68] Benner's model, as well as describing and explaining how expertise is acquired, is also about the nature of professional knowledge. It encapsulates a fundamental distinction that is to be found in theories of knowledge (i.e. epistemology) between two types of knowledge: 'declarative knowledge' (i.e. 'knowing that') which can easily be codified and is most often acquired formally; and 'procedural knowledge' (i.e. 'knowing how') which is most often acquired informally and experientially and is difficult to codify. It follows from this distinction that it is sometimes possible to 'know how' without 'knowing why',[69] and that we can know more than we can tell: these are the hallmarks of intuitive practice.

Benner's model of how nurses develop their expertise closely follows the pattern of the Skill Acquisition Model from novice, through advanced beginner, competent, proficient, and eventually to expert. Novice nurses learn through instruction, acquire factual, declarative knowledge and learn rules and apply them context-free irrespective of the nuances of the situation. At the other end of the developmental spectrum are experts. Expert nurses, in a similar way to Klein's expert firefighters, perceive and process a constellation of cues that enable them recognize patterns that activate action scripts, which are then used to inform action. In perceiving situations holistically they use their situation awareness to focus on the most salient cues and use their prior experiences as prototypes for action.[70]

By way of example, Benner uses expert nurses' finely-tuned ability to sense impending medical 'shock',[i] a condition which is often difficult to recognize in practice. Expert nurses were able to sense impending shock intuitively as a result of many hours of direct observation and care of patients who had experienced shock. Expert nurses' judgements are holistic in that seemingly small but significant changes (faint signals) become highly salient only in the light of the patient's past history and their current situation. Hence, to an expert a faint signal can be a strong sign. Benner borrows the term 'connoisseurship' from the philosopher Michael Polanyi of 'we know more than we can tell' fame, to refer to this highly-tuned sensing ability which serves as a method of appraising and judging a complex and fast-moving situation. Connoisseurship, which literally means 'one who knows',[71] is a skill that can only be gained by doing and reflecting in and reflecting on action.[72] It transforms the casual and superficial looking at a situation into a deeper sensing and seeing. Connoisseurship is arrived at experientially through educating attention and cultivating sensibility.[73] Benner cited the example of a patient in ICU whom the nurse had to 'watch his colour, his eyes, if he tremored [and] you really had to pick up on it, much more than his numbers, much more than his monitoring ... you had to more or less look at him, and *just know*'.[74]

Benner described expert intuition in nursing—which distinguishes expert human judgement from that of a computer or a beginner—as 'understanding without a rationale'.[75] Experts' intuitive understanding without a rationale gives them a grasp of a particular situation such that some interpretations stand out as more plausible than others. Intuitively grasping the gist of a situation enables experts in time-pressured high-stakes situations to take immediate actions rather mechanically assess signs and symptoms. There is no better illustration of this than the case of a patient who was haemorrhaging and had stopped breathing whom the nurse had taken care of in a previous successful resuscitation:

> I just started calling out the drugs that I needed to get for this guy, so we started to push these drugs in. In the meantime, I said, 'Can we have some more blood?' I was

---

[i] Shock is a life-threatening, generalized form of acute circulatory failure with inadequate oxygen delivery to, and consequently oxygen utilization by, the cells, see: https://bestpractice.bmj.com/topics/en-gb/3000121

just barking out this stuff. I can't even tell you the sequence. I was saying, 'We need this'. I needed to anticipate what was going to happen and I could do this because I had been through this a week before with this guy and knew what we had done [and what had worked].

The difference between a merely proficient nurse and an expert is that the proficient nurse still has to think what to do. In the situation described above the expert's focus shifted seamlessly from problem to immediate action, she was just 'barking out this stuff' without the need to think it through. As in the case of Klein's firefighters, thinking it through laboriously was simply not an option. Benner characterizes nurses who operate at this level as balancing an openness to what the situation presents with an anticipation of what is likely to happen. They are attuned such that they shape their actions on a careful reading of the patient's responses so as to arrive at the gist of the situation[76] based on a nuanced interpretation of the patient's needs without conscious deliberation.

The concept of gist is a key idea in Valerie Reyna's 'fuzzy trace theory' (FTT) of intuition. In FTT Reyna makes a distinction between two kinds of representations of information in memory. 'Verbatim representations' capture the precise and surface-level details of one's experiences, for example the verbatim success rate for a business start-up is 20 per cent. 'Gist representations' capture the bottom line and deeper meanings of one's experiences and are fuzzier, for example the gist of 'Linda' is that she is both a bank teller and an active feminist (see Chapter 2). Reyna's theory positions verbatim and gist as opposite ends of a continuum. As a result of learning and experience, people develop a preference for the fuzzy end of the spectrum and come to rely on gist-based intuitions to execute tasks efficiently and effectively. Even so, verbatim representations are relied on by experts, but only when the situation demands absolute precision, for example in formulating the exact dosage of a drug in nursing, or in presenting precise financial data in business. One of the upsides of gist-based reasoning is that it goes beyond surface-level details into deeper meanings. One of the downsides of gist-based interpretations is that they make decision-makers vulnerable to mistaking generalized inferences for specific memories, for example by inferring from an active feminist whom we once met to the new instance, Linda, whom she sounds just like.[77] As a result we run the risk of overgeneralizing from prototypes and exemplars when judging specific cases.

Lessons in Intuitive Expertise from Nursing

Benner distilled intuitive expertise in nursing to four critical success factors. First, 'clinical grasp': expert nurses take their time in getting settled, which means getting a sense for who the patient is, their immediate demands and concerns, and the likely pattern of responses. Second, 'embodied know-how': swift and adept action through knowing that is lodged in sensations in the body, hands, eyes, and ears and which gives a felt-sense in the form of an intuition. Third, 'big picture': a sense of the future, anticipated trajectories and future possibilities for the patient and family (akin to foreseeing) and a peripheral vision which accommodates the needs of other patients and the responsibilities and capabilities of other members of the team. Fourth, 'seeing the unexpected': expert nurses have a realistic knowledge of what is to be expected of particular type of patients, as in cases that 'are going down the drain': 'You can just see it. Tiny little trends and you can just follow them, and you just know'.[78] But when their expectations are violated the expert has sufficient practical know-how to search for evidence that helps with the interpretation of 'jarred expectations'.[79] This awareness creates the possibility for noticing when things are going awry because their practical understanding of what a well-understood situation feels like also enables them to sense when the situation does not add up. Experts are much more adept than novices in expecting the unexpected and, moreover, have a much better idea of how to handle it.

These four critical success factors can be extrapolated to business. Clinical grasp requires a basic knowledge of the business that you are in. For example, Bill Gates's knowledge and experience with computers can be traced back a long way to his pre–high school years. By the time he set up Microsoft in 1975 at the age of just twenty Gates had an in-depth knowledge of the fast-developing business of computing. Embodied know-how means being alert to signs and signals from all five senses. For example, Howard Schulz attended to the visceral signals from his body during the epiphany he experienced in a visit to Italy, which led to him spotting the potential for high street coffee shops in the United States. Being 'big-picture conscious' means standing back and looking at the whole, for example, by deliberately creating time for big-picture thinking so that the things on one's 'to do' list don't crowd out peripheral things. Seeing the unexpected involves being attuned to situations as dynamic and being vigilant towards unanticipated changes and the wider and unintended consequences of one's actions. Business managers swim in a sea of uncertainty, and intuition can give them a sense of direction in which they should go and for the possible directions in which events may turn. Intuition supports foresight. A faint signal can be the first indicator of an emerging issue that may become significant in the future.[80] The faint signals that intuition picks up on can end up being strong indicators. For example, in the financial system prior to the crash of 2007 and 2008 there were numerous faint signals (for example, sustained rise in house prices, new financial innovations, etc.) that at the time did not reveal that a credit crunch was on its way; they only made sense post hoc when they were put together into a bigger picture. The policymakers at the United States Federal Reserve noted problems in housing and banking but thought that they were isolated issues and unlikely to 'tear down the U.S. economy as they ultimately did', thinking instead that they would be moderate and short-lived.[81] Few experts at the time exhibited the necessary foresight that might have prevented this financial calamity from happening (see Chapter 1).

Intuitive Expertise in Business

The credit crunch and banking in general is a world away from nursing, but nonetheless research reveals how experienced finance practitioners, in common with nurses, use their intuitive expertise when making high-stakes decisions. Raanan Lipshitz and Nurit Shulimovitz of the University of Haifa were interested in the role that intuition plays in credit decisions in the finance business.[82] They interviewed fourteen experienced, i.e. expert, bank loan officers responsible for mid-range loads of up to $500k in a large commercial bank in Israel. Contrary to expectations for a numbers-driven business, the loan officers reported that gut feelings, such as 'it did not smell right' or 'my stomach was all in knots', helped to guide decisions of whether or not to offer a loan to potential clients. Out of the critical incidents captured in the interviews, five of the intuition-based decisions were positive (which signalled 'approach') whilst fourteen were negative (signalling 'avoid'). These findings are consistent with the idea that expert intuition in banking, and more generally, tends to err on the side of caution.

In this research, intuitions were found to be most often triggered in face-to-face meetings with potential clients. The bankers themselves found it difficult to explain the reasons behind their visceral reactions to certain clients' applications. However, subsequent scrutiny of the interviews revealed a number of key behaviours that stood out. In the case of the negative hunches (which were the majority of intuitive decisions) these were potential clients' 'dubious behaviours' (such as suspicious appearance, withholding financial information, and unusual utterances), 'peddling an unpersuasive story' (such as fantasizing about success) and 'failing to "walk the talk"' (such as not putting money into an account by a certain date).

Lipshitz and Shulimovitz made four practical recommendations for banks. First, hard financial data alone cannot capture the gist of a complex situation involving people and money. Second, greater acknowledgement should be given to the role of experienced-based hunches and gut feelings in deciding whether or not to lend the bank's money. Third, methods should be developed for training loan officers so that they are sensitized to their intuitions and understand when and when not to trust them. Finally, bank loan offers should not shy away from integrating soft, impressionistic, 'gisty' information with hard, financial data into an overall holistic assessment of a client's loan application. Lipshitz and Shulimovitz's research offered a counter to the view that financial decisions have to be made rationally and solely on the basis of numbers and without the interference of 'distracting' intuitions or emotions.[83]

Lipshitz and Shulimovitz's interviewees were experts at the levels of mid-ranked loan officers in a bank, which begs the question: does the recognition of and reliance on expert intuition in banking and finance extend up the hierarchy to senior executives? Ann Hensman and I undertook and in-depth study of intuitive decision-making amongst fifteen senior executives in a FTSE-100 British multinational banking and financial services company headquartered in London. In the research Ann asked executives to recall a transaction or a project they were involved in where they had a gut feeling that a course of action was right or wrong. In the preamble she explained that by 'gut feeling' we meant 'knowing, without knowing how or why you know'.

Contrary to expectations we found that even at the most senior levels in banking and finance, expert intuition is both recognized and used in taking decisions. This is significant not least because many of the decisions these executives took were of strategic importance for the bank. We discovered that banking executives' experiences of intuitions were compelling and alluring but in their industry were likely to be perceived as having less validity than analytical decision-making. For example, one executive remarked that 'I think you should go with your gut instinct. Whatever you think initially is probably going to be right, not all the time but in most cases'. Another executive expressed caution that 'acting on instinct and gut feel [in this industry] is still seen as a bit of an invalid reason for making a decision'. In keeping with due diligence, the banking executives saw their intuitions as hypotheses, and like any hypothesis they should be opened up to testing and potential falsification: 'I probably rely on gut feel before I do on anything else, but it doesn't stop me going through the process'. Another one commented that the 'gut feeling is always the first thing, and then I would try to go through it in a more formulated fashion to try and prove myself wrong'. Like these senior bankers, managers in general should temper any extreme certainty they have about their own intuitions (which are 'sometimes wrong, but rarely in doubt') with the necessary caution by subjecting their intuitions to requisite scrutiny, for example by using the 'devil's advocacy' test (see Chapter 11).

In keeping with Benner's notion of embodied know-how, we found that banking executives' intuitions manifested both verbally and non-verbally and were often most expressed through imagery or metaphor. For example, one executive remarked that 'sometimes I have a voice in my head—and I think most people do, although some don't like to admit it—but the voice in your head will say something'. Intuition also cropped up in a variety of non-verbal ways, ranging from a visceral felt-sense, as in 'the whole decision was really geared by a hugely strong, physical feeling that this was just not right, to do it this way' to more unusual manifestations as in 'Whenever I meet somebody I make a judgment. I don't know… it might be a physical thing… but you just look at a person and they give off an aura'. These findings suggested to us that executives in banking, and more generally, should: be open to and mindful of intrapersonal non-verbal channels of communication (i.e. between their unconscious and conscious selves) mediated through processes such as visual and aural imagery. They should also recognize gut feelings as a potentially valid form of 'data' which complements hard financial figures; not shy away from expressing their hunches using images, analogies, figures of speech, and metaphors in order to interpret them. This is healthy: it opens-up intuitions both to self-examination and the scrutiny of others.

These recommendations resonate with the findings from other research on intuition in business decision-making. In Laura Huang and Jone Pearce's study (see Chapter 1) of how angel investors use their intuition in high-stakes financial decisions, one investor recalled one deal in particular:

> Those are the deals that really make you sweat … the ones where you start saying 'on the one hand, how can I not …, and on the other hand, how could I possibly.' He was playing in a $65 billion market, and I believed that what he was trying to do could capture a really large chunk [of it]. But there was something about him that reminded me of why I lost [a large sum of money] on [a prior investment].

He had that same zany glare in his eyes as [prior entrepreneur], and was using the same 'if… then' statements that just took me back to my past nightmare and told me to back away from this one … back away from a $65 billion market … who does that? It was one of the most painful choices and I lost a lot of sleep over that one.[84]

Other entrepreneurship research by Leonie Baldacchino and colleagues supports the idea that it is not either intuition or analysis that is important in business-venting decisions (and in managerial decision-making in general); rather it is skilful deployment of both intuition and analysis. Baldacchino and colleagues explained their findings as follows: as entrepreneurs gain relevant experience, they develop the complex domain-relevant schemas (mental models) that enable them to both process information unconsciously and intuitively and to connect the dots between faint signals (or cues). This helps them to sense and potentially foresee emerging trends in the business environment giving first-mover advantage. Because this process takes place automatically and unconsciously it frees up scarce cognitive resources that can be devoted to other more effortful cognitive processes, such as analysing, interpreting, and mental simulation, all of which help entrepreneurs to assess the viability of a proposed venture. This cognitive versatility, analogous to ambidexterity, enables experienced entrepreneurs to switch cognitive gears at will in order to handle the information-processing demands of the task at hand.[85]

J. F. Coget in his research in the film industry observed a different type of ambidexterity in the way that Hollywood directors used their intuition. Movie sets are fraught places: for example, every minute lost costs money, equipment is complex, the weather can be fickle, and actors are often unpredictable and temperamental. Coget found that to cope with these complexities and uncertainties, experienced film directors used their intuition in two complementary ways. They used it to intuitively diagnose and solve small issues such as choosing types of shots or deciding if a special effect was likely to become dangerous. They also used their intuition to keep track, literally, of the bigger picture and their vision for the movie, and where necessary to update it in the moment, as in the case of the director who had an argument with an actress but rather than defusing her anger decided intuitively in the moment to use it as part of the narrative. Coget also witnessed a different type of ambidexterity amongst Californian winemakers who used chemical analyses to solve sugar and acidity issues with the wine but used their intuitive tasting experience to sense the grapes' ripeness.[86] These findings show that intuitive experts are not consumed by fine detail or overwhelmed by the bigger picture but are able to zoom-in and zoom-out at will.

Team and Collective Intuition

Individual intuitions can become team or collective intuitions through a sense-making process of interpretation. This is important because if and how individual managers' intuitions are integrated into business operations and strategy impact on employees, organizations, investors, and may even affect entire industries. Intuitive decisions can only be agreed upon and implemented successfully in organizations if they are interpreted and integrated collectively into the business' processes, routine, procedures, and systems.[87] In a study of senior police officers' decision-making, Cinla Akinci and I discovered that intuitive 'hits' (where intuition gets it right) or 'misses' (where it gets it wrong) that are not interpreted and internalized collectively can impede organizational learning and the building of organizational memory.[88] When this happens, organizations run the risk of repeating previous mistakes or not capitalizing on the lessons of prior successes, and in business, as well as in life more generally, those who fail to learn the lessons of previous intuitive misses are destined to repeat them.[89]

Senior managers and executives are, by dint of their experiences, likely to have developed high-level expertise. By virtue of their position in the organization, they are able to exercise their intuitions when making decisions. If and how well executive intuition works in top management teams depends on a number of factors related both to the leaders themselves and the organizational context they are operating in. Codou Samba and colleagues identified four different types of top management team (TMT) intuition.[90] 'Dominant actor intuition' in a TMT reflects the intuition of one top manager and likely occurs when a powerful leader such as the CEO has an autocratic leadership style. Dominant actor intuition confers the advantages of speed and decisiveness. Samba and her colleagues give the example of Steve Jobs, who tended to rely on his own intuitions in spite of the fact that there was extensive knowledge capital embedded in Apple's TMT. The second type, 'shared intuition', is a consequence of TMT members selecting people who happen to be like them. This process of homogenization leads the members of the TMT to have similar intuitions about strategic issues. This is not de facto a bad thing, and in fact can lead to speedy decision-making, however it can also lead to cognitive inertia, the creation of an echo chamber for the leader's and team's ingrained beliefs and values, and eventually end up as groupthink. This type of TMT intuition is likely to be quite rare because the team is likely to be forced by circumstances to seek a more diverse outlook. In the third type, 'actor-driven collective intuition', the dominant actor, which may be the CEO, secures the TMT's validation of their intuition, but who the dominant actor actually *is* can change depending on circumstances and the type of expertise required. Its advantage is inclusion and adaptability, but a drawback could be slowness. Finally, 'team-driven collective intuition' is synergistic in that it is a shared intuition that is produced through social interactions and is the preferred type of TMT intuition. It is collective in that it involves the intuitions of different members of the team. It is synergistic in that the collective intuition is greater than the sum of the individual intuitions. The TMT intuits together in a shared process of interpretation of individual intuitions and their integration into organizational systems and processes.[91] Developing this level of integration is likely to be difficult and time-consuming. However, as strategic management research Kathleen Eisenhardt noted, TMTs that do not develop good collective intuitions are likely to be less successful because without this level of integration, the TMT is, cognitively speaking at least, a 'group of strangers'.[92]

Collective intuition is built by cooperative learning, dialogue, and feedback. When it works effectively it builds a valuable, rare, and difficult-to-imitate source of competitive advantage. The process begins typically with an individual's creative intuitions, which are expressed in metaphors, for example Thomas Edison expressed his idea for a kinetoscope, a primitive machine for viewing motion pictures and the forerunner of movies, by analogy to his phonograph: 'I am experimenting upon an instrument which does for the Eye what the phonograph does for the Ear, which is the recording a reproduction of things in motion, and in such a form as to be both cheap, practical and convenient'.[93] These creative intuitions become interpreted with the wider group of stakeholders through conversation and dialogue. They then become integrated into an organization as a shared understanding (for example, for what a kinetoscope might eventually achieve) and eventually institutionalized collectively not only in 'hard' inventions, production routines, manufacturing systems, and organizational structures but also in 'softer' shared values, team culture and climate, for example the psychological safety which is a prerequisite for opening up creative intuitions to a collective interpretation.[94] This whole process was captured by Mary Crossan and colleagues in their four-I model of organizational learning (intuiting, interpreting, integrating and institutionalizing, see Chapter 11).

Problems arise when the suppression of individual team members' intuitions blocks collective interpretation and sense-making. This creates organizational learning dysfunctions, for example by repeating bad intuitive decisions or sticking to outdated mental models, which can end up being value-destroying rather than value-creating. A case in point is the UK 'big four' supermarket bosses whose ingrained assumptions that bigger stores are always better (the supermarket 'space race') were wrong-footed by so-called 'deep discounters', customers' changed shopping habits, and the rise of online grocery retailing.[95] Senior managers' collective intuitions about the way British consumers shopped were out of step with how consumers were actually behaving. In order to catch up, the big grocery supermarkets had to shift their mindset. They had to make it easier for time-pressured consumers to buy whenever and wherever it suited them by shopping more often, closer to home and online. But this was not before some of the biggest players in this intensely competitive market got their fingers burned by having to mothball or repurpose newly-built big out-of-town stores.[96]

Summary

1. Many of the insights into how intuition works can be traced back to research on intuition in chess.
2. Expert chess players have an intuitive feeling for a position and the best next-move based on tens of thousands of patterns held in long-term memory.
3. It takes in the order of 10,000 hours of deliberate, high-quality practice to become an expert.

4. Expertise is acquired in a process that begins with novice, passes through advanced beginner, competeht, and proficient stages, and culminates with expert/masterful performance.
5. Novice performance is decontextualized, rule-following, and deliberative; expert performance is situation-specific, holistic, and intuitive.
6. Novices rely on surface-level verbatim knowledge whist experts rely on deeper-level, gist-based knowledge.
7. Critical success factors for expert performance include having a complete grasp of the situation, embodied know-how, being big-picture conscious, and being equipped to expect the unexpected.
8. Expert managers are open to gut feel as a form of data, they do not shy away from expressing their hunches, and use figures of speech and metaphors to open themselves up to interpretation.
9. Surfacing and sharing individual intuitions helps to build collective intuitions, which can be a hard-to-imitate source of competitive advantage.
10. Interpretation of individual intuitions leads eventually to their institutionalization in the processes/procedures and climate/culture of an organization.

Endnotes

1. Gobet, F., & Chassy, P. (2009). Expertise and intuition: A tale of three theories. *Minds and Machines*, 19(2): 151–180.
2. Simon, H. A. (1987). Making management decisions: The role of intuition and emotion. *Academy of Management Perspectives*, 1(1): 57–64, p. 59.
3. De Groot, A. D. (1965). *Thought and Choice in Chess* (first Dutch edition in 1946). The Hague: Mouton Publishers, p. 337.
4. Ibid.
5. Ibid., pp. 337, 367.
6. Busato, V. (2006). In Memoriam: Adriaan de Groot. Association for Psychological Science. Available online at: https://www.psychologicalscience.org/observer/in-memoriam-adriaan-dingeman-de-groot-1914-2006 Accessed 22.02.2022.
7. De Groot, A. D. (1965). *Thought and Choice in Chess* (first Dutch edition in 1946). The Hague: Mouton Publishers, p. 186.
8. Ibid., p. 195.
9. Ibid., p. 285.
10. Ibid., p. 311.
11. Ibid., p. 199.
12. Ibid., p. 262.
13. Ibid., p. 199.
14. Ibid., p.261.
15. Ibid., p. 274.
16. Ibid., p. 278.
17. Ibid., p. 274.

18. Ibid., p. 310.
19. Ibid., p. 304.
20. Ibid., p. 308.
21. Miller, G. A. (1956). The magical number seven, plus or minus two: Some limits on our capacity for processing information. *Psychological Review*, 63(2): 81–97.
22. Chase, W. G., & Simon, H. A. (1973). The mind's eye in chess. In W. G. Chase (Ed.). *Visual Information Processing* (pp. 215–281). New York: Academic Press. Chase, W. G., & Simon, H. A. (1973). Perception in chess. *Cognitive Psychology*, 4(1): 55–81.
23. Chase, W. G., & Simon, H. A. (1973). Perception in chess. *Cognitive Psychology*, 4(1): 55–81.
24. Simon, H. A. (1987). Making management decisions: The role of intuition and emotion. *Academy of Management Perspectives*, 1(1): 57–64, p. 61.
25. Schön, D. A. (1983). *The Reflective Practitioner*. Aldershot: Ashgate, p. 42.
26. Ericsson, K. A., Prietula, M. J., & Cokely, E. T. (2007). The making of an expert. *Harvard Business Review*, 85(7/8): 114–122.
27. Baldridge, M. (2012). Rafael Nadal: The making of a champion. *Bleacher Report*. Available online at: https://bleacherreport.com/articles/1234812-wimbledon-2012-rafael-nadal-the-making-of-a-champion-part-one Accessed 06.04.2022.
28. Gladwell, M. (2013). Complexity and the ten-thousand hour rule. *The New Yorker*, 21 August 2013. Available online at: https://www.newyorker.com/sports/sporting-scene/complexity-and-the-ten-thousand-hour-rule Accessed 21.02.2022
29. Ericsson, K. A., Krampe, R. T., & Tesch-Romer, C. (1993). The role of deliberate practice in the acquisition of expert performance. *Psychological Review*, 100(3): 363–406, p. 379
30. Gladwell, M. (2013). Complexity and the ten-thousand hour rule. *The New Yorker*, 21 August 2013. Available online at: https://www.newyorker.com/sports/sporting-scene/complexity-and-the-ten-thousand-hour-rule Accessed 21.02.2022
31. Campitelli, G., & Gobet, F. (2011). Deliberate practice: Necessary but not sufficient. *Current Directions in Psychological Science*, 20(5): 280–285.
32. Gladwell, M. (2013). Complexity and the ten-thousand hour rule. *The New Yorker*, 21 August 2013. Available online at: https://www.newyorker.com/sports/sporting-scene/complexity-and-the-ten-thousand-hour-rule Accessed 21.02.2022.
33. Macnamara, B. N., & Maitra, M. (2019). The role of deliberate practice in expert performance: revisiting Ericsson, Krampe & Tesch-Römer (1993). *Royal Society Open Science*, 6(8): 190327.
34. Sample, I. (2019). Blow to 10,000-hour rule as study finds practice doesn't always make perfect. *The Guardian*, 21 August 2019. Available online at: https://www.theguardian.com/science/2019/aug/21/practice-does-not-always-make-perfect-violinists-10000-hour-rule Accessed 08.08.2022.
35. Kirzner, I. M. (1999). Creativity and/or alertness: A reconsideration of the Schumpeterian entrepreneur. *The Review of Austrian Economics*, 11(1): 5–17, p. 6.
36. Knowledge @ Wharton (2009). How entrepreneurs identify new business opportunities. Wharton University of Pennsylvania, 9 November 2009. Available online at: https://knowledge.wharton.upenn.edu/article/how-entrepreneurs-identify-new-business-opportunities/ Accessed 22.02.2022.
37. Miller, M. (no date) Busting the myth of the 10,000 hours rule. *Six Seconds*. Available online at: https://www.6seconds.org/2020/01/25/the-great-practice-myth-debunking-the-10000-hour-rule/ Accessed 22.02.2022.

38. Klein, G. A. (2017) Retiring the Dreyfus five-stage model of expertise. *Psychology Today*, 2 November 2017. Available online at: https://www.psychologytoday.com/gb/blog/seeing-what-others-dont/201711/retiring-the-dreyfus-five-stage-model-expertise Accessed 22.02.2022.
39. Ibid.
40. Ericsson, K. A., Prietula, M. J., & Cokely, E. T. (2007). The making of an expert. *Harvard Business Review*, 85(7/8): 114–122.
41. Macnamara, B. N., Hambrick, D. Z., & Oswald, F. L. (2014). Deliberate practice and performance in music, games, sports, education, and professions: A meta-analysis. *Psychological Science*, 25(8): 1608–1618. In this study the effect size for 'professions' was 1 percent. The professions studied were computer programming, military aircraft piloting, soccer refereeing, and selling insurance.
42. Ericsson, K. A., Prietula, M. J., & Cokely, E. T. (2007). The making of an expert. *Harvard Business Review*, 85(7–8): 114–21.
43. Macnamara, B. N., Hambrick, D. Z., & Oswald, F. L. (2014). Deliberate practice and performance in music, games, sports, education, and professions: A meta-analysis. *Psychological Science*, 25(8): 1608–1618.
44. Hogarth, R. M. (2001). *Educating intuition*. Chicago: Chicago University Press.
45. Salas, E., Rosen, M. A., & DiazGranados, D. (2010). Expertise-based intuition and decision making in organizations. *Journal of Management*, 36: 41–973, p. 947.
46. Ericsson, A., & Pool, R. (2016). *Peak: Secrets from the New Science of Expertise*. London: Random House., p. xix.
47. Klein, G. A. (2004). *Intuition at Work*. New York: Currency.
48. Sadler-Smith, E. (2010). *The Intuitive Mind: Profiting from the Power of Your Sixth Sense*. Chichester: John Wiley & Sons.
49. Klein, G. A. (2017) Retiring the Dreyfus five-stage model of expertise. *Psychology Today*, 2 November 2017. Available online at: https://www.psychologytoday.com/gb/blog/seeing-what-others-dont/201711/retiring-the-dreyfus-five-stage-model-expertise Accessed 22.02.2022.
50. Ibid.
51. Dreyfus, H. L., & Dreyfus, S. E. (2005). Peripheral vision: Expertise in real world contexts. *Organization Studies*, 26(5): 779–792, pp.791–792, emphasis added.
52. Csikszentmihalyi, M. (1996). *Flow*. London: Rider, pp. 111–113.
53. Dreyfus, H. L., & Dreyfus, S. E. (2005). Peripheral vision: Expertise in real world contexts. *Organization Studies*, 26(5): 779–792.
54. Benner, P. (2001). *From Novice to Expert*. Upper Saddle River: Prentice Hall.
55. Csikszentmihalyi, M. (1996). *Flow*. London: Rider, p. 113.
56. Klein, G. A. (2017) Retiring the Dreyfus five-stage model of expertise. *Psychology Today*, 2 November 2017. Available online at: https://www.psychologytoday.com/gb/blog/seeing-what-others-dont/201711/retiring-the-dreyfus-five-stage-model-expertise Accessed 22.02.2022.
57. Glöckner, A., & Ebert, I. D. (2011). Legal intuition and expertise. In Sinclair, M. (Ed.). *The Handbook of Intuition Research*. Cheltenham: Edward Elgar, pp. 157–167.
58. Harteis, C., & Billett, S. (2013). Intuitive expertise: Theories and empirical evidence. *Educational Research Review*, 9: 145–157.
59. Bakken, B., & Haerem, T. (2011). Intuition in crisis management. In Sinclair, M. (Ed.). *The Handbook of Intuition Research*. Cheltenham: Edward Elgar, pp. 122–132.

60. Benner, P. (2001). *From Novice to Expert*. Upper Saddle River: Prentice Hall, p. vi.
61. Benner, P. (2004). Using the Dreyfus model of skill acquisition to describe and interpret skill acquisition and clinical judgment in nursing practice and education. *Bulletin of Science, Technology & Society*, 24(3): 188–199, p. 189.
62. Ibid.
63. Queiroz, R. (2012). The importance of phronesis as communal business ethics reasoning principle. *Philosophy of Management*, 11(2): 49–61.
64. Stiglitz, J. (2010). *Freefall: America, Free Markets, and the Sinking of the World Economy*. New York: W.W Norton & Company.
65. Sadler-Smith, E. (2019). *Hubristic Leadership*. London: SAGE.
66. Benner, P. (2001). *From novice to expert*. Upper Saddle River: Prentice Hall, p. xxi.
67. Akinci, C., & Sadler-Smith, E. (2020). 'If something doesn't look right, go find out why': how intuitive decision making is accomplished in police first-response. *European Journal of Work and Organizational Psychology*, 29(1): 78–92.
68. Simon, H. A. (1987). Making management decisions: The role of intuition and emotion. *Academy of Management Perspectives*, 1(1): 57–64.
69. Sadler-Smith, E., & Shefy, E. (2004). The intuitive executive: Understanding and applying 'gut feel' in decision-making. *Academy of Management Perspectives*, 18(4): 76–91.
70. Benner, P. (2001). *From Novice to Expert*. Upper Saddle River: Prentice Hall, p. 3.
71. Bleakley, A., Farrow, R., Gould, D., & Marshall, R. (2003). Making sense of clinical reasoning: judgement and the evidence of the senses. *Medical Education*, 37(6): 544–552.
72. Polanyi, M. (1958/1998). *Personal Knowledge: Towards a Post-Critical Philosophy*. London: Routledge.
73. Bleakley, A., Farrow, R., Gould, D., & Marshall, R. (2003). Making sense of clinical reasoning: judgement and the evidence of the senses. *Medical Education*, 37(6): 544–552.
74. Patricia Benner, R. N., Christine Tanner, R. N., & Catherine Chesla, R. N. (Eds.). (2009). *Expertise in Nursing Practice: Caring, Clinical Judgment, and Ethics*. Springer Publishing Company, pp. 144–145, emphasis added.
75. Benner, P., & Tanner, C. (1987). How expert nurses use intuition. *The American Journal of Nursing*, 87(1): 23–34, p. 23.
76. Reyna, V. F. (2012). Risk perception and communication in vaccination decisions: A fuzzy-trace theory approach. *Vaccine*, 30(25): 3790–3797.
77. Corbin, J. C., Reyna, V. F., Weldon, R. B., & Brainerd, C. J. (2015). How reasoning, judgment, and decision making are coloured by gist-based intuition: A fuzzy-trace theory approach. *Journal of Applied Research in Memory and Cognition*, 4(4): 344–355.
78. Benner, P., Benner, P. E., Tanner, C. A., & Chesla, C. A. (2009). *Expertise in Nursing Practice: Caring, Clinical Judgment, and Ethics*. Springer Publishing Company. p. 157.
79. Ibid., p. 156.
80. Dufva, M. (2019). What is a weak signal? Sitra. Available online at: https://www.sitra.fi/en/articles/what-is-a-weak-signal/ Accessed 22.02.2022.
81. Reuters (2013). Fed missed warning signs in 2007 as crisis gained steam. 18 January 2013. Available online at: https://www.reuters.com/article/us-usa-fed-idUSBRE90H13Q20130118 Accessed 22.02.2022.
82. Lipshitz, R., & Shulimovitz, N. (2007). Intuition and emotion in bank loan officers' credit decisions. *Journal of Cognitive Engineering and Decision Making*, 1(2): 212–233.
83. Earle, T. C. (2009). Trust, confidence, and the 2008 global financial crisis. *Risk Analysis: An International Journal*, 29(6): 785–792, p. 790.

84. Huang, L., & Pearce, J. L. (2015). Managing the unknowable: The effectiveness of early-stage investor gut feel in entrepreneurial investment decisions. *Administrative Science Quarterly*, 60(4): 634–670, p. 646.
85. Baldacchino, L., Ucbasaran, D., & Cabantous, L. (2022). Linking experience to intuition and cognitive versatility in new venture ideation: A dual-process perspective. *Journal of Management Studies* (in press). Available online at: https://doi.org/10.1111/joms.12794
86. Coget, J.F. (2011). The critical decision vortex. In Sinclair, M. (Ed.). *The Handbook of Intuition Research*. Cheltenham: Edward Elgar, pp. 133–144.
87. Crossan, M. M., Lane, H. W., & White, R. E. (1999). An organizational learning framework: From intuition to institution. *Academy of Management Review*, 24(3): 522–537.
88. Akinci, C., & Sadler-Smith, E. (2019). Collective intuition: Implications for improved decision making and organizational learning. *British Journal of Management*, 30(3): 558–577.
89. This paraphrases the famous quote of the Spanish philosopher George Santayana (1863 to 1952) 'those who cannot remember the past are condemned to repeat it'.
90. Samba, C., Williams, D. W., & Fuller, R. M. (2019). The forms and use of intuition in top management teams. *The Leadership Quarterly*, (in press).
91. Ibid., p.8.
92. Eisenhardt, K. M. (1999). Strategy as strategic decision making. *Sloan Management Review*, 40(3): 65–72.
93. Hughes, V. (2014). Where do new ideas come from? *National Geographic*, 18 June 2014. Available online at: https://www.nationalgeographic.com/science/article/where-do-new-ideas-come-from. Accessed 14.03.2022.
94. Crossan, M. M., Lane, H. W., & White, R. E. (1999). An organizational learning framework: From intuition to institution. *Academy of Management Review*, 24(3): 522–537.
95. Butler, S. (2013). Tesco and the end of the supermarket space race. *The Guardian*, 12 September 2013. Available online at: https://www.theguardian.com/business/2013/sep/12/tesco-ends-supermarket-space-race Accessed 14.03.2022.
96. The end of the space race. *The Economist*. 20 April 2013. Available online at: https://www.economist.com/britain/2013/04/20/the-end-of-the-space-race Accessed 06.04.2022.

8
The Moral Sense

Overview

The main idea of this chapter is that moral judgement is based mostly on automatic (System 1, intuitive) processes rather than deliberative (System 2, analytical) processes. The 'moral intuitions' which are the product of these System 1 processes resonate with Darwin's idea of the 'moral sense'. In intuitive models of moral judgement, the 'moral mind' defaults to 'automatic' mode; for the 'manual' mode to be operative it has to be selected deliberately. The 'social intuitionist model' of moral judgement (SIM) and the related idea of 'moral foundations theory' (MFT) are explored. The work of Jonathan Haidt and his colleagues and their work on moral intuitions and intuitive ethics is centre stage. Applications of MFT in business are discussed.

Darwinian 'Moral Sense'

The idea that our mental lives are influenced by intuition and emotion as well as intellect is not new. The Scottish philosopher David Hume (1711 to 1776) in his *Treatise of Human Nature* (1740) proposed that our 'passionate nature' enables us through 'sympathy' to share in the emotions we infer intuitively to be present in others. Hume's contemporary, Adam Smith (1723 to 1790), in his second most famous book[1] *The Theory of Moral Sentiments* (1759) argued that our moral judgements are created empathetically by putting ourselves in the shoes of others and asking how they would view our conduct if they knew all of the circumstances surrounding our actions. For example, if we witnessed a man blatantly breaking the law by stealing a drug from a pharmacy but we also knew that the drug was grossly overpriced, that he could not afford to buy the drug, and that the man's wife needed the drug to save her life, would we view his conduct as morally good or bad? For Smith, moral judgements are a deliberate act of 'moral imagination' by which we empathize or sympathize with another person. By means of this imaginative act we consciously place ourselves mentally in their position in order to intuitively grasp their thoughts, emotions, and actions.[2]

Following David Hume and Adam Smith, the 'moral sense' that Darwin wrote about in *The Descent of Man* (1871) is a product of evolution through natural selection. Human evolution was conspicuous by its absence from *The Origin of Species* (1859). However, Darwin remarked tantalizingly right at the end of the book that

Intuition in Business. Eugene Sadler-Smith, Oxford University Press. © Eugene Sadler-Smith (2023).
DOI: 10.1093/oso/9780198871569.003.0008

'[through his theory] much light will be thrown on the origin of man and his history'.[3] Darwin applied his theory of evolution through natural selection to human nature and its origins, including the nature and origins of moral behaviour in *The Descent of Man*. He was influenced by Adam Smith's idea that 'the sight of another person enduring cold, hunger or fatigue revives in us some recollection of these states, which are painful even in idea'. The emotional response of sympathy impels us to recognize and relieve the sufferings of others.[4]

The moral sense, in Darwin's own words, is the 'best and highest distinction between man and the lower animals'. It leads naturally to the golden rule which lies at the 'foundation of morality': 'As ye would that men would do to you, do ye to them likewise'.[5] Darwin reconciles the tricky issues of both self-interest and sympathy for others by postulating that groups of people with strong emotional ties, forged by sentiments such as sympathy and empathy, will be at an advantage over groups that are bound together less cohesively. Those groups 'which included the greatest number of the most sympathetic members, would flourish best, and rear the greatest number of offspring'.[6] The Darwinian moral sense explains how human beings not only take pleasure in the company of others but also 'feel a certain amount of sympathy for them, and to perform various services for them'. However, these sympathies and services are by no means 'extended to all individuals'.[7]

The Darwinian moral sense makes sense from an evolutionary perspective. *Homo sapiens* is the most gregarious of all the primates, hence survival in the ancestral environment was entwined with the existence and flourishing of 'the tribe'.[8] But if this is so, what are the implications for 'selfish genes' and their 'gene survival machine' (i.e. the body) given that the members of social groups in ancestral environments were likely to include both genetically related and unrelated individuals? Any explanation of morality which implicates emotions such as sympathy and empathy and behaviours such as altruism and reciprocity towards non-kin requires also a non-selfish (i.e. cooperative) explanation. Ironically, in the foreword to the thirtieth anniversary edition of his highly influential 1976 book *The Selfish Gene* and in a noteworthy volte-face, Richard Dawkins acknowledged that a 'good alternative' to the book's chosen title 'would have been *The Cooperative Gene*'.[9] Dawkins acknowledged that cooperation and mutual assistance can flourish without departing from the fundamental laws of genetics. However, as far as the selfish gene meme[10] was concerned, the horse had already bolted. Genes were branded forever as selfish.[11]

The Darwinian moral sense is a capability that was designed into *Homo sapiens* by evolution in order to cope with the vagaries and vicissitudes of social living, i.e. of 'tribal life'. A corollary of this is that our intuitive moral sense is perhaps better adapted to relations between 'us' (the members of our tribe) rather than with 'them' (the other tribe) in the competition for scarce resources. The Harvard moral psychologist Joshua Greene in his book *Moral Tribes: Emotion, Reason and the Gap Between Us and Them* (2014) described our moral brains as designed to allow us to reap the benefits of cooperation within groups in order to facilitate competition between groups for scarce resources. In other words, intragroup cooperation is advantageous for intergroup competition. This cooperation supports the members of one 'tribe' in outcompeting the members of other 'tribes'. Genes that favour within-group cooperation are selected for because they will give, in Darwin's words, 'an immense advantage to one tribe over another'. Hence, selection operates on groups as well as on individuals.[12] Cooperation—and the thoughts, emotions, and behaviours that support within-group cooperation such as care and the relief from suffering that it brings—is not an end in itself, it is a means to an end. In Dawkins' view this end is the passing on of our genetic material.

Intuition and the Moral Sense

But where does intuition fit with this view? The underlying logic of reciprocity which supports tit-for-tat behaviour ('you scratch my back, and I'll scratch yours') could be achieved through deliberative reasoning (System 2) processes. But as we know, System 2 thinking is comparatively slow and effortful. Relying on System 2 to reason out every moral dilemma and social interaction that we are involved in would not be an efficient way for group living to proceed. It would be analogous to the firefighters that were discussed in Chapter 5 going into a group huddle before every life-or-death emergency to thrash out a detailed plan from first principles. A much more efficient way to arrive at moral judgements, as is the case with intuitive expert judgement, is to let System 1 do the heavy-lifting. In the moral domain, the heavy-lifting is leveraged through the mechanisms of feelings, for example in a flash of approval or disapproval of someone else's actions. These intuitive flashes of moral approval or disapproval are, by definition, affectively charged (since intuitions are affectively-charged judgements[13]). Moreover, intuitions are first to arrive on the scene of a moral problem because they are the products of fast, automatic System 1 processes. They oil the wheels of those moral judgements that make cooperative behaviour and group living possible, including automatic intuitive responses to issues concerning care for others, fairness, cheating, loyalty, and respect for authority.

The moral intuitions that are the products of System 1 processes have a head start in the race to win our attention in two ways. Firstly, they have a head start in terms of speed of psychological processing and invariably win the race with slower System 2 processes. Second, they have a head start phylogenetically (evolutionarily) because they have been honed over hundreds of thousands of years of human evolution through natural selection to enable us to navigate our social world effectively and efficiently. As a result, moral intuitions have become the default. The evolutionary psychologists Leda Cosmides and John Tooby illustrate these points with the example of 'free-riders' who enjoy the benefits of something without incurring the efforts or costs involved. Human beings have a moral intuition to punish free-riders, and procedures for punishing free-riders exist across cultures. This is advantageous because a social group's collective behaviours are more likely to be successful when free-riding is punished. The judgement that free-riding should be punished is a fast, automatic 'moral heuristic' (i.e. a moral intuition) which uses limited information to judge quickly and effortlessly if and how much punishment a free-rider deserves.[14]

However, Cosmides and Tooby also point out that our moral intuitions need to be handled delicately and used with care. They were designed for the 'small world' of kin, friends, and close neighbours, not for the large worlds of business corporations and economies composed of multitudes of anonymous, unrelated people. Moral intuitions evolved in ancestral environments, but how they manifest in modern organizations must be made sense of and reconciled with their original purposes in mind.

The Intuitive Dog and Its Analytical Tail

The title for this section is adapted and borrowed from an article published in the prestigious journal *Psychological Review* in 2001. It was written by the eminent social psychologist Jonathan Haidt (pronounced 'height') of New York University's Stern School of Business.[15] The article was called 'The emotional dog and its rational tail'.[16] Haidt's hypothesis is as simple as it is profound: moral judgement is based mostly on automatic (System 1, intuitive) processes rather than deliberative (System 2, analytical) processes. Metaphorically speaking, rational analysis (which is like the 'tail') is used largely to mobilize evidence to support moral intuitions (which is like the 'dog').[17]

By way of a different but complementary analogy, one of Haidt's colleagues, Joshua Greene author of *Moral Tribes*, thinks that our 'moral mind' can be thought of as a camera that has two modes of operation, a 'manual (analytical) mode' and an 'automatic (intuitive mode) mode'. When the camera is switched on it defaults to automatic. For the manual mode to be operative it has to be deliberately selected for.[18] Haidt's theory turns the traditional idea that rationality is in the driving seat of moral judgement on its head. It is a dual-process (i.e. 'two minds') theory of moral cognition in which the analytical tail (System 2) is no longer wagging the intuitive dog (System 1).

Much of the research in support of Haidt's hypothesis is from experimental lab studies in which participants' moral emotions, such as compassion, gratitude, pride, disgust, etc., are aroused and analysed. One of the ways in which Haidt and his colleagues evoked the moral emotion of disgust was by presenting participants with fictional taboo vignettes, such as 'the man who ate his already-dead dog'[i], and then gauging their responses:

> My dog was killed by a car in front of my house. I had heard that in some other countries people occasionally eat dog meat, and I was curious to find out what it tasted like. So I cut up the body and cooked it and ate it for dinner. How wrong is it for me to eat my already-dead dog for dinner?

---

[i] Haidt uses dogs in his arguments in two separate ways: (1) as a metaphor in the title of his article; (2) as an illustrative moral dilemma.

When people, for example business students in the lecture hall, are told the above story, many of them respond immediately, and often with outright revulsion, with the hard-to-shift opinion that is was wrong for me to eat my dead dog.[19] When asked to justify their intuitive response they search for reasons. Impassioned exhortations such as 'it was your pet', 'how could you do such a thing', and 'it was loyal to you, how could you eat it?' are common. When challenged through devil's advocacy, which strips away the (ir-)rationality of their arguments, students frequently resort to the justification, 'I know it's wrong, but I just can't come up with a reason. It's just *not right*'. When they realize that rational arguments against eating the already-dead dog are not going to work, they drop the rational argument. By resorting to an 'it's just wrong' response they end up being morally dumbfounded.[20] By contrast, when students are presented with moral psychologist Lawrence Kohlberg's 'Heinz dilemma' (named after the fictitious man, Heinz, who steals a drug to save his dying wife, alluded to at the beginning of this chapter), they logically weigh issues of justice and fairness. They marshal coherent and convincing rational arguments in favour of Heinz's actions.[21] In the original experiments by Haidt and his colleagues it was not possible to whip up any dumbfounding in the case of Heinz because it is not necessary as a rational argument can be made. The students could articulate the rational principle 'life is more important than property' and could not be persuaded to abandon it.[22]

Why is the already-dead dog dilemma so potent? It is potent because it immediately and intuitively elicits the powerful moral emotion of disgust.[23] The emotional response is so powerful that people cling to the judgement that it is wrong to eat an already-dead dog in the absence of a logical justification. In the UK, dogs are very popular animals, many people keep them as pets. Pets have become humanized to the extent that for some people their dog is part of the family. Eating dog meat is definitely taboo and would be reviled in the UK. On the other hand, in some parts of the world eating dog meat is accepted. In the UK, business students tortuously offer up all sorts of specious reasons for why eating the already-dead dog is wrong and rarely change their minds. Their moral intuitions are strong and sticky.

The already-dead dog dilemma is one of several fictional vignettes that Haidt and his colleagues have used in their experiments to illustrate two things. First, it shows the immediacy and power in moral judgement of uncontrollable intuitive (System 1) processes and judgements. Second, it shows how analytical (System 2) processes are mobilized in order to justify and preserve the strong and sticky initial intuition. Haidt's argument is that most moral judgements are made intuitively in a flash and are relatively impervious to disconfirmation. He also makes the important point that they are not judgements about preferences (such as liking dogs), they are moral statements that somebody did something wrong (by eating the already-dead dog). If it were simply about liking or not liking dogs it would be wrong for the dog-eater to be punished simply because he did something that some people happen to dislike but which is not de facto immoral.[24] However, becasue it is about transgressing a moral principle, that, presumably, warrants a sanction in an animal-loving society.

Social Intuitionist Model of Moral Judgement

As noted earlier, the idea that our mental lives are influenced by both intuition and intellect, and that intellectual processes may not be as under our control as we like to think they are, is not new. David Hume distinguished between reason which 'exerts itself without feeling any sensible emotion' and 'calm passions' which are distinct from 'violent [primary] emotions' and do not 'cause any disorder in the soul' but nonetheless 'often determine the will'.[25] 'Calm passions', which we might refer to as moral intuitions, are not like primary emotions such as love, joy, surprise, anger, or sadness. Metaphorically speaking, they are experienced as a subtle shift in the contours of the internal body landscape.[26] Because they are affectively charged, moral intuitions provide us with compelling guidance on how to behave., they are experienced as a felt-sense but do not rise to the level of a fully-fledged emotion.[27]

Jonathan Haidt defines 'moral intuitions' as the 'rapid, effortless moral judgements and decisions that we all make every day'.[28] He called his theory of moral judgement the 'social intuitionist model' (SIM). Its two principles, consistent with Hume ('reason is the slave of the passions') and contrary to Plato ('reason should rule'), as follows: Principle 1: intuitions come first and strategic reasoning second; Principle 2: reasoning seeks out evidence for intuitive judgements. Haidt's hypothesis is that in moral arguments the intuitive dog, not its rational tail, is in charge. The rational tail is metaphorically 'waved' however to reason in favour of moral intuitions: 'moral reasons are the tail wagged by the intuitive dog'. An implication is that to change people's minds and 'win an argument' you have to talk directly to the dog. Talking to the dog begins with speaking to its emotional system 'respectfully' and 'warmly' in a spirit of openness to dialogue before stating one's own case.[29]

The social intuitionist model is replete with analogies. One that Haidt and colleagues offered and which became especially relevant in the era of the Trump presidency is that of the president and the press secretary: the president (System 1) 'goes with his gut' and the unfortunate press secretary (System 2), in the case of President Trump it was Press Secretary Sean Spicer, is left in the unenviable position of having to justify and rationalize the president's decisions. No amount of rational argument from the members of the press will have any effect on the president because reasoning has been outsourced to the press secretary.[30] One further metaphor that has been offered by Haidt in making his case for the pre-eminence of intuitive moral judgement is that the reasoning process is like a lawyer defending a client (the intuition) rather than as an investigator seeking the truth.[31]

In the traditional rationalist model, the process of moral judgement works by firstly reasoning about an ethical dilemma and secondly coming to a moral judgement. Viewed through the rational lens, moral emotions, such as compassion or displeasure, may sometimes be taken into account, but reasoning is the driving force. For example, an employee witnesses a co-worker using their company computer during the working day to work on freelance jobs.[32] This elicits a conscious intentional reasoning process in which the colleague's behaviour is analysed (moral reasoning), and their behaviour is evaluated as morally bad (moral judgement), with accompanying feelings of disapproval. Moral reasoning is followed by moral judgement and emotion has only a bit-part role to play.

The social intuitionist model turns this process on its head. Viewed through this lens, moral judgements arise automatically and effortlessly in response to an eliciting situation. A positively or negatively charged judgement (an evaluation of 'that's good' or 'that's bad', or of 'like' or 'dislike') appears involuntarily in conscious awareness. It arrives in a flash without any immediate awareness of the processes by which it was arrived at. It is analogous to the feeling of liking or disliking a piece of music or a work of art (an aesthetic judgement). One is struck immediately with a feeling or liking/approval or disliking/disapproval. In the previous example, witnessing a co-worker using the company computer to work on freelance jobs in work time automatically elicits a feeling of disapproval as 'that's bad'. Their behaviour is evaluated intuitively as morally bad (moral judgement). A conscious intentional reasoning process then provides a post hoc analysis of why their behaviour is judged to be wrong (moral reasoning). The sequencing of the processes in the social intuitionist model is 'intuition-then-judgement-then-reasoning'.

The social intuitionist model is 'intuitionist' because an affectively charged moral intuition (the outcome of non-conscious System 1 processes) is the source of the moral judgement. The judgement of 'that's good/right, or virtuous' or 'that's bad/wrong, or a vice' is accompanied by a flash of approval or disapproval. This is followed by a verbally persuasive post hoc moral reason, which is a deliberative, conscious System 2 process.

The social intuitionist model is 'social' because one way in which people can make sense of as well as justify and defend their initial intuitions is by sharing their responses with others (as well as by mulling it over themselves). Haidt included the social component for a number of reasons. First, he wanted to capture the give and take of moral debate. In public discussion and debate, other people can challenge our initial intuitions, which then may cause us to change our minds, for example through rational argument, devil's advocacy, reflection, etc. Second, one person's intuitively-derived moral judgement may also exert a direct effect on another person's moral judgement by sparking their moral intuitions. For example, one person's reaction of disgust to a moral dilemma can be echoed and elicit disgust in others.

The social part of the model can account for the emergence of groups norms and ethical climates in business organizations which may end up promoting ethical or unethical behaviours. Ethical climate provides employees with norms that simplify moral judgements. The climate and its norms, which provide decision-makers with cues for how to behave, make moral judgements more intuitive.[33] The upside of this is that through exposure and experience the organizational ethical climate can habituate ethical behaviours through a process of organizational learning that begins with interpretation of moral intuitions and ends with their institutionalization. The downside is that an organizational ethical climate in which immoral behaviours are intuitively recognized as being acceptable supports and enables moral misdemeanours. In the case of the Enron corporate scandal, the company's unethical culture gave rise to a groupthink in which unethical behaviour was condoned. It was institutionalized from the deeply dysfunctional and defective leadership of its bosses Kenneth Lay and Jeffrey Skilling. Their toxic tone from the top had a profound effect on the moral behaviour of its employees and ended up mattering more than ethical codes by the creation of an unethical organizational climate.[34]

The social intuitionist model's intuition-judgement-reasoning process is efficient because the vast majority of everyday moral judgements can be handled automatically (analogous to pattern recognition in recognition-primed decision-making). Only in exceptional situations, such as when two moral intuitions conflict, intuition and analysis conflict, or the social situation demands a thorough examination of the case, is moral reasoning mobilized (analogous to mental simulation in recognition-primed decision-making).[35] For the most part, moral judgement is set to automatic mode and switched to manual only occasionally when the situation requires (for example if a formal analysis is required) or when we proactively chose to switch from intuition to analysis.

The Neurobiology of Moral Intuitions

Evidence for a biological basis for moral intuitions can be found in the work of the neurologist Antonio Damasio and colleagues. Chapter 6 described his work, which discovered the role played by the ventro-medial (middle-bottom) region of the prefrontal cortex (the VMPFC) in the infusion of gut feelings into rational decision-making. To recap some of the key points from Chapter 6, Antonio Damasio and his colleagues' discovered in their Iowa Gambling Task (IGT) experiments that people with damage to the VMPFC (referred to as 'VMPFC patients') continued to choose disadvantageously from the loaded 'bad' decks of cards in the Iowa Gambling Task (see Chapter 6). Participants with an intact VMPFC (referred to as 'normal' participants) learned unconsciously to avoid the bad decks. Normals' gut feelings guided them towards a strategy by which they were able to make modest gains in the gambling task. VMPFC patients accrued large losses because they lacked the gut feelings that could have steered them away from the bad decks. The normals experienced increased skin conductance responses prior to making their choices. These were the physical signals (somatic markers) that guided them towards advantageous behaviours. The VMPFC patients did not show any such responses.

Damasio and his team also conducted experiments in which they showed normals and VMPFC patients gruesome images and monitored their skin conductance responses. These images aroused strong neurophysiological responses in normals. VMPFC patients showed no neurophysiological response even though the patients knew that they should feel something. Damasio and colleagues referred to this phenomenon as 'acquired sociopathy'. It seems as though damage to the VMPFC can inure people to the requirements and standards of social norms. It can result in personality change and a range of anti-social behaviours, such as obstinacy, vacillation, capriciousness, impatience, and profanity.[36]

Another study used the well-known 'trolley problem' to compare VMPFC patients' and normals' responses to personal (pushing one person off a footbridge over a railway track to stop a runaway trolley car hitting five people) versus impersonal (turning the runaway trolley away from five people but towards one person) moral dilemmas.[37] In the personal moral dilemma, the VMPFC patients overwhelmingly endorsed pushing the person off the footbridge, whereas the normals were averse to doing so. In the impersonal moral dilemma, there was no difference between normals and VMPFC patients. The researchers concluded that impeded functioning of the VMPFC meant that the VMPFC patients' were bereft of emotional responses against personally and directly inflicting harm on another person. This made their moral choices hyper-utilitarian consistent with Haidt's social intuitionist model. This is further evidence that affect (including moral intuitions and emotions) plays an important role in the generation of moral judgements rather than affect following on from a moral judgement.

Moral Foundations Theory

The 'moral sense' which Darwin wrote about in *The Descent of Man* (1871) anticipated some of the moral intuitions identified by modern behavioural and brain sciences by almost a century-and-a-half. The moral sense and moral intuition need an integrative framework which connects them to evolutionary theory, genetics, biology, psychology, and anthropology. One such unifying framework is 'moral foundations theory' (MFT). Moral foundations theory was created by a group of social and cultural psychologists including Jonathan Haidt, Jesse Graham, and Craig Joseph in the early 2000s. As well as the fundamental idea that an individual's virtues, vices, and moral judgements are intuitively generated, MFT also helps to explain why individuals and groups differ in what they see as good/right and bad/wrong and why virtues and vices are culturally variable. It helps to explain why eating your already-dead dog is judged as wrong, but only sometimes.

The main idea of moral foundations theory is social-intuitionist: System 1 processes (in the form of moral intuitions) are in the 'driving seat' and System 2 processes (in the form of reasoning) only have a role to play after the fact in justifying intuitive moral judgement to others, and sometimes to oneself.[38] But moral foundations theory goes further in proposing that our moral intuitions have five foundations. These function like 'taste buds' or taste receptors on the 'moral tongue'.[39] The five moral receptors were evolved in response to the challenges that our species faced in its ancestral environment. They were adaptive in relation to the safety of self and kin, managing group processes and negotiating hazards in the challenging physical environment of the Pleistocene (which ended about 12,000 years ago). The foundations are social because adaptive mechanisms, such as the detection of cheating, support effective group-living. The evolution of these mechanisms favoured the reproductive success of individuals who could sense patterns in the social world and use them to conduct social interactions and resolve social problems efficiently.

For example, one of the primary adaptive challenges that any species faces is the protection of its young and of vulnerable or injured members of its social group. The perception of suffering, distress in, or threats to, its young or to a member of its group elicits a fast, automatic (i.e. intuitive) affective response, for example concern and compassion, which then motivates behaviour towards avoiding or relieving suffering or distress. Additionally, group-living would be supported by responses that approved of individuals who displayed the virtues of caring and kindness and disapproved of the vices of being unkind and uncaring. These behaviours would be selected for in the ancestral environment. The relevant moral module in this instance is referred to in moral foundations theory as 'care'; its contrastive is 'harm'. 'Care/harm' is one of five moral modules on which cultures construct their ethical frameworks. These ethical frameworks are distinctive locally but only within broad parameters circumscribed by the moral foundations, for example the moral reaction to eating an already-dead dog is that it is frowned upon in some cultures but not in others, whilst in those other cultures the moral emotion of disgust, which caused already-dead dog eating to be frowned upon, might be elicited by a different moral issue.

The five moral modules are the foundations of an evolved system of 'intuitive ethics'. They are (with their contrastives in brackets):[40] (1) 'care' ('harm') reaps the benefits of protection and care of young and vulnerable or injured members of the group. It is triggered by suffering and distress. It manifests affectively as compassion, empathy, and sympathy, and ethically as the virtues of caring and kindness and the vices of cruelty and unkindness. In business this could manifest as charitable giving or CSR initiatives; (2) 'fairness' ('cheating') reaps the benefits of dyadic, i.e. two-way, cooperation. It is triggered negatively in response to cheating/deception, eliciting disapproval. It is triggered positively, thus eliciting approval, in response to cooperation. It manifests affectively as anger/guilt or gratitude and ethically as the virtues of fairness, justice, honesty, and trustworthiness and the vices of dishonesty and untrustworthiness. In business this could manifest as flashes of disapproval for free-loading co-workers; (3) 'loyalty' ('betrayal') reaps the benefits of group, i.e. tribe, cooperation. It is triggered by threats or challenges to the group social structure. It manifests affectively as group pride and belongingness and the disapproval of defectors and traitors. It manifests in the virtues of loyalty, patriotism, and self-sacrifice, and the vices of disloyalty, treachery, and treason. In business this could manifest as brand loyalty or organizational commitment; (4) 'authority' ('subversion') reaps the benefits of the forging of beneficial vertical/hierarchical relationships within groups. It is triggered positively by signs of dominance/submission and negatively by agitation/sedition. It manifests affectively as esteem, deference, and respect or fear, and as the virtues of obedience and deference and the vices of disrespect, insolence, and subversion. In business this could manifest as respect for a boss on the basis of their legitimate, expert or referent power (in terms of French and Raven's five sources of power); (5) 'purity'[41] ('degradation') reaps the benefits of the avoidance of contamination from agents in the environment such as toxins, parasites, and microbes. It is triggered by waste, unpalatable substances, pathogens, microbes, decaying organic matter, or diseased people. It manifests affectively as disgust and revulsion and as the virtues of cleanliness, piety, and temperance and the vices of lust, excess, gluttony, and intemperance. In business this could manifest as the marketing of personal hygiene and household cleaning products[42]

Moral foundations theory makes a distinction between the original triggers in the ancestral environment (sometimes called the 'proper environment') for which the module evolved and current triggers in the present-day environment (sometimes called the 'actual environment') to which the module is co-opted. For example, in the case of fairness, a current trigger would be queue-jumping (since there were likely no queues as we know them in the ancestral environment, although there may have been a pecking order). For authority a current trigger would be respect for supervisors, managers and executives (see above) whereas in the ancestral environment it would be respect for the leader or elders of the tribe.[43]

The modules are prewired[44] not hardwired. This implies that humans are not born with care or any of the other modules fully formed, rather the modules are 'innate' or 'innately prepared'. By innately prepared, the moral foundations researchers mean that the modules are organized in advance of experience (through genetics) and are brought into their full form through social and cultural experiences. How the moral modules manifest ultimately depends both on genetics (nature) and environment (nurture). As an example of how culture shapes the final form that modules take, Haidt points out that in Western societies the scope of the care module has expanded so that we have come to feel compassion in response to many more types of animal suffering, such as battery hens and the testing of cosmetics on animals, than was the case only a few decades ago. Appealing to this moral module in business was pioneered in the 1980s by The Body Shop and its then novel but now widely accepted maxim of 'Against Animal Testing' in its fight for animal rights.

The malleability of the moral modules is such that they can be fine-tuned negatively. Haidt and his colleague Craig Joseph point out that it is possible to teach adults to be cruel to certain classes of people. They give the example of how racism can be induced by invoking the purity module in order to trigger flashes of disgust at certain groups. They noted how Hitler manipulated the moral modules to trigger flashes of disapproval against various cultural and religious groups in Nazi Germany as a prequel to the Holocaust.[45] Current triggers can be modified by culture in only a very short time and be made to apply to a broad domain of social and moral judgements. The original triggering neural mechanisms, which are the basis for moral intuitions, remain intact for longer periods and would require much more time to be modified through genetic evolution.[46] For this reason moral foundations theorists refer to the moral mind as having a 'first draft', which gets 'heavily edited' by experience and culture:[47]

> The mind is like a book. The genes write the first draft into neural tissue (although there may be no genes 'for' any specific modules or for any specific paragraphs in the book). Experience (nurture) then revises the draft. Some chapters of the book are heavily edited by experience in some cultures but only lightly edited in others.[48]

For example, people in all cultures have innately prepared moral concerns about purity. In some cultures this is encoded in norms about whether it is right to eat one's already-dead dog. In the UK, it is definitely not considered to be right, whereas in other non-Western cultures eating dog meat is perceived differently.[49] Hence, moral foundations theory can account both for similarities amongst peoples (for example, moral judgements relating to purity are an automatic response) and for differences between peoples, cultures, and business organizations in their moral codes, which means that what counts as impure, for example, can sometimes vary quite considerably. The culture and ethical climate of a business organization can play an important role in 'editing' and thus shaping the moral codes of employees in terms of the five moral modules. Enron shaped employees' moral code towards unethical behaviours.

Jesse Graham and colleagues use the taste metaphor and the five taste receptors on the human tongue (sweet, sour, salt, bitter, umami) to explain how this works. Cuisines, like moral codes, are cultural constructions that are shaped by history, but at the end of the day any cuisine has to please tongues that evolved to taste sweet, sour salt, bitter, and umami. Likewise, the 'moral cuisine' of any culture has to be constructed on the basis of the five prewired moral modules (care, fairness, loyalty, authority, and purity).[50] Evolutionary prewiring made learning moral intuitions relating to the five moral modules highly efficient and effective. It is analogous to a domain-specific prewiring for fear of certain objects such as snakes, which is easy to invoke, but not others such as flowers, for which it is hard to invoke an instinctive fear[51] (aside from members of the small and unfortunate group of people who are 'anthophobic', i.e. have a fear of flowers).

The Moral Sense in Business

Moral intuition and moral foundations theory have a number of applications in business. One of the most promising areas is in marketing. Values-based marketing involves aligning a company's core values tightly with its business strategy. It creates a deeper and more meaningful relationship between brands and customers by appealing to its customers' values. The emphasis shifts from being product-centric to customer-centric. For example, Kraft was one of the first companies to stop advertising junk food to children when it realized that it was out of step with changes in customers' values and ethics. The CEO at the time, Roger K. Deromedi, commented in an interview that 'Our relationship with consumers is about trust. If you don't align with society and you get out of step with that, then you're going to destroy shareholder value.'[52] Ben and Jerry's Ice Cream was one of the first-movers in value-based marketing in the early 2000s. Ben and Jerry's had a vision to 'seek out progressive, values-driven strategies and corporate practices', including the values of economic and social justice and eliminating negative environmental impact.[53] In so doing Ben and Jerry's were, perhaps naïvely but nonetheless insightfully, appealing to the moral foundations of care for individuals and the environment.

Core values can be brand-specific. For example, in the sports' equipment company Under Armour's 'I will what I want campaign', the espoused values were: freedom, purpose, tradition, security, achievement, and pleasure.[54] A question for values-based marketing executives is 'which values?'. So far in value-based marketing, the values have tended to be quite general. They have not been linked to any specific moral philosophy or moral theory. Moral foundations theory offers businesses a morally robust, generic set of ethically based values on which to base their values-based marketing strategies. This would mean that advertisements could be designed deliberately to intuitively elicit moral emotions in the five moral domains of care, fairness, loyalty, authority, and purity. In doing so they are more likely to create deeper, more purposeful and meaningful relationships between the customer and the product or service on offer. They are also based on up-to-date scientific evidence about our species' innately prepared moral responses to given stimuli.

The social psychologist Sena Koleva and her colleagues have explored how the moral foundations can be applied in the branding and selling of products and services through value-based, or more appropriately moral foundations-based, marketing. They offer the example of a 'Huggies' advertisement which depicts a mother lovingly caring for her baby, which is designed to trigger positive moral intuitions by appealing to the care moral foundation. IKEA's values of cost-consciousness and simplicity resonate with the moral foundations of care and purity.[55] Koleva and colleagues also point out that moral foundations can be mobilized to make products more appealing even when they have little to do with morality; for example, a car can be marketed for its safety features (the care moral module), affordability (fairness), 'made in Britain' (loyalty), and environmental credentials (purity). This creates a patchwork of moral associations that connect with a broad audience. Messages can be tailored to a single dominant moral foundation; for example, zero emissions for an electric vehicle (purity) would connect with consumers who have specific moral concerns around climate change and sustainability. Moral foundations can be used to create seemingly incongruous combinations; for example, Persil's 'dirt is good' advertising campaign cleverly weaves the idea that progressive parents have free-thinking children who play outdoors, get dirty, and expose themselves beneficially to various natural pathogens, hence making them more disease-resistant (the care module), whilst the soap powder product (Persil) makes their children's clothes clean again (the purity module).

Valued-based marketing utilizes the fact that the underlying System 1 processes from which the moral intuitions emanate tend to be imagistic, metaphorical, and narrative-based. This is important if the aim is to mobilize pro-social or pro-environmental behaviour. For example, dramatic images of environmental destruction are more likely to appeal to care- and purity-related moral intuitions than are verbatim statistics about climate change. The latter is attuned to the analytical System 2, whilst the former is attuned to the heuristic System 1. For example, in 2021, levels of CO_2 reached 415ppm, the highest ever in recent geological history. This is an important piece of objective, scientific data. However, being a simple fact means that it appeals more to abstract, analytical System 2 processing and people need backgournd knowledge to understand how bad this really is. However, the sterile figure of 415pmm is unlikely to arouse potent moral emotions from System 1. Hence it will be less likely to mobilize pro-environmental behaviours.[56] When formulated and presented through vivid imagery or compelling stories, for example Al Gore's documentary film *An Inconvenient Truth* (2006) or the engaging chronicle in Nathaniel Rich's book *Losing Earth* (2019), climate change narratives stand a much better chance than purely analytical narratives of influencing pro-environmental behaviour, since they will heighten 'hot' intuitive moral emotions and hence catalyse a behavioural rather than a purely 'cold' cognitive response.[57]

Humans are storytelling animals.[58] Stories appeal to System 1 (also known as the experiential system, see Chapter 5) because they are emotionally engaging, evoke images, and present the temporal unfolding of events that parallels lived experience.[59] The appeal and comprehensibility of narratives and images, mean that individuals can be persuaded more readily to make choices and take actions. This is a consequence of the coherence, fidelity, and potency of stories and images. The emotions that many stories evoke are moral emotions. For example, the Bible teaches ethics through parables ('earthly stories with heavenly meanings') rather than through abstract analytical discourse. Advertisers have long-recognized that visual images evoke stronger affective responses than words.[60] Combining visual images and a compelling story communicate directly with System 1 and amplifies the potency of the evoked emotions, with consequential effects on moral judgement and decision-making.

Another potential application of moral foundations identified by Sena Koleva and her colleagues is fostering values-based organizational cultures. Values-based organizations (VBOs) have a culture that is shaped by a set of ground rules which form the basis for everything that the organization does, both in its internal exchanges between employees and in its external exchanges between the organization and its stakeholders, including its community and the natural environment. Managers and leaders play a vital role in shaping a values-based culture through the standards that they embody and the ethical example they set.[61] For example, the high premium that South West Airlines' placed on the value of service based on the moral foundation of care meant that a pilot at Los Angeles airport once held up his plane's departure so that a man who was stuck in security and travelling to visit his dying grandson could make the flight.[62] Conversely, the leadership at WorldCom created a dysfunctional ethical culture in which the vice of cheating (the company inflated its assets by almost $11bn making it one of the biggest accounting scandals ever) rather than the virtue of fairness became normalized in the tone from the top of the organization.

Moral foundations provide a general framework for building a value-based culture that is intertwined with employees' moral intuitions in the five domains. In this way, the fit between the person (their moral intuitions) and their organization (its ethical climate) can be enhanced with a positive effect on employees' satisfaction, commitment, loyalty, and performance.[63] A values-based, or moral foundations-based, culture gives organizations and people a way to unite around a common set of ethical values of care, fairness, loyalty, authority, and purity. These foundations are both robust and malleable, in that they are biologically prewired but shaped by learning and experience to be culturally-specific. Koleva and colleagues single out loyalty as essential to the internal health and hence the success of work groups and to the establishment of virtuous behavioural norms in the workplace. For example, the American online shoe and clothing retailer Zappos began the process of building a value-based culture by eliciting from employees core values ('What we live by') expressed as a small number of very simple rules: be humble, be passionate, be determined, be open, be honest, be adventurous, and be open-minded.[64] The first step in building a moral values-based organization would be to uncover the moral foundations that matter most to its stakeholders. The next step would be to take the necessary steps to create a culture in which the foundations can flourish. Once habituated and established, the foundations serve as a moral compass that a particular group of stakeholders, for example employees, can reference when they are confronted by ethical challenges.[65]

One of the strengths of the moral foundations approach is that it is pluralist. Workplace moral values and cultures cannot be assumed to be universal or to manifest in the same ways across different cultures and subcultures. For example, in politics, conservatives rely more heavily on the foundations of authority, fairness, and purity. For liberals, the authority foundation may be seen to be too close to oppression, and the purity module is tainted by the attitudes of some conservatives that lead to discrimination against certain groups in society.[66] In spite of the indisputable intergroup differences, Haidt reminds us that versions of care, fairness, loyalty, authority, and purity are valued across most cultures and that moral foundations theory links this long-established fact (for example, as evidenced in the various ancient wisdom traditions) with an evolutionarily, psychologically, and neuroscientifically robust account of the moral intuitions that are the drivers of most of our day-to-day moral judgements in our personal and professional lives.

Summary

1. The main idea of this chapter is that nature has prepared us innately to respond intuitively to ethical dilemmas based on affective responses emanating from the moral modules of care/harm, fairness/cheating, loyalty/betrayal, authority/subversion, and purity/degradation.
2. These modules and their associated cognitive and affective processes are the soft wiring of human beings' 'moral sense'.
3. This moral sense enables us to respond automatically and intuitively (and hence efficiently) to many of the ethical dilemmas that we face in our day-to-day lives.
4. Intuitive moral judgements are often justified after the fact (post hoc) by analytical reasoning.
5. The idea that intuitions come first and reasoning second is contrary to rationalist models of moral judgement.

6. The idea that intuitions come first (via reflexive System 1 processes) and reasoning second (via reflective System 2 processes) is consistent with dual-process theory.
7. An innately prepared moral sense designed for social living was adapted in ancestral environments to reap the benefits of cooperation *within* rather than *between* social groups.
8. Moral intuitions were designed for the small world of kin and the immediate members of one's tribe rather than the modern world of large-scale urban living and organizational life.
9. Whilst moral intuitions do oil the wheels of group-living, they need to be handled with care lest they bias our ethical judgements and moral behaviours hence moral judgements should proceed both reflexively and reflectively.

Endnotes

1. Smith's most famous book is *The Wealth of Nations* (1776) but some, such as the politician and author Jesse Norman, have argued that his *Theory of Moral Sentiments* (published in 1759 a century before Darwin's *Origin of Species*) has been overshadowed unjustly.
2. Norman, J. (2018). *Adam Smith: What He Thought, and Why It Matters*. London: Penguin.
3. Darwin, C. (1959) *On the Origin of Species*. London: John Murray, p. 462.
4. Laurent, J., & Cockfield, G. (2007). Adam Smith, Charles Darwin and the moral sense. In Cockfield, G., Firth, A., & Laurent, J. (Eds.). (2007). *New Perspectives on Adam Smith's The Theory of Moral Sentiments*. Cheltenham: Edward Elgar Publishing, pp. 141–162.
5. Darwin, C. (1871). *Descent of man, and selection in relation to sex*. London: John Murray, p. 127.
6. Ibid., p. 107.
7. Ibid.
8. Sadler-Smith, E. (2012). Before virtue: Biology, brain, behaviour, and the 'moral sense'. *Business Ethics Quarterly*, 22(2): 351–376, p. 356.
9. Dawkins, R. (2006). *The Selfish Gene: 30th Anniversary Edition*. Oxford: Oxford University Press, p. ix.
10. Richard Dawkins coined the word 'meme' in his 1976 bestseller *The Selfish Gene*. The word 'meme' is ascribed to an idea, behaviour or style that spreads from person to person within a culture. https://www.wired.co.uk/article/richard-dawkins-memes
11. Mutalik, P. (2017). Are genes selfish or cooperative. *Quanta Magazine*, 14 September 2017. Available online at: https://www.quantamagazine.org/are-genes-selfish-or-cooperative-20170914/ Accessed 18.02.2022.
12. Darwin, C. (1871). *Descent of Man, and Selection in Relation to Sex*. London: John Murray, p.132. For a discussion of potential mechanisms for the explanation of altruistic behaviours towards non-kin see Sadler-Smith, E. (2012). Before virtue: Biology, brain, behaviour, and the 'moral sense'. *Business Ethics Quarterly*, 22(2), 351–376, pp. 356–357.
13. Dane, E., & Pratt, M. G. (2007). Exploring intuition and its role in managerial decision making. *Academy of Management Review*, 32(1): 33–54.

14. Cosmides, L., & Tooby, J. (2006). Evolutionary psychology, moral heuristics and the law. In Gigerenzer, G., & Engel, C (Eds.). *Heuristics and the Law*. Cambridge, MA: MIT Press, pp. 181–212.
15. In his 2012 book *The Righteous Mind* (p. 48), Haidt regrets not calling his article 'The intuitive dog and its rational tail' which would have avoided any inference that morality is always driven by emotion per se.
16. According to Google Scholar it has been cited by other researchers over 500 times a year on average since it was published. By way of comparison Kahneman and Tversky's seminal article of 1974 on heuristics and biases which forever changed the face of decision research has been cited around 400 times a year (based on a Google Scholar search on 04.10.21): (1) Haidt, J. (2001). The emotional dog and its rational tail: A social intuitionist approach to moral judgment. *Psychological Review*, 108(4): 814–843 had 10,319 citations; (2) Tversky, A., & Kahneman, D. (1974). Judgment under uncertainty: Heuristics and biases. *Science*, 185(4157): 1124–1131 had 43,105 citations.
17. Haidt, J. (no date). Extended biography. Available online at: http://righteousmind.com/wp-content/uploads/2015/08/JonathanHaidt_ExtendedBiography.pdf Accessed 18.02.2022.
18. Greene, J. (2014). *Moral Tribes: Emotion, Reason, and the Gap between Us and Them*. London: Penguin, p. 300.
19. I have never owned a dog. I did not eat my own or anyone else's dead dog. It is a fictitious vignette.
20. Haidt, J., Bjorklund, F., & Murphy, S. (2000). *Moral Dumbfounding: When Intuition Finds No Reason*. Unpublished manuscript, University of Virginia, 191–221.
21. Kohlberg, L. (1984). *Essays in moral development. Vol. II. The psychology of moral development*. San Francisco: Harper & Row; Haidt, J. (2012). *The Righteous Mind*. London: Allen Lane, p. 36.
22. Haidt, J. (2012). *The Righteous Mind*. London: Allen Lane, pp. 37, 44
23. Haidt, J., Bjorklund, F., & Murphy, S. (2000). *Moral Dumbfounding: When Intuition Finds No Reason*. Unpublished manuscript, University of Virginia, pp. 191–221.
24. Haidt, J. (2012). *The Righteous Mind*. London: Allen Lane, p. 44.
25. Hume Texts Online. Available online at: https://davidhume.org/texts/t/full, T 2.3.3.8, SBN 417; https://davidhume.org/texts/t/full, T 2.3.3.9, SBN 417-8. Accessed 18.02.2022.
26. Damasio, A. R. (1994). *Descartes' error*. Penguin: Random House, p. 154
27. Greene, J. (2014). *Moral tribes: Emotion, reason, and the gap between us and them*. London: Penguin, p.300; Haidt, J. (2012). *The Righteous Mind*. London: Allen Lane, p. 45.
28. Ibid.
29. Ibid., p. 48.
30. Haidt, J., Bjorklund, F., & Murphy, S. (2000). *Moral Dumbfounding: When Intuition Finds No Reason*. Unpublished manuscript, University of Virginia, pp. 191–221, p. 3
31. Haidt, J. (2001). The emotional dog and its rational tail: a social intuitionist approach to moral judgment. *Psychological Review*, 108(4): 814–834, p. 820.
32. Michigan State University (2022) 5 Common Ethical Issues in the Workplace. Available online at: https://www.michiganstateuniversityonline.com/resources/leadership/common-ethical-issues-in-the-workplace/ Accessed 18.02.2022.
33. Kim, D., & Vandenberghe, C. (2020). Ethical leadership and team ethical outcomes: the roles of team moral efficacy and ethical climate. *Academy of Management Proceedings*, (1): 17,273. Briarcliff Manor, NY 10,510: Academy of Management.

34. Sims, R. R., & Brinkmann, J. (2003). Enron ethics (or: culture matters more than codes). *Journal of Business Ethics*, 45(3): 243–256.
35. Haidt, J. (2001). The emotional dog and its rational tail: a social intuitionist approach to moral judgment. *Psychological Review*, 108(4), 814–834, p. 820.
36. Evans, G. (2020). Phineas Gage. *Simply Psychology*. Available online at: https://www.simplypsychology.org/phineas-gage.html Accessed 18.02.2022.
37. Young, L., Bechara, A., Tranel, D., Damasio, H., Hauser, M., & Damasio, A. (2010). Damage to ventromedial prefrontal cortex impairs judgment of harmful intent. *Neuron*, 65(6): 845–851.
38. Suhler, C. L., & Churchland, P. (2011). Can innate, modular 'foundations' explain morality? Challenges for Haidt's moral foundations theory. *Journal of Cognitive Neuroscience*, 23(9): 2103–2116.
39. Haidt, J. (2012). *The Righteous Mind*. London: Allen Lane.
40. Based on the following tabulated summaries: Haidt, J. (2012). *The Righteous Mind*. London: Allen Lane; Haidt, J., & Joseph, C. (2007). The moral mind: How 5 sets of innate moral intuitions guide the development of many culture-specific virtues, and perhaps even modules. In Carruthers, P., Laurence, S., & Stich, S. (Eds.). *The Innate Mind*, Vol. 3. New York: Oxford University Press, pp. 367–391.
41. Purity is also referred to as 'sanctity' by some moral foundations theorists.
42. Haidt, J. (2012). *The Righteous Mind*. London: Allen Lane, p. 125. In the original formulation by Jonathan Haidt and Craig Joseph published in 2004 there were four moral modules: 'suffering' (renamed 'care'), 'hierarchy' (renamed 'authority'), 'reciprocity' (renamed 'loyalty'), and 'purity' (renamed 'sanctity'), see: Haidt, J., & Joseph, C. (2004). Intuitive ethics: How innately prepared intuitions generate culturally variable virtues. *Daedalus*, 133(4): 55–66.
43. Haidt, J. (2012) . *The Righteous Mind*. London: Allen Lane, p. 124.
44. Haidt, J. (2012) *The Righteous Mind*. London: Allen Lane, p. 130.
45. Haidt, J., & Joseph, C. (2004). Intuitive ethics: How innately prepared intuitions generate culturally variable virtues. *Daedalus*, 133(4): 55–66, p. 63.
46. Haidt, J. (2012) . *The Righteous Mind*. London: Allen Lane, p. 124.
47. Koleva, S., Beall, E., & Graham, J. (2017). Moral foundations: Building value through moral pluralism. In Sison, A. J., Beabout, G. R., & Ferrero, I. (Eds.). *Handbook of Virtue Ethics in Business and Management*. Dordrecht: Springer, pp. 521–530, p. 524.
48. Haidt, J., & Joseph, C. (2011). How moral foundations theory succeeded in building on sand: A response to Suhler and Churchland. *Journal of Cognitive Neuroscience*, 23(9): 2117–2122, p. 2120.
49. Koleva, S., Beall, E., & Graham, J. (2017). Moral foundations: Building value through moral pluralism. In Sison, A. J., Beabout, G. R., & Ferrero, I. (Eds.). *Handbook of Virtue Ethics in Business and Management*. Dordrecht: Springer, pp. 521–530, p. 524.
50. Graham, J. et al. (2013). Moral foundations theory: The pragmatic validity of moral pluralism. In Devine, P., & Plant, A. (Eds.). *Advances in Experimental Social Psychology*, Vol. 47. Burlington: Academic Press, pp. 55–130.
51. Ibid.; Mineka, S., & Cook, M. (1988). Social learning and the acquisition of snake fear in monkeys. In Zentall, T. R., & Galef, Jr., B. G. (Eds.). *Social Learning: Psychological and Biological Perspectives* (pp. 51–73). Mahwah, NJ: Lawrence Erlbaum Associates.

52. Royston, M. (2006). What is values-based marketing. *Credit Unions*. Available online at: https://www.creditunions.com/articles/what-is-values-based-marketing/ Accessed 18.02.2022
53. Cross, V. (no date). The goals of values-based marketing. *Chron*. Available onlie at: https://smallbusiness.chron.com/goals-valuesbased-marketing-21639.html Accessed 18.02.2022
54. Campaign Creators (2018) We're talking about… Values-based marketing. *Campaign Creators*. Available online at: https://www.campaigncreators.com/blog/what-were-talking-about…values-based-marketing Accessed 18.02.2022.
55. Edvardsson, B., Enquist, B., & Hay, M. (2006). Values-based service brands: narratives from IKEA. *Managing Service Quality*, 16(3): 230–246.
56. Morris, B. S., Chrysochou, P., Christensen, J. D., Orquin, J. L., Barraza, J., Zak, P. J., & Mitkidis, P. (2019). Stories vs. facts: triggering emotion and action-taking on climate change. *Climatic Change*, 154(1): 19–36.
57. Morris, B. S., Chrysochou, P., Christensen, J. D., Orquin, J. L., Barraza, J., Zak, P. J., & Mitkidis, P. (2019). Stories vs. facts: triggering emotion and action-taking on climate change. *Climatic Change*, 154(1): 19–36.
58. Dautenhahn, K. (2002). The origins of narrative: In search of the transactional format of narratives in humans and other social animals. *International Journal of Cognition and Technology*, 1(1): 97–123.
59. Epstein, S. (2013). *Cognitive experiential theory*. Oxford: Oxford University Press, p. 32.
60. Ambler, T., Ioannides, A., & Rose, S. (2000). Brands on the brain: Neuro-images of advertising. *Business Strategy Review*, 11(3): 17–30.
61. SHRM (no date). What does it mean to be a values-based organization? Available online at: https://www.shrm.org/resourcesandtools/tools-and-samples/hr-qa/pages/whatdoesitmeantobeavalues-basedorganization.aspx Accessed 18.02.2022.
62. Avon, N. (2011). Pilot holds flight for man going to see dying grandson. CNN, 15 January 2011. Available online at: http://edition.cnn.com/2011/TRAVEL/01/14/southwest.pilot.holds.flight/index.htm Accessed 18.02.2022; Rhoades, A. (no date). Building a high-performance culture through culture. LLR. Available online at: https://www.llrpartners.com/growth-bit/values-based-culture-rhoades/ Accessed 18.02.2022.
63. Judge, T. A. (1994). Person–organization fit and the theory of work adjustment: Implications for satisfaction, tenure, and career success. *Journal of Vocational Behaviour*, 44(1): 32–54; Silverthorne, C. (2004). The impact of organizational culture and person-organization fit on organizational commitment and job satisfaction in Taiwan. *Leadership and Organization Development Journal*, 25(7): 592–599.
64. Zappos (no date). What we live by. *Zappos*. Available online at: https://www.zappos.com/about/what-we-live-by Accessed 18.02.2022.
65. Deutch, K. 2016). 5 ways to create a value-driven company culture. *Gusto Blog*. Available online at: https://gusto.com/blog/people-management/5-ways-to-create-a-values-driven-company-culture Accessed 18.02.2022.
66. Haidt, J., & Joseph, C. (2004). Intuitive ethics: How innately prepared intuitions generate culturally variable virtues. *Daedalus*, 133(4): 55–66.

9
The Social Sense

Overview

The main idea of this chapter is that many of our everyday social judgements are accomplished intuitively through the processes of mirroring, mentalizing, and thin slicing. The process of mentalizing combined with mirroring gives us the ability to anticipate and make sense of the thoughts that may be driving another person's behaviour. Whilst mirroring is automatic, fast, and unconscious, mentalizing can be more deliberate. Both are required in order to arrive at complex social judgements. The process of 'thin slicing', discovered by Naline Ambady, is fast and automatic and occurs outside of conscious awareness; it is used to arrive at judgements about another person's affective state, motivations and intentions. Matthew Lieberman's dual-system model (a 'reflexive' X-System and a 'reflective' C-System) of social cognition is discussed as an overall framework that captures both the social and the moral senses. The applications of mentalizing, social intuition, thin slicing, and the X- and C-Systems in business are explored.

Mentalizing

Consider the following fictional vignette.

> A thief who has just stolen a bottle of whiskey from a convenience store is making his getaway. As he is running along the road, a police officer who just happens to be walking by sees him drop his mobile phone. The police officer does not know that the man is a thief, she just wants to tell him that he has dropped his phone. The police officer shouts out 'Hey you. Stop!' The thief turns around, sees the police officer, stops in his tracks, produces the bottle of whiskey, confesses that he has just stolen it from the shop and pleads for leniency.[1]

When most people are asked 'why did the thief do that?' they are likely to make the inference that the thief thought—mistakenly as it happens—that the police officer knew he had committed a crime. As mere readers of the vignette they do not have access to the thief's state of mind but nonetheless they make an attribution about his false belief which helps them to make sense of what is driving the thief's behaviour. This ability to make inferences about the mental state of another person automatically without deliberation (i.e. intuitively) is called 'mentalizing'. It goes under various synonyms, including 'mind-reading', 'folk psychology', and 'theory of mind' (ToM). It involves the invaluable and powerful social skill of being able to making social inferences by intuiting the contents of someone else's mind.

In terms of the development of this ability, explicit mentalizing becomes evident from between the ages of four and six years, as in this example:

> Milly has some chocolate and puts it into a blue cupboard. Milly goes out. Now her mother comes in and moves the chocolate to a green cupboard. Milly comes back to get her chocolate. Where will Milly look for the chocolate?

Milly will look in the blue cupboard, because this is where she falsely believes the chocolate to be. By the time a child gets to around 4 years old they can understand that Milly holds a false belief about the whereabouts of the chocolate and can explain it when asked. By around this age, children have developed the remarkable ability to 'mind-read'. Younger children are unable to infer that Milly will look in the blue rather than the green cupboard; similar experiments have also shown that people with autism have a diminished ability to mind-read in daily life.[2]

Homo sapiens is the only species with a well-developed theory of mind,[3] and this highly evolved ability to mentalize enables humans to do three remarkable things: first, to infer what a person believes about the world by perspective-taking; second, to represent and interpret the mental states of one's self and others through speaking; and third, to share in the experiences and emotions of others by empathizing.[4] The social cognitive neuroscientist Matthew Lieberman refers to mentalizing as one of the 'signature achievements' of the human mind and speculated that 'humans may be alone in the *Universe* when it comes to their ability to thoroughly appreciate the nature of others' minds'.[5] Mentalizing has far-reaching consequences for social intuition. Our 'all-purpose mind-reading machine' is recruited many hundreds of times every day to make 'educated guesses' about what is in another person's mind; without it we would be 'absolutely lost', unless we happened to live a completely solitary existence where there are no other human minds to read.[6] Mentalizing is intuitive in that it is triggered automatically, and this can be in response to a wide range of verbal and non-verbal cues including body movements, vocalizations, and facial appearance and expression. Mentalizing is one of the primary processes that drives our social intuitions.

The mirror mechanism (discussed in Chapter 6) takes us part way to understanding how our social intuition works. Through the mirror mechanism we are able to 'echo' the movements of another person and experience vicariously their emotional state. The mirror mechanism, which is not unique to humans, evolved to support continuous tracking of the emotions and intentions of others. It helps us, for example, to recognize intuitively from someone's facial expression that they are afraid. However, this intuitive reading of a facial expression only tells us so much; it does not tell us necessarily about the source of their fear (if indeed they themselves are aware of it) or about the mental state that precipitated their fear. Also, even though mirror neurons which are the neural substrate of the mirroring mechanism may be a necessary prerequisite for higher-level social intuitions, they are also present in other species such as monkeys, but monkeys do not possess any mentalizing ability.[7] Social intuitions require additional components over and above mirror neurons; they are necessary but not sufficient. When these lower-level components such as mirror neurons and higher-level, uniquely human components such as mentalizing are connected together, we are able to accomplish social intuitions. Although the potential to be able to resonate with another person may be wired into us by evolution, it is our experiences of and our learnings about other people with whom we come into contact—what they look like, how they behave, and what they say—which builds our complex intuitions about other people's motivations and intentions. It is both nature and nurture which confers on us the remarkable ability to be able to judge whether another person is likely to be trustworthy or untrustworthy, whether they intend to deceive us, and whether they should be approached or avoided. Social intuition is 'mentalizing-plus'.

One of the higher-level components that supports mentalizing is simulation. Simulating what someone else is likely to be thinking or feeling helps us to envisage anticipated future states of our social world and is essential for predicting and planning how we behave with respect to others in our social orbit. One way in which we do this is by consciously and effortfully considering what we would think or feel if we were in their situation, and which is also involved in moral judgement (see Chapter 8). The proviso here is that how accurate our simulations are likely to be depends on how similar we are to, or how experienced we are with, the type of person whose mind we are simulating. Simulation is a conscious and deliberate analytical (System 2) process (see Chapter 4). Simulating someone else's thoughts and feelings involves the conscious effort, for example by fast-forwarding a 'video' of the social situation. In this respect, simulation is not an intuitive process, and even though it may become habituated through learning and experience, it is nevertheless deliberate and effortful. Whilst the activations of mirror neurons may give us an experiential grasp of the mind of another person, simulation gives us a rationale for their behaviours and their presumed motives and intentions, which are made through logical inferences and by consciously imagining ourselves in their situation.

Intuitive processes, such as empathizing with another person's emotional state ('they look unhappy, I know how that feels') via the actions of mirror neurons that give a 'motor resonance',[8] provide a quick-and-dirty evaluation of a social situation. The initial intuitive evaluation is affectively charged (i.e. valenced) by gut feelings or hunches. This affectively 'hot' initial evaluation may then be accepted, corrected, or rejected in two ways: firstly, affectively 'cold' higher-level conscious processing, such as simulating how we might feel by using our mind as a proxy for theirs (for example, 'they look unhappy, is that how I would feel in their situation?'); secondly, and/or by making a logical inference (for example, 'they look unhappy, was it something I said?').

Recruiting higher-level processes such as simulation and inference provides opportunities for rapid intuitive responses to be scrutinized and corrected if necessary and where time and informational resources permit.[9] The degree of iterative activity between reflexive System 1 and reflective System 2 processes depends on a number of factors including the persons' thinking style (for example, whether they have a preference for analysis or intuition, see Chapter 11), the opportunities provided by the situation for reflection and recalibration (for example, if there is sufficient time), and what the consequences of the decision are (for example, low consequence decisions are not likely to warrant extensive reappraisals).[10]

Our social sense, which in the past was crucial for our very survival and which is essential for efficiently and effectively navigating the modern world, is accomplished by both mirroring and mentalizing. Mirroring helps us to appreciate quickly and easily the emotional and other states of another person (*what* they are doing, for example crying), whilst mentalizing helps us to understand and make sense of their motives and intentions and arrive at a satisfying answer to *why* they are doing what they are doing (for example, why they are crying)[11]. Mirror neurons are the intuitive (i.e. sensing) foundation of a lower-level mind-recognizing system, whilst mentalizing is the analytical (i.e. solving) foundation of a higher-level mind-reading system. Matthew Lieberman summarizes the workings of this dual-system as follows: 'the mirror system chops the world of living movement into pieces and it repackages them into the psychological elements that the mentalizing system can work from'; our primate relatives have a mirror system and live in a world of *what* others are doing, whereas *Homo sapiens* has both a mirroring system and an 'advanced mentalizing' system and lives in a world of *why* others are doing *what* they are doing.[12] Monkey and apes may be able to recognize behaviours, but they are not able to read the minds of others. *Homo sapiens*' social judgement system has both experiential (intuitive, and concerned with 'what') and rational (analytical, concerned with 'why') components.

Leaders and managers in business mentalize all of the time. For example, a salesperson needs strong mirroring capabilities and mentalizing skills in order to create a positive ambience and build rapport with potential customers. Take the example of adaptive selling in marketing: a good salesperson must be able to adopt a tailored, client-centred approach that adapts quickly and effortlessly to the needs, wants, and problems of the customer. Social intuitions built on mirroring (which builds rapport) and mentalizing (which helps in customizing the offering) contribute to sales success.[13] Salespersons with good mentalizing skills are able to sense when their approach is not working, experiment with different tactics, be flexible, and can utilize a variety of strategies based on their prior experiences. They are able to do so because they can figure out, often intuitively at first, what the customer's needs are and what kind of product and service would best suit the customer. They possess the micro-skills of being able to easily build rapport with small talk, discern verbal and non-verbal cues in customer interactions, and easily act in a way that gives a conversation a positive spin. These are all skills that can be developed through observational learning of a role model allied to high-fidelity experiences (for example, role play and simulation) and good-quality (i.e. timely, accurate and relevant) feedback.[14]

The capability to intuit the needs of customers and the market is at the heart of Henry Ford's famous dictum: 'If I'd have asked my customers what they wanted, they'd have said "a faster horse". Ford was able to mentalize what customers were likely to want. His intuitions gave him foresight. Likewise, Steve Jobs mastered the art of mentalizing what customers would want before they knew it themselves; as he once said, 'it's not the customers' job to know what they want.'[15] Jobs made design intuitively obvious. He had the mentalizing knack to be able to stand in the customers' shoes and applied his mentalizing skills to inventing and innovating new designs. For example, in developing the idea of the desktop as a metaphor for a physical office he was able to see the task from the user's perspective: 'if you walk into an office, there are papers on the desk. The one on the top is the most important.'[16] Jobs was masterful in mind-reading what users were likely to want, and like Henry Ford had an acute intuitive foresight that enabled him to recognize and exploit opportunities for how to do things better and do better things in business.[17]

Thin Slicing

The distinguished American anthropologist and linguist Edward Sapir (1884–1939) wrote that 'we respond to gestures with an extreme alertness, one might almost say, in accordance with an elaborate secret code that is written nowhere, known by none, and understood by all.'[18] He described the mental processes by which this secret code works as being of 'that little understood sort for which the name "intuition" has been suggested'.[19] Sapir's 'secret code' is a quick, effortless, and efficient way of making inferences intuitively about other people. It is how we adapt to the social world by perceiving and processing other people's behaviours. If this is correct, then how much information is required to make an inference and a judgement and how long might it take?

This was the question that intrigued the eminent social psychologist Nalini Ambady (1959–2013) of Stanford University.[20] In the 1990s she and her colleagues designed an ingenious experiment to test this idea based on the method of 'thin slices'. A thin slice is a short sample of behaviour that provides information regarding aspects of a person's personality (for example, introverted or extraverted), affective state (for example, positive or negative mood), and interpersonal relations (for example, warm and approachable or cold and aloof). The processes that underlie 'thin slicing' are fast and automatic and occur outside of conscious awareness. Thin slicing is intuitive and tacit; as such it renders verbal reasoning and explanations about another person's behaviours both difficult and unnecessary. Ambady was interested in two questions: how accurate is a thin slice, and how short is a 'short sample' of behaviour?

To answer this question, Ambady and her co-researchers created short silent video clips (three of ten seconds each) of college teachers in action. They showed the clips to students who were not members of the teachers' class (referred to as 'strangers'). These strangers were asked to rate the teachers on a number of non-verbal expressive behaviours, including how 'active', 'confident', 'enthusiastic', and 'optimistic' the teachers were. The strangers' ratings were then compared with actual students' ratings of how effective the teachers were in the classroom. Teachers rated higher by their students in end-of-semester evaluations were rated by strangers as more optimistic, confident, dominant, active, enthusiastic, likable, warm, competent, and supportive. The correlations between semester-long student evaluations and second strangers' ratings were remarkably high considering that they were based on three ten-second slices of behaviour.

Ambady and colleagues then raised the bar. They shortened the clips from three times ten seconds to three times two seconds to see what the effect might be, i.e. from a thirty-second sample to a six-second sample of behaviour. They found that significantly shortening the clips made very little difference to their findings. Semester-long students' evaluations and six-second strangers' evaluations still showed a high level of agreement, whether the total length of the clips was thirty seconds or just six seconds. Ambady's research presented compelling evidence that thin slices of expressive behaviours convey a wealth of information that is related strongly to a number of real-life variables, including teaching effectiveness. Ambady extended the thin slice studies to other real-world contexts including studies of surgeons (those rated as domineering were more likely to have been sued for malpractice in the past) and physical therapists (the patients of therapists rated as using distancing behaviours were more likely to experience longer-term decline). There have been numerous other applications of the technique, and the findings have been remarkably consistent in predicting outcomes ranging from racial bias to personality disorders.[21]

If thin slicing is a fast, automatic, unconscious System 1 process then its accuracy ought not to be impeded by concurrently carrying out a task that requires effortful System 2 processing. Ambady and her colleagues tested this in a repeat of the teacher effectiveness experiments. This time, one group of participants were asked to follow an analytical reasoning strategy by listing the attributes they would be looking for. Another group of participants were given a cognitive loading distraction task (counting backwards from 1,000 in nines). The assumption was that the analytical group would be using System 2 processes whilst the cognitive load group had to rely on System 1 because their System 2 was otherwise engaged. The correlations between participants' thin slice judgements and students' evaluations were significantly lower when they followed the analytical reasoning strategy compared to the thin slice judgements of participants who were given the distraction task and were forced to rely solely on unconscious processing. Deliberating about teachers' attributes appeared to distract attention away from salient aspects of teacher behaviours which are hard to analyse but relevant to their effectiveness and instead focused attention on aspects of teacher behaviour which were easier to consciously spot, analyse and verbalize but were less relevant.[22] Thin slicing appears to be an efficient and effective way to make social judgements on the basis of a 'global gestalt impression',[23] which intuitively conveys the gist of another person's behaviour. The process is impeded by conscious deliberation, adding further weight to the idea that making social judgements based on thin slices is a automatic, unconscious and reflexive System 1 process.

Mood can also affect how well someone makes an intuitive thin slice judgement. Ambady and colleagues tested the idea that happy people tend to process social information heuristically while sad people tend to process it systematically. They found that experimentally induced sadness diminishes the accuracy of thin slice judgements. Sad people were less accurate and took more time to make their judgements compared to happy participants. However, when sad participants were given a cognitive load task, and hence forced artificially to rely on their intuition, their judgements were quicker and more accurate.[24]

Thin slice judgements are based on tacit knowledge that has been acquired implicitly. They make verbal explanations and reasoning unnecessary and are intuitive in that they occur automatically and outside of conscious awareness. As such they are an efficient way to arrive at social judgements by making use of limited information and hence do not make demands on higher-level cognitive processes and resources.[25]. By and large, evaluations based on thin slice first impressions remain uncorrected, except when a logjam occurs in System 1 and cognitive effort needs to be expended because the information received is novel, confusing, or inconsistent (for example, someone's behaviour seems 'out of sorts' or atypical).[26] In this situation, System 2 is mobilized to make sense of the situation by inquiring into our intuitive impressions. Research in evolutionary psychology suggests that thin slice judgements are hardwired into the human organism and that the human mind is designed to delegate social judgements to is reflexive sub-systems.[27]

Thin Slicing in Business and Management

In the world of business, Ambady and her colleagues studied whether thin slices of salespersons' behaviours agreed with their managers' evaluations and actual sales performance. In this research they extended the scope of the thin slices to encompass verbal behaviours. Participants rated twenty-second audio clips of interviews with a sample of salespersons on their 'interpersonal skills' (for example, 'empathic', 'enthusiastic', and 'warm') and 'task-related skills' (for example, 'confident', 'decisive', and 'persevering'). Thin slice judgements of interpersonal and task-related skills were positively related not only to managers' evaluations of the salesperson but also to their actual sales performance.[28] In a study of law firms it was found that judgements of 'competence', 'dominance', and 'maturity' based on perception of the faces of the Managing Partners (MPs) of America's top hundred law firms was associated with their firms' success.[29] A study of thirty-second video clips of CEOs at initial public offering (IPO) roadshows found that viewers' intuitive perceptions of CEOs in terms of 'competence', 'trustworthiness', and 'attractiveness' was positively associated with an IPO firm's market value at the initial proposal price date, the final offer price, and the end of the first day of trading.[30]

In a potentially controversial study which followed a slightly different line of inquiry, students' (selected because they would be naïve judges) ratings of power-related traits based on CEOs' facial appearance (after controlling for age, affect, and attractiveness) were found to be positively associated with company profits. Whilst acknowledging that more successful companies might be choosing individuals with a particular facial appearance to be their CEOs or that individuals with a particular appearance might emerge as more successful in their work as CEOs, Ambady concluded that at least some element of financial success seems to be associated with CEO appearance.[31]

The study of CEO faces was extended to the neuroimaging laboratory. A team of researchers including Ambady used functional magnetic resonance imaging (fMRI) to examine responses to images of CEOs' faces in an effort to locate the brain regions involved in thin slice judgements. They found greater left amygdala response to CEOs' faces was associated with ratings of CEOs' leadership capabilities. Other research has shown that individuals without functioning amygdalae have an impaired ability to intuitively evaluate the approachability and trustworthiness of others based on facial images.[32] It appears that the amygdala, which is part of the limbic system and associated with System 1 processes linked to emotional processing, is activated when we make intuitive judgements based on thin slices of behaviours. This backs up Damasio's Iowa Gambling Task studies that showed how the amygdala is involved in infusing gut feelings into intuitive decision-making (see Chapter 6). In this case the amygdala appears to be involved in generating signals as to whether another person is likely to be approachable and trustworthy and which may also extend to evaluations of their leadership capabilities.

Overall, these findings show that perceptual judgements made on the basis of thin slice observations of non-verbal and verbal behaviours can be surprisingly accurate predictors of real-world behaviours. Thin slice judgements rely on System 1 processes. They are fast and automatic and can be conducted in parallel with other cognitive tasks. Thin slice judgements are more accurate when they are made without deliberation.[33] Ambady explained these findings in terms of the 'affordances' (that is the stimulus information provided by an object) that verbal and non-verbal behaviours provide for making inferences about other aspects of a person's behaviour, including their abilities and competencies. Individuals unwittingly and involuntarily communicate certain aspects of behaviour that are adaptive for perceivers to be able to detect unconsciously and automatically. This suggest that we have evolved as a species to be able to detect and decipher the 'honest signals' that we all give out unconsciously and involuntarily.

However, thin slices are only valid as predictors of behaviour when the perceived attributes of the person are relevant to the criterion variable. For example, the attributes of active, confident, enthusiastic, and optimistic are valid and relevant cues and likely to be correlated with the criterion of teaching effectiveness. In this case implicit knowledge about the person is being correctly applied and the judgement is likely to be valid. On the other hand, the attributes such as eye colour and or shoe size are invalid and irrelevant cues as to whether or not a person is likely to be a good teacher. More significantly, thin slices based on implicit racial, gendered, and other stereotypes open the door to unconscious biases, prejudice, and discrimination. The potency of thin slices is compounded by the fact that intuitive thin slice judgements are formed quickly and unwittingly and tend to be resistant to disconfirmation (first impressions, even when they are inaccurate and biased, count and tend to stick). As with intuitive judgements in general, thin slices can be powerful when used in the right way under the right circumstances but perilous when used in the wrong way under the wrong circumstances.

Honest Signals and Linguistic Markers

Thin slices present honest signals from the sender which are processed and interpreted intuitively by the receiver. They are the basis of an efficient and effective communication system based on expressions, gestures, and calls that automatically coordinate and manage behaviours between individual members of a social species. Media and behavioural scientist Alex (Sandy) Pentland of MIT and author of *Honest Signals* argues that our ancestors used non-verbal signals to coordinate their actions before language evolved and that spoken language was layered on top of this older primate signalling system.[34] Non-linguistic signals which are often exercised and communicated non-consciously, such as body language, facial expression, and tone of voice, are significant indicators of other people's affective states, motives, and intentions. Such clues for 'people reading' can predict behavioural outcomes in areas as diverse as negotiating, dating, selling, bluffing, and criminal activities.[35] Honest signals are, by their nature, authentic and difficult to fake. Hence, like the thin slices researched by Ambady and colleagues, they provide us with reliable verbal and non-verbal signals that not only help to read other people intuitively but they also oil the wheels of group living.

Pentland's research group at MIT has identified four components of this intuitive signalling system. 'Mimicry' is the reflexive copying of one person by another in a social exchange, resulting in postural echoing, interjections, etc.; for example head-nodding during a conversation. 'Activity' indicates interest and excitement, as would be signalled by signs of affirmation or encouragement. 'Influence' is the extent to which one person's verbal behaviours causes another person's pattern of speech to match theirs, for example by elevating their levels of excitement or anxiety. 'Consistency', which is related to fluidity of speech, is perceived by the receiver as a marker of authority and expertise, for example by being able to speak unfalteringly on a complex topic. By examining intuitive back-and-forth signals in a wide variety of social encounters, Pentland and his team have accurately predicted the outcomes in business-related applications such as job interviews and salary negotiations. They estimate that honest signals account for roughly 40 per cent of the variation in outcomes in some of these areas, a figure which is comparable to some estimates of the influence of genetics on certain aspects of behaviour.[36]

Pentland explains the power of pervasiveness of honest signals in terms of his version of a dual-process model which he referred to as 'habitual versus attentive'. He describes the habitual mind as representing an evolutionarily older system which is attuned to non-verbal signalling and which learns new behaviours though experience and mimicry. As well as being fast, the habitual mind is adept in complex social trade-offs and associations and in identifying cheating behaviours through a process of sensing. However, unlike its System 2 counterpart the attentive mind, the habitual mind is not particularly adept at abstract reasoning and relies on System 2 for the complementary process of solving.

Developing this dual-system approach to honest signals, linguistic researchers Kayla Jordan and James Pennebaker used linguistic analysis to try and understand people's thinking processes and position individuals on an intuitive–analytic thinking style continuum. They found that analytic thinkers tend to use more nouns, articles, and prepositions, whereas intuitive thinkers tend to use more pronouns, auxiliary verbs, and adverbs. They combined this into a composite measure of analytical thinking and implemented the algorithm into their computerized text analysis package Linguistic Inquiry and Word Count (LIWC). They studied the speeches of Donald Trump in the 2016 election campaign and found him to be the least analytical of all the Republican candidates and far less analytical than his Democratic opponent Hilary Clinton. Jordan and Pennebaker describe Trump as an 'outlier' amongst presidential candidates and presidents for the way in which he appears to eschew analytical (System 2) thinking.[37]

In my own research with Vita Akstinaite, we used the LIWC software to compare Trump's Covid-19 public pronouncements with those of New Zealand's Prime Minister Jacinda Ardern during the crucial early stages of the pandemic in 2020. We found that Trump's speeches were low on 'analysis' and 'authenticity' and high on 'emotional tone'. For Ardern we found the opposite: she was high on analysis and authenticity and low on emotional tone. At the time of our research the US and New Zealand had the highest and lowest death rates respectively during the pandemic amongst English-speaking countries. We interpreted these markers as possible indicators of Trump's hubristic incompetence in his crisis management of the coronavirus pandemic.[38] Analysis, authenticity, and emotional tone in a leader's speech could be used as an early indication of how they might behave in managing a crisis, i.e. good management is associated with high authenticity, high analysis, and low emotional tone, and vice versa.

These findings are illuminating and potentially useful in that the honest signals that people unwittingly and intuitively transmit in their speech provide hard-to-conceal linguistic markers for their likely behaviours and underlying cognitive and emotional processes. These markers could be used as an early warning system to intervene and offset the potential negative effects of certain types of leader behaviours, such as extreme overconfidence, which leads to hubristic arrogance and contempt

Social Intuition

Social intuition is the rapid and automatic evaluation of another person's cognitive or affective state through the perception and non-conscious processing of verbal and/or non-verbal indicators. The ability to make inferences about the intentions, knowledge, goals, and desires of others helps us to understand and predict others' behaviours and adjust our own behaviours correspondingly.[39] Because we have no direct access to the mind of another person, natural selection has favoured the evolution of mechanisms that use certain perceptual cues, such as motion, gaze, posture, and vocalizations, that help us to make potentially useful inferences. Over the course of *Homo sapiens*' evolution this social intuition is likely to have had significant fitness benefits, for example the skill of empathizing, i.e. the drive to identify another person's emotions and thoughts and respond to these appropriately.[40]

The Cambridge clinical psychologist Simon Baron-Cohen argues that research evidence gathered over several decades strongly suggests that there is female superiority in empathizing. This manifests in sharing and turn taking (girls show more concern for fairness), responding empathetically to distress in others (from the age of 1 year old, girls show greater concern through more sad looks), using 'theory of mind' (by the age of 3 years, girls are ahead), sensitivity to facial expressions (women are better at decoding non-verbals) and language style (girls' speech is more cooperative, reciprocal, and collaborative). Baron-Cohen speculates that these differences might reflect natural selection for empathy among females because this would have led to better caregiving and the supportive processes of socializing. Incidentally, Baron-Cohen also argues for stronger drive to systematize (i.e. use input output rules to analyse, predict, and identify relationships between objects in the physical environment) amongst males.[41] Evolutionary speculations aside, if indeed females are superior to males in empathizing (or males in systematizing) this begs the question of course: which came first? For example, are the words girls use cooperative, reciprocal, and collaborative because society expects this of them and has brought them up to do so?

Irrespective of speculations about social intuition's evolutionary origins and any related sex differences that may or may not exist, the ability to decode social signals in social interactions is also a product of implicit learning.[42] Implicit social learning occurs when complex behavioural regularities are learned without us being fully aware of how they are learned or what has been learned.[43] This process happens throughout our lives, but especially so in the early years.[44] The social cognitive neuroscientist Matthew Lieberman of the University of California Los Angeles and author of *Social: Why Our Brains Are Wired to Connect* (2013), describes social intuition as the capability to make rapid judgements about the emotions, personality, intentions, attitudes, and skills of others. Social intuitions are based on the perception of various verbal as well as non-verbal cues, including subtle facial expressions, body postures, and non-verbal gestures. For example, speed-dating relies on the principle that in a brief simulated date—typically four minutes—people communicate enough about their personality, motives, and intentions through their face, body, and voice that they can arrive at a decision about whether they would like to meet again and maybe build a relationship. This ability to non-verbally decode another person's behaviour is acquired early on, for example childhood learning of social skills depends on mimicry and develops continuously throughout the life span.[45]

Social intuition extends from romance to politics and, as the thin slice researchers discovered, the human face seems to be the focal point of this non-verbal decoding process. The face is so important in social interaction that we use it to make judgements beyond what might reasonably be inferred from a person's face alone. The psychologist Alexander Todorov and his colleagues looked at the extent to which quick, unreflective judgements based on facial appearance predicted the outcomes of US congressional elections. They presented participants in an experiment with pairs of headshot photos of winners and runners-up in the elections for the US Senate (2000, 2002, and 2004) and House (2002 and 2004) who were then asked to judge which one of the pair looked more competent (the photo was excluded if a participant recognized the candidate). The candidate who was perceived as more competent from nothing more than a black-and-white headshot was the actual winner in 72 per cent of the Senate elections and 67 per cent of the House races. When they cut the exposure to the photos down to one second, the accuracy remained high at 68 per cent, and even when they used statistical techniques to partial out the age and attractiveness of the candidates (i.e. so that the judgement was purely on the perception of competence), the effect remained. It seems that voters' decisions are anchored to an intuitive inference of competence based on facial appearance information.

The social cognitive neuroscientist Matthew Lieberman asks us to imagine how difficult, and well-nigh impossible, it would be to navigate the social interactions of our daily lives if we were unable to 'make sense of the minds of others' or if we could not 'count on others to make sense of [our] minds'. This metaphorical mind-reading process relies on us having a 'theory of mind'. Having thoughts about our own and other people's minds—a theory of our own mind and of the mind of another person— enables us to understand the thoughts that enable and constrain our own and other people's behaviours. As noted earlier, the theory of mind works by the process of mentalizing. Lieberman suggests that the brain regions that are involved in this process comprise a 'default network' (or 'default mode network') of subsystems which becomes *less* active when we are doing cognitive, motor, or visual tasks and *more* active when we are passively daydreaming, reminiscing, and future planning. It is analogous to the mind 'putting its feet up' or the light coming on after people have left the room. The key point that Lieberman makes about the default network and the honing of social intuitions is that in this 'free time' the default network resets to thinking about other things. One of the main things that the human brain defaults to thinking about is other people. Lieberman argues that we, as the most social and biggest brained of all the primates, are built by nature to do so.[46] The implication for intuition is that by repeatedly defaulting to thinking effortlessly about other people and their behaviours, motives, and intentions we become, quite early on in our lives, intuitive experts in the subtleties of social living and the complexities of navigating the social world.[47]

A theory of mind and the associated process of mentalizing are vital for social functioning. Mentalizing enables us to ascribe mental states, for example intentions and emotions, to ourselves and others. This information is used to make sense of and predict behaviours based on our readings of our own mental states and those of other people.[48] In mentalizing, we use both our observations of others' behaviours and our subjective experience of our own minds as a proxy for other minds. One way we can do this is by using propositional 'if–then' logic (for example, by inferring that if someone has not had a good night's sleep they are likely to be techy and irritable) or by imagining (for example, trying to get into the mind of, or walk in the shoes of, an employee who has been verbally abused by a bullying boss).[49]

Some of the time this works well. However, it can also lure us into the trap of substituting the easy-to-answer question of, for example, 'do I like this?' or 'what do I think?' for the harder-to-answer question of 'does this other person like this?' or 'what does the other person think?'. As a consequence, our intuitive social judgements can entice us into making erroneous self-serving assumptions and inferences about other people's mental states and their motives and intentions. Such mistakes can not only be highly embarrassing, but they can also come at a high social cost in terms of competence, reputation, and trustworthiness.

Social intuitions are the gut feelings and hunches that we have towards other people that are experienced in the absence of a reason that is easy to articulate.[50] We think we know something about their affective state, motivations, or inferred behaviours without knowing how or why we know. For example, someone's story that does not 'stack up' or a situation they are in that does not 'smell right'. These social intuitions are the products of experiences and learnings in which cues and outcomes are implicitly connected, for example the inference that a certain gesture or posture, such as arm folding, indicates a particular state of mind. From an evolutionary perspective, the idea of social intuition is consistent with a social brain hypothesis which claims that one of the main selective pressures among cognitively advanced group living species such as primates is to generate social knowledge about other individuals with whom we are likely to both cooperate and compete.[51] If this is correct then the ability to generate knowledge about others intuitively is a valuable cognitive capability. Evolutionary anthropologists define social intuition as the capacity to attain knowledge about others, including their mental states, in order to predict their behaviours and ultimately influence their behaviour in our own interests. As such, this social sense is an adaptive response to social complexity in the ancestral environment which likely had a significant impact on reproductive success.[52] As a fundamental human capability, social intuitions are no less important in business than they were amongst our cave-dwelling ancestors.

Reflexion, Reflection, and Social Cognition in Business

Business is essentially a social process. Much of a manager's working day is spent interacting with colleagues, co-workers, other managers, direct reports, clients, and customers. As a social world, business is riven with complexity, ambiguity, and uncertainty, but it is a world that has to be made sense of intuitively in order to be navigated efficiently and effectively. According to a growing body of work in social psychology, our automatic social cognitions, such as categorizing and empathizing, are underpinned by a 'reflexive system' of thinking, whilst our deliberative social cognitions, such as planning and hypothetical thinking, are underpinned by a 'reflective system' of thinking.[53] This is another variation on the theme of two minds in one brain, but this time applied specifically to the social domain.

Matthew Lieberman coined the term 'social cognitive neuroscience' (SCN) to describe a programme of research that uses fMRI and related neuroscientific techniques to examine the neuronal substrates of social cognitive processes, such as fairness, empathy, and social intuition. In the SCN model, Liebermann uses the term 'X-system processes' to describe social cognitive processes that are automatic and spontaneous and occur without conscious awareness, for example the intuitive perception, recognition, and reaction to another person's mood. The 'X' in 'X-system' refers to the fact that such processes are refle_x_ive. The term 'C-system processes' is used to describe social cognitive processes that are controlled, deliberative, and conscious, for example overt conscious thought about the internal mental states of others. The 'C' in 'C-system' refers to the fact that such processes are refle_c_tive.

Lieberman makes the important point that even though each system has a collection of attributes that are distinct from those of the other system, the two systems are not hermetically sealed from each other. They interact so as to be able to work hand in hand to achieve specific goals through, in the terms set out in this book, the complementary processes of solving for the C-system and sensing for the X-system. The attributes of the X- and C-systems align with many of those of a number of two-minds models, such as Kahneman's distinction between System 1 and System 2 and Epstein's experiential and rational systems. The X-system's attributes include: parallel processing; fast operation; slow learning; spontaneous; reflexive responses; sensory; and evolutionarily older. The C-system's attributes include: serial processing; slow operation; fast learning; intentional; reflective responses; linguistic; and evolutionarily newer.

Lieberman and his colleague Ajay Satpute of Northeastern University in Boston singled-out a small number of brain regions that appear to be the bases[54] of these two high-level systems of social cognition. The neural substrates of the X-system include the amygdala, basal ganglia (including caudate nuclei), and the ventro-medial prefrontal cortex (VMPFC). Moreover, there appear to be strong interconnections between these brain regions. It is worth noting that these are some of the brain regions that other researchers have identified as being implicated in System 1-type processes, for example, the role of the amygdalae and VMPFC in somatic marking of risky decisions (in Antonio Damasio's and his colleagues' IGT studies) and the precuneus–caudate nucleus circuit in the quick and automatic perception of complex patterns and best next-move generation in board games (in Tanaka and his colleagues studies of shogi players). The neural substrates of the C-system are concentrated in the prefrontal cortex (lateral PFC, ventro-lateral PFC, medial PFC, dorsomedial, PFC) along with areas of the parietal cortex (medial and lateral) and temporal lobe (medial), see Figure 9.1.

The amygdala — often referred to in the singular when there are in fact two amgydalae, one in each hemisphere—is one of the neural correlates of automatic affective processing.[55] It is associated with 'quick and dirty' flight or fight responses, it responds quickly and automatically to subliminal presentations for example of fearful stimuli such as angry facial expressions and is biased towards negatively valanced emotions and avoidance behaviours. Because the brain's evolved capacities prioritize

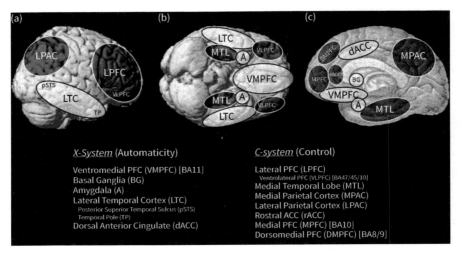

Figure 9.1 Neural correlates of the C-system (refle*c*tive cognition) and X-system (refle*x*ive cognition).
Source: Lieberman, M. D. (2007). Social cognitive neuroscience: a review of core processes. *Annual Review of Psychology*, 58: 259–289. Reproduced by permission of Annual Reviews.

the processing of fear and anxiety, the amygdala often steps in to help us protect ourselves from threats. But in doing so, even though it can be thought of as an evolutionary residue of flight or fight, it can also crowd-out C-system rational processing. The popular science writer Daniel Goleman used the term 'amygdala hijacking' to refer this situation when, for example, someone is especially vulnerable to intense emotions such as anger, anxiety, fear, and rage and is unable to think 'straight' (i.e. rationally and analytically).

In business there are numerous sources of fear and anxiety that can catalyse the amygdala into action, everything from criticism from a colleague to proposals for organization change can provoke an intuitive fight-or-flight, i.e. X-system, response. In negotiations where the financial stakes are high, such as in mergers and acquisitions, emotions running amok can lead to the negotiating parties losing sight of the bigger picture. If runaway emotions surface, they can significantly slow down or even destroy negotiations. Emotional contagion between parties can also occur which can have both positive and negative effects, for example, an upwardly virtuous cycle catalysing affirmatory behaviour or a downwardly vicious spiral sparking retaliatory behaviour. On the other hand, affective commitment to a potential relationship can emerges out of the social and emotional consequences of repeated negotiations between the same parties.[56] Emotions also play an important role in how we assess risk. People weight equivalent gains and losses differently, we feel better about avoiding a £100 loss than securing a £100 gain. This is one of the main ideas in Kahneman and Tversky's prospect theory.[57] As the fear centre of the brain, it is the amygdala that is especially attuned to losses and hence can have a significant effect on business decisions where losses might be envisaged.

Although the amygdala is classified as part of the X-system in social cognitive neuroscience, it has strong connections to other brain systems and regions and influences higher-level cognitive functions (such as decision-making) in response to emotional stimuli (such as a potential financial loss). Hence, rather than being seen as a discrete component of a lower-level system (the X-system) that is simply about flight or fight, in humans the amygdala modulates other neural circuits and brain systems (including System 2 or the C-system). In doing so it exercises and unconscious influence on higher-level cognitive processing, risk assessment, and social behaviours.

Another neural region associated with X-system processing is the ventro-medial prefrontal cortex (VMPFC). As we discovered in Chapter 6, research by the eminent neurologist Antonio Damasio and his colleagues using an artificial gambling task (the Iowa Gambling Task) demonstrated that the VMPFC is involved in the experiential learning of relationships between stimuli (such as good and bad decks of cards) and outcomes (large versus small financial gains and losses) and that the gut feelings (somatic markers) generated by the VMPFC influence decision-making in advance of conscious awareness.

The VMPFC has also been shown to have other biasing effects on intuitive decision-making in addition to its effects on judgements of risky behaviours. For example, 'framing' is a source of cognitive bias in which large changes in preferences are sometimes caused by trivial variations in the way a problem is worded (framed). For example, framing that 'our Earnings per share (EPS) in Q3 were $1.25, compared to Q2, where they were $1.21' does a better job of presenting the EPS data that saying, 'our EPS in Q3 were $1.25 compared to expectations of $1.27'.

A team of researchers based at the University Hospital Munster presented twenty-one experimental participants with thirty fictitious headlines in four well-known German news magazines of varying credibility. Sample headlines were: 'since 1995 the number of polar bears decreased more than 5 per cent' and 'American research institute proved that coffee can promote the generation of cancer.' Participants were required to judge whether the headlines were true or false, and whilst they were doing so their brains were monitored using fMRI. The researchers' aims were to test whether the credibility of the magazine that the headline appeared in (i.e. how the headline was 'framed') had any effect on whether headlines were judged as true or false, and identify the brain regions that were activated when these true/false judgements were being made.[58]

Yet again the VMPFC is centre-stage. Participants who showed higher susceptibility to framing bias showed increased levels of activity in the VMPFC. The magazine-specific differences (credible versus less credible) were attributed to the emotions aroused (positive versus negative) by the different brands which then biased participants' judgements (true versus false). Participants' intuitions about the magazine influenced their judgement as to the veracity of the content of the headline, even though the wording was exactly the same and only the magazine logo associated with it varied. In this experiment the intuitive system erroneously sensed the credibility of the content because of where it was presented (i.e. framed), irrespective of the content itself.

The VMPFC is associated with the integration of emotions into decision-making. The X-system can be manipulated into judging information as true or false depending on where the information comes from and how it is framed. However, the ability to sense the credibility of an input could be adaptive in the real world since it stands to reason that the source of information (for example, credibility, trustworthiness, political leanings, etc.) should be taken into account in judging the content of the information itself. On the face of it, intuitively judging information as dubious when it comes from a source that is recognized as untrustworthy could be a quick and efficient (i.e. fast and frugal) way of arriving at an advantageous 'avoid' decision. Intuitively judging information as credible when it comes from a source that is recognized to be trustworthy, on the other hand, could be a quick and efficient way of arriving at an advantageous 'approach' decision. Of course the effectiveness and the ethics of this process depend on how the judgement of trustworthiness is arrived at in the first place.

Trust is a vital component of social intuition in business and professional decision-making more broadly. Intuitively trusting in something as superficial as a person's physical appearance in social judgements can be fraught with biases. In a study of legal decision-making, participants were presented with two vignettes describing two different crimes ('car theft' and 'robbery resulting in murder') accompanied by a photograph of the supposed defendant. The photographs had previously been rated by a panel as being of a highly trustworthy appearance or a highly untrustworthy appearance. Participants were then required to evaluate supposed defendants' culpability following the presentation of evidence, for example, the 'accused admits to using marijuana', 'the accused tried to run from the police', etc. The researchers found that less evidence was required to convict an 'untrustworthy looking' defendant of the same crime compared to a 'trustworthy looking' defendant. This effect was particularly pronounced in the case of severe crimes, and in such cases participants were more confident in their guilty decision. These results are worrisome given that reliance on gut instinct about the defendants' demeanour, particularly the face, are frequently cited in legal decision-making as components of credibility assessments. The intuitive assessment of a defendant taints the presentation of evidence, which automatically puts at a disadvantage those defendants who, for whatever reason, the jurors happen to perceive as untrustworthy.[59]

The links to social judgement in business are palpable. In hiring decisions (for example, which candidate to employ), entrepreneurial decisions (for example, which pitch to back), marketing decision (for example, which ad campaign to run with), who in the team to trust (for example, giving them additional responsibilities and opportunities). Across a wide range of social judgements in the workplace, appearances have the potential to effortlessly deceive the X-system into making inaccurate inferences and biased judgements. Needless to say, such X-system judgements can be a potent source of bias and discrimination unless they are corrected by C-system interventions.

Summary

1. The main idea of this chapter is that we have a lifetime's experience of the opportunities and challenges of social living which manifests as social intuitions.
2. Social intuitions are the products of mirroring, mentalizing, and thin slicing.
3. Social intuitions are underpinned by a reflective X-system (aligned with System 1) and a reflective C-system (aligned with System 2).
4. It is adaptive for our brains to have evolved a fast, automatic, and accurate system for intuitively making sense of social judgements and dilemmas.
5. This habitual system helps us to make sense of and respond quickly and for the most part accurately to other people's affective states, motives, intentions, and behaviours.
6. Our intuitive social sense is vital for group living in which it is neither possible nor desirable to analyse every social encounter from first principles.
7. These intuitive processes can be efficient and effective when used in the right way under the right circumstances.
8. Social judgements can be biased as a result of unwarranted inferences and extrapolations and the way in which social situations are presented and framed and may lead to erroneous, inaccurate, and potentially discriminatory social judgements.

Endnotes

1. Frith, U., & Frith, C. D. (2003). Development and neurophysiology of mentalizing. *Philosophical Transactions of the Royal Society of London. Series B: Biological Sciences*, 358(1431): 459–473, p. 463.
2. Ibid., pp. 459–473.
3. Baron-Cohen, S. (1999). The evolution of a theory of mind. In Corballis, M., & Lewa, S. (Eds.). *The Descent of Mind: Psychological Perspectives on Hominid Evolution* (pp. 261–277). Oxford: Oxford University Press.
4. Frith, C. D., & Frith, U. (2006). The neural basis of mentalizing. *Neuron*, 50(4): 531–534.
5. Lieberman, M. (2013). *Social: Why Our Brains Are Wired to Connect*. Oxford: Oxford University Press, p. 111, emphasis added.
6. Ibid., pp. 127, 120.
7. Frith, U., & Frith, C. D. (2003). Development and neurophysiology of mentalizing. *Philosophical Transactions of the Royal Society of London. Series B: Biological Sciences*, 358(1431): 459–473.
8. Lieberman, M. (2013). *Social: Why Our Brains Are Wired to Connect*. Oxford: Oxford University Press, p. 139.
9. Van Overwalle, F., & Vandekerckhove, M. (2013). Implicit and explicit social mentalizing: dual processes driven by a shared neural network. *Frontiers in Human Neuroscience*, 7: 560.
10. Cunningham, W. A., & Zelazo, P. D. (2007). Attitudes and evaluations: A social cognitive neuroscience perspective. *Trends in Cognitive Sciences*, 11(3): 97–104.

11. Lieberman, M. (2013). *Social: Why Our Brains Are Wired to Connect*. Oxford: Oxford University Press, p. 147
12. Ibid., p. 150.
13. Chakrabarty, S., Widing, R. E., & Brown, G. (2014). Selling behaviours and sales performance: the moderating and mediating effects of interpersonal mentalizing. *Journal of Personal Selling & Sales Management*, 34(2): 112–122.
14. Nadler, J., & Thompson, L. van Boven, L. 2003. Learning negotiation skills: Four models of knowledge creation and transfer. *Management Science*, 49(4): 529–540.
15. Anthony, S. (2012). 3ways to predict what consumers want before they know it. *Fast Company*, 16 February 2012. Available online at: https://www.fastcompany.com/1669070/3-ways-to-predict-what-consumers-want-before-you-know-it Accessed 18.03.2022.
16. Isaacson, W. (2011). *Steve Jobs*. London: Little Brown, p. 127.
17. Lieberman, M. (2013). *Social: Why Our Brains Are Wired to Connect*. Oxford: Oxford University Press, p. 130.
18. Sapir, E. A. (1949). Communication. In Sapir, E. (1949). *Selected Writings in Language: Culture and Personality*. University of California Press, p. 556.
19. Cited in Modjeska, C. N. (1968). A note on unconscious structure in the anthropology of Edward Sapir. *American Anthropologist*, 70(2): 344–348, p. 346.
20. Stanford Report (213) Nalini Ambady, Stanford psychology professor, dies at 54. *Stanford Report*, 31 October 2013. Available online at: https://news.stanford.edu/news/2013/october/nalini-ambady-obit-103013.html Accessed 18.02.2022.
21. Ambady, N., & Weisbuch, M, (2010). Nonverbal behaviour. In Fiske, S. T., Gilbert, D. T., & Lindzey, G. (Eds.). *Handbook of Social Psychology* (pp. 464–497). New York: McGraw-Hill; Richeson, J. A., & Shelton, J. N. (2005). Brief report: Thin slices of racial bias. *Journal of Nonverbal Behaviour*, 29(1): 75–86.
22. Millar, M. G., & Tesser, A. (1986). Effects of affective and cognitive focus on the attitude-behaviour relationship. *Journal of Personality and Social Psychology*, 51: 270–276; Wilson, T. D., & Schooler, J. W. (1991). Thinking too much: Introspection can reduce the quality of preferences and decisions. *Journal of Personality and Social Psychology*, 60: 181–192.
23. Ambady, N. (2010). The perils of pondering: Intuition and thin slice judgments. *Psychological Inquiry*, 21(4): 271–278, p. 274.
24. Ambady, N., & Gray, H. M. (2002). On being sad and mistaken: Mood effects on the accuracy of thin slice judgments. *Journal of Personality and Social Psychology*, 83: 947–961.
25. Ambady, N. (2010). The perils of pondering: Intuition and thin slice judgments. *Psychological Inquiry*, 21(4): 271–278.
26. Ibid.
27. Ambady, N., & Weisbuch, M. (2010). Nonverbal behaviour. In Fiske, S. T., Gilbert, D. T., & Lindzey, G. (Eds.). *Handbook of Social Psychology* (pp. 464–497). New York: McGraw-Hill.
28. Ambady, N., Krabbenhoft, M. A., & Hogan, D. (2006). The 30-sec sale: Using thin-slice judgments to evaluate sales effectiveness. *Journal of Consumer Psychology*, 16(1): 4–13.
29. Rule, N. O., & Ambady, N. (2011). Face and fortune: Inferences of personality from Managing Partners' faces predict their law firms' financial success. *The Leadership Quarterly*, 22(4): 690–696.
30. Blankespoor, E., Hendricks, B. E., & Miller, G. S. (2017). Perceptions and price: Evidence from CEO presentations at IPO roadshows. *Journal of Accounting Research*, 55(2): 275–327.

31. Rule, N. O., & Ambady, N. (2008). The face of success: Inferences from chief executive officers' appearance predict company profits. *Psychological Science*, 19(2): 109–111.
32. Adolphs, R., Tranel, D., & Damasio, A.R. (1998) The human amygdala in social judgment. *Nature*, 393: 470–474; Adolphs, R., Baron-Cohen, S., & Tranel, D. (2002). Impaired recognition of social emotions following amygdala damage. *Journal of Cognitive Neuroscience*, 14: 1264–1274.
33. Ambady, N. (2010). The perils of pondering: Intuition and thin slice judgments. *Psychological Inquiry*, 21(4): 271–278, p. 274.
34. Pentland, A. (2010). To signal is human: Real-Time data mining unmasks the power of imitation, kith and charisma in our face-to-face social networks. *American Scientist*, 98(3): 204–211.
35. Pentland, A. (2010). *Honest Signals: How They Shape Our World*. Cambridge, MA: MIT Press, p. 111.
36. Pentland, A. (2010). To signal is human: Real-Time data mining unmasks the power of imitation, kith and charisma in our face-to-face social networks. *American Scientist*, 98(3): 204–211.
37. Jordan, K. N., & Pennebaker, J. W. (2017). The exception or the rule: Using words to assess analytic thinking, Donald Trump, and the American presidency. *Translational Issues in Psychological Science*, 3(3): 312–316.
38. Sadler-Smith, E., & Akstinaite, V. (2023). Did destructive leadership help create the conditions for the spread of Covid-19, and what are the early warning signs? *Leadership* (in press).
39. Barrett, H. C. (2008). Evolved cognitive mechanisms and human behaviour. In Crawford, C., & Krebs, D. (Eds.). *Foundations of Evolutionary Psychology*. New York: Lawrence Erlbaum Associates, pp. 173–189.
40. Ibid.
41. Baron-Cohen, S. (2008). The evolution of brain mechanisms for social behaviour. In Crawford, C., & Krebs, D. (Eds.). *Foundations of Evolutionary Psychology*. New York: Lawrence Erlbaum Associates, pp. 415–432.
42. Norman, E., & Price, M. C. (2012). Social intuition as a form of implicit learning: Sequences of body movements are learned less explicitly than letter sequences. *Advances in Cognitive Psychology*, 8(2): 121–131.
43. Lewicki, P., Hill, T., & Czyzewska, M. (1992). Nonconscious acquisition of information. *American Psychologist*, 47: 796–801.
44. Lieberman, M. D. (2000). Intuition: a social cognitive neuroscience approach. *Psychological Bulletin*, 126(1): 109–137.
45. Pentland, A. (2010). *Honest Signals: How They Shape Our World*. Cambridge, MA: MIT Press, p.38.
46. Lieberman, M. (2013). *Social: Why Our Brains Are Wired to Connect*. Oxford: Oxford University Press, p. 120.
47. Ibid., p. 21.
48. Frontiers in Psychology (no date). Misunderstanding others: Theory of mind in psychological disorders. Available online at: https://www.frontiersin.org/research-topics/16742/misunderstanding-others-theory-of-mind-in-psychological-disorders Accessed 18.02.2022.
49. Lieberman, M. (2013). *Social: Why Our Brains Are Wired To Connect*. Oxford: Oxford University Press.

50. Satpute, A. B., & Lieberman, M. D. (2006). Integrating automatic and controlled processes into neurocognitive models of social cognition. *Brain Research*, 1079(1): 86–97.
51. Voland, E. (2007). We recognize ourselves as being similar to others: Implications of the 'social brain hypothesis' for the biological evolution of the intuition of freedom. *Evolutionary Psychology*, 5(3): https://doi.org/10.1177/147470490700500301.
52. Ibid.
53. Hodgkinson, G. P., & Healey, M. P. (2011). Psychological foundations of dynamic capabilities: Reflexion and reflection in strategic management. *Strategic Management Journal*, 32(13): 1500–1516.
54. Lieberman refers to the brain regions that are associated with the X- and C-systems as their neural correlates. Others also refer these brain regions as the neural substrates of the relevant processes, for example the amygdala is a neural correlate or neural substrate of a number of X-system processes. See: Lieberman, M. D. (2007). Social cognitive neuroscience: a review of core processes. *Annual Review of Psychology*, 58: 259–289.
55. Ibid., p. 267.
56. Barry, B., Fulmer, I. S., & Van Kleef, G. A. (2004). I laughed, I cried, I settled: The role of emotion in negotiation. In Gelfand, M. J., & Brett, J. M. (Eds.). *The Handbook of Negotiation and Culture*. Stanford, CA: Stanford Business Books, pp.71–94.
57. Tversky, A., & Kahneman, D. (1992). Advances in prospect theory: Cumulative representation of uncertainty. *Journal of Risk and Uncertainty*, 5(4): 297–323.
58. Deppe, M., Schwindt, W., Kraemer, J., Kugel, H., Plassmann, H., Kenning, P., & Ringelstein, E. B. (2005). Evidence for a neural correlate of a framing effect: Bias-specific activity in the ventromedial prefrontal cortex during credibility judgments. *Brain Research Bulletin*, 67(5): 413–421.
59. Porter, S., ten Brinke, L., & Gustaw, C. (2010). Dangerous decisions: The impact of first impressions of trustworthiness on the evaluation of legal evidence and defendant culpability. *Psychology, Crime & Law*, 16(6): 477–491.

10
The Creative Sense

Overview

The main idea of this chapter is that intuition 'senses' whilst insight 'sees'. Other differences between intuition and insight are discussed and illustrated with examples such as Archimedes' fabled 'Eureka' moment and various 'light-bulb' moments from business. Close examination of the Standard Model of creativity reveals it to have five not four stages. The pivotal point in the model, as far as sensing is concerned, is 'intimation' (approximating to 'creative intuition'). The role of unconscious thought in decision-making and creative thinking is explored. The example of the Mann Gulch fire illustrates how insight and intuition work together under straightened circumstances. Whether the idea of an 'intuitive insight' is an oxymoron is debated. If and how 'holistic hunches' should be used in business as a way of 'exploring' (as opposed to 'exploiting') is discussed. The vital role of creative intuition in 'sensing' direction and foreseeing in art, science, technology, and business is established, and evidence from extraordinary human achievement is cited as evidence.

Intuition 'Senses'

One of the most famous examples of intuition's sensing capability is the story of the 'Getty kouros' with which Malcolm Gladwell begins his bestselling book about intuition, *Blink: The Power of Thinking Without Thinking* (2005). The J. Paul Getty Museum in Los Angeles is one of the world's great art museums. In the early 1980s, a dealer in antiquities, Gianfranco Becchina, offered the Getty an eight-foot-high marble statue of a boy, a 'kouros' (a male youth) for purchase. The kouros was purportedly from sixth century BC Greece. The Getty took the kouros on loan initially and submitted it to rigorous scientific testing by a University of California geologist using various X-ray and crystallographic techniques. The results confirmed that it was marble from Cape Vathy quarry on the Greek island of Thasos in the Northern Aegean and that its patina suggested it was suitably ancient. Science seemed to have solved any doubts that there could have been about the statue's provenance. The Getty Museum was as sure as it felt it needed to be that the kouros was genuine. They agreed to buy it for just under $10 million.

Professor Evelyn B. Harrison (1920–2012) an eminent scholar of Greek sculpture from the Institute of Fine Arts at New York University, had the opportunity to view the kouros at the Getty before it went on display to the public. Instinctively and intuitively, she did not like what she saw: it did not give her the impression of being old; the curls over the forehead looked unpleasantly 'doughy'; the collarbones were 'boringly understated' and there was no 'verve to their curves'; the pectorals were 'flat and depressed'; and the knees were 'stiffly carved', 'inorganic', and 'almost ugly'. Harrison's response was as understated as it was unequivocal: she said that she was 'very sorry' to hear that the Getty Museum was about to complete the purchase.[1]

Professor Harrison's assessment of the Getty kouros demonstrated how her deep knowledge and decades of experience of studying Greek sculpture merged into an instantaneous judgement that there was something seriously not right about the Getty kouros.[2] In a specially arranged colloquium in Athens in 1992, another expert commented that it aroused in him an 'intuitive revulsion'.[3] The two-second glance of an expert trumped a year of rigorous scientific analysis by geologists and technicians. Following the refurbishment of the galleries in 2018, the kouros was removed from public view and is now in museum storage. The caption alongside a photo of the kouros in the catalogue reads poignantly: 'About 530 BC, or modern forgery'.[4] The case of the Getty kouros demonstrated quite strikingly how an expert's intuitive sensing capabilities can, at least as far as aesthetic judgement is concerned, surpass scientists' analytical solving capabilities.

Insight 'Sees'

The terms 'insight' and 'intuition' are sometimes used interchangeably, but they are not the same thing. Harrison's experience with the Getty kouros was an intuition; she had a nagging doubt which made her sense that something was wrong, but she did not have a light-bulb moment at which she could say exactly that the kouros was a fake. Intuition's distinctive feature is sensing, insight's distinguishing features are fourfold: first, insight involves a rapid transition from 'not knowing' to 'knowing'; second, there does not appear to be any conscious step-by-step reasoning process involved; third, where insight does occur there is often a period where there is a failure to solve a perplexing problem to the extent that the problem solver gets stuck at a mental impasse; fourth, following the impasse there is an illuminative breakthrough in a Eureka moment, at which point the solution to the problem is revealed. Scientific writers on the subject have waxed lyrical on its properties: 'Like dynamite, the insightful solution explodes on the solver's cognitive landscape with breath-taking suddenness';[5] 'That glorious moment when one suddenly sees the solution to a problem'.[6] By these and other accounts, insight is a much more dramatic event than the subtle felt-sense that characterizes intuition.

A well-known example of an insight problem is the 'matchstick problem': 'Given six matches, make four equilateral triangles, with one complete match making up the side of each triangle'. The matchstick problem is initially hard because people attempt to solve it using a narrow two-dimensional representation of the goal. As a result they confine their attempts to making two-dimensional arrangements. In two dimensions, the matchstick problem is impossible to solve. The breakthrough comes if the problem-solver realizes that a solution cannot be achieved without thinking outside the two-dimensional box. The matchstick problem is solved easily when the matches are used in three dimensions to form a tetrahedron (a triangular-based pyramid with four faces and six straight edges).[7]

When insight occurs, the problem-solver becomes aware of the logical structure of the problem. They know, *and* they know how and why they know. In the matchstick problem, the insight is the sudden realization that the solution does not lie in a single plane. This insight then allows the problem to be solved. Moreover, the solution is not a fuzzy or vague felt-sense. It is explicit and tangible and can be communicated in words or images.[8] In other words, there is nothing particularly intuitive about solving the matchstick problem or many of the other puzzles that psychologists have used to study insight in their laboratories. Intuitions on the other hand are notoriously difficult to interpret and communicate to others, this is why Evelyn Harrison had to resort to metaphors such as 'doughy', 'understated', lacking 'verve', and 'inorganic' to describe her intuitive sense about the fake kouros. Whilst intuition involves sensing, insight is literally seeing into the structure and the solution of the problem. Hence intuition *senses* whilst insight *sees*.

In our own research, Vita Akstinaite and I have studied the differences between intuition and insight by comparing managers' answers to two questions: 'what happens when you intuit'; versus 'what happens when you have an insight?'.[9] Using computerized text analysis (CTA) software (which counts words in various predetermined categories, for example cognitive processes, emotional processes, etc.) we found that the 'linguistic markers' of insight were words to do with 'future-focus', 'positive emotions', and 'seeing'. The linguistic markers of intuition were words to do with 'negative emotions', 'feelings', and 'the body'. For example, managers described what happens when they have an insight as 'the connections I make in my head make brilliant and powerful sense', 'it is like a flash of lightning in the night sky', and 'the way forward suddenly becomes clearer and more obvious'. Examples of what happens when managers intuit included 'something does not feel right', 'I feel uncomfortable, initially for no apparent reason', 'I have sensations, feelings in my stomach', 'thoughts/questions come to mind instinctively', 'it feels right or wrong', and 'I get a weird feeling in my stomach if something isn't right'. These linguistic markers support the idea that insight involves seeing, whilst intuition involves sensing. They also add weight to the view that intuition often errs on the side of caution.

Whether insightful seeing or intuitive sensing is more important in scientific discovery and technological invention is open to debate. For example, the science fiction writer Isaac Asimov remarked that 'The most exciting phrase to hear in science, the one that heralds new discoveries, is not "Eureka" but "That's funny"'. (in the sense of strange). It is in these 'hmmm … that's funny' moments that intuition's sensing function comes into its own. The reality is that both seeing and sensing have a role to play in creative discovery and problem-solving.

Archimedes and the Original Eureka Moment

The pre-eminent, and undoubtedly clichéd, story of insight is that of Archimedes (circa 287–212 BC) and his Eureka moment. Archimedes was a Greek citizen of Syracuse in Sicily and mathematician, inventor scientist, and confidante of King Hieron II. The king had ordered his metalsmith to make a wreathlike crown for a deity. But the king's intuition told him that the metalsmith might have dishonestly adulterated the expensive gold with cheaper silver in order to pocket the difference. King Hieron needed proof. The clue to the problem's solution lay in the fact that silver is less dense than gold. To determine if the crown was pure gold or a gold-silver alloy, its volume needed to be known so as to be able to work out its density. Who better than the brilliant Archimedes to solve the problem of how to measure the volume of a highly irregular and precious object without destroying it?

The University of Massachusetts astronomer Alan Hirshfeld, in his book *Eureka Man: The Life and Legacy of Archimedes* (2009), described what is reputed to have happened when Archimedes was taking his regular bath which he happened to like filled to the brim with water:

> Archimedes noticed water splashing over the rim. The more of him that was immersed, the more the water overflowed. Eureka! The mundane had become the momentous; to find the crown's volume all he had to do was immerse the crown in a vessel full of water and measure the spillage. The crown was indeed too large for the original weight of gold. The metal smith was guilty.[10]

Archimedes is alleged to have jumped out of the bath and run down the street naked and dripping with water exclaiming Eureka! The King's problem of how to measure the crown's volume could now be solved without destroying it in the process. Whether the metalsmith was quite so lucky is not recorded. Archimedes' Eureka moment has bequeathed to us the principle of displacement, which is used to this day in hydrostatics and numerous other applications. Eureka is a Greek word meaning 'I have found it!' (εὕρηκα, *heúrēka*). This is why insights are called Eureka moments. Archimedes' bathing experience was the perceptual clue that gave his perplexed mind the unexpected jolt that was needed. He had an abrupt and unexpected revelation of how displacement could be used to measure volume. Archimedes was able to *see* the solution to his problem. This is insight.

Neuroscientists Mark Beeman and John Kounios used functional magnetic resonance imaging (fMRI) to locate where in the brain activations occur when problems are solved in Eureka moments. They gave participants co-called remote associate tests (for example, what word connects crab, pine, and sauce?)[i] and found that, at the moment that the insightful solution pops into someone's awareness, there is increased activation in a small fold of tissue in the right brain's temporal lobe called the anterior

---

[i] The solution is 'apple'.

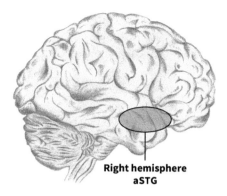

Figure 10.1 The right hemisphere aSTG associated with solving laboratory insight problems.
Source: Brain image drawn by Sarah Sadler-Smith, based on an image by Vasilisa Tsoy/Shutterstock.com

superior temporal gyrus (aSTG, Figure 10.1) which lies underneath an area of the skull just above the right ear. When they gave the participants in their experiment methodical, analytical problems to solve, activation in the aSTG was absent. It seems as though the more broadly tuned neurons in this small area of the right hemisphere are able to collect and connect together information from a wide area of cortical space and make connections between distantly related ideas.[11]

Eureka Moments in Business

It is not only bathing that can create the conditions for Eureka moments. They also seem to be precipitated by a change in perspective or a distraction from the problem. Harry Beck, an electrical draughtsman and the designer of the iconic London Tube map, had his light-bulb moment when he reconfigured the London underground railway map to be not like a map but like an electrical circuit diagram. Beck spaced the stations more or less equally on the map rather than spacing them geographically as they were on the ground. The powers that be did not like it, but the public loved it and it became the template and style guide for transport maps the world over. Beck's perspective shifted from 'map' to 'circuit', and the problem was solved.

Insight had a vital role to play in establishing many of our most iconic brands and daring new business ventures. When Steve Jobs witnessed Xerox's work on developing a novel graphical user interface in 1979 he was convinced 'within 10 minutes' that 'every computer would work this way someday. You knew it with every bone in your body'.[12] More recently, the entrepreneur and former tech employee, Julie Stevanja, founder of the leading multi-brand retailer for women's sportswear Stylerunner, which became a $50 million fashion empire, had her light-bulb moment whilst she was sitting on the mat in the middle of her yoga class.[13] The origins of the GoPro camera is said to have involved an entrepreneur, Nick Woodman, taking some time out on a surfing holiday in Bali. Woodman tied a 35 mm camera to his wrist with a strap improvised from old wet suits and bits of plastic to shoot himself and his friends surfing. This insight inspired him to innovate the GoPro, the innovative waterproof, lightweight camera with a wrist harness. By 2020, 26 million GoPros had been sold in a hundred countries across the globe. Or take the case of the US food giant General Mills' revelation for Yoplait Go-Gurt, a portable, low-fat yogurt for kids in the form of a squeezable tube. The insight was a product of real-life observations of children playing in school yards. The researchers had the light-bulb moment that a tube of yogurt that could be held in one hand and eaten without a spoon would be an ideal way for children to eat yogurt on the go in their breaks.[14]

Stories of entrepreneurial and intrapreneurial insights are the stuff of business legends. 3M's Post-it Notes were the products of an insight from two of its top scientists. Spencer Silver and Art Fry joined the dots between Silver's non-sticky glue that was looking for an application and Fry's frustration that the page markers in his hymn book kept falling out and ending up on the floor during church services. Incidentally, Post-its' iconic canary yellow colour was purely serendipitous—the lab next door happened to have scrap yellow paper to hand. Edwin Land invented the Land Camera, which later became the world's first and bestselling instant picture camera, the Polaroid camera. Land's Eureka moment came in 1943 while on holiday in Santa Fe with his family. His 3-year-old daughter wanted to know 'why can't I see the pictures now?'. Within the hour, Land had visualized and put together in his mind the necessary components for the instant picture Land Camera 'stimulated by the dangerously invigorating plateau air of Santa Fe'.[15] Four years later, the Polaroid camera was launched, and the company dominated the instant photography market for the next six decades. Land, who was much admired by Steve Jobs, had a dictum: 'Don't do anything someone else can do.'

These light-bulb moments present an idealized, romanticized notion of cavalier thinkers and eccentric inventors coming up with revolutionary scientific discoveries and groundbreaking innovations out of the blue. They pervade the folklore of invention and innovation. However, Eureka moments are only one part of a more elaborate process which is as much about perspiration as it is about inspiration, involving long fuses as well as light-bulb moments.

The Standard Model

The Standard Model of creative thinking in psychology involves four steps. Step 1 is 'preparation': the problem solver is immersed in a novel, important, interesting and unsolved problem in their field, for example scientists in the nineteenth-century were perplexed by the problem of the chemical structure of benzene. Such problems can be so puzzling that scientists reach an impasse. Step 2 is 'incubation': ideas 'churn' in the melting pot of the unconscious, for example when the discoverer of the structure of benzene, Kekulé, was dozing by the fire and had a dream of snakes swallowing their own tails thus forming a ring shape; Step 3 is 'illumination' (or insight): the 'pieces of the puzzle' come together. Once the 'dots are joined', the answer to the problem becomes visible and obvious, for example the benzene molecule has a ring, not a linear structure. Kekulé interpreted the tail-swallowing snakes as the vital clue he needed to solve the problem. Step 4 is 'verification': the insight is tested in a protracted process of evaluation and elaboration, for example by collecting further evidence to prove the insight. Preparation and verification bookend the creative process. They are the '99 percent' that Thomas Edison was referring to when he said that creativity and invention is 'one percent inspiration and 99 percent perspiration'.[16]

The origin of the standard four-stage 'preparation-incubation-illumination-verification' model of creativity dates back to the early decades of the last century. Graham Wallas (1858–1932) presented it in Chapter 4 ('The Stages of Control') of his 1926 book *The Art of Thought*. Wallas was a social and political scientist, educator, and one of the four original founders of the London School of Economics (LSE). Wallas's book presents one of the first modern scientific accounts of the process of creative discovery. In it he set out to document the train of psychological events that great scientists go through in making breakthrough discoveries. He based the model on two main case studies: the German physician and physicist Hermann Helmholtz (1821–1894), and the French mathematician Henri Poincaré (1854–1912). Wallas quoted from Helmholtz's autobiographical writings to illustrate the importance of the preparation stage:

> An investigator, or an artist, who is continually having a great number of happy ideas, is undoubtedly a privileged being ... I have often been in the unpleasant position of having to wait for lucky ideas ... They often steal into the line of thought without their importance being at first understood; then afterward some accidental circumstance shows how and under what conditions they have originated ... But to reach that stage was not usually possible without long preliminary work.

Wallas also quoted several examples from Poincaré's autobiographical writings on *Mathematical Reasoning*. Poincaré reached an impasse: 'for fifteen days I strove to prove ... I seated myself at my work table, stayed an hour or two, tried a great number of combinations and reached no results'. He experienced a light-bulb moment as he stepped onto a bus: 'At the moment when I put my foot on the step the idea came to me, without anything in my former thoughts seeming to have paved the way for it'. On another occasion Poincaré allowed a perplexing problem to incubate during a clifftop walk during which the solution occurred to him with a 'brevity, suddenness and immediate certainty'.[17] Poincaré, like Helmholtz and Kekulé, could literally *see* the solution to the problem once the insightful moment had occurred.

More Than Meets the Eye

The four-stage Standard Model has dominated thinking about the creative process for the best part of a century. However, there is more to the Standard Model than meets the eye. Wallas was intrigued particularly by the role that the unconscious plays in the creative process. He saw illumination as the end point in a 'train of associations'. These associations are mostly either unconscious or on the periphery or fringe of consciousness, which he described as the 'penumbra' that surrounds our focal consciousness. There is more to this model than meet the eye because there is an aspect of the Standard Model that has been overlooked but stands out in a close reading of Wallas's writings.[18] He refers to that moment when the mind has been 'simmering over something', when a 'dim feeling' arises that the 'fully conscious flash of success is coming'.[19] He devoted no less than twelve pages of his twenty-nine-page 'Stages of Control' chapter of *The Art of Thought* to this 'dim feeling'. Wallas referred to this phenomenon as 'intimation'. We might call it 'creative intuition' and it supports the process of foreseeing.

Intimation is the bridge between incubation and illumination. The Standard Model has five not four stages: preparation; incubation; intimation; illumination; verification. Like intuition, intimation involves feelings: 'dim feelings, [and] faint intuitions' and a 'vague feeling of the unexpected'. Intimation is a felt-sense that needs to be 'encouraged and coaxed' before it emerges fully into consciousness. Wallas found support for his ideas in the work of one of the founders of modern psychology, Wilhelm Wundt (1832–1920), who said that intimations are the 'pioneer', i.e. the harbinger, of knowledge and that novel thoughts come to consciousness first in the form of a feeling. Intuition researcher Clare Petitmengin described the process as an 'unfolding forwards' in which the intuition at first shows on the surface of consciousness, which is followed by a slow ripening of the idea but also where the intuitor experiences an absence of control; it is not a case of '*I* have an idea or *I* see an image' but '*there is* an idea or *there is* an image'.[20] The sense of ownership seems to lie somewhere else.

This means that in terms of their proximity to consciousness, intimations are in the liminal (i.e. transitional) zone between the unconscious and the conscious, in other words they occupy the fringes of consciousness,[21] see Figure 10.2.[22] They are both automatic and 'felt'.[23] Wallas likened his personal experience of intimation to this feeling 'as if my clothes did not fit me'. He was firmly of the view that if the intimation lasts for an appreciable time it can be made sufficiently conscious by an effort of attention. In an appeal to what we might term 'intuitive awareness' or 'interoceptive awareness' (see Chapter 11), Wallas concluded his discussion of intimation with the

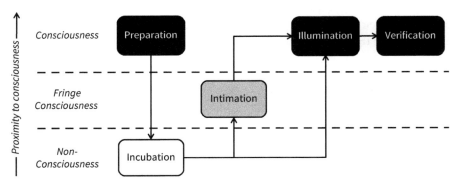

Figure 10.2 Five stages of the creative process in terms of different levels of consciousness.

(*Source*: Sadler-Smith, 2015)

recommendation that we can improve in the art of thought by 'directing our attention from time to time to the feeling of Intimation and bringing our will to bear on the cerebral processes which it indicates'. In so doing, he also urged creative thinkers to proceed with caution for fear of scaring their intimations away 'as a fish is scared by the slightest ripple'.[24]

Insight in the Real World

The Standard Model, especially the four-stage version, is simple and appealing. However, in reality the creative process, especially outside the psychology laboratory and autobiographical writings of famous scientists from history, is more complex. Studies of natural occurrences of insight seem to suggest it is the product of a 'slower-burn' creative process. In a major study of 'natural insights', naturalistic decision researchers Gary Klein and Andrea Jarosz studied 120 examples of insight taken from interviews with scientists, technicians, inventors, and others in a variety of different fields including technology, science, the military, business management, and finance. What they discovered poured some cold water on the traditional idea of the Eureka moment as the main way in which creative problem solving works.

As well as finding evidence of intimations or creative intuitions (although they did not use these terms as such), Klein and Jarosz' research also paints a more nuanced picture of how insight happens. Some insights were spurred by impasses, but most were not. Some insights were accompanied by a Eureka moment, but many were not. Many insights were triggered by inconsistencies and contradictions which were actively inquired into and investigated rather simply explained away. When inconsistencies were sensed, intuitions catalysed inquiry. In the majority of incidents, the person's expertise was a critical factor in arriving at an insight. Almost half of the incidents were gradual rather than sudden. Where insights were all of a sudden, this was as result of new information becoming available. Gradual insights were associated with long-standing hunches. Intuition researcher William Duggan of Columbia Business School calls this 'strategic intuition' and he argues that for your strategic intuition to work 'you must disconnect the old dots, [and] let new ones connect on their own'.[25]

Klein and Jarosz give the example of Wall Street analyst Meredith Whitney's sense of something out-of-kilter at the New York–based investment bank Bear Stearns and her deliberate search to find out if the bank was in trouble. Her intuitions prompted her inquiries to make sense of a situation that did not stack up. An accumulation of evidence about Bear Stearns' contracting assets and high leverage of up to fifty to one confirmed her hunch that the firm was about to go under. She commented that 'this has happened to me several times ... where I know things in my gut. But I can't believe that I'm the only person who is putting it together'.[26] Whitney's intimations were correct in foreseeing Bear Stearns' demise: the company went bust in the 2008 financial crisis.

Klein and Jarosz uncovered a different kind of insight in the case of financial fraud investigator, and self-confessed 'maths geek',[27] Harry Markopolos's hunches about the disgraced financier Bernie Madoff (1938–2021). Madoff was an American financial fraudster who was responsible for the largest 'Ponzi' scheme in history. A Ponzi scheme is a form a financial pyramid selling in which earlier investors are paid using funds from later investors. It is named after the 1920s swindler and con man Charles Ponzi. Madoff's $65 billion Ponzi scheme earned him a 150-year prison sentence in 2009. Markopolos said he smelt a rat as far back as 1999 when his own firm asked him to create a financial product that could give Madoff-like stellar returns.[28] Like Professor Harrison with the fake Getty kouros, Markopolos suspected that he was dealing with a fraud within minutes of examining publicly available information about Madoff's feeder funds.

However, Markopolos had to spend almost a decade on Madoff's trail. He contacted politicians and badgered journalists. But no one would listen because they were taken in by Madoff's name and reputation. In the official US Securities and Exchange Commission's report of 2009, one witness remarked that investigations 'cannot go on indefinitely [just] because people have a hunch'.[29] But the Madoff case proved that they can—and sometimes should. Markopolos's account of the Madoff investigation is called *No One Would Listen: A True Financial Thriller*; it demonstrated what can happen when an independent and determined expert has a strong hunch and is fearless in calling out fraud. Markopolos was both perplexed by and sceptical about Madoff's ability to make profits irrespective of what the markets were doing. He had a gut feeling that Madoff was up to something and followed through on it with dogged determination. Markopolos's hunch paid off, and Madoff paid the penalty.

Both Whitney's and Markopolos's insights were slow burns rather than Eureka moments. Switching from swindling to science, a similar phenomenon was observed in drug development at AstraZeneca, where one scientist had a feeling that something was wrong in the data: 'you look at the pattern and you feel that "no, this is not right". ... you screen them again ... and then there's still something that is not right and then you must go further [to] get to the bottom of the thing that is not right.'[30] The Astra Zeneca scientists' experiences of creative discovery are more like the intuition-based inquiry that Cinla Akinci and I found in police officers' first-response decisions than the puzzle-induced insights following impasses that psychologists have studied traditionally in their laboratories.[31] Intuition prompts efforts to make sense of data that do not initially make sense because they are sparse, noisy, vague, uncertain, and ambiguous.

In our own research Cinla Akinci and I looked for evidence of Eureka moments when we interviewed managers, scientists, and technologists in UK companies who had won the prestigious Queen's Award for Innovation. We did find evidence for insightful moments, but other factors played equally important roles. One stand-out feature was that award-winning innovators were highly motivated by the double hurdle of challenge and curiosity. They deliberately sought out difficult problems to solve. One of them remarked 'we don't do stuff that's easy because ... [others] can all do that and we don't make any money out of it'. Another interviewee explained how their company deliberately sought-out hard problems where no one else had been 'brave enough to actually say, you know what, I think we can do this'. In solving the harder problems, they gave vent to their curiosity, played around with large a number of ideas and in doing so came up with new ones.

That said, they did use formal brainstorming and 'idea capture' techniques right out of the innovation management textbooks, but they also kept informal notebooks crammed with scribbles and sketches of inventions. They experimented and literally played with physical objects and materials such as balloons and eggs to investigate the tensile strength of novel materials in the case of a company came up with the seemingly incongruous invention of a canvas made out of concrete. These extraordinary innovators accepted that a majority of the ideas would never reach fruition. But by generating ideas, exploring their feasibility, and discarding the ideas judged unworkable, they satisfied their powerful intrinsic motivators of challenge and curiosity. They were energized by the promise and potential for finding a big breakthrough idea that would solve their hard problem and make money as well.

Likewise, in haute cuisine, creative intuitions are not so much an exclusive product of Eureka moments, they are more akin to an artistic compositional process. Intuition researchers Marc Stierand and Viktor Dörfler discovered that the world's leading chefs, such as Ferran Adrià of the three Michelin-starred El Bulli in Catalonia ('the most imaginative generator of haute cuisine on the planet'[32]), weave together emotion ('feeling the creative idea'), harmony ('structural intuitions' in the dish), sensibility (an 'inner guiding force') as well as simplicity (as 'essence of complexity') and authenticity (the 'distinctive voice of the chef/creator'). Creative intuition in haute cuisine can be consequential: losing a Michelin star can cut a restaurant's sales by as much as 50 per cent, whilst gaining one can have the opposite positive effect.[33]

Studying insight in naturalistic (i.e. field) as opposed to artificial (i.e. laboratory) settings reveals that insight occurs through multiple pathways involving detecting contradictions (as in the Meredith and Markopolos examples), needing to make a breakthrough (as in the Mann Gulch example, see below), deliberately looking for hard problems and playing with ideas (as in the Queen's Award companies), and seeing connections (as in the example of Charles Darwin encountering Malthus's essay on population and competition for resources, which sparked his insights about selection of the fittest). As well as appearing in illuminative moments, breakthrough ideas also come about after a slow burn on a long fuse. Often. intuition is the back-seat driver with an impeccable sense of direction, and which impels the idea on a forward trajectory.

Thinking Without Thinking

Life is full of complex problems and consequential decisions which require solutions, for example which car to buy, which apartment to rent, which course to study, which job to take, and the one which perplexed Darwin greatly: whether to marry or not. The exhortation to 'look before we leap' is sound advice. But is it possible to overthink complex problems? Dutch social psychologist Ap Dijksterhuis, the creator of Unconscious Thought Theory (UTT), thinks so. He was intrigued to find out if unconscious thought has a 'generative power' of its own which could help us to arrive at accurate judgements in complex decisions without the need to think too hard.[34] According to UTT—which is not an uncontroversial theory[35]—the best way to find a solution to a complex problem is: first become prepared by gaining as much information as possible about the problem; second distract yourself from the problem for a period of time so as to allow for incubation; third make an intuitive, gut-feel decision.

Dijksterhuis backs up his claims for UTT with experimental evidence from a series of laboratory studies. In one of these, people who did not think too hard about their consumer choices (for example, by being distracted deliberately in the experiment by doing an anagram) end up more satisfied with their choice of a complex item (such as a video camera) than with their choice of a simple item (such as a bottle of shampoo). Conversely, people who thought hard were more satisfied with their choice of the simple item than with their choice of the more complex item.[36] In another study, Dijksterhuis and his colleagues found that experts' predictions of the scores of soccer matches were more accurate when they did not think consciously about their forecasts. For non-experts, thinking a lot or a little did not make much difference to how accurate their forecasts were.[37]

Not thinking too hard about a complex problem is thought to give superior results for a number of reasons. First, unconscious thought is presumed to have superior processing capacity (analogous to a broad bandwidth parallel processor) to conscious thought (analogous to a narrow bandwidth serial processor). Second, conscious processing is constrained by an attentional bottleneck because of the limits of a working memory which can hold and manipulate only a small number of items (approximately seven) at any one time. Third, conscious thought tends to give greater weight to factors that happen to be under the attentional spotlight and overlook those that are not, this is analogous to looking for our lost keys under the nearest streetlight.[38] For example, when evaluating the decision of which car to buy conscious thought is good at solving the problem of which vehicle is likely to be the most fuel-efficient based on unambiguous, verbatim information. But it is not so good when it comes to integrating large amounts of information from diverse and sometimes intangible sources such as fuel efficiency, comfort, appearance, and brand into an overall gist for which one is the best.[39]

Unconscious thought is especially relevant where complex decisions involve qualitative and aesthetic factors which are, by their nature, hard to quantify objectively, as was the case with the Getty kouros incident which opened this chapter. Angela Ahrendts, former CEO of British luxury brand Burberry and later a senior VP for retail at Apple, recognized the dangers of overthinking and the power of intuition in marketing and retail management in her TEDx talk of 2013:

> Intuition is a form of wisdom, the gift of knowing without reasoning. When you're not forced to overthink things it's amazing the clarity that emerges and how rapidly you can adapt. Intuition is usually more right than wrong. But we love to convince

ourselves otherwise. Why is it that we value thinking over feeling? Why aren't we taught to follow our natural inclinations to protect the possibilities instead of just accepting the probabilities?[40]

UTT makes the strong claims that unconscious thought helps decision-makers to intuitively sense what the optimal judgement is likely to be and that unconscious thought can outperform conscious thought in complex decisions.[41] Dijksterhuis's UTT is arguably a theory of intuition rather than of insight. He defines intuition as the 'feeling of knowing what to do'. Unconscious thought uses the subjective quality of an object's attributes, such as comfort and aesthetics, which are combined into an overall gist rather than objective, verbatim, numerical information. A team led by Madelijn Strick and Dijksterhuis reviewed the evidence for the effect of unconscious thought on decision-making across ninety-two separate research studies. They found strong support for the existence of the unconscious thought effect. Strick and Dijksterhuis concluded that it is less a question of *whether* the unconscious thought effect exists and more a question of *when* the unconscious thought effect is important in judgement and decision-making.

A number of factors determine if and how unconscious thought has a positive effect on judgement and decision-making. First, when the problem is complex and there are a higher number of choice options, unconscious thought appears to be better at integrating an abundance of decision attributes and information. Second, unconscious thought appears to be effective when the problem involves both verbal information and visual imagery because unconscious thought is capable of holistic (i.e. parallel or broad bandwidth) processing. Third, unconscious thought works better when decisions involve real-world alternatives and interesting, lively decision materials, such as which apartment to rent or which high-value item to buy. Fourth, unconscious thought is better suited to situations where decisions need to be taken under time pressure because unconscious System 1 processes are automatic and fast.[42]

Also, unconscious thought can be made more effective through priming. For example, it is possible to activate unconscious incubation in advance of a complex task. The American author Norman Mailer and Pulitzer Prize winner for fiction explained how he went about the unconscious pursuit of a conscious goal in the complex and arduous task of novel writing:

> Over the years, I've found one rule. It is the only one I give on those occasions when I talk about writing. It's a simple rule. If you tell yourself you are going to be at your desk tomorrow, you are by that declaration asking your unconscious to prepare the material. You are, in effect, contracting to pick up such valuables at a given time. Count on me, you are saying to a few forces below: I will be there to write.[43]

Mailer made a metaphorical contract with his unconscious mind that it would pick up its share of the heavy lifting offline and that he, in the form of his conscious mind, would be there to take the ideas forward. For the English author Martin Amis, his novels do not actually start with a conscious decision. Their genesis is to be found in his unconscious, out of which emanates 'a throb or a shiver, a frisson, and you recognise the feeling and you know that here is a bit of fiction offering itself to you ... it's more as if it's chosen me than you've chosen it.'[44] In musical composition, the twentieth-century Russian composer Igor Stravinsky said of his most famous composition *The Rite of Spring* (1913) that he wrote what he 'heard' and that he was merely the 'vessel through which *The Rite of Spring* passed'. The twentieth-century English composer Benjamin Britten had 'considerable faith in the ability of his unconscious mind to solve daytime problems while he slept'.[45] Creative intuition is lauded in the arts and in science.

Many of the stories and anecdotes of creative intuitions involve lone individuals, often portrayed as geniuses, struggling with hard problems. Given that business management is a social as well as an economic arena, the romantic ideal of the lone intellect is more likely to be the exception rather than the rule. In the case of Steve Jobs, many of the intuitive insights on which Apple was founded were arrived at by sensing patterns, associations, and coherences between seemingly disparate elements. For example, having attended calligraphy classes at Reed College, Steve Jobs came to recognize the power of typography, and this evolved into an obsession with fonts, typefaces, and icons. These evolved into concrete images and metaphors such as the trash can for junk. Jobs' initial ideas were fuzzy and nebulous, and it was language that played a pivotal role in making his creative intuitions more concrete through his talking them through with designers such as Susan Kare. He hit it off with Kare because they both had a creative instinct for simplicity and aesthetics. As a result, Apple was the first computer to have beautiful typography. Jobs appears to have something in common with the Nobel Laureate Paul Dirac (Physics, 1933) whose dictum was 'a theory with mathematical beauty is more likely to be correct'.

Creative intuitions start out in the mind of an individual, however to become an invention or an innovation they have to be surfaced, shared, and interpreted. Through interpretation, for example by dialoguing with a like mind, highly personal intuitive creations shift from being a subjective, tacit sense of the possible to an objective, explicit, and conceivable solution. Albert Einstein in a letter to the French mathematician Jacques Hadamard remarked that 'conventional words or other signs have to be sought for laboriously only in a secondary stage, when the associative play' which takes place before any logical construction is sufficiently established. Hadamard himself spoke of mathematicians as being 'logical in the enunciation of their ideas, after having been intuitive in their discovery', in this sense mathematicians, scientists, and artists may be thought of as being *both* 'intuitive creators' (via System 1's sensing capacity) *and* 'intellectual makers' (via System 2's solving and interpretive capacities).

The Hard Work of the Slow Burn

Unconscious though theory (UTT) researcher Madelijn Strick and her colleagues point out that it would a mistake to assume that because unconscious thought occurs by definition outside of conscious awareness that unconscious thought does not require cognitive resources. Unconscious thought is a consumer of mental resources, but it does so 'offline', so to speak. Our attention, by definition, cannot be directed towards unconscious processing.[46] However, because conscious processing and attention are correlated in our lived experience, we assume, not unreasonably, that if there is nothing to attend to, there is nothing going on. But there may be a lot going on behind the scenes. UTT postulates that unconscious processing occurs without conscious attention (the so-called 'deliberation-without-attention' effect) but not without utilizing resources, albeit in a tacit form. Indeed, one of the most important contributions of UTT to the study of judgement and decision-making is the proposal that people can 'think' unconsciously as well as consciously.[47] Creative intuition is not constrained by the brain's computational capabilities, moreover its parallel processing capacities, which also happen very quickly, make thinking without thinking possible.[48]

As far as unconscious thought and creativity are concerned, a naïve inference from unconscious thought theory might be that scientists, artists, inventors, and entrepreneurs should simply engage in daydreaming or distractions and let serendipity and unconscious thought do the heavy lifting. However, this is a mistaken and misleading conclusion. Even though unconscious thought research suggests that unconscious processing can be effective in 'joining the dots' to form novel configurations, in order for unconscious processing to work, there has to be enough dots to be connected. Dijksterhuis and colleagues have reminded us of three important principles of creativity: first, unconscious thought cannot create knowledge; second, conscious learning is needed to establish the requisite knowledge base; third, unconscious thought draws on this knowledge base to come up with creative connections.[49]

This assertion is backed up by a number of well-known examples. Some of Darwin's most important ideas about evolution through natural selection are detectable with hindsight in his early writings. Darwin's reading of Malthus's *An Essay on the Principle of Population* (1798) made him realize how competition for resources could explain how species evolve. This helped him to join the dots he had already acquired over decades of study and investigation, in order to configure his hunches into a compelling and coherent theory which became after many years the revolutionary idea put forward in *The Origin of Species* (1859).[50] Steve Jobs, in an interview with *Wired* magazine, described creativity as 'just connecting things', but he also pointed out that you have to have things to connect in the first place and, 'unfortunately, that's too rare a commodity ... a lot of people in our industry ... don't have enough dots to connect, and they end up with very linear solutions'.[51] Deep immersion gives scientists, inventors, artists, and entrepreneurs not only a sense of which problems are worth tackling but also helps them to make the connections which create novel and useful solutions to important and complex problems. Without this slow burn, creative problem-solving may simply turn into an aimless wandering in the dark.[52] One of the paradoxes of creative intuition is that thinking without thinking is far from easy, even though the thinking may be unconscious. In this sense, creative intuition, and other forms such as expert intuition, are fast but not frugal. As educational researchers

Christian Harteis and Stephen Billett point out, the intuitions that support fast, complex, and consequential decisions (such as those of a firefighter or a nurse) or the emergence of creative ideas (such as those of an artist, scientist, or an entrepreneur) are compiled from of complex knowledge patterns, developed by implicit learning over many years of effort and engagement with the complex and messy problems of professional practice.[53]

Insight and 'Creative Desperation'

When psychologists study insight in the laboratory they tend to use puzzles that are well-defined, tightly structured, and for which there is a single, clear-cut solution; for example, the 'matchstick problem' (see above) or the 'nine-dot problem' (given nine dots composed of a three-by-three grid, join all nine dots with four straight lines without taking your pen off the paper), which have only one solution.[ii] In this 'puzzle paradigm', tasks are designed deliberately to stymie subjects. This can lead them to a sudden realization of the solution, most likely after having reached an impasse having had the benefit of a period of incubation. The impasse is forced for the purposes of the experiment and the role of expertise is eliminated by the use of unfamiliar and artificial tasks.[54] Researchers can then study performance, reaction times, brain activity, etc. with precision in order to identify and understand the cognitive processes and neural substrates of such insights.

However, in the real, world problems tend to be much more ill-defined, loosely structured, and generally messy. An impasse is not always reached and solutions may be on a much longer fuse or slower burn than it is possible to study or concoct in time-constrained laboratory sessions. For example, the problem of designing a graphical user interface for personal computers that will have mass-market appeal is an ill-defined problem (because the parameters for what constitutes the 'right' answer are very broad) and has a loose structure (because there is more than one likely solution). Steve Jobs' sense of the potential of a graphical user interface (GUI) that would appeal to a mass market was not fully worked out when he first encountered it at Xerox in 1979, even though seeing the interface on a bitmapped screen lifted a veil from his eyes and allowed him to 'see what the future of computing was destined to be'.[55] The estimate of 'six months' for how long it would take to implement proved to be wildly optimistic. Such problems stand in stark contrast to the puzzles used traditionally in laboratory experiments. In real-world problem-solving, insight is more nuanced than the Standard Model of creativity and experimental findings suggest. This is especially the case when the challenges of ill-definition and loose structure are compounded by fast-moving conditions in life-threatening situations.

One of the most famous examples of the power of insight under time pressure (and which creates challenges for the Standard Model of the creative process) is the infamous Mann Gulch Fire.[56] It was made famous in the eminent organizational

---

[ii] Clue: the nine-dot problem is solved by literally thinking outside the three-by-three box.

theorist Karl Weick's seminal 1993 *Administrative Science Quarterly* article entitled 'The collapse of sensemaking in organizations: The Mann Gulch disaster'. It took place in Montana 1949 and claimed the lives of fifteen 'smokejumpers' in a blaze that burned nearly 5,000 hectares of the Helena National Forest park. A smokejumper is a firefighter who is dropped near to the site of a fire by parachute. Mann Gulch is a steep valley which leads down to the Missouri River.[57] On 5 August 1949, a team of eighteen smokejumpers led by Wagner Dodge parachuted into Mann Gulch to control a forest fire that had been started by a lightning strike. Analyses of what actually happened have proven hard to verify and must be taken as reconstructions.[58] The smokejumpers landed at 04.00 hrs but as the team headed down the valley towards the fire, turbulent winds gusting to 40 mph turned the fire into a 'blow-up', creating 'spot fires' all over the valley and causing it to spread rapidly. At 05.45 hrs the smokejumpers turned around and moved up the valley to a safer location. However, on looking back, Dodge realized that they would not be able to outrun the 600 feet-per-minute tsunami of flames that was chasing them up the valley and would soon engulf them. The first smokejumper was caught at 05.56, the rest were caught by 06.00. Two smokejumpers escaped in a rocky area off to the left of the Gulch. Dodge escaped by the most counter-intuitive of means—at 05.55 he decided to light a fire of his own.

Decision researcher Gary Klein has re-analysed the details of the investigation and has actually visited the site himself. He explains Dodge's insightful moment as follows. Dodge realized that he could not reach safety by trying to outrun the fire (because it was moving at hundreds of feet per minute) against a steep slope (because at the top of the Gulch the gradient is 75 per cent), nor could he get to the rocky area to the left (because it was 200 yards away and the fire was thirty seconds behind him). In an act of what Klein called 'creative desperation', Dodge came up with the idea of lighting what later came to be known as an 'escape fire'. In the words of the Forest Service investigation:

> Dodge sized up the situation better than most of his crew, who either thought they could outrun the fire or saw no other alternative. Some if not all of the crew stopped briefly to see what Dodge was doing and listen to his pleas for them to get into the burned-out area he was preparing. Someone is reported to have said: 'To hell with that, I'm getting out of here!' No one stayed with Dodge. The crew members split up afterward, with the majority continuing to run up the canyon.[59]

The escape fire quickly turned the bone-dry grass into thick black ash. Dodge then lay down in the ash to take refuge from the looming wall of flame. He recounted that fierce winds from the firestorm lifted him off the ground three times during the few minutes that it took for the fire to pass over him. At 06.10 he was able to sit up and move about. Tragically by then the other smokejumpers who had tried to run away up the canyon had been consumed by the flames.

Dodge's inspired and insightful outside-of-the-box thinking was that he was running through thick, heavy, dry bunchgrass and this was the fuel for the fire itself. In making sense of the situation, he realized that he could not do anything about the slope of the ground or the speed of the fire. But he could neutralize the fire's fuel by burning it. Like Archimedes' principle of displacement, Dodge's insight joined the dots to make a novel combination, literally fighting fire with fire to create a protective buffer zone.[60] Perhaps the colleagues who perished thought that Dodge had gone crazy or just given up. We will never know, but cognitive psychologists attribute their refusal to join Dodge to a phenomenon known as 'functional fixedness'. They were fixated cognitively because they could only think of fire as a deadly threat rather than a potential saviour.[61] As a result of Dodge's sudden realization in the face of desperation that fire could literally be fought with fire, escape fires became a recognized practice after Mann Gulch.[62]

Did Dodge have an insight, or an intuition, or both? There appears to have been a Eureka moment of sorts, but it was not a proven solution, and the circumstances meant that the decision was literally a matter of life and death. Could Dodge see insightfully into the structure of the problem directly? Yes: he quickly came to the conclusion he should try burning the fuel before it could burn him. Did Dodge sense intuitively that burning the grass was his only way of surviving this calamity? Yes: he sensed how critical the situation was and that it demanded a novel solution, he formulated his plans and made an intuitive judgement to go with his gut.[63] Did he have any guarantee of success? No: his insight was a hypothesis on which he took an intuitive gamble. It could have gone disastrously wrong. Could Dodge's intuition be classed as expertise-based? Management researchers Chet Miller and Duane Ireland think not because Dodge's tactic:

> was not part of fire training at the time, nor had Dodge had any prior experience with it. Dodge needed to take a risk, create variance from plan, and experiment with a new direction. His hunch, based on past experience with fire but not a straightforward replay of past learning, proved wise.[64]

Dodge was unable, in the literal and metaphorical heat of the moment, to sell his hunch to the members of his team, who perished. For Dodge, the challenge of saying why the hunch made sense to him was compounded and constrained by the speed and dynamism of the desperate situation he found himself in. Nonetheless the desperation of the situation forced him to intuit an insightful solution. In this messy and time-pressured life-or-death situation, Dodge had both an insight for what to do and an intuition that it could work. As a result he was able to foresee the potential consequences of fighting fire with fire.

Intuitive Insights: An Oxymoron?

At Mann Gulch, Dodge had the insight that he could light a fire to burn the fuel that was threatening him. Dodge also exercised his intuitive judgement in gambling that acting on this insight might just save his life. He had an intuitive insight. In the world of business, Mary Crossan of Ivey Business School and Iris Berdrow of

Bentley College found that the process of strategic renewal at Canada Post Corporation (CPC) was driven by entrepreneurial-style intuitive insights of one visionary key individual. This person was the first to envision the radical change from physical to electronic delivery of mail in the early 2000s.[65] But if intuition and insight are distinct phenomena,[66] how can it make sense to talk of intuitive insights? Many intuition researchers have been dogged in their determination to reserve insight for those moments when people can see into the structure of a problem and intuition for 'knowing without knowing how or why we know',[67] thus preserving the distinction between seeing (insight) and sensing (intuition). Is it possible for some insights to be intuitive?

In an effort to resolve this issue, intuition researcher Viktor Dörfler distinguishes between 'intuitive insights' and 'intuitive judgements' in the field of creativity.[68] In so doing, he challenges the assumption that intuition is exclusively a judgement (as in the definition 'affectively charged judgements that arise through rapid, non-conscious, holistic associations'[69]). Dörfler's reasoning goes as follows: just as there can be intuitive judgements (as in domains as diverse and chess, firefighting and management) and non-intuitive judgements (as in standard analytical problem-solving and decision-making), so there can be intuitive insights (where solutions to ill-defined and loosely structured problems are required) and non-intuitive insights as well (where solutions to well-defined, tightly structured problems are required). Rather than contradicting the assumption that all intuitions are judgements, which is largely the making of decision researchers, Dörfler adds a new angle to the study of intuition in business, especially where creativity and innovation are involved as follows.

Solving the well-defined and tightly structured puzzles and problems favoured by laboratory researchers (such as the nine-dot problem and the matchstick problem, see above) and mythologized in stories such as Archimedes' Eureka moment, involves non-intuitive insight (the nine-dot, matchstick, and Hieron's crown problem all had predetermined solutions that were waiting to be discovered). But as Dörfler points out, ill-structured and loosely structured problems call for intuitive insight. Most real-world problems are likely to involve both intuitive insights in order to generate alternatives or come up with novel solutions and intuitive judgements in deciding which of the insightful alternatives to choose or novel solutions to trust. Wagner Dodge intuited a number of alternatives (to run, or climb, or light a fire) and intuited that one of these (lighting a fire) to be viable and worth pursuing. Intuitive insights support the process of foreseeing.

This distinction is also to be found in the fuzzy front end (FFE) of the new product development (NPD) process. Intuitive insights are used divergently to generate and explore a large number of alternatives in feeding the funnel of NPD, whilst intuitive judgements are used convergently to filter and prioritize alternatives into a manageable number from a choice set (a larger number) to a consideration set (a smaller number).[70] In the divergent stage, quantity of ideas takes precedent over quality, and ideas that initially may seem ridiculous, like paying to stay in a stranger's home (Airbnb), often turn out to be brilliant.[71] Feeding the innovation funnel can be a laborious and all-consuming process. The famous British business person and inventor Sir James Dyson invented the bagless vacuum cleaner which bears his name. It was the end product of literally thousands of prototype designs. In Dyson's own words: 'after four years of building and testing 5,127 prototypes of my cyclonic vacuum, I finally cracked it. Perhaps I should have punched the air, whooped loudly, and run down the road from my workshop shrieking "Eureka!"'. He did not do an impersonation of Archimedes because for Dyson, feeding the ideas funnel was more about the intelligent pursuit of diligent research, slogging through prototype after prototype and the acceptance of failure than any folklorish flash of brilliance.[72]

Automated Expertise versus Holistic Hunches

The idea of intuitive insights as an explorative tool recaps a discovery made by one of the pioneers of intuition research in management, Weston H. Agor, in his study of several thousand senior managers in the US in the 1980s. Agor described how executives reported using intuition as an 'explorer'. By this he meant giving intuition free rein to foresee a path that might be worth following. The executives in Agor's study did so by avoiding the rigid system of step-by-step decision-making they had been trained to use. Instead, they allowed their minds to flow where they, or it, wanted to go. They did this in variety of ways ranging from 'sifting through the sand' of prior experiences to simply toying with concepts and ideas. The main aim was not to 'choke off' intuition. On the other hand, inhibiting intuition through the use of rules, boundaries, and restrictions only serves to reinforce the cognitive fixedness and intellectual inertia which constrain creativity and foresight.[73]

Management researchers Chet Miller and Duane Ireland's distinction between intuition as 'holistic hunch' and intuition as 'automated expertise' parallels Dörfler's distinction between intuitive insights and intuitive judgements. Intuition as holistic hunch results in judgements being made by subconscious processes. These involve synthesizing diverse experiences and combining information in novel ways. The outcome of this process of intuiting is accompanied by strong feelings of rightness. On the other hand, intuition as automated expertise results in judgements being made through partially subconscious processes. This involves matching to, or recall of, similar situations that have been encountered in the past and replaying past learnings. The process of automated expertise is accompanied by feelings of familiarity.

In assessing whether and when holistic hunch or automated expertise should be used, Miller and Ireland started from the premise that an organization's strategic decisions can be focused on either 'exploitation' (capitalizing on existing ways of doing things) or 'exploration' (searching for new technologies and markets). Exploration is critical for organizational success in fast-moving sectors and markets, whilst exploitation is advantageous in stable sectors and markets. This resonates with research findings which show that intuition is a more effective decision-making tool in unstable environments (where exploration is required) but is a less effective decision-making tool in stable environments (where exploitation is required).[74]

Intuition as holistic hunch supports exploration because playing one's hunches often involves risk-taking, experimentation, and departures from current practices. It is a feature of entrepreneurial alertness, which is the 'antenna' that some people have that enable them to recognize gaps, make connections, spot opportunities and foresee outcomes.[75] However, in playing a hunch there is always the possibility of failure. Miller and Ireland do not see this as a bad thing necessarily. Improvisations and experiments are by their nature uncertain and not all of them will yield positive outcomes, yet Wagner Dodge saved his life through improvising his escape fire at Mann Gulch. Failures and the lessons that can be learned from them can create new knowledge. James Dyson saw the rejection of his invention of the bagless vacuum cleaner by big companies as a learning opportunity: 'Failure is so much more interesting because you learn from it. That's what we should be teaching children at school, that being successful the first time, there's nothing in it. There's no interest, you learn nothing actually.'[76]

Miller and Ireland advise that using intuition as automated expertise for exploration is using the 'wrong tool from the tool box'. Likewise, in situations calling for exploitation, intuition as holistic hunch is unlikely to work if all that is required is the straightforward use of past learnings. Miller and Ireland's message for managers is simple. First, where organizations are committed to an exploitation focus, they should limit the role of holistic hunch in their decision processes. Second, where organizations are committed to an exploration focus, they should create the conditions for intuitive insights to flourish. However, both come with a health warning. In both exploitation and exploration, standard decision-making tools such as devil's advocacy should be used where possible to test the robustness of holistic hunches and automated expertise.

Researchers in Austria led by Kurt Matzler surveyed the relationships between entrepreneurs' decision-making style (intuition and deliberation[77]), firms' orientation (exploration versus exploitation[78]), and business performance (growth and profitability compared to competitors). An intuitive decision-making style was positively related to explorative success but not significantly related to exploitative success. They recommended that organizations who have an exploration focus should dare to follow their holistic hunches but also be sensitive to when not to trust them.[79] Researchers in the United States discovered that successful entrepreneurs balanced intuitive and analytical approaches rather than being gung-ho, 'go-with-your-gut' types. Reassuringly, in the same research, accountants were found to be strongly inclined towards analysis, whilst actors were inclined strongly towards intuition.[80] These findings resonate with the thoughts of the great Austrian management thinker Peter Drucker who believed in intuition 'only if you discipline it'[81] and cautioned against the thoughtless playing of gut feelings by 'hunch artists' because this can 'kill businesses'.[82]

Another great Austrian, the political economist Joseph Schumpeter (1883–1950), in his magnum opus *The Theory of Economic Development*, recognized the anticipatory nature of intuition: 'the success of everything depends on intuition, the capacity of seeing things in a way which afterwards proves to be true, even though it cannot be established at the moment'.[83] Schumpeter here is referring to the power of intuitive foresight in creativity, alertness and opportunity recognition. Bill Gates explained in his business autobiography the intuitive insight they had at Microsoft about the future of personal computing. They had a holistic hunch that there could be a computer in every office and every home: 'We set up shop betting on cheap computing power and producing software when nobody else was'; the book's title was *The Road Ahead*.[84] Gates also commented in an interview with CNN in response to the question of whether he has 'some sort of sounding board': Gates: 'Well, if I think something's going to catch on, I trust my own intuition'; CNN: 'And you're never wrong?'; Gates: 'No, I'm often wrong, but my batting record is good enough that I keep swinging every time the ball is thrown.'[85]

Creative Intuition in Scientific Discovery

Business can learn much about intuition and foresight from studies of creative thinking in scientific discovery. The pivot point in Graham Wallas's Standard Model of creativity with which this chapter began (preparation, incubation, intimation, illumination, and verification) is intimation (which was his word for intuition, or more precisely for creative intuition). The word itself comes from the Latin for 'to announce' (*intimare*). Intimations, or creative intuitions, are poised between incubation and illumination. As such, they occupy the liminal space between the unconscious and the conscious, the zone Wallas referred to as fringe consciousness. Creative intuitions may presage or announce that something novel may be about to happen. They may also give the sense, that is the foresight, that a particular path of scientific or technical discovery is worth pursuing.

The standard textbook definitions of creative intuition include 'a vague anticipatory perception that orients creative work in a promising direction'[86] and 'feelings that arise when knowledge is combined in novel ways'.[87] They fit with intuition's sensing capacity. There are many situations in the context of scientific discovery and innovation where scientists and inventors became aware of possible solutions of paths towards a solution, i.e. they *sensed* the way forward, without necessarily knowing why they knew.[88] The philosopher of science Sir Karl Popper (1902–1994) recognized the 'irrational element or creative intuition' in scientific discovery which is consistent with the anticipatory perceptions which Wallas called intimations and which we might refer to as a process of foreseeing.[89]

If creative intuition has any importance as a method of discovery, then we might expect to find it at the highest level of human achievement and endeavour, as revealed in the work of Nobel Laureates. Viktor Dörfler and Colin Eden interviewed nineteen science Nobel Laureates to try and find out more about creative intuitions in scientific discoveries. They came to the strong conclusion that, for the Nobel Laureates they interviewed, no significant research result has been achieved 'without intuition playing a major part in the process'.[90] Prominent examples include physics Nobel Laureates James Cronin (1980), who said 'you kind of have a sense of what's going to work and what's not going to work', and Yoichiro Nambu (2008), who commented that 'something that's clicked in my mind, that seems interesting or something that's maybe promising'. Medicine Nobel Laureate Michael S. Brown (1985) described his team's experiences of creative intuition as follows:

> As we did our work, I think, we almost felt at times that there was almost a hand guiding us. Because we would go from one step to the next, and somehow we would know which was the right way to go. And I really can't tell how we knew that, how we knew that it was necessary to move ahead.[91]

George Stigler (Nobel Laureate of economics, 1982) considered himself to have 'good intuition and good judgement on what problems are worth pursuing'. Stanley Cohen (Nobel Laureate of medicine, 1986) his research is guided by a 'feeling of ... "this is an important result" and "Let us follow this path", I am not always right, but I do have feelings about what is an important observation and what is probably trivial'.[92]

The Swedish neuropharmacologist Arvid Carlsson (Nobel Laureate of medicine, 2000), who is best known for his work on the neurotransmitter dopamine, likened the process of drug development to 'walking in a labyrinth' with many decision points where the 'thing is to not jump in the wrong direction too many times'. For Carlsson, creative intuition is the thing that 'leads your decision in a certain direction' in spite of the fact that in the early stages the whole picture is very fragmentary.[93] Carlsson came to appreciate the value of intuitive thinking in science from one of his mentors, Bernard Brodie. Brodie is one of the founders of modern pharmacology and Carlsson recalled that he had 'remarkable intuition. When he sensed that a research area was "hot" he did not hesitate to go into it'.[94] More recently, the cosmologist Stephon Alexander noted that intuition is the lifeblood of a great physicist: 'we intuit first, then confirm with math'.[95] The perception of intuition, or at least creative intuition, in the hard sciences stands in stark contrast to the view of intuition in much of the social sciences and business management, where it was until relatively recently viewed with suspicion. As in the arts, creative intuition is extolled in the sciences.

Creative Intuition in Invention

Nobel Laureates' experiences of creative intuitions resonate with those of engineers involved in new product development. Many engineers testify to relying 'strongly on their own intuition for determining the directions(s) in which new technology should be moved'.[96] Creative intuitions are at the fuzzy front end (FFE) of new product development (NPD). In the FFE, a product concept is formulated and then a decision is made as to whether or not to invest the necessary resources to develop the idea, and the sums involved can be significant. The FFE occupies the space between when an idea is first conceived and when it is judged ready for formal development.[97] Creative work in the FFE is 'insight-driven, prototype powered and foresight-inspired'.[98] It involves the generation of a large number of potential ideas and is fuzzy to the extent that it is intuitive, open-minded, and rough around the edges.[99] Innovation researcher Katrin Eling and her colleagues argued that the unconscious mind comes into its own in the FFE because it has both high processing capacity and can access tacit knowledge. This makes it capable of recognizing patterns and extracting the gist of a problem and sensing potential solutions holistically. This gives intuitive thinking the edge over analytical thinking in the need to combine information, sense opportunities, and make connections between ideas in the early stages of NPD.[100]

James Dyson, referred to earlier, trusted his intuitive judgement in the early stages of developing his bagless vacuum cleaner. As well as being bagless, the Dyson vacuum cleaner had a feature that was unheard of previously: a clear bin which meant that you could see the dirt. Dyson and his engineers were very excited at being able to watch the dirt and see how much had been collected. His hunch was that this would work. However, retailers were appalled: "'You'll never sell that. People don't want to see the dirt". We [Dyson] said no, we like it'. But when Dyson and his team did the research, they found out that the retailers were right: people said they did not want to see the dirt. However, like Geoff Bezos and his decision to go with Amazon Prime, and flying in the face of the naysayers (see Chapter 1), Dyson decided to gamble on his gut feelings. As it turned out, he was right. The Dyson vacuum ended up having a see-through bin. He could not prove that people would buy it. The market research showed the opposite. But as Dyson remarked, 'you have to be brave, you have to risk a lot of money, you have to go into the unknown. It's risky.'[101] As well as being intuitive and risky, proving creative intuitions can be a lengthy and laborious, slow burn of a process. Belief and dogged determination play as important a role as the creative idea itself. Dyson found that this required sweat and sacrifice:

> By [prototype number] 2,627, my wife and I were really counting our pennies … By 3,727, my wife was giving art lessons for some extra cash … It didn't happen overnight, but after years of testing, tweaking, fist-banging, and after more than 5,000 prototypes, it was there … Or nearly there. I still needed to manufacture it and go sell it.'[102]

Mats Sundgren and Alexander Styhre, who studied the role of creative intuition in the pre-clinical drug development at the pharmaceutical company AstraZeneca (AZ), found that successful drug development requires both formal processes and procedures *and* creative and intuitive thinking. In drug development, as in Nobel Prize–winning science and bagless vacuum cleaner development, creative intuition gives the early stages of the process both the impetus of a new idea and a sense of direction. Observations from AZ scientists captured how this worked for them: 'the ability to predict things with pretty good precision'; 'a kind of feeling. It is like what vision is for planning'; 'almost emotional; it's like that things look good. For example, if I have a synthesis that I am working with, I can get a feeling that "this should work."'[103] In spite of the fact that creative intuition is a key part of the drug development process, Sundgren and Styhre lamented the fact that intuition's role in scientific creativity and discovery is underappreciated, seriously misunderstood, and poorly institutionalized in many research-based organizations.

Automating Creative Intuition?

Could a machine ever match the intuitive mind's capacity to sense creative connections and give direction to scientific discovery and artistic invention? Data scientists have used algorithmic creativity to compose music, paint paintings, and write poetry. Whether these efforts have been successful is open to debate. The Oxford mathematician Marcus du Sautoy in *The Creativity Code* (2019) asked whether algorithmic creativity presents an existential threat to human creativity. He argues that although AI has a role to play in making us more creative by assembling data and generating alternatives, AI lacks the capability to exercise 'transformational creativity', in which something new is created that shocks us. Could AI have written *The Rite of Spring*, or *Hamlet*, or conceived of Jackson Pollock's drip paintings, or Damien Hirst's shark in formaldehyde?

If AI is currently able to produce a script for the 2019 Lexus ES advertisement then in time and given the right kinds of inputs could AI compose a Hamlet-like drama? Algorithmic creativity is limited in that it can only play by the rules that humans give to it. Humans, on the other hand, not only play by the rules, but they also throw out old obsolete rules and create bold, new, daring ones through which we are able to see our world differently. Creative artists and scientists are rule-makers, rule-takers, *and* rule-breakers. Algorithmic creativity might be able to produce a passable Bach-like three-part fugue or a Picasso-like cubist painting, but could it have come up with the revolutionary *ideas* of counterpoint and cubism in the way that Bach and Picasso did? It is impossible for me to feel what it means to *be* Bach or anyone else for that matter, but through Bach's music I at least get a glimpse of how he saw and felt about his world. As du Sautoy points out, art is *self-discovery*—the painter paints and the composer composes what she *is*. If there is no self, then there is nothing to paint or compose about. Would a self-portrait painting by a computer by definition be merely a photograph? Du Sautoy's conclusion is that until a machine can become conscious and empathetic it cannot be more than a tool for replicating and extending human creativity which transcends what a computer is currently capable of.[104]

Hiroaki Kitano, CEO and President of the Sony Computer Science Lab, whilst acknowledging that scientific breakthroughs still depend heavily on human beings' creative intuitions, speculates as to whether AI could be equipped with the necessary creative intuition for discovery that could enable computers to ask the 'right' questions for major scientific breakthroughs and 'thereby render scientific intuition obsolete'.[105] The jury is out on that question. Until that day arrives, if it ever does, human creative intuition is a distinctive and sustainable source of added value and competitive advantage for technology-based organizations and organizations in general in the information age. Through its capability to detect anomalies, make connections, extract the gist, and sense direction creative, intuition is a rare, valuable, difficult-to-imitate and hard-to-substitute resource in science, technology, and business.[106] Creative intuition is one of the few infinite resources that we have at our disposal and, as noted by one of the most influential French philosophers of the twentieth century, Henri Bergson, intuition is at the heart of the truly creative act, such that 'true creativity starts with intuition and is followed by intellectual thought processes, never the other way around'.[107]

Summary

1. The main idea of this chapter has been that intuition 'senses' a direction or a potential solution whilst insight 'sees' the solution, usually after a period of incubation or unconscious thought.
2. The idea that analysis 'solves' creates a triad of sensing (intuition), solving (analysis), and seeing (insight).
3. The four-stage Standard Model of creativity (preparation, incubation, illumination, verification) has five stages, with intimation (creative intuition) at the pivot point between incubation and illumination.
4. Studies of creativity in the real world show that many creative solutions are not the product of a Eureka moment but emerge after a slow burn on a long fuse.
5. Creative solutions to pressing problems are also the products of the social context in which they occur, as well as random factors such as serendipity.
6. Creative intuitions are invaluable in sensing and setting direction in scientific discovery, technical invention, and entrepreneurship and innovation.
7. Insight and intuition are different, but some insights can be intuitive, hence intuitive insights.
8. Whether or not artificial intelligence could ever mimic or replace human creativity is an open question, and taking a firm position could create a hostage to fortune, but since computers do not have selves, the prospects for algorithmic creativity which can match human creativity do not look good.

Endnotes

1. *The Getty Kouros Colloquium* (1992). Athens: Kapon Editions.
2. McCredie, J.R. (2013). Evelyn Byrd Harrison (1920–2012). *American Journal of Archaeology*. AJA Online, available online at: https://www.ajaonline.org/online-necrology/1605 Accessed 20.02.2022.
3. *The Getty Kouros Colloquium* (1992). Athens: Kapon Editions, p. 44.
4. The Getty Museum. Available online at: https://www.getty.edu/search/?qt=kouros&pg=1 Accessed 20.02.2022.
5. Durso, F. T., Rea, C. B., & Dayton, T. (1994). Graph-theoretic confirmation of restructuring during insight. *Psychological Science*, 5(2): 94–98, p. 98.
6. Gruber, H. E. (1995). Insight and affect in the history of science. In Sternberg, R. J., & Davidson, J. E. (Eds.). *The Nature of Insight* (pp. 397–431).

7. Gilhooly, K. J., & Fioratou, E. (2009). Executive functions in insight versus non-insight problem solving: An individual differences approach. *Thinking & Reasoning*, 15(4): 355–376, p. 356.
8. Dane, E., & Pratt, M. G. (2007). Exploring intuition and its role in managerial decision making. *Academy of Management Review*, 32(1): 33–54. p. 40
9. Sadler-Smith, E., & Akstinaite, V. (2021). Identification of Linguistic Markers of Insight and Intuition Using Computer-Assisted Text Analysis. *The Journal of Creative Behaviour* (in press).
10. Hirshfeld, A. (2009). *Eureka Man: The Life and Legacy of Archimedes*. New York: Walker and Company, p. 4.
11. Kounios, J., & Beeman, M. 2015. *The Eureka Factor*. London: Heinemann, p. 70.
12. Goodell, J. (1994). Steve Jobs in 1994: The Rolling Stone interview. *Rolling Stone*, 17 January 2011. Available online at: https://www.rollingstone.com/culture/culture-news/steve-jobs-in-1994-the-rolling-stone-interview-231132/ Accessed 22.02.2022.
13. Murphy, A. (2018). How a former tech employee, 37, has built a $50MILLION fashion empire after experiencing a genius 'light bulb moment' during a yoga class. *Daily Mail*, 15 November 218. Available online at: https://www.dailymail.co.uk/femail/article-6391011/How-Australian-entrepreneur-built-50-MILLION-fashion-empire-light-bulb-moment-yoga-mat.html Accessed 22.02.2022.
14. Valero, P. B. (2018). Thick data in product development: The Go-Gurt Case. *Antropologia 2.0*. Available online at: https://blog.antropologia2-0.com/en/thick-data-in-product-development-the-go-gurt-case/ Accessed 21.03.2022.
15. Sadler-Smith, E. (2008). *Inside Intuition*. Abingdon: Routledge, p. 250.
16. Csikszentmihalyi, M. (1996). *Creativity: The Psychology of Discovery and Invention*. New York: Harper Collins.
17. Sadler-Smith, E. (2008). *Inside Intuition*. Abingdon: Routledge.
18. Sadler-Smith, E. (2015). Wallas' four-stage model of the creative process: More than meets the eye? *Creativity Research Journal*, 27(4): 342–352.
19. Wallas, G. (1926). *The Art of Thought*. London, UK: Jonathan Cape, p. 97.
20. Petitmengin, C. (2014). Researching the micro dynamics of intuitive experience. In Sinclair, M. (Ed.). *The Handbook of Research Methods on Intuition*. Cheltenham: Edward Elgar Publishing, pp. 188–198.
21. Zander, T., Öllinger, M., & Volz, K. G. (2016). Intuition and insight: Two processes that build on each other or fundamentally differ?. *Frontiers in Psychology*, 7(1395): 3.
22. Sadler-Smith, E. (2015). Wallas' four-stage model of the creative process: More than meets the eye? *Creativity Research Journal*, 27(4): 342–352.
23. Gendlin, E. (1978). *Focusing*. New York: Bantam.
24. Wallas, G. (1926). *The art of thought*. London, UK: Jonathan Cape, pp. 101, 105.
25. Duggan, W. (2007). *Strategic Intuition: The Creative Spark in Human Achievement*. New York: Columbia University Press.
26. Dawes, R. (2009). *House of Cards*. New York: Simon and Schuster, p. 40.
27. Clark, A. (2010). The man who blew the whistle on Bernard Madoff. *The Guardian*, 24 March 2010. Available online at: https://www.theguardian.com/business/2010/mar/24/bernard-madoff-whistleblower-harry-markopolos Accessed 22.02.2022.
28. Ibid.
29. US Securities and Exchange Commission (2009). *Investigation of Failure of the SEC to Uncover Bernard Madoff's Ponzi Scheme*. Available online at: https://www.sec.gov/files/oig-509.pdf Accessed 22.02.2022, p. 35.

30. Sundgren, M., & Styhre, A. (2004). Intuition and pharmaceutical research: the case of AstraZeneca. *European Journal of Innovation Management*, 7(4): 267–279, p. 274.
31. Akinci, C., & Sadler-Smith, E. (2020). 'If something doesn't look right, go find out why': how intuitive decision making is accomplished in police first-response. *European Journal of Work and Organizational Psychology*, 29(1): 78–92.
32. Carlin, J. (2006). If the world's greatest chef cooked for a living, he'd starve, *The Guardian*, 11 December 2006.
33. Stierand, M., & Dorfelr, V. (2014). Researching intuition in personal creativity. In Sinclair, M. (Ed.). *Handbook of Research Methods on Intuition* (pp. 249–263). Cheltenham: Edward Elgar Publishing, p. 252.
34. Dijksterhuis, A., & Meurs, T. (2006). Where creativity resides: The generative power of unconscious thought. *Consciousness and Cognition*, 15(1): 135–146, p. 1005.
35. Waroquier, L., Marchiori, D., Klein, O., & Cleeremans, A. (2010). Is it better to think unconsciously or to trust your first impression? A reassessment of unconscious thought theory. *Social Psychological and Personality Science*, 1(2): 111–118.
36. Dijksterhuis, A., Bos, M. W., Nordgren, L. F., & Van Baaren, R. B. (2006). On making the right choice: The deliberation-without-attention effect. *Science*, 311(5763): 1005–1007.
37. Dijksterhuis, A., Bos, M. W., Van der Leij, A., & Van Baaren, R. B. (2009). Predicting soccer matches after unconscious and conscious thought as a function of expertise. *Psychological Science*, 20(11): 1381–1387.
38. Bargh, J. A. (2011). Unconscious thought theory and its discontents: A critique of the critiques. *Social Cognition*, 29(6): 629–647.
39. For differences between verbatim and gist see Valerie Reyna's fuzzy trace theory of intuition, which is discussed in Chapter 10, see: Reyna, V. E. (2013). Intuition, reasoning and development: A fuzzy-trace theory approach. In Barrouillet, P., & Gauffroy, C. (Eds.). *The Development of Thinking and Reasoning* (pp. 193–220). Psychology Press.
40. https://www.youtube.com/watch?v=mZNlN31hS78; https://www.druckerforum.org/blog/human-essence-as-a-key-to-prosperity-part-i-of-ii-by-ellina-watanabe/
41. https://www.researchgate.net/publication/289541850_Intuition_and_unconscious_thought
42. Strick, M., Dijksterhuis, A., Bos, M. W., & Nordgren, L. (2011). A meta-analysis on unconscious thought effects. *Social Cognition*, 29(6): 738–762.
43. Bargh, J. A. (2011). Unconscious thought theory and its discontents: A critique of the critiques. *Social Cognition*, 29(6): 629–647, p. 638
44. Milles, G. (2015). A telegram from the unconscious: Martin Amis on creativity and style. Jobs.ac.uk. Available online at: https://blog.jobs.ac.uk/language-and-literature/a-telegram-from-the-unconscious-martin-amis-on-creativity-and-style/ Accessed 22.02.2022
45. Sadler-Smith, E. (2008). *Inside Intuition*. Abingdon: Routledge, p. 16.
46. Dijksterhuis, A., Bos, M. W., Nordgren, L. F., & Van Baaren, R. B. (2006). On making the right choice: The deliberation-without-attention effect. *Science*, 311: 1005–1007.
47. Bargh, J. A. (2011). Unconscious thought theory and its discontents: A critique of the critiques. *Social Cognition*, 29(6): 629–647.
48. Betsch, T., & Glöckner, A. (2010). Intuition in judgment and decision making: Extensive thinking without effort. *Psychological Inquiry*, 21(4): 279–294.
49. Zhong, C. B., Dijksterhuis, A., & Galinsky, A. D. (2008). The merits of unconscious thought in creativity. *Psychological Science*, 19(9): 912–918.

50. Gruber, H.E. (1995). Insight and affect in the history of science. In Sternberg, R. J., & Davidson, J. E. (Eds.). *The Nature of Insight* (pp. 397–431). Cambridge, MA: MIT Press.
51. Wolf, G. (1996). Steve jobs: The insanely great thing. *Wired*, 1st February 1996. Available online at: https://www.wired.com/1996/02/jobs-2/ Accessed 22.02.2022.
52. Zhong, C. B., Dijksterhuis, A., & Galinsky, A. D. (2008). The merits of unconscious thought in creativity. *Psychological Science*, 19(9): 912–918.
53. Harteis, C., & Billett, S. (2013). Intuitive expertise: Theories and empirical evidence. *Educational Research Review*, 9: 145–157.
54. Klein, G., & Jarosz, A. (2011). A naturalistic study of insight. *Journal of Cognitive Engineering and Decision Making*, 5(4): 335–351.
55. Isaacson, W. (2011). *Steve Jobs*. New York: Simon and Schuster, p. 96.
56. Weick, K. E. (1993). The collapse of sensemaking in organizations: The Mann Gulch disaster. *Administrative Science Quarterly*, 38(4): 628–652.
57. Forest History Society (no date). Mann Gulch fire 1949. Available online at: https://foresthistory.org/research-explore/us-forest-service-history/policy-and-law/fire-u-s-forest-service/famous-fires/mann-gulch-fire-1949/ Accessed 22.02.2022.
58. Rothermel, R. C. (1993). *Mann Gulch Fire: A Race That Couldn't Be Won*. Ogden, UT: Intermountain Research Station.
59. Ibid., p. 6.
60. Weick, K. E. (1993). The collapse of sensemaking in organizations: The Mann Gulch disaster. *Administrative Science Quarterly*, 38(4): 628–652.
61. Kounios, J., & Beeman, M. 2015. *The Eureka Factor*. London: Heinemann, p. 36.
62. The Film (no date). What is an escape fire? Available online at: http://www.escapefiremovie.com/escape-fire-defined Accessed 22.02.2022
63. Weick, K. E. (1996). *Sensemaking in Organizations*. Thousand Oaks: SAGE.
64. Miller, C. C., & Ireland, R. D. (2005). Intuition in strategic decision making: Friend or foe in the fast-paced 21st century?. *Academy of Management Perspectives*, 19(1): 19–30.
65. Crossan, M. M., & Berdrow, I. (2003). Organizational learning and strategic renewal. *Strategic Management Journal*, 24(11): 1087–1105.
66. Hogarth, R.M. (2001). *Educating Intuition*. Chicago: Chicago University Press.
67. Sadler-Smith, E., & Shefy, E. (2004). The intuitive executive: Understanding and applying 'gut feel' in decision-making. *Academy of Management Perspectives*, 18(4): 76–91.
68. Dörfler, V., & Ackermann, F. (2012). Understanding intuition: The case for two forms of intuition. *Management Learning*, 43(5): 545–564.
69. Dane, E., & Pratt, M. G. (2007). Exploring intuition and its role in managerial decision making. *Academy of Management Review*, 32(1): 33–54, p. 40.
70. Eling, K., Griffin, A., & Langerak, F. (2014). Using intuition in fuzzy front-end decision-making: A conceptual framework. *Journal of Product Innovation Management*, 31(5): 956–972.
71. Divergent thinking and the innovation funnel (no date). *IDEO Blog*. Available online at: https://www.ideou.com/blogs/inspiration/brendan-boyle-on-divergent-thinking-and-the-innovation-funnel Accessed 21.03.22.
72. Dyson, J. (2021). *Invention: A Life*. New York: Simon and Schuster, pp. 1–2.
73. Kounios, J., & Beeman, M. 2015. *The Eureka Factor*. London: Heinemann, p. 36.
74. Khatri, N., & Ng, H. A. (2000). The role of intuition in strategic decision making. *Human Relations*, 53(1): 57–86; Sadler-Smith, E. (2004). Cognitive style and the management of small and medium-sized enterprises. *Organization Studies*, 25(2): 155–181.

75. Kirzner, I. M. (1999). Creativity and/or alertness: A reconsideration of the Schumpeterian entrepreneur. *The Review of Austrian Economics*, 11(1): 5–17; Tang, J., Kacmar, K. M. M., & Busenitz, L. (2012). Entrepreneurial alertness in the pursuit of new opportunities. *Journal of Business Venturing*, 27(1): 77–94.
76. Cadwalladr, C. (2014). James Dyson's interview. *The Guardian*, 9 May 2014. Available online at: https://www.theguardian.com/technology/2014/may/09/james-dyson-interview-engineering-education Accessed 22.02.2022.
77. For example: 'I am a very intuitive person' versus 'Before making decisions, I usually think about the goals I want to achieve'.
78. For example: 'How innovative is your company compared to your strongest competitors?' versus 'Our focus is on improving efficiency and reducing costs'.
79. Matzler, K., Uzelac, B., & Bauer, F. (2014). The role of intuition and deliberation for exploration and exploitation success. *Creativity and Innovation Management*, 23(3): 252–263.
80. Groves, K., Vance, C., & Choi, D. (2011). Examining entrepreneurial cognition: An occupational analysis of balanced linear and nonlinear thinking and entrepreneurship success. *Journal of Small Business Management*, 49(3): 438–466.
81. Drucker Forum (2014). Human essence as a key to prosperity. 14th peter Drucker Forum. Available online at: https://www.druckerforum.org/blog/human-essence-as-a-key-to-prosperity-part-i-of-ii-by-ellina-watanabe/ Accessed 22.02.2022.
82. Miller, C. C., & Ireland, R. D. (2005). Intuition in strategic decision making: Friend or foe in the fast-paced 21st century?. *Academy of Management Perspectives*, 19(1): 19–30, p. 24.
83. Schumpeter, J. A. (1934/1983). *Theory of Economic Development*. Abingdon: Routledge, p. 85.
84. Cited in Duggan, W. (2013). *Strategic Intuition*. New York: Columbia University Press, p. 87.
85. CNN (2002). One on one interview with Bill Gates. CNN Available online at: http://edition.cnn.com/2002/TECH/industry/02/28/gates/ Accessed 22.02.2022.
86. Policastro, E. (1995). Creative intuition: An integrative review. *Creativity Research Journal*, 8(2): 99–113, p. 99.
87. Dane, E., & Pratt, M. G. (2009). Conceptualizing and measuring intuition: A review of recent trends. *International Review of Industrial and Organizational Psychology*, 24(1): 1–40, p. 5.
88. Hogarth, R. M. (2001). *Educating intuition*. Chicago: Chicago University Press, p. 254.
89. Marton, F., Fensham, P., & Chaiklin, S. (1994). A Nobel's eye view of scientific intuition: discussions with the Nobel prize-winners in physics, chemistry and medicine (1970–86). *International Journal of Science Education*, 16(4): 457–473.
90. Dörfler, V., & Eden, C. (2014). Research on intuition using intuition. In Sinclair, M. (Ed.). *Handbook of Research Methods on Intuition* (pp. 264–276). Cheltenham: Edward Elgar Publishing, p. 266.
91. Sadler-Smith, E. (2008). *Inside Intuition*. Abingdon: Routledge, p. 66.
92. Sadler-Smith, E. (2008). *Inside Intuition*. Abingdon: Routledge, p. 67.
93. Sundgren, M., & Styhre, A. (2004). Intuition and pharmaceutical research: the case of AstraZeneca. *European Journal of Innovation Management*, 7(4): 267–279, p. 276.
94. Carlsson, A. (1998). Arvid Carlsson. In Squire, L. R. (Ed.). *The History of Neuroscience in Autobiography* (pp. 28–67). San Diego: Academic Press, p. 35.

95. Lewton, T. (2021). Stephon Alexander interview: Is the universe a self-learning AI? *New Scientist*, 8 September 2021. Available online at: https://institutions-newscientist-com.surrey.idm.oclc.org/article/mg25133510-900-stephon-alexander-interview-is-the-universe-a-self-learning-ai/ Accessed 15.04.2022.
96. Sim, E. W., Griffin, A., Price, R. L., & Vojak, B. A. (2007). Exploring differences between inventors, champions, implementers and innovators in creating and developing new products in large, mature firms. *Creativity and Innovation Management*, 16(4): 422–436, p. 428.
97. Kim, J., & Wilemon, D. (2002). Focusing the fuzzy front-end in new product development. *R&D Management*, 32(4): 269–279.
98. Mootee, I. (2011). Strategic innovation and the fuzzy front end. *Ivey Business Journal*. Available online at: https://iveybusinessjournal.com/publication/strategic-innovation-and-the-fuzzy-front-end/ Accessed 22.02.2022.
99. Mootee, I. (2011). Strategic innovation and the fuzzy front end. *Ivey Business Journal*. Available online at: https://iveybusinessjournal.com/publication/strategic-innovation-and-the-fuzzy-front-end/ Accessed 22.02.2022.
100. Eling, K., Griffin, A., & Langerak, F. (2014). Using intuition in fuzzy front-end decision-making: A conceptual framework. *Journal of Product Innovation Management*, 31(5): 956–972.
101. Cadwalladr, C. (2014). James Dyson's interview. *The Guardian*, 9 May 2014. Available online at: https://www.theguardian.com/technology/2014/may/09/james-dyson-interview-engineering-education Accessed 22.02.2022
102. Malone-Kircher, M. (2016). James Dyson on 5,126 vacuums that didn't work—and the one that finally did. *New York*, 22 November 2016, Available online at: https://nymag.com/vindicated/2016/11/james-dyson-on-5-126-vacuums-that-didnt-work-and-1-that-did.html Accessed 22.02.2022.
103. Styhre, A., Wikmalm, L., Olilla, S., & Roth, J. (2010). Garbage-Can decision making and the accommodation of uncertainty in new drug development work. *Creativity and Innovation Management*, 19(2): 134–146, p. 137.
104. Du Sautoy, M. (2019). *The creativity code: Art and innovation in the age of AI*. Cambridge, MA: Belknap.
105. Kitano, H. (2016). Artificial intelligence to win the Nobel prize and beyond: Creating the engine for scientific discovery. *AI Magazine*, 37(1): 39–49.
106. Bruner, J. S. (1977/1999). *The Process of Education*. Cambridge, MA: Harvard University Press; Dörfler, V., & Eden, C. (2014). Research on intuition using intuition. In Sinclair, M. (Ed.). *Handbook of Research Methods on Intuition* (pp. 264–276). Cheltenham: Edward Elgar Publishing.
107. Hardman, T. J. (2021). Understanding creative intuition. *Journal of Creativity*, 31 (in press): 3.

11
Making an Impact through Intuition

Overview

The main idea of this chapter is that the informed and intelligent use of intuition can create positive impact for individuals and organizations as well as wider society and the economy. In order for this to happen, intuition needs to be cultivated and nurtured, and this can be achieved by (in alphabetical order): 'coaching' (to build expertise), 'debiasing' (to overcome errors), 'diagnosing' (to find out what your preferred thinking style is), 'incubating' (to put the unconscious mind to work on a problem), 'inferring' (to come up with an inference-to-best-explanation), 'integrating, imagining, and iterating' (to build on the complementary strengths of intuition and analysis), 'interocepting' (to hone intuitive awareness), 'interpreting' (to make sense of intuitions), 'learning' (to understand when intuition works and when it does not), 'practising' (because quality, not just quantity, of practice makes perfect), and 'seeking feedback' (because taking intuitive decisions without feedback is one of the best ways to develop bad intuitions). 'Intuitive intelligence' is a vital component of management and leadership; the ability to recognize if, when, and how to 'go with your gut' is one of the keys to impactful performance in the volatile, uncertain, complex, and ambiguous workplaces of the twenty-first century.

Impact and Intuition

Perhaps the most impactful piece of scientific research of the twenty-first century has been the development of the various coronavirus vaccines which, apart from having saved millions of lives, are also estimated to have achieved a global financial benefit of $17.4 trillion, worth about $5,800 of value-added per course and dwarfing the price of $6 to $40 per course.[1] The vaccine research by the scientists at the University of Oxford, Astra Zeneca, BioNTech, Moderna, Pfizer, and others impacted immeasurably on the health and well-being not just of individual human beings but of entire populations and saved the global economy from an even worse catastrophe than the one which we were all forced to endure.

Research impact is the demonstrable contribution that the creation of new knowledge makes to individuals, organizations, wider society, and the economy. Stakeholders have become more vocal in querying the value-added contribution of research, especially that which is publicly funded. Hence the question of if, and how, academic

Intuition in Business. Eugene Sadler-Smith, Oxford University Press. © Eugene Sadler-Smith (2023).
DOI: 10.1093/oso/9780198871569.003.0011

research has a demonstrable and useful impact on society has risen up the policy and practice agendas in recent years. The research community in business schools has woken up to the need to explain the 'so-what' value of its work to its stakeholders and find ways to make and demonstrate a difference.

Intuition, like any other area of management research, must be able to answer its 'so-what?' question. Impact through intuition works in three ways. First, by building individual managers' knowledge of intuition and developing their intuitive decision-making skills and capabilities, for example by helping them to know when and when not to 'go with their gut' (see Chapter 1, for example). This is called 'capacity-building impact' and involves *changing self*.[2] Second, by influencing how organizations do business, for example by developing ways in which employees' creative intuitive insights can be captured and transformed into organizational value-adding products, processes, and services (see Chapter 10, for example). This is called 'instrumental impact' and involves *changing practices*. Third, by improving our understanding of how intuitive decision-making is accomplished in managerial work, for example by showing how intuition and analysis can complement each other when taking decisions in dynamic, uncertain, and complex situations (see Chapter 4, for example). This is called 'conceptual impact' and involves *changing ideas*.

This book is mostly about changing self, leading to changing practices. Its main aim is to help readers to understand intuition in business and apply their newly-acquired knowledge to create positive change that will have a beneficial impact on themselves and their organizations and hence on the economy and wider society. To this end, one of the main arguments of this book, based on the premise of 'two minds in one brain', is that analysis makes its best impact by solving, whilst intuition makes its best impact by sensing.

As far as solving is concerned, there is plenty of guidance for managers in the popular business press on how to develop their analytical skills, for example the *Financial Times' The Decision Maker's Playbook* and *Harvard Business Review Guide to Making Better Decisions* to name but two. Much of the business school curriculum as well as the business press portrays analysing as the most dependable, reliable, and trustworthy way to solve problems and take decisions, for example, by acquiring and analysing data, breaking complex problems into manageable chunks,[3] using data analytics to make predictions, and managing risk and uncertainty.[4]

Analysing is by no means an infallible cure-all, nor is it the only decision-making skill that managers need. As well as being adept at solving by analysing, managers also need to be equally adept at sensing, and one of the ways in which managers can sense, and sometimes foresee, is by using their intuition. Tools and techniques that can be used to develop managers' sensing capabilities are necessary not to displace but rather to complement managers' solving capabilities. It is perhaps surprising that there is a paucity of scientific and evidence-based guidance for managers on how to educate, train, and develop their intuition. On the other hand there is a wealth of material available which promises to be able to ignite and awaken parapsychological, magical, and supernatural intuitions, for example *Intuition Magic, Ignite Your Psychic Intuition*, and *Awaken Your Third Eye*.[5] This chapter offers an alternative in the form of evidence-based guidance on how to 'sharpen your sixth sense' through the methods of coaching, debiasing, diagnosing, incubating, inferring, integrating, imagining and iterating, interocepting, interpreting, learning, practising, and seeking feedback. These are some, but by no means all, of the ways to make intuition impactful in business and beyond.

Coaching

Elite sports performers have always appreciated how invaluable the relationship with a good coach can be in elevating performance to a level at which they can execute skilled performance intuitively. For example, Rafael Nadal's coach and uncle, Toni, said of him that: 'We have proven that a normal kid from Manacor—with effort, with sacrifice—has managed to achieve the many goals which he set when he was young'.[6] One of the reasons that expert coaching is so effective in developing sports intuition is that a coach is able to give immediate and accurate feedback on performance both on the training ground and in a real game. In recent decades, managers in business organizations have come to recognize coaching's potential such that it has become one of the most popular learning and development methods and integral to the fabric of the learning culture of many businesses.[7] The relationship between coaching and intuition in business works in two ways: first, intuitive decision-making is a skill that can be developed through coaching; second, coaches themselves, as well as good managers who see coaching as part of their job, use intuition as part of their day-to-day practice of leading and managing people.

Developing Intuition through Coaching

Good intuitions are built up through learning and experience, but quality of experience is at least as important as quantity of experience. Developing intuitions directly from experience works well in environments in which there are clear and predictable relationships between cues (for example, thin slices of non-verbal behaviours) and outcomes (for example, lecturers' performance in the classroom). This was one reason why the experienced fire ground commanders studied by Klein and colleagues (see Chapter 7) were able to respond intuitively to emergencies in time-pressured, dynamic conditions. The cues they recognized, such as the sight, smell, and sound of a blaze, could be associated with the type of fire and used to predict outcomes. In order to explain how this works, Kahneman and Klein contrasted 'high-validity' versus 'low-validity' environments. In high-validity environments it is possible to learn cues that are associated with outcomes and hence make intuitive predictions, i.e. to forecast an outcome. In low-validity environments it is not possible to make valid and reliable associations between cues and outcomes, and hence intuitive predictions and forecasting outcomes are not possible.[8]

The environments in which an experienced firefighter is able to intuit accurately whether a building is about to collapse or an experienced neonatal nurse is able to predict correctly if a child is likely to get seriously ill are high-validity environments. The environment in which a retail day trader might attempt to predict the future value of individual company stocks is a low-validity and hence high-risk decision-making environment. Because of the nature of the environments in which their skills have been built, we would be wiser to trust the intuitions of the experienced firefighter and the nurse than the inexperienced day trader. It is easier to coach intuition in high-validity than low-validity environments because in high-validity environments there are discernible cue-to-outcome relationships that can be learned through experience and coaching.

Learning from experience works less well and is harder to coach in situations where the relationships between cues and outcomes are more ambiguous and fluid, as in the example of predicting the future value of individual stocks—something which is inherently unpredictable and risky. In business settings, it is often difficult to attribute outcomes to a specific set of well-defined cues. For example, the relationship between decisions taken in designing and launching a marketing campaign and relevant outcomes, such as sales, may be hard to discern because so many factors in the internal and external environment may affect the outcome. In such environments, developing intuitions, coaching for them, and trusting them can be much less straightforward than in environments where there is timely and unambiguous feedback on consequences of intuitive decisions is available. Intuition researchers Emre Soyer and Robin Hogarth in *The Myth of Experience* (2021) describe how in such environments more experience, especially in the absence of a coach, can actually lead to worse decisions because without the intervention of a coach we may naturally look for evidence that will confirm our beliefs and gloss over information that might contradict them. 'Confirmation bias' is a natural tendency of a human mind that actively looks for connections.

If intuition is not to be complicit in building confirmation biases and falling foul of other sources of error, coaching can provide a much-needed helping hand. Soyer and Hogarth advocate the use of an 'experience coach' who can help mangers to ask penetrating questions of the decision-maker (i.e. the person being coached), the environment, and whether or not it is a suitable one in which to use intuition. For example: how complex and uncertain is the environment, do cues in the environment reliably predict outcomes, which cues are the most reliable, and how likely is it that the current problem resembles those of the past? As far as the decision-makers themselves are concerned, other important questions include: what is their level of mathematical and statistical literacy (to avoid heuristics and biases); have they received timely and accurate feedback on past decisions; are they incumbered by false beliefs in their intuitive judgement that makes it simply self-serving and self-fulfilling; are they guilty of over-confidence; are they, especially CEOs, on the road to the 'thinking big' that leads to hubristic incompetence?[9] Last but not least, does an experience coach add value by administering a 'healthy dose of scepticism' into the use of intuition in the decision-making process?[10]

It is also possible, armed with sufficient knowledge, self-confidence, and awareness, to become one's own experience coach. This process can work in two ways. The first way is by using Soyer and Hogarth's coaching questions as a way of unpicking the environment that you are operating in and testing whether or not it is likely to be a place where it is a good idea to trust your intuition. The second way is to take every opportunity to learn from experts by asking them the right questions. Gary Klein suggests that we can become our own intuition self-coach by: probing experts for incidents and stories about their intuitive hits and misses, for example 'why did your intuition work in that advertising campaign, and why did it fail in the another one?'; trying to figure-out what cues and patterns experts look for in complex, ambiguous, and uncertain situations, for example asking an experienced hiring manager, 'what things other than on the CV do you look for when assessing a job candidate?'; asking experts how their actions contrast with the way a novice would have dealt with the situation, for example asking a successful entrepreneur, 'what is different between how you pitched for the project compared to a how a novice might have done so?'; and finally getting specific rather than general advice, for example by asking a marketing manager 'exactly how do you go about making customer satisfaction your number one priority rather than it being just a vague and meaningless aspiration?'.[11]

Intuition in Coaching Practice

Skilled coaching practitioners use intuition in their work.[12] Good coaching demands active and empathetic listening skills such as paying attention, withholding judgement, and reflecting, clarifying, sharing, and summarizing with the client.[13] Over and above these explicit listening skills, experienced coaches are able to intuitively listen 'in between' the words in a coaching conversation and read client's non-verbal signals as well.[14] Non-verbals such as posture and eye contact can be strong markers for a client's emotional state, which can be picked up intuitively, and once noticed are impossible to ignore. By picking up on these a coach can mentalize (see Chapter 9) what might be going on inside the head of the person they are coaching.

There are also some general ground rules and principles for using intuition in coaching. In my own research with coaching experts, Penelope Mavor and the late David Gray, we interviewed professional coaches about how they use intuition in their coaching practice. We found that intuition is used in coaching in three ways. Firstly, intuitive coaches give themselves permission and also seek their client's consent to access and use intuition. Second, intuitive coaches listen to their body (for how to do this see the section on 'Interocepting' below). Third, an intuitive coach is emotionally unattached to and objective about their intuitions.[15]

Other research into how coaches use intuition found that some 'stayed put' (they kept their intuition to themselves) whilst others 'entered the intuitive territory' (they shared their intuition with their client).[16] In situations where the coach stayed put, on the downside they ran the risk of missing out on an intuitive insight by dismissing or muting their intuition; on the upside, by holding back judiciously but keeping their intuitions in mind, they could accumulate more evidence and tread more carefully in taking the process forward. In situations where coaches 'entered the intuitive territory', on the downside they took the risk of being presumptuous, 'showing-off' about how intuitive they were, and sometimes getting it wrong. On the upside, by opening up to intuition, coaches created a space for 'not knowing' and tentatively sharing their gut feelings about the client and the challenges they may be facing. For intuition to be used effectively in coaching, it is important that the coach: has access to a deep well of coaching experience; has the skills to pay attention to and interpret intuitions; recognizes when noise and biases may be impairing their intuitive judgements; is prepared to treat intuitions as hypotheses and wait for objective evidence to vindicate or refute them.[17]

Debiasing Decisions

One of the main sources of error in decision-making are systematic biases. By way of analogy: in the sport of rifle shooting, if all the shots hit the bull's eye, performance is accurate, whereas if all the shots are consistently to the bottom left they are repeatedly biased (and inaccurate); the likely reason is a systematic error, for example as a result of a misaligned sight on the gun.[18] As we discovered in Chapter 2, heuristics are one of the main sources of bias in human judgement because they lead to systematic (i.e. regular and predictable) errors. There are a number of sources of bias which lead to bad intuitions, for example the representativeness heuristic (as in 'The Linda Problem'), the availability heuristic (as in overestimating the likelihood of being involved in a shark attack), anchoring and adjustment (as in starting a negotiation with an excessively high or low opening gambit), and the affect heuristic (as in overestimating the risks and underestimating the benefits of something, such as nuclear power, because it happens to evoke negative feelings). These kinds of heuristics—as opposed to the fast-and-frugal variety discussed in Chapter 3—systematically and predictably improve one's chances of making a bad intuitive judgement call; they should be avoided wherever possible. Debiasing judgements and decisions, and hence purging them of those intuitions that can be a hinderance, is one way to improve decision-making and become more intuitively intelligent.

In *Noise: A Flaw in Human Judgement* (2021), Daniel Kahneman and his colleagues Olivier Sibony and Cass Sunstein (the latter of *Nudge* fame) identify two main approaches to debiasing: debiasing before a judgement, i.e. 'ex ante'; debiasing after a judgement has been arrived at, i.e. 'ex post'.

Debiasing Intuitions Ex Ante

Kahneman and colleagues suggest two ways in which the process of arriving at judgements can be debiased beforehand. The first of these involves training managers to understand and be able to recognize the logical and statical sources of their biases. For example, if managers understand the role that stereotyping plays in the biases associated with the representativeness heuristic, managers can then become attuned to the likelihood of falling foul of unconscious biases in hiring employees, performance appraisal, promotion decisions, selecting a leaders, etc. Armed with this knowledge, they could take appropriate action, e.g. not overlooking the data and subjecting their gut feelings to devil's advocacy. Another beforehand way of training managers to overcome biases associated with heuristics is through the method Kahneman refers to as 'boosting', which aims to improve mangers' statistical literacy. For example, educating aspiring entrepreneurs about base rates of business venturing failures and the ease of availability and recall of high-profile entrepreneurial successes could help them to ground their assessments accurately and arrive at a realistic evaluation of their chances of success. However, Kahneman is somewhat guarded about the chances of successfully deprogramming the human brain of its in-built tendencies to commit logical and statistical errors of judgement. Moreover, even informed judges who are able to apply statistical reasoning principles to judgements in their professional domain, such as business venturing, are far from immune from committing the same errors in other non-professional spheres, for example the chances of winning a lottery.[19]

Debiasing Intuitions Ex Post

Corrective action can be taken after an initial intuitive estimate has been arrived at but before any action is taken. For example, mangers typically underestimate project costs and delivery times as a result of the 'planning fallacy'. Estimates for project schedules and budgets can be debiased by looking at historical data for similar projects, taking risks and uncertainties into account, and not being overly optimistic about one's own skills and abilities.[20] In an extreme example of the dangers of hubristic overconfidence, the former UK Prime Minister Boris Johnson intuitively estimated the cost of one of his vanity projects of building a bridge between Scotland and Northern Ireland to be 'about £15 billion'. The professional auditor's correction was that the actual price tag would be more like £335 billion. The cost massively outweighed any benefits. It was recommended that the project be abandoned forthwith.[21] Looking to the lessons of the past, expecting the unexpected, and being wary of overconfidence (and ever watchful for hubris) are amongst the ways in which decisions can be debiased before they are put into action.

In dual-processing terms debiasing occurs when System 2 intervenes to modify or correct System 1's default intuitive judgements. System 2 intervention is a wise thing to do when being biased is likely to have significant consequences, for example when the stakes are high and it is important to avoid costly slip-ups. But as Kahneman reminds us, debiasing requires extra effort. For example, debiasing in business venturing by finding the relevant reference values of business failure rates and then objectively evaluating the available evidence is effortful and resource intensive. It is likely to run up against the buffers of bounded rationality in terms of the constraints of time, and informational and computational complexity. On the other hand, if a self-aware, risk-seeking venture capitalist's conscious priority is to take a high-stakes gamble by trying to spot the next Netflix or Facebook business opportunity, then the risks of investing in a speculative start-up that might ultimately fail may be knowingly worth taking, in spite of the risks. As Kahneman noted, the decision-makers' challenge in such situations is to accurately judge the extreme cases in the full knowledge that there is a potentially high financial and reputational cost of overestimating the prospects of success.[22]

Kahneman's summary words of advice on this matter are salutary: 'we are not all rational, and some of us may [even] need the security of distorted estimates to avoid paralysis [by analysis]'. He goes on to caution that if we consciously choose to delude ourselves by acting on extreme predictions of success we will 'do well to remain aware of [our] self-indulgence'.[23] The value of correcting our biases either ex post or ex ante is metacognitive in that it requires us to reflect on whether we actually know as much as we think we know. It is an antidote to overconfidence, thinking big, and epistemic hubris that may lead ultimately to unintended negative consequences and nasty surprises borne of unbridled intuitions.[24]

Diagnosing

In the same way that most people are either left-handed or right-handed, people also differ in how they prefer to think, problem-solve, and decide. Some people prefer to be intuitive, whilst others prefer to be analytical in solving problems and taking decisions. This aspect of individual difference is known as 'cognitive style', also referred to as 'thinking style' or 'decision-making style'. The extent to which a person is intuitive or analytical is likely to depend on a number of factors including genetics, personality, family background, learning, experiences, job demands, etc.[25] Some people tend to be more detail conscious and analytical whilst others tend to be big-picture conscious and intuitive. There are relationships between cognitive styles and personality, for example an analytical style shows a stronger relationship to conscientiousness and openness to experience than does an intuitive style.[26] Certain types of education and training or job types, including in different fields of business, can also encourage analytical thinking (for example, finance) or intuitive thinking (for example, marketing). An important point about style is that one cognitive style is not necessarily better than the other, they are just different and more or less suitable depending on the setting. Intuition is more appropriate when experienced participants have to take quick decisions in dynamic conditions or where a solution that is good enough will suffice. Analysis is more appropriate in situations that are computationally complex, where an optimal rather than good enough solution is sought, and where detailed justification is required.[27]

Cognitive Styles

Simple self-scoring questionnaires can be used to assess a person's preferences for intuition and analysis.[28] Table 11.1 shows a short questionnaire that can be used to

Table 11.1 Questions for diagnosing your analysis/intuition cognitive style.

When taking decisions	Strongly Disagree	Disagree	Neutral	Agree	Strongly Agree
1. I give more attention to the big picture rather than the fine details.	0	1	2	3	4
2. I prefer facts and figures over hunches and gut feelings.	0	1	2	3	4
3. I prefer to be spontaneous rather than reserved.	0	1	2	3	4
4. I can usually feel when something is right or wrong, even if I can't explain why.	0	1	2	3	4
5. I give more emphasis to hard data rather than gut feelings.	0	1	2	3	4
6. I think it's important to always weigh up the pros and cons when taking a decision.	0	1	2	3	4
7. I like to take my time and consider a situation from every angle.	0	1	2	3	4
8. I rarely go wrong when I listen to my initial impressions and gut feelings.	0	1	2	3	4
9. I have taken a lot of important decisions using my intuition.	0	1	2	3	4
10. I think it is always better to look before you leap and be safe rather than sorry.	0	1	2	3	4

Scoring key: (a) to calculate your intuition total out of a possible maximum of 20 points, add up your scores for questions 1, 3, 4, 8, and 9; (b) to calculate your analysis total, add up scores for questions 2, 5, 6, 7, and 10.

diagnose cognitive style informally. This information can be used to improve the aspect of your style that you prefer least, with the ultimate goal of developing the skill to be able to switch cognitive gears and become cognitively versatile.

There are numerous inventories and questionnaires available to assess individual differences in cognitive style in research settings. For example, Seymour Epstein, originator of the Cognitive Experiential Theory (CET) (see Chapter 5) developed the 'Rational Experiential Inventory' (REI) to investigate individual differences in experiential and rational processing. The REI gives two scores, one for analysis and one for intuition, on the assumption that experientiality and rationality are independent, i.e. the two scores are uncorrelated and as dimensions of thinking style they are at right angles to each other. These two separate scores can then be mapped in relation to each other on a two-by-two grid to show where someone sits in terms of

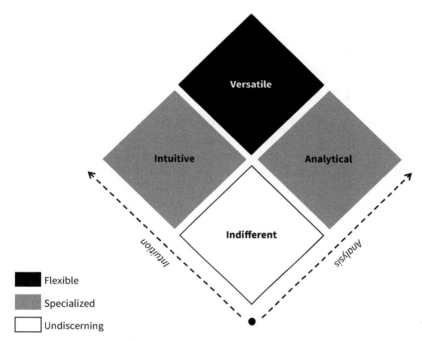

Figure 11.1 Four cognitive styles (for descriptions see text).
Source: Sadler-Smith, E. (2002). The role of cognitive style in management education. Academy of Management Conference, Denver, August 2002 (Best Paper Proceedings)

both intuition (which can be considered equivalent to Epstein's experientiality) and analysis (equivalent to rationality), see Figure 11.1.

Figure 11.1 shows a typology of intuition/analyse cognitive styles.[29] A two-by-two format similar to that in Figure 11.1 was used by management researchers Gerard Hodgkinson and Ian Clarke to specify four cognitive style types: 'intuitive' (high on intuition, low on analysis); 'analytical' (high on analysis, low on intuition); 'cognitively versatile' (high on analysis and high on intuition); and 'cognitively undiscerning' (low on analysis and low on intuition).[30] According to Hodgkinson and Clarke, the intuitive and analytical styles have strengths and weaknesses as follows.

Analytics are detail conscious, logical and rational, and data-driven; they eschew intuition. For example, a highly analytical salesperson will take rational decisions based on a detailed customer profile and product specifications and use these to craft the best offering for the customer.[31] One of the downsides to this style if that when a person with an analytical style is confronted by abundant information in circumstances where they need to take incisive action, they may become overburdened, so much so that they succumb to 'analysis paralysis'.[32]

Intuitives, on the other hand, are big-picture conscious, able to perceive the whole when presented with a quagmire of detail, they see patterns and associations, and embrace feelings and appreciate that affect can be a valuable form of data. For example, a highly intuitive salesperson would rely on selling strategies based on remembered stories of what worked well in the past in converting prospect clients.[33] They may overlook the fine details and be swayed by their gut feelings, such that 'if it feels right it must be right', but as we know confidence is no guarantee of accuracy.[34] If the intuitive style is taken to its extreme, then effective decision-making may capitulate to what strategic management researcher Ann Langley referred to as 'extinction by instinct'.[35]

Cognitively indifferent or undiscerning individuals deploy both analysis and intuition minimally, it is possible that such individuals simply depend on the opinions of others and 'received wisdom'[36] without bothering to think intuitively or analytically for themselves. On the other hand, they may solve problems and take decisions in ways that are neither intuitive nor analytical, that do not fit with the two-minds model, and cannot be captured using cognitive styles questionnaires.

Cognitively versatile individuals are, metaphorically speaking, ambidextrous; they have preferences for both analysis and intuition, they are able to switch cognitive gears flexibly from intuition to analysis in order to focus on the fine detail when necessary and switch vice versa from analysis to intuition in order to see the bigger picture when it is necessary to do so. They have the capabilities to be both data-driven and feelings-focused and embody the much sought-after combination articulated by Herbert Simon: 'The effective manager does not have the luxury of choosing between "analytic" and "intuitive" approaches to problems. Behaving like a manager means having command of the whole range of management skills and applying them as they become appropriate'.[37]

Cognitive Styles in the Workplace and Beyond

Researchers have used self-report questionnaires similar to that in Table 11.1 to analyse cognitive styles in relation to a variety of business management-related factors, such as job level, job type, person–job fit, etc. Research shows consistently that senior managers are more intuitive than junior managers and that junior managers are more analytical than senior managers, with middle managers somewhere in the middle. The gap between intuition and analysis for senior managers is much narrower than is the gap between analysis and intuition for junior managers, suggesting that senior managers have a more balanced cognitive style profile.[38] Research also shows that people with different job types have different cognitive styles. Actors have been found to be more intuitive than analytical, whilst accountants unsurprisingly and reassuringly are more analytical than intuitive. Successful entrepreneurs on the other hand are somewhere in between accountants and actors both on intuition and analysis which suggests that, like senior managers, their cognitive style profile is more balanced.[39] In terms of the fit between a person and their job, intuitives are more satisfied than analytics in unstructured jobs, whilst analytics are more satisfied than intuitives in structured jobs.[40]

Cultural psychologists have studied the differences between particular national groups in terms of cognitive style. They found that Chinese people appear to be more holistic and intuitive than Westerners in their thinking processes, and in terms of their values, East Asians, relative to Westerners, appear to rate intuitive reasoning as more important than analytical reasoning. This same research also found that Westerners tend to handle conflicts by polarizing a choice into two seemingly contradictory elements, whereas East Asians opt to avoid polarizing and instead seek to find a compromise or balance between conflicting positions. These difference translate into business decision-making, for example a study of Chinese fund managers found that they tended to use intuition more than Western fund managers in the investment decision-making process. In an interview, one Chinese fund manager remarked that 'Investment is like some arcane martial art [that] can only be taught by experience … rather than by words'.[41]

Cognitive styles research into the question of 'are there sex differences in intuition and analysis?' does not appear to support the stereotype of female intuition. Even where there are measurable intuition/analysis cognitive style differences between the sexes they have tended to be small and statistically uninteresting and mostly based on student samples. However, there may be other sources of such differences that the self-report questionnaires are unable to detect, for example differences in how males and females use intuition and adeptness in different types of intuition.

Incubating

In the preparation-incubation-illumination-verification Standard Model of the creative process[42] discussed in Chapter 10, the preparation stage often leads to an impasse in the problem-solving process, for example the mental blockage Amazon had over what a loyalty scheme might look like and the breakthrough which led to Amazon Prime. This is followed typically by a period of incubation, characterized by mental quietude or distraction, which is the prequel to a sudden moment of illumination. The paradox seems to be that a blockage is necessary for a breakthrough. The impasse can be a moment of dissatisfaction and disorientation, but it is also productive in that it signals that the mind is ready to enter a quieter incubation stage.

Incubation and Insight

Incubation creates the mental space and time for activations to spread across the brain's networks of associations and for new and unusual connections to be made. In the incubation phase these unconscious processes can be supported and enabled by mental distraction and relaxation. The ancient Greek philosopher Heraclitus observed in his fragmentary writings that 'Even a soul submerged in sleep is hard at work and helps make something of the world' (Fragment 90).[43] IKEA's founder Ingvar Kamprad did not deliberately come up with the idea for flat-pack furniture. He had his Eureka moment in 1956 when he happened to watch an employee remove the legs from a customer's table to fit it into their car. The result was that flat-pack furniture was born and an entire industry was transformed. It is unlikely that Kamprad would have arrived at this insight had he not been immersed in the furniture business and been ruminating for a long time about the problem of how to pack furniture.

Incubation has been studied by psychologists for many decades, and studies show unequivocally that when compared to working on a problem uninterrupted, taking a break from a problem and returning to it later really does increase the chances that a solution will be found.[44] Neuroscience suggests that there are two non-conscious mechanisms at work: 'spreading activation' in which previously ignored but relevant memories are revived and connected to the problem at hand; 'problem restructuring' in which the mental representation of the problem is reorganized into a more appropriate format after previously unsuccessful attempts at solving, for example configuring the six matchsticks problem (see Chapter 10) from a two- to a three-dimensional mental representation.

Creating the Conditions for Insights

The good news is that it possible, and easy, to create the conditions that make Eureka moments more likely.[45] One of the easiest ways of doing this is to sleep on the problem. A number of documented scientific discoveries have emerged out of dreamlike states. The German organic chemist August Kekulé (1829–1896) made his discovery of the ring structure of benzene whilst dozing by the fire; he fell into a slumber and he dreamt of snakes swallowing their own tails, hence the 'ring' breakthrough. This seemingly effortless insight was prefaced by hard, focused mental effort of years working at the benzene problem.[46] Sleep is thought to promote insight through a process in which the mental blocks that prevent a fragile and weakly consolidated idea from becoming firmly fixed are removed. The idea may then become conscious soon after waking, as in the case of a member of the pop group The Beatles, Paul McCartney, waking with the melody of the hit song 'Yesterday' in his head. The general rule seems to be that sleep, whether as a short nap or longer night-time slumber, seems to create the time and the mental space for connections between remotely associated concepts and ideas to be created and solidify, analogous to the idea of 'wet cement drying' and which cannot be speeded up.[47]

Cognitive psychologists John Kounios and Mark Beeman described the unconscious mental processes that lead to insights via incubation as working as follows. Information stored in the brain has connections to other pieces of information, for example in the business brain, 'strategy' is connected to 'vision', is connected to 'mission', is connected to 'long-term', is connected to 'planning', etc., and in the manager's mind these ideas simmer in and out of awareness. When thinking about these things in a work context, 'strategy' would normally elicit a connection to 'vision'. However, in a different context, for example, walking in the woods prior to a business strategy away day (the pressing problem), 'strategy' might elicit a connection to 'tree' or 'branches' or 'roots' or 'birds', and as a result, new serendipitous connections can be made which elicits connections such as 'roots are like company values', 'birds are like stakeholders', and 'branches are like options'.[48] This example illustrates that grappling with a pressing problem sensitizes one to finding a solution and then putting oneself in a different context automatically filters and changes our perception of the world and creates the conditions for novel connections to emerge.[49]

The French chemist Louis Pasteur (1822–1895) observed in a lecture in 1854 that 'chance favours the prepared mind'. More recently the Harvard educationalist and creativity expert David Perkins remarked that 'knowledge sharpens the eye of the beholder'.[50] In this sensitized state and armed with the right knowledge it is okay, and may even be advisable and ultimately worthwhile, to reach a road block. Stepping back from the problem and switching to a new and possibly unusual context can 'cleanse the mental palette'.[51] Relaxation, new sources of stimulation and novel ways of looking at the world help to catalyse novel connections.

Inferring

One of the most famous fictional intuitors is Sherlock Holmes. Part of his problem-solving genius was his precocious ability to infer plausible hypotheses on the basis of seemingly minimal information. For example, when he first met Dr Watson, Holmes inferred immediately and correctly that Watson, an army doctor, had recently returned home from the Afghan campaign. Watson was surprised by Holmes' insight and was convinced that someone had told him, to which Holmes remarked: 'Nothing of the sort. I knew you came from Afghanistan. From long habit the train of thoughts ran so swiftly through my mind, that I arrived at the conclusion without being conscious of intermediate steps. There were such steps, however. The train of reasoning ran …' At which point Holmes enumerates his train of thought 'gentleman', 'medical type', 'air of a military man', 'his face is dark' but 'his wrists are fair', 'undergone hardship and sickness', 'just come from the tropics' and then asked himself, 'where could an English army doctor have seen much hardship and got his arm wounded? Clearly in Afghanistan. The whole train of thought did not occupy a second. I then remarked that you came from Afghanistan, and you were astonished'. Holmes intuitively generated a plausible hypothesis about Watson which provided an 'inference-to-best-explanation'.

Abduction

Holmes' method of inference-to-best-explanation is a method of logical inquiry known as abduction.[52] It is most often associated with the work of the American pragmatist philosopher Charles Sanders Peirce (1839–1914) and is part of an 'epistemological triangle' of deduction, induction, and abduction.[53] Abduction involves inferring from an observed effect (for example, Watson's appearance) to probable cause (i.e. Watson's time spent as an army doctor in Afghanistan). It is a process of generating and adopting an explanatory hypothesis which has the potential to yield an insight. However, such a hypothesis is speculative, provisional, and fallible. Holmes amplified the information available to him in order to arrive at an inference which was a plausible, albeit provisional, hypothesis. Holmes' inference worked well at the level of a strong 'maybe?'. There are links to insight in that the inference is arrived at quickly and without conscious effort, but unlike insight in the Standard Model, there is no incubation. Inferring through the process of abduction is a product of a prepared, keen, and flexible mind, which gives rise to an informed speculation and is lent weight by a feeling of rightness attributable to a sense or attunement in the mind 'to the truth of things'.[54]

When we infer in the manner of Peirce's method of abduction, and amply illustrated by Holmes, we perceive faint, clue-like signs which instigate a search process and result in an inference to best explanation. There is no implication that the problem-solver arrived at the 'instinctive guess' without reasons; far from it, an intuitive logic is at play which is so complex and so rapid that it need not be analysed by the 'person within whose brain it takes place'.[55] The end result is a 'conceptual leap' that bridges the gap between puzzling observational data and a best-fitting explanation, thus bringing elements of the problem space together that were previously not associated with each other into a plausible inference.[56] There may be an 'Aha!' moment as in Holmes' insight, but inferring towards the conceptual leap can also be a process that unfolds over time, it may be punctuated by several insights and driven both by intuitive 'free play' and controlled analytical reasoning. James Dyson's conceptual leaping towards the final realization of the bagless vacuum cleaner was a staccato, drawn-out process of intuitive sensing, insightful seeing, and analytical solving.

Conceptual Leaping

Inference to best explanation in a process of conceptual leaping is an alternative to the magical light-bulb moment explanation for creative intuitions. But unlike the process of incubation to illumination (and for which conditions favourable to insights can be created such as taking a 'walk in the woods' or a nap), with conceptual leaping the process is less easy to pin down but by no means less plausible. Building on the suggestions of strategic management researchers Malvina Klag and Ann Langley, creating the conditions that improve the chances of a conceptual leap occurring might involve: embracing both doubt/naïveté and experience/expertise simultaneously; using both active engagement to seed ideas and detached incubation to grow ideas; relying on deliberation to generate variety and serendipity to inject chance and novelty.[57] This dialectical process, i.e. acting through the juxtaposition of opposing and seemingly paradoxical cognitive forces such as naïveté and expertise, takes advantage of the creative tensions generated between deliberation-versus-serendipity, engagement-versus-detachment, and knowing-versus-not-knowing.

Inferring and conceptual leaping comes with a health warning. Harvard Professor of Education and Organizational Behaviour, Chris Argyris (1923–2013) used a 'ladder of inference' to illustrate how our self-generated beliefs can lead us to erroneous inferences if we leave them untested. For example: 'Jane arrived at 9.15 for a 9.00 meeting; Jane knew the meeting started at 9.00; Jane is often late; Jane is unreliable; Jane can't be counted on'. Is this an inference-to-best-explanation? The intuitive inference that Jane cannot be counted on is a product of several leaps of abstraction which take us to the top of the ladder very quickly. We cannot avoid automatically using intuitive inferences to create meaning in our day-to-day living; they help us to think and decide quickly and with minimal effort and clear the cognitive space for other work. However, we can ascend the ladder more cautiously by: reflecting on our own intuitive leaps of abstraction ('reflecting'); making our intuitive leaps more visible to others ('revealing'); inquiring into others' intuitive leaps ('inquiring'). By reflecting, revealing, and inquiring, our intuitive reasoning processes become more visible both to ourselves and those around us.[58]

Integrating, Imagining, and Iterating

Intuition and analysis are the two components of a dual-system of thinking, problem-solving, and decision-making. They are, metaphorically at least, the two minds in one brain. An implication which can sometimes be overlooked, especially when intuition is in the focus of attention, is that effective problem-solving and decision-making is a product of *both* analysis *and* intuition. In business it is unlikely that many of the day-to-day problems that managers have to solve and the decisions that they have to take are purely intuitive or purely analytical. Consequently, both intuition and analysis have vital and often complementary roles to play in judgement and decision-making. One of the challenges for decision-makers is to integrate them successfully; a way of rising to this challenge is through the linked processes of 'integrating', 'imagining', and 'iterating'. Moreover, the relationship between human intuition and artificial intelligence creates the opportunity for the development of a hybrid intelligence.

Integrating

When intuition and analysis are in agreement, they can be integrated to give an unequivocal outcome. For example, if intuition says 'yes' and analysis says 'yes' it would be safe to move ahead. To take the recruiting example: if the job candidate creates a favourable intuitive impression amongst the interview panel and this is backed up by hard evidence from the available data (test scores, CV, assessment centre performance, references, etc.) this, metaphorically, is a 'green flag'. Likewise if intuition says 'no' and analysis says 'no' then this is a 'red flag'. A green light signals 'approach' or 'proceed'; a red light signals 'avoid' or 'stop'. This mode is integrative in that both intuition and analysis have their say.

Imagining

Imagination can also have a role to play in this process. For example, in Klein's recognition-primed decision model, an intuitively generated option can be tested out by mental simulation. The decision-maker imagines their intuition playing out. This is using imagination to analyse, or stress-test (albeit hypothetically), an intuition. But imagining can also be used to test an analytical solution by getting a sense of how it would *feel* if it were to be implemented. Imagining is a powerful decision-making tool in business and in life more generally because it is a way of 'looking before you leap' (where the intuition is mentally simulated to test if it might work) and 'feeling before you act' (where the analysis is mentally simulated to see how it would feel).

Iterating

A contrary scenario can be imagined to the 'yes/yes' or 'no/no' scenario outlined in 'integrating' above: for example, imagine an entrepreneur pitching to backers for funding to support a new business venture in which the aspiring entrepreneur gives a polished presentation which a business angel finds attractive. Intuition says 'yes' based on person perception. The potential market is massive and the investor is sorely tempted to move quickly to obtain first-mover advantage. However, she is an experienced business angel and always looks before she leaps. Before proceeding to making an offer, she scrutinizes the business viability data and the finances in forensic detail. This reveals that whilst the market is potentially huge, there are serious flaws in the marketing and operational aspects of the proposed new business venture. Analysis says 'no'. Poised at the metaphorical traffic lights, the signal is amber. In this situation the investor could err on the side of risk-taking and make an offer taking a bet on high risk/high returns, or she could err on the side of caution and walk away. Either way, at least there has been a check and balance.

On the other hand, rather than approaching or avoiding on the first iteration, if the investor senses potential high-value opportunity she could recommend that the business plan is revised and resubmitted. In the ensuing process, intuition and analysis work together iteratively to move the project forward. In doing so, the proposal evolves, as do both parties' conceptions and perceptions of it. It is not difficult to imagine a similar scenario working in other areas of business, such as a pitch from a creative agency for an advertising campaign or a hiring decision in which the first impressions are favourable but analytical scrutiny gives cause for concern. How much weight is given to intuition rather than analysis, or vice versa, is likely to depend on a variety of factors including the decision-maker's cognitive style, situation (is it a stable or an unstable environment and is there sufficient time to iterate), and its consequences (is the outcome consequential or non-consequential).

The iterating between intuition and analysis works both ways: when analysis says 'yes' but intuition senses some as yet unspecified reason for caution and therefore says 'no' the amber light in this scenario could be a valid reason to go back to the figures or the plans and check them through thoroughly and resubmit them for further scrutiny by intuition and analysis. The process iterates until the tensions between intuition and analysis are reconciled (for example, they will not necessarily go away, but at least they are admitted to and a middle way is found) or resolved and intuition and analysis reach agreement, hence the amber light turns green, or the situation is deemed to be irreconcilable and the amber light turns red.

Hybrid Intelligence

The relationships between intuition and analysis take on a different complexion and the challenges are of a different type when the analysis is conducted by a computer. The need for human intuition to judge the outputs of artificial intelligence is amplified when there are issues of emotion and empathy at stake. For example, artificial intelligence may be advanced enough to judge which of a number of alternatives for a marketing campaign is likely to be the best, however at the end of the day it may be that human judges must be the final arbiters because they, unlike the computer, are able to walk in the shoes of the potential customer and empathize in ways that a computer, because it does not have a body, is unable to do. The information age opens up possibilities for a 'hybrid intelligence' that leverages the strength of human and artificial intelligences, and of human intuition in sensing and artificial intuition in solving, but how this might work in business, and other spheres of activity, is only now beginning to emerge.

Interocepting

Intuitions are affectively charged; they involve feelings and these are described metaphorically as gut feelings, hunches, vibes, etc. These feeling states differ from primary emotions, such as happiness sadness, fear, and anger, and instead are felt as a subtle change in the contours of the internal body landscape.[59] A term used to capture this change is 'bodily felt-sense' or 'felt-sense', borrowed from the work of the philosopher and psychotherapist Eugene T. Gendlin (1926–2017). Gendlin was not satisfied with the idea of 'feeling' or 'reflection of feeling' in the process of introspecting in psychotherapy because of the connotation with specific, and often intense, emotions such as anger, joy, sadness, etc. Clearly such intense emotions are experienced, but Gendlin's view was that most of the time the feeling of what happens is somewhat different. Similarly, the feeling of what happens when we experience an intuition is quite distinct from what happens when we experience a primary emotion.

Gendlin was keen to point out that the felt-sense is broader than 'just getting in touch with your gut feelings'. 'Intuitive felt-sense' is used here as a subcategory of Gendlin's 'felt-sense'. The intuitive felt-sense is not a purely internal state (unlike a mood), it is a feeling of how we 'are' in response to an external situation; for example, how an experienced manager is in response to a particular candidate for a job interview who makes her 'feel uneasy', or a mathematically watertight balance sheet that feels like it does not 'add up' to an experienced accountant, or a business opportunity that feels 'too good to be true' to a seasoned start-up investor. The intuitive felt-sense is intertwined with how we interpret or construe the situation, for example an expert's intuitive response to situations with which they are intimately familiar will be quite different to that of a novice, whilst on the other hand both the expert and novice would likely have the same intense emotional reaction posed by a fierce dog. The intuitive felt-sense is not as sharply defined as an emotion and it cannot be separated from the situation or the person's interpretation of the situation. In Gendlin's jargon it may be described as a 'person-situation composite that is concretely felt'.[60]

Interoception and the Felt-Sense

Interoception refers to the perception of the internal state of the body, and in general this includes various bodily states such as heart rate, breathing, and thermal properties. Interocepting is also the sensing of bodily signals, as well as bodily states, such as gut feelings which are elicited in response to a triggering situation, for example the job candidate, the spreadsheet, or the pitch. As a bodily signal, the intuitive felt-sense is accessible through the process of interocepting. Communing with the intuitive felt-sense through the process of interocepting is, in the words of educationalist Guy Claxton, a 'ruminative mental art' that is the prequel to its interpretation.[61]

The intuitive felt-sense can manifest in variety of different 'voices' including words, images, and bodily sensations. The words which are used as a proxy for the intuitive felt-sense are typically metaphorical ('intuition is a warning sign') and analogical ('intuition is like an alarm bell'). Visual images through which the intuitive felt-sense manifests mediate between the conscious and the unconscious and they themselves may have a metaphoric quality (a 'bright light' or a 'dark shadow'). The above quotes are from my own research with HR managers and business students in which they were invited to 'interocept' on the felt-sense which emerges out of the process of intuiting; their responses were prompted by the general question 'what happens when you intuit?' This technique, which relies on de-nominalizing the noun (intuition) into the verb (intuit), can also be applied to specific situations, for example 'what happened when you intuited in relation to the job candidate who made you feel uneasy, or the spreadsheet that did not add up, or the pitch that sounded too good to be true?'. This is a good technique for getting people to talk about (i.e. interpret) their intuitions. More on interpreting follows in the next section.

The intuitive felt-sense varies in terms of three dimensions: level (high-versus-low, for example, a strong, nagging doubt or anxiety), valence (positive-versus-negative, for example, intuitions may err on the side of caution because of greater sensitivity to losses rather than gains) and locus (for example, in our own research one police officer remarked to us that when he intuited there was 'nothing going on below the neck').[62] The combination of level and valence are an impetus to action. For example, a positively valenced, high-level intuitive felt-sense would be a strong 'approach' signal, whilst a negatively valenced, low-level felt-sense would be a weak 'avoid' signal. It is possible to develop the skill of interocepting through the method of 'focusing' which was developed by Gendlin as a psychotherapeutic method. Focusing on the intuitive felt-sense involves asking questions such as: where is the felt-sense located; what is the intensity of the felt-sense; is there an image or a metaphor which captures it; is the felt-sense stable or does it shift; what is the felt-sense trying to tell me that words cannot express?[63]

Metaphors

Metaphors are especially useful as quality-words[64] in interocepting and interpreting the intuitive felt-sense because they are one of the ways in which the intuitive system encodes reality.[65] Primary metaphors are an inherent part of our cognitive system, both conscious and unconscious; they are acquired automatically, and are correlation- and bodily-based, for example 'more is up'.[66] Primary metaphors are useful tools for expressing internal subjective states and are relevant to interoception and the intuitive felt-sense because they are grounded in source domains that relate to embodied experiences, such as temperature, size, vision, location, orientation, etc.[67] For example, a metaphorical expression for a negatively valenced intuition about someone's story that does not stack up is 'I smell a rat'. In terms of the primary metaphor 'bad is stinky':

> *Bad is stinky.*
> Subjective judgement: Evaluation
> Sensory motor occurrence: Smell
> Example: 'His story just stinks; I smell a rat'.
> Primary experience: Being repelled by foul-smelling objects, such as rotten food.
> Cross-mapping: 'His story may not be true therefore he is a person to be further investigated/avoided'.[68]

Primary metaphors enable the intuitor to cross-reference from their subjective and hard-to-express experiences to concrete and easier-to-express examples.[69] For example, the mapping 'up is good whereas down is bad', as in the metaphor 'things just don't stack up' (orientation), signifies that the situation is 'not up' and therefore 'not good'; likewise, 'I see what you mean' (vision) signifying 'seeing-as-knowing'.[70] Primary metaphors are elemental in that it is not possible to regress any further to more 'primordial' descriptions.[71] Responses to the question of 'what happens when you intuit in relation to "X"?' can be guided towards metaphorical and analogical expression by prompting the intuitor to say what their intuiting is 'like'. Primary metaphors are a consequence of associative learning and ultimately of neurons that are accustomed to firing together also ending up wiring together.[72]

One of the greatest English poets of the twentieth century, Ted Hughes (1930–1998), was troubled from his early years by the challenge of putting his creative thoughts into words. He remarked that if we are without a process for breaking into the inner life then our thoughts of mind 'lie in us like fish in the pond of a man who cannot fish'.[73] Hughes described how he developed as a result of deliberate practice a 'trick or skill' of holding the 'dim sorts of a feeling about something' still so as to be able to 'get a really good look at them'.[74] Interocepting is a way of seizing the essence of the intuitive felt-sense which, like the fish in Hughes' pond, can be a slippery 'catch'.[75] Without a method for capturing our intimations and intuitions 'in flight', they may end up also lying in us like the fish in a pond of a person who cannot fish. One of the aims of this chapter is to help managers to be able to 'fish' in the ocean of their unconscious so as to become more aware of their intuitions as a prequel to their interpretation.

Interpreting

'Intuiting' is the first step in a four-stage process of organizational learning as described by Mary Crossan and colleagues follows: 'intuiting' is the preconscious recognition of patterns and possibilities, for example an inventor intuiting novel connections and new or emergent relationships for a new product; 'interpreting' involves articulating and explaining an intuition through words or other symbols to one's self and others, for example, the inventor talking with others to develop the language necessary to describe what had up until that point been a personal intuition of an idea for a new product; 'integrating' is the further development of the shared understanding of the intuition and taking coordinated action, for example, the inventor, through conversation and dialogue, both developing her own understanding and also integrating the perceptions and understanding of the group of colleagues or potential investors into a shared understanding (a 'shared mental model'); 'institutionalizing' is the process of ensuring that routinized actions occur and organizational mechanisms are put in place that are based on the intuition, for example, developing formal processes, procedures, and structures into an organized system for exploiting the intuitive insight as an invention and ultimately turning it into a value-creating innovation.[76]

Interpreting and the 'Four I's

Crossan and her colleagues called their model the 'four I' (intuiting, interpreting, integrating, institutionalizing) model of organizational learning. In business organizations, or collectives of any kind, interpreting is the pivotal stage because it is where the intuitor begins to name and explain a thing that originated as a highly personal and subjective intuitive felt-sense. As a social process, interpreting creates a common language and common understanding of the subjectively experienced intuition. It is where the intuition crosses the threshold from being an individual felt-sense to a collective intuition shared by the group.

The process of interpreting begins with efforts to articulate the intuition. Intuitions, as products of the non-verbal experiential system, are embodied, but they rely on words, or other symbols, to be externalized. Interocepting segues into interpreting. As noted above, metaphors provide one means by which intuitions can make the transition from the internal world of the intuitor to the external world of colleagues and customers. Metaphors are used to describe subjective states through the use of words, which conjure up parallel yet unrelated images from common experience. For example, the intuitive statement 'I smell a rat' uses the sensory modality of smell and the image of a rat to represent something that has bad connotations (see above). Likewise, the intuitive phrase, 'things just don't stack up' communicates the point that something is not quite right or 'out of kilter' (this is thought to originate from an old English word 'kelter' meaning good health or good condition). Metaphors as discussed above are vivid, sometimes quirky, phrases which help to distil the complex properties of an intuitive feeling into an image that can be understood quickly and easily by another person.[77] The same goes for the use of analogies, for example 'intuition is like a radar' or 'intuition is like a personal GPS'.

Metaphors and Interpreting Intuitions

As noted above, metaphors are one of the ways in which we interpret intuitions: they help us to articulate and understand how people perceive and make sense of them. They allow the private to become public.[78] If used constructively, they promote dialogue and learning. For example, if one person thinks of their organization as a finely tuned machine, whereas another thinks of it as an amorphous, soft living organism, this is likely to bring out important differences in the ways they express and make sense of the organization of which they are both a part. In their four-I model Crossan and colleagues give the example of the metaphor that Steve Jobs used to articulate his intuitive vision for the personal computer 'as like a domestic appliance'. The use of a different metaphor, for example as a personal assistant, might have led to very different actions and Apple might have become a somewhat different company. As Jobs' intuitions about the personal computer developed, they became collectivized and the shared language changed to become more concrete and literal.

One of the keys to using intuitions productively in organizations seems to be making them explicit. In the new product development process, it has been suggested that novel ideas can be made explicit by asking 'ideators' or intuitors questions such as: 'why is this idea good?' to encourage elaboration and justification, which helps others to understand the potential of the idea; 'how could the idea be improved?', which triggers critical evaluation of the idea and the improvement of the idea. This highlights the fact that intuitions need not be fixed things; they are malleable, and language can shape them and through interpreting good intuitive ideas, can be made even better.[79] The expression of intuitions in inquiry or dialogue— either literally or more metaphorically, and not necessarily only in words since pictures can also play a role in interpretation—creates the space for shared meanings to develop and for new interpretations to emerge.

The Upsides and Downsides of Intuition's Ineffability

Management researchers Nora Meziani and Laure Cabantous draw attention to the possibility that intuition's tacitness and ineffability can energize and motivate managers to overcoming its innate 'resistance' to being expressed. In this way, paradoxically, intuition's ineffability is a good thing because the presence of resistances can actually encourage people to clarify their intuitions and in so doing illuminate the aspects of the initial felt-sense that have eluded capture or may have gone unnoticed even by them.[80] As a result, more sophisticated interpretation of the intuitive felt-sense is developed and the intuition itself may change in the process.

When this intuitive sense-making process fails, things can go badly wrong. Meziani and Cabantous give the example of the 1986 Space Shuttle Challenger disaster. The O-ring booster rocket seal expert from the manufacturer Morton-Thiokol, Roger Boisjoly, knew intuitively that launching in low temperatures was very risky, but he could not capture and communicate his intuition in a way that would satisfy the managers at NASA. The managers concluded that Boisjoly's intuitions were nothing more than a 'dangerous' guess. A report into a previous accident involving the launch of Skylab 1 concluded that NASA's management systems which place emphasis on rigour, detail, thoroughness, and formalism 'while nearly perfect, such a system can submerge the concerned individual and depress the role of the intuitive engineer or analyst. It may not allow full play for the intuitive judgement or past experience of the individual'.[81] This insight proved to be tragically prescient: in the ensuing catastrophe all seven astronauts lost their lives.

Using Interpreting to Build Collective Intuitions

Interpreting individual managers' intuitions helps to build collective intuitions, defined as common judgements that arise rapidly and automatically based on shared holistic associations (i.e. shared mental models).[82] Collective intuition emerges after sustained debate and discussion and can only develop in a climate in which individuals both feel free to express their own intuitions (even if they are only partially formed) and are prepared to listen to those of others.[83] Collective intuition is a synthesis of individual intuitions built up over time; it gives the members of the organization a common sense of how to act and of the right thing to do. Collective intuitions are both a centre of gravity (which provides an anchor) and a compass (which provides a sense of direction). For example, one of the senior managers in the study of intuition in banking by Ann Hensman and myself commented that: 'you tend to have a common standpoint on certain issues; because of a policy, because of experience, because of culture in the organization. [In] those sorts of decisions I would be very confident that a peer of mine would have made exactly the same decision'.[84]

Collective intuitions are much less portable than individual intuitions since they are part of the organizational culture. Building collective intuitions are a valuable, rare, difficult to imitate cognitive resource. Intuitive organizational knowledge in the form of routines and recipes are often not explicitly written down in organizations but people intuitively know what they are, and they are continually reinforced by behaviours. Organizational culture defines values and behaviours, and successful companies are able to develop a behavioural 'secret sauce', embedded in their collective intuitions, that propels the business towards its vision.[85] For example, at the online shoe and clothing retailer Zappos, whose parent company is Amazon, its values are taken-for-granteds and captured in the company's core values or 'Oath of Employment, that 'everyone helps even when it isn't their job'.[86] However, collective intuitions can be a double-edged sword if they are not periodically surfaced, debated, and challenged.[87] Taken to an extreme, a toxic organizational culture with its baseline of things that are intuitively taken for granted can actually hold back or even destroy a company; one need only think of Enron to appreciate how destructive an organizational culture and collective intuitions about 'what okay behaviour looks like' can be.

Learning

Intuition helps us to sense and make predictions about regularities in our physical and social environments. Whilst the psychological processes of intuiting apply across a wide variety of complex problem-solving and decision-making situations (they are 'domain-general'), the intuitions themselves are 'domain-specific'. For example, intuition in playing chess does not translate to chess, or firefighting, or business venturing, or vice versa. Intuitions are acquired implicitly and experientially through observing how other people perform actions that are successful and unsuccessful and through making associations between cues and observed outcomes. This type of learning is reinforced by two factors: feedback on outcomes (which ratify and reinforce causal mechanisms) and rewards and punishments (which strengthen observed associations).

Conducive Contexts for Developing Good and Bad Intuitions

Some environments are conducive for learning good intuitions because there are associations between cues and outcomes which means that the lessons of experience will be reliable. Other environments are less conducive for learning good intuitions because the associations between cues and outcomes are unreliable (for example, they may be non-existent or false), hence the lessons of experience are typically unreliable. Intuition researcher Robin Hogarth in his book *Educating Intuition* distinguished between two different types of learning environments or 'learning structures'.[88] In a 'kind learning structure' decision-makers receive abundant, immediate, and accurate feedback on their actions and the 'rules of the game' remain largely constant. Daniel Kahneman and Gary Klein call these high-validity learning environments.[89] On the other hand, in a 'wicked learning structure' feedback on actions is absent, delayed, and inaccurate; this is potentially dangerous because having an experience in such an environment will lead inevitably to learning, however the lessons that are learned may be invalid and unreliable and result in bad intuitive judgement. Kahneman and Klein call these low-validity learning environments.[90]

Hogarth uses meteorology as an example of a kind learning environment. Meteorologists have extensive knowledge of weather and climate as well as access to extensive real-time data. They also receive accurate, timely, and diagnostic feedback on whether their weather forecasts are correct or not. On this basis, weather forecasting is a valid learning environment for developing 'meteorological intuition'. Hogarth also gives the example of an emergency room in hospital as an example of a wicked learning environment. Emergency room physicians have expert knowledge of medicine, unfortunately they may not always receive feedback on the longer-term effects of their treatment decisions if the patient is moved to a different part of the hospital or discharged. In this situation it is more difficult for the physician to develop accurate knowledge about the efficacy of their clinical decisions; this can be an impediment to developing good intuitions.[91]

In business, the learning environment of evaluating training courses has the potential to be wicked. For example, consider the case of a training manager who gathers feedback from course delegates using end-of-course 'happiness sheets'. Imagine that these data reveal that the trainees had a good time, liked the trainer, and generally enjoyed themselves. On this basis the training manager might feel justified in concluding that the investment in the training was money well spent. However, the traditional happiness sheet feedback tells the training manager nothing about whether the training was applied to the job in the trainees' actual workplace, whether it had any effect on job performance, and what its impact on the bottom line was. A training manager who develops an intuition for what works well in training based on end-of-course happiness sheets could, and in all likelihood would, develop bad intuitive judgement about what works well in training. This situation is a wicked learning environment for a training manager. On the other hand, a training manager who gathers end-of-course feedback and follows this up with evaluations of if and how well the learning was applied on the job, whether it improved job performance, and whether there was any impact on the bottom line is much more likely to develop good intuitions for what works well in training. This is a kind learning environment for a training manager. In this situation the manager actively seeks feedback from a wide range of sources including trainees' reactions, impact on job performance, and return on investment. As a result the manager is much more likely to develop good intuitive judgement about training.

Noise and Overcoming It

Noise, or random error, is a complicating factor in developing good intuitions because it contaminates learning structures. Again, by way of Kahneman and colleagues' rifle-shooting analogy used earlier: if all the shots hit the bull's eye, then performance is accurate, but if the shots are scattered all over the target, performance is inaccurate due this time, not to systematic error, but to some random and hard-to-predict factor or noise, for example, as a result of the shooter experiencing a nervous twitch. Random scatter or noise, along with systematic deviations as a result of heuristics and biases, is one of the main sources of error in judgement.[92] If data is inherently noisy as a result of random scattering in the decision-making environment, then seeking feedback from recent events is unlikely to build good intuitions because the relationships between cues, decision, and outcomes may be neither valid nor reliable. Noisy environments are wicked learning structures, and feedback from them can be misleading. Where there is noise, the right lessons are not learned from experience and the result is likely to be poor intuitive judgement.

In business, the environment for personnel section decisions can often be noisy, and feedback on outcomes of hiring decisions can be suboptimal. In hiring decisions, noise is compounded by the fact that different interviewers can arrive at wildly different assessments of the same candidate, the results of a selection decision made today is unlikely to be known for weeks, months, or even years, and in the meantime many other factors can intervene to obfuscate outcomes.[93] One way of reducing the effect of noise in such situations is by using multiple interviews, combining interviews with objective data, using structured interviews, having interviewers' rate candidates separately and before interviewers communicate with each other, and by feeding back knowledge of outcomes over the longer term to interviewers.[94] Intuition has a role to play in this process, but it should not be allowed to dominate because it could simply add to the noise. Delaying or parking intuition until the time is right ot use it can help to overcome the effects of noise and build what Daniel Kahneman, co-author of the bestseller *Noise*, refers to as better 'decision hygiene'.[95]

Practising

One of the world's greatest soccer players, the Portuguese star Ronaldo, used to spend so much time practising that Manchester United's manager, Sir Alex Ferguson, used to have to yell at him and order him to 'Go home!'. Gary Klein in his book *Intuition at Work*, in which he elucidates for a non-specialist audience his recognition-primed decision (RPD) model, lets his readers into the three secrets for improving their intuition: practice, practice, practice, but with the caveat that quality as much as quantity of practice is vitally important. Intuition, like any other business skill, is developable. It is built through experiential and observational learning and honed through practising under the right circumstances for the right amount of time and under the right guidance.

Intuition begins with experience, but to be effective experiences must be meaningful. Meaningful experiences in real-life, or in high-fidelity simulations of real-life situations, allow decision-makers to build complex domain-relevant schemas (also known as mental models) that enable them to recognize patterns and prototypes that either tell them what to do (this is recognition-primed decision-making, RPD) or tell them that the situation needs further investigation if it is to be made sense of (this is intuition-based inquiry[96]).

As we discovered in Chapter 7, the Swedish psychologist K. Anders Ericsson discovered that even the most gifted performers need a minimum of ten years (or around 10,000 hours) of intense training and deliberate high-quality practice to become an expert. The mantra 'practice, practice, practice' at one level implies 'more is better', but this is not necessarily so. Developing intuitive expertise requires deliberate and stretching practice through specific and sustained efforts, with expert guidance and feedback: this is high-quality practice. Expert chess players spend much more time deliberately practising the game than playing the game, as do expert sports people and musicians. Perhaps one of the more surprising things about management is that mangers spend much more time 'playing' the game than deliberately practising. To counter this, Gary Klein, in his book *Intuition at Work*, adapted a quality-practice programme that he developed originally for military training based on the recognition-primed decision model for use with executives, business leaders, and managers. Klein's quality practice programme has three elements.

Knowing the Decision Requirements of Your Job

Klein recommends that managers identify the difficult, important, and frequent (DIF) decisions that they have to take. Each decision can then be analysed by specifying what it is that makes the decision difficult, what errors might be made in taking the decision, and how an expert might take the decision compared to a novice (what are the 'tricks of the trade'). For example, construction projects can be difficult because of the creation of unrealistic expectations as a result of bad planning and underestimating the time taken to get things done. Resultant typical errors include going over budget and over schedule (this is the planning fallacy). To rectify this, talking to expert construction project managers might reveal that they focus on the long-term by breaking forecasts down into daily, weekly, and monthly goals and coming to an informed judgement about whether they are achievable. Over the long-term this simple and straightforward analytical strategy will become frozen into a habit which gives managers an intuitive feel for what is realistic and what is not.[97]

Practising Difficult Decisions In Context

Whilst it would be ideal to practice DIF decisions in context, sometimes that is neither realistic nor safe, for example, performing an emergency landing of an aircraft is difficult and important but cannot be practised in the real world. Where difficult and important decisions cannot be practised in authentic settings, Klein recommends that some other method such as simulation, decision games, or scenario-planning exercises be used either individually but ideally in a small group in which dialogue, debate, and the surfacing of individual mental models can take place.

Reviewing Decision-Making Experiences

Experience is one of the best teachers, but only when there is accurate feedback on performance. Blindly undertaking DIF decisions without debriefings and reviews means that the lessons of history do not get learned. One way of reflecting on intuitive decisions is to try to understand the decision process, why particular decisions were taken, how events played out as a result, and what the factors were that led to success or failure. For intuitive decisions this could take the form of a 'critical incident' analysis which entails identifying a previous DIF decision that was taken intuitively where a good outcome was achieved (an intuitive 'hit'), and post-morteming the decision. The same procedure could be carried out with an intuitive DIF decision that worked out badly (an intuitive 'miss'). By combining the analyses across hits and misses and across different managers and contexts, a rich picture can be built up of the factors that enable good intuitive decision-making and those that constrain good intuitive decisions. Reviewing hits and misses and identifying their enabling and constraining factors will help decision-makers to improve their intuitions; in so doing they will build what Klein refers to as their 'intuitive muscle power' as a result of learning the lessons of history.

Seeking Feedback

Feedback plays a vital role in developing good intuitive decision-making skills because lack of knowledge of outcomes as a result of absent or poor feedback builds bad intuitions. In some situations, feedback can be quick to the point of being instantaneous. For example, a chess player who makes a move intuitively gets unequivocal and immediate feedback on how good their intuition was (they are able to reflect-in-action). In addition, after a game a chess player will be able to make sense of why their intuition did or did not work, having won or lost the game (they are able to reflect-on-action[98]). Optimal feedback, such as that which is available to chess players, is accurate, timely, and diagnostic. This helps to make chess a kind learning structure which makes it a good environment in which to develop accurate intuitions. In wicked learning structures, where feedback is inaccurate, delayed, and undiagnostic, decision-makers do not get to find out if their intuitions have been effective. Receiving suboptimal feedback in a wicked learning structure is one of the best ways to develop bad intuitions.

Getting Immediate Feedback

In soccer, referees' judgements and decisions are vital to the smooth and effective running of a game. Soccer referees make up to 250 decisions per game, and many of these have to be taken intuitively given the pace and energy of the game. A team of researchers from the Universities of Heidelberg and Potsdam studied the effects of feedback on the accuracy of soccer referees' decisions. The researchers used a video-based online training tool to see if referees' decision-making performance in 'foul/no-foul' decisions could be improved by feedback.[99] Foul/no foul, like many other sports decisions, is a decision that has to be executed within a few seconds and without deliberation. The video-based training tool was designed to give speedy, accurate, and relevant feedback. It was a kind learning structure (as opposed to a wicked learning structure characterized by missing, noisy, delayed, and biased feedback). The researchers compared the learning success for three different groups: an immediate feedback group who received feedback on whether their decision was good or bad immediately after their decision; a delayed feedback group who received feedback at the end of the game; and a control (no feedback) group. Feedback was only on whether the decision was correct or not, and no explanations were required or given. The immediate feedback group showed significant improvements between their pre- and post-test scores, whereas the delayed and control group showed no such improvement. The results supported the hypothesis that in order to learn how to make good intuitive judgements, decision-makers benefit most from immediate outcome feedback on the correctness of their decisions.

Incidentally, the introduction of video assistant referees (VAR) into soccer is likely to improve referees' intuitive decision-making through the provision of immediate feedback during the course of a real game. Ultimately the use of such methods could raise the overall standard of refereeing as a result of optimal feedback, which allows referees to review and revise their decisions immediately and also for this to be verified by a second official and goal-line decision technology. The associated costs are that it takes more time and reduces the fluidity of the game and also could de-controversialize refereeing, which may be to the chagrin of some fans and commentators who enjoy criticizing referees. Analogically, a type of VAR could be applied in management in the form of immediate and candid reviews of decisions by off-the-pitch bystanders, for example by asking a trusted colleague or mentor 'how did I do?'

The use of technology to improve decision-making is not confined to sports. Recent advances in information technology make it possible in business to obtain real-time stock quotes and for investors to change portfolios on daily and even hourly bases. Technology also gives managers real-time updates on the effects of pricing decisions and on responding to competitors prices, and in inventory and stock control decisions to meet changes in customer demand. The enormous volumes of data that are now available to managers provide unparalleled opportunities for learning, and through learning, for developing better intuitions via timely, accurate, and diagnostic feedback.[100] And yet we might ask: is frequent and more feedback necessarily better? One of the disadvantages of more and frequent feedback is that it may lead decision-makers to focus on the most recent data (which may be 'noisy') and lose sight of the bigger picture and longer-term trends.

Feedback and Learning Structures

Feedback is timely, accurate, and diagnostic in a kind learning structure. It is possible to contribute actively to the creation of a kind learning structure by consciously developing the habit of seeking feedback in order to deliberately test out our intuitive hypotheses, for example by devil's advocacy. Good practice in devil's advocacy includes: challenging the intuition not the intuitor; using logic not opinion; providing alternative interpretations and solutions; acting in the interests of the project or the team not personal agendas; and knowing when to stop.[101] Good practice also entails creating a psychologically safe climate for inquiry and dialogue, for example by actively seeking feedback oneself and reciprocating by offering feedback to others.[102]

It is also possible, although it may sound illogical, to seek feedback before the event in the form of a 'pre-mortem'. A post-mortem is a procedure in which an analysis is undertaken, for example an autopsy, in order to understand the causes of failure, for example why a person died. Intuition researcher Gary Klein recommends that rather than waiting for a project to fail it is helpful to investigate what could be wrong with the plans from the very beginning. Klein's method for pre-morteming includes: looking into a metaphorical crystal ball in order to imagine a 'fiasco', then asking, 'what could have caused this', generating a list of possible reasons for failure, consolidating the list, and revisiting the plan to address the items of greatest concern. Intuition plays an invaluable role in the generating reasons for failure stage because here different managers will have their own experiences of similar situations in the past and their own reasons for seeing potential weaknesses in the project.[103] Pre-morteming in a group is a way to build good intuitions collectively and reap the benefits of a wide range of different intuitions and experiences.

Conclusion

1. The main idea of this chapter is that intuition is a sense that can be sharpened to create impact by building individual managers' knowledge of intuition and developing their intuitive decision-making skills and capabilities; this is 'capacity-building impact' and involves changing self.
2. Coaching features in intuition in two ways: intuitive decision-making is a skill that can be developed through coaching; coaches use intuition as part of their coaching practice.
3. Intuitions can be debiased in two ways: debiasing before a judgement, i.e. 'ex ante' (e.g. training managers to understand sources of bias); debiasing after a judgement has been arrived at, i.e. 'ex post' (e.g., corrective action can be taken after an initial intuitive estimate has been arrived at but before any action is taken).
4. People differ in how they prefer to think, problem-solve, and decide; this is called cognitive styles; there are four analysis/intuition cognitive styles: versatile (ambidextrous), intuitive and analytical (both specialized), and indifferent (undiscerning).
5. Incubation creates the mental space and time for activations to spread across the brain's networks of associations and for new and unusual connections to be made resulting in Eureka moments; incubation can be promoted by distraction, sleeping on the problem, etc.
6. Abduction entails inferring from an observed effect to probable cause; it is a process of generating and adopting an explanatory hypothesis which has the potential to yield an insight; inferences can also be arrived at by conceptual leaping.
7. Intuition and analysis are linked by the processes of integrating, iterating, and imaging; mental simulation is one way to imagine how an intuition might play out and also how a person would feel if they followed their intuition.
8. By interocepting we can gain access to our internal bodily state (e.g., gut feelings); through interoception we can become more intuitively aware.
9. Interpreting involves articulating/explaining an intuition; it is the second step in a process of intuiting, interpreting, integrating, and institutionalizing.
10. Intuitions are built by learning and experience; kind learning environments are conducive for developing good intuitions; wicked learning environments are conducive for developing bad intuitions.
11. Intuitions are honed through extensive practice; quality of practice is as important as quantity of practice; high-quality practice extends intuitive expertise through optimal feedback, i.e. accurate, timely, and diagnostic, and builds good intuitions.

Endnotes

1. Castillo, J. C., Ahuja, A., Athey, S., Baker, A., Budish, E., Chipty, T., ..., & Więcek, W. (2021). Market design to accelerate COVID-19 vaccine supply. *Science*, 371(6534): 1107–1109.
2. UK Research and Innovation (2021). Defining Impact. Available online at: https://www.ukri.org/councils/esrc/impact-toolkit-for-economic-and-social-sciences/defining-impact/ Accessed 28.03.2022; MacIntosh, R., Beech, N., Bartunek, J., Mason, K., Cooke, B., & Denyer, D. (2017). Impact and management research: Exploring relationships between temporality, dialogue, reflexivity and praxis. *British Journal of Management*, 28(1): 3–13.
3. Mueller, S., & Dhar, J. (2019). *The Decision-Maker's Playbook*. Harlow: Pearson Education.
4. *The Harvard Business Review Guide to Making Better Decisions*. (2020). Boston, MA: Harvard Business Review Press.
5. Keen, L. (2019). *Intuition Magic: Understanding Your Psychic Nature*. California: Keen Press; Brady, T. (2011). *Ignite Your Psychic Intuition: An A-Z Guide for Developing Your Sixth Sense*. No place: Llewellyn Publications; Shumsky, S. (2015). *Awaken Your Third Eye: How Accessing Your Sixth Sense Can Help You Find Knowledge, Illumination and Intuition*. Pompton Plains, NJ: New Page Books.
6. Jureko, J. (2022). Rafael Nadal: The tough love that shaped a 21-time grand slam champion. BBC News. Available online at: https://www.bbc.co.uk/sport/tennis/60183861 Accessed 09.04.2022.
7. Ibarra, H., & Scoular, A. (2019). The leader as coach. *Harvard Business Review*, 97(6): 110–119.
8. Kahneman, D., & Klein, G. (2009). Conditions for intuitive expertise: a failure to disagree. *American Psychologist*, 64(6): 515–526.
9. Cairns, D. L. (1996). Hybris, dishonour, and thinking big. *The Journal of Hellenic Studies*, 116: 1–32.
10. Soyer, E., & Hogarth, R. M. (2020). *The Myth of Experience: Why We Learn the Wrong Lessons, and Ways to Correct Them*. Paris: Public Affairs, p. 199.
11. Klein, G. A. (2004). *Intuition at Work*. New York: Currency, pp. 223–224.
12. Skiffington, S., & Zeus, P. (2003). *Behavioural Coaching*. Sydney: McGraw Hill.
13. Centre for Creative leadership (2021). Use active listening skills to coach others. Available online at: https://www.ccl.org/articles/leading-effectively-articles/coaching-others-use-active-listening-skills/ Accessed 21.02.2022.
14. Passmore, J (2006). *Excellence in Coaching: The Industry Guide*. London: McGraw-Hill.
15. Mavor, P., Sadler-Smith, E., & Gray, D. E. (2010). Teaching and learning intuition: Some implications for HRD and coaching practice. *Journal of European Industrial Training*, 34(8/9): 822–838.
16. Sheldon, C. (2018). Trust your gut, listen to reason: How experienced coaches work with intuition in their practice. *International Coaching Psychology Review*, 13(1): 6–20, p. 16.
17. Ibid.
18. Kahneman, D., Sibony, O, & Thaler, R. (2021). *Noise*. London: William Collins, p. 4.
19. Ibid., p. 238.

20. ActiTime (no date). The planning fallacy and how to deal with it. Available online at: https://www.actitime.com/project-time-estimation/planning-fallacy Accessed 21.02.2022.
21. Financial Times (2021). Boris Johnson's bridge to Northern Ireland impossible to justify. *Financial Times*, Sunday 28 November.
22. Kahneman, D. (2011). *Thinking, Fast and Slow*. London: Allen Lane, p. 193.
23. Ibid.
24. Sadler-Smith, E., & Cojuharenco, I. (2021). Business schools and hubris: Cause or cure?. *Academy of Management Learning & Education*, 20(2): 270–289; Sadler-Smith, E. (2019). *Hubristic leadership*. London: SAGE.
25. Sadler-Smith, E. (2010). *The Intuitive Mind*. Chichester: John Wiley & Sons, p. 40.
26. Witteman, C., Van den Bercken, J., Claes, L., & Godoy, A. (2009). Assessing rational and intuitive thinking styles. *European Journal of Psychological Assessment*, 25(1): 39–47.
27. Klein, G. A. (2004). *Intuition at Work*. New York: Currency, p. 57.
28. Hodgkinson, G. P., & Sadler-Smith, E. (2011). *Investigating intuition: Beyond self-report*. In M. Sinclair (Ed.). *Handbook of Intuition Research* (pp. 52–66). Cheltenham: Edward Elgar.
29. Sadler-Smith, E. (2002). The role of cognitive style in management education. Academy of Management Conference, Denver, August 2002 (Best Paper Proceedings).
30. Hodgkinson, G. P., & Clarke, I. (2007). Conceptual note: Exploring the cognitive significance of organizational strategizing. *Human Relations*, 60(1): 243–255.
31. Vieira, V. A., Faia, V. D. S., Gabler, C. B., & Cardoso, R. N. (2020). The impact of intuition and deliberation on acquisition-retention ambidexterity and sales performance: comparing the Dual-Process and Uni-Process Models. *Journal of Personal Selling & Sales Management*, 41(1): 56–69.
32. Langley, A. (1995). Between 'paralysis by analysis' and 'extinction by instinct'. *Sloan Management Review*, 36: 63–76.
33. Vieira, V. A., Faia, V. D. S., Gabler, C. B., & Cardoso, R. N. (2020). The impact of intuition and deliberation on acquisition-retention ambidexterity and sales performance: comparing the Dual-Process and Uni-Process Models. *Journal of Personal Selling & Sales Management*, 41(1): 56–69.
34. Kahneman, D., Sibony, O, & Thaler, R. (2021). *Noise*. London: William Collins, p. 138
35. Langley, A. (1995). Between 'paralysis by analysis' and 'extinction by instinct'. *Sloan Management Review*, 36: 63–76.
36. Hodgkinson, G. P., & Clarke, I. (2007). Conceptual note: Exploring the cognitive significance of organizational strategizing. *Human Relations*, 60(1): 243–255, p. 247.
37. Simon, H. A. (1987). Making management decisions: The role of intuition and emotion. *Academy of Management Perspectives*, 1(1): 57–64, p. 63
38. Hodgkinson, G. P., & Sadler-Smith, E. (2003). Complex or unitary? A critique and empirical reassessment of the Allinson-Hayes Cognitive Style Index, *Journal of Occupational and Organizational Psychology*, 76: 243–268.
39. Groves, K., Vance, C., & Choi, D. (2011). Examining entrepreneurial cognition: An occupational analysis of balanced linear and nonlinear thinking and entrepreneurship success. *Journal of Small Business Management*, 49(3): 438–466.
40. Brigham, K.H., et al., (2007). A person-organization fit model of owner-managers' cognitive style and organizational demands, *Entrepreneurship Theory & Practice*, 32: 29–51.

41. Wu, H. (2022). Intuition in investment decision-making across cultures. *Journal of Behavioral Finance*, 23(1): 106–122.
42. Sadler-Smith, E. (2016). 'What happens when you intuit?' Understanding human resource practitioners' subjective experience of intuition through a novel linguistic method. *Human Relations*, 69(5): 1069–1093.
43. Heraclitus' Fragment 90 cited in Kounios, J., & Beeman, M. (2015). *The Eureka Factor*. London: Heinemann, p. 92.
44. Sio, U. N., & Ormerod, T. C. (2009). Does incubation enhance problem solving? A meta-analytic review. *Psychological Bulletin*, 135(1): 94–120.
45. Sio, U. N., & Ormerod, T. C. (2009). Does incubation enhance problem solving? A meta-analytic review. *Psychological Bulletin*, 135(1): 94–120.
46. Sadler-Smith, E. (2008). *Inside Intuition*. Abingdon: Routledge.
47. Kounios, J., & Beeman, M. (2015). *The Eureka Factor*. London: Heinemann, pp. 95–96
48. Shrimpton, D. (2019). 'The business tree model'—dependencies, interdependencies and relationships. *Medium*. Available online at: https://medium.com/@davidshrimptonds/the-business-tree-model-dependencies-interdependencies-and-relationships-eb2dfa633b14 Accessed 21.02.2022.
49. Kounios, J., & Beeman, M. (2015). *The Eureka Factor*. London: Heinemann, p. 101.
50. Perkins, D. 2000. *Archimedes' Bathtub*. New York: WW Norton, p. 198.
51. Kounios, J., & Beeman, M. (2015). *The Eureka Factor*. London: Heinemann, p. 109
52. Lipscomb, M. (2012). Abductive reasoning and qualitative research. *Nursing Philosophy*, 13(4): 244–256.
53. Aliseda, A. (2000). Abduction as epistemic change: A Peircean model in artificial intelligence. In Flach, P. A., & Kakas, A. C. (Eds.). Abduction and induction. *Applied Logic Series*, 18. Dordrecht: Springer, pp. 45–58.
54. Charles Sanders Peirce Cited in: Nubiola, J. (2005). Abduction or the Logic of Surprise. *Semiotica*, 153: 117–130, p. 127.
55. These are the words Chester Barnard (see Chapter 1) used to describe the operation of non-conscious mental processes, i.e. intuition, see: Barnard, C.E. (1938). *The Functions of the Executive*. Cambridge, MA: Harvard University Press.
56. Klag, M., & Langley, A. (2013). Approaching the conceptual leap in qualitative research. *International Journal of Management Reviews*, 15(2): 149–166, p. 151
57. Ibid., p. 152.
58. Senge, P.M. et al. (1994). *The Fifth Discipline Fieldbook*. London: Nicholas Brealey, pp. 243–245.
59. Damasio, A. R. (1999). *The Feeling of What Happens: Body and Emotion in the Making of Consciousness*. New York: Houghton Mifflin Harcourt.
60. Gendlin, E. (1968). The experiential response. In Hammer, E. F. (Ed.). *Use of Interpretation in Treatment* (pp. 208–227). New York: Grune and Stratton, p. 210.
61. Claxton, G. (2000). The anatomy of intuition. In Atkinson, T., & Claxton, G. (Eds.). *The Intuitive Practitioner* (pp. 32–52). Milton Keynes: Open University Press, p. 46.
62. Akinci, C., & Sadler-Smith, E. (2020). 'If something doesn't look right, go find out why': how intuitive decision making is accomplished in police first-response. *European Journal of Work and Organizational Psychology*, 29(1): 78–92.
63. Listening Partnership (no date). Body language and coaching: Going right to the heart. Available online at: https://www.listeningpartnership.com/insight/body-language-matters/ Accessed 21.02.2022; Gendlin, E. (1978). *Focusing*. New York: Bantam.

64. Gendlin, E. (1978). *Focusing*. New York: Bantam.
65. Epstein, S. (2014). *Cognitive-Experiential Theory*. Oxford: Oxford University Press, p. 39.
66. Ortiz, M. J. (2011). Primary metaphors and monomodal visual metaphors. *Journal of Pragmatics*, 43(6): 1568–1580.
67. Sadler-Smith, E. (2016). 'What happens when you intuit?' Understanding human resource practitioners' subjective experience of intuition through a novel linguistic method. *Human Relations*, 69(5): 1069–1093.
68. Adapted from: Feldman, J. A. (2008). *From Molecule to Metaphor: A Neural Theory of Language*. Cambridge, MA: MIT Press, p. 201.
69. Lakoff, G., & Johnson, M. (1980). The metaphorical structure of the human conceptual system. *Cognitive Science*, 4(2): 195–208.
70. Feldman, J. (2008). *From Molecule to Metaphor: A Neural Theory of Language*. Cambridge, MA: MIT Press.
71. Cornelissen, J. P., & Kafouros, M. (2008). The emergent organization: Primary and complex metaphors in theorizing about organizations. *Organization Studies*, 29(7): 957–978; Gibbs, R. W. (2006). Metaphor interpretation as embodied simulation. *Mind & Language*, 21(3): 434–458.
72. Feldman, J. (2008). *From Molecule to Metaphor: A Neural Theory of Language*. Cambridge, MA: MIT Press.
73. Hughes, T. (1967). *Poetry in the Making*. London: Faber and Faber, pp. 56–57.
74. Ibid., p. 58.
75. Claxton, G. (2000). The anatomy of intuition. In Atkinson, T., & Claxton, G. (Eds.). *The Intuitive Practitioner* (pp. 32–52). Milton Keynes: Open University Press, p. 46.
76. Crossan, M. M., Lane, H. W., & White, R. E. (1999). An organizational learning framework: From intuition to institution. *Academy of Management Review*, 24(3): 522–537.
77. Davis, S. H., & Davis, P. B. (2003). *The Intuitive Dimensions of Administrative Decision-Making*. Lanham: Scarecrow Press, p. 179.
78. Feldman, J. (2008). *From Molecule to Metaphor: A Neural Theory of Language*. Cambridge, MA: MIT Press.
79. Sukhov, A., Sihvonen, A., Netz, J., Magnusson, P., & Olsson, L. E. (2021). How experts screen ideas: The complex interplay of intuition, analysis and sensemaking. *Journal of Product Innovation Management*, 38(2): 248–270.
80. Meziani, N., & Cabantous, L. (2020). Acting intuition into sense: How film crews make sense with embodied ways of knowing. *Journal of Management Studies*, 57(7): 1384–1419.
81. Boisjoly, R. P., Curtis, E. F., & Mellican, E. (1989). Roger Boisjoly and the Challenger disaster: The ethical dimensions. *Journal of Business Ethics*, 8(4): 217–230, p. 224.
82. Akinci, C., & Sadler-Smith, E. (2019). Collective intuition: Implications for improved decision making and organizational learning. *British Journal of Management*, 30(3): 558–577.
83. Dotlich D. L., Cairo, P. C., & Rhinesmith, S. H. (2006). *Head, Heart and Guts*. San Francisco: Jossey-Bass, p. 167.
84. Hensman, A., & Sadler-Smith, E. (2011). Intuitive decision making in banking and finance. *European Management Journal*, 29(1): 51–66, p. 58.
85. DiLeonardo, A., Phelps, R. L., & Weddle, B. (2020). Establish a performance culture as your 'secret sauce'. McKinsey & Company. Available online at: https://www.mckinsey.com/business-functions/people-and-organizational-performance/our-insights/the-

organization-blog/establish-a-performance-culture-as-your-secret-sauce Accessed 21.02.2022.
86. Zappos Insights (no date). Zappos 10 Core Values. Available online at: https://www.zapposinsights.com/about/core-values#oath Accessed 21.02.2022.
87. Van der Heijden, K. et al. (2002). *The Sixth Sense*. Chichester: John Wiley & Sons, pp. 159–160.
88. Hogarth, R. M. (2001). *Educating Intuition: A Challenge for the 21st Century*. Chicago: Chicago University Press, pp. 89–90.
89. Kahneman, D., & Klein, G. (2009). Conditions for intuitive expertise: a failure to disagree. *American Psychologist*, 64(6): 515–526.
90. Ibid.
91. Hogarth, R. M. (2021). *Educating Intuition: A Challenge for the 21st Century*. CREI: Catalunya.
92. Kahneman, D., Sibony, O., & Thaler, R. (2021). *Noise*. London: William Collins, p. 4.
93. Hogarth, R. M. (2001). *Educating Intuition: A Challenge for the 21st Century*. Chicago: Chicago University Press, p. 203.
94. Kahneman, D., Sibony, O, & Thaler, R. (2021). *Noise*. London: William Collins p. 307.
95. Nesterak, D. (2021). A conversation with Daniel Kahneman about 'Noise'. *Behavioural Scientist*. Available online at: https://behavioralscientist.org/a-conversation-with-daniel-kahneman-about-noise/ Accessed 11.04.2022.
96. Akinci, C., & Sadler-Smith, E. (2020). 'If something doesn't look right, go find out why': how intuitive decision making is accomplished in police first-response. *European Journal of Work and Organizational Psychology*, 29(1): 78–92.
97. Page, M. (no date). Top 6 construction project challenges. Michael Page. Available online at: https://www.michaelpage.com/advice/management-advice/top-6-construction-project-challenges Accessed 10.04.2022.
98. Schön, D. A. (1987). *Educating the Reflective Practitioner*. San Francisco: Jossey-Bass.
99. Schweizer, G., Plessner, H., Kahlert, D., & Brand, R. (2011). A video-based training method for improving soccer referees' intuitive decision-making skills. *Journal of Applied Sport Psychology*, 23(4): 429–442.
100. Lurie, N. H., & Swaminathan, J. M. (2009). Is timely information always better? The effect of feedback frequency on decision making. Organizational Behaviour and Human Decision Processes, 108(2): 315–329.
101. Eckfeldt, B. (2020). How to play devil's advocate in a constructive way. *Inc Magazine*, 22 May 2020. Available online at: https://www.inc.com/bruce-eckfeldt/how-to-play-devils-advocate-in-a-productive-way.html Accessed 10.04.2022.
102. Hogarth, R. M. (2001). *Educating Intuition: A Challenge for the 21st Century*. Chicago: Chicago University Press, p. 270.
103. Klein, G. A. (2004). *Intuition at Work*. New York: Currency, pp. 88–90.

Index

abduction 273–4
accountancy, intuition and 9
actor-driven collective intuition 182
    dominant 182
adaptive toolbox 56, 57
Adriá, Ferran 239
affect heuristic 46, 48–9, 121
    bias and 121
    see also mood
Agor, Weston H, intuition in decision-making 136
Ahrendts, Angela 240
AI (artificial intuition) 253–4
    'Face-Trace' technology 122
    new techniques 21–4
Akinci, Cinla 238
Akstinaite, V 231
Alexander, S 251
algorithms
    AI 23–4, 253
    statistical prediction 21–2
altruism 70, 190
Amazon Prime, launch 5, 252
Ambady, N, thin slicing 212–13
Amis, Martin 241
amygdala
    approximate location 147*f*, 222*f*
    decision-making 148
analysis/intuition
    cognitive style, questions for diagnosis 268*t*
    decision-making 115–19
    innovation projects 116
    paradoxical thinking 116
analytical mind
    mental stimulation 89, 90
    two-minds model 104–8
analytical–rational thinking (system 2) 117, 189
anchors 108
animals, in advertising 107
anterior insula 150–1*f*
anterior superior temporal gyrus (aSTG) 233*f*
Apple 80, 115, 182, 240, 242, 281
Archimedes, original 'Eureka' moment 232–3
Ardern, Jacinda 80, 217
art expertise 173
artificial grammar 106
Ashkanasy, Neil 14
Asimov, I 231
associative learning 120
    and hedonic principle 119–20

AstraZeneca 238, 252
Atanasiu, R, simplification principle 74
attitudes, and practices, decoupling 109
attribute substitution 40, 123
'authority *vs* subversion' (MFT) 198
autism 209
automatic *vs* controlled information processing 83
autotelic/exotelic activity 172
availability heuristic 44
    boom and bust cycles 47

Bakken, B 174
Barnard, Chester 1, 8–10, 82–3
    The Functions of the Executive 8
Baron, R, business opportunity recognition 141
Baron-Cohen, S 218
basal ganglia, caudate nucleus 144*f*
base rate fallacy 40
bat and ball problem, intuitive answer 38
Bear Sterns (bank) 237
Beatles, The 168, 272
Becchina, G 229
Bechara, A 146
Beck, J 233
Beeman, M 232, 272
behavioural finance, boom and bust cycles 47
Ben & Jerry's ice cream, marketing 200
Benner, Patricia
    embodied know-how 180
    nursing theory 174–7
Berdrow, Iris 246
Bergson, H 254
Bezos, Jeff 5
bias
    decision-making 265
    framing 223
    and intuition 97
    and representativeness heuristic 44
    systemic, in decision-making 265
    see also debiasing; framing bias; heuristics and biases
Bible, The 202
bicycle control 105
Billett, S 244
Bin Laden, Osama 6
biofeedback techniques, interoceptive awareness 152–3
board games 142–3
body consciousness 150–3

Boeing 707 16
bounded rationality 7–8, 35–7, 57–9
  fast and frugal heuristics 56, 59–60
  less can be more 57–8, 73
  limitations 36
  multi-attribute methods (Simon) 35
  quasi-rationality 82–3
Boyatzis, R 155
brain
  activation in 'Eureka' moments 232–3
  anterior superior temporal gyrus (aSTG) 233*f*
  location of amygdala 147*f*, 222*f*
  orbitofrontal cortex (OFC) 138–40*f*
  see also ventro-medial prefrontal cortex (VMPFC)
brand name recognition 63–4, 107, 113–15, 122, 138, 149, 240
  framing bias 223
  leverages 122
Branson, Richard 16
Britten, Benjamin 242
Brodie, B 251
Brown, Gordon 80
Brown, Michael S 251
Burberry 240
burglary, 'take the best' heuristic 67–8
business
  business opportunity recognition 141
  critical success factors 177–8
  deliberate practice in management 170
  'Eureka' moments 233–4
  expertise, expert sense 178–83
  intuition-based inquiry 96–7
  intuitive expertise 178–83
  moral intuition/sense 200–3
  negotiation skills 106
  recognition-primed decision-making (RPD) 91–2
  social sense
    reflexion, reflection and social cognition 220–4
    thin slicing, in management 214–16
  ventures/entrepreneurship 42–4
business angels 1, 3–4
business viability data (BVD) 3

C-system, neural correlates 222*f*
Calabretta, G, dynamics of analysis and intuition 116
Calderwood, R 84
Cameron, David 108
Canada Post Corporation 247
cardioception, cardiac signals 150–1
'care *vs* harm' (MFT) 198
Carlson, Chester, photocopying machine 141
Carlsson, Arvid 251

caudate nucleus
  approximate location 144*f*
  dopamine neurons 145
  fMRI analysis 145
CEO, problems, examples 6–7
Chaiken, Shelly, dual heuristic–systematic model 106–7
charity donations 108
Chase, William 10
chess 142–3, 163–6, 168
  intuition and 164
choice
  overload 73–4
  simplicity as a virtue 73
Clarke, Ian 269
classical rationality 34–5, 58
  models of decision-making 8
    Franklin, Priestley 34
  satisfice, *vs* maximise 36, 58
climate change
  attitudes and practices, decoupling 109
  System-1, System-2 processing 201–2
Clinton, Hilary 217
Clinton-Cirocco, A 84
coaching 262–5
cognitive bias, framing 223–4
cognitive continuum theory 81–3
  and bounded rationality 83
  evolutionary origins 83
  intuition and analysis 82, 83
cognitive inertia 125
cognitive neuroscience
  core processes 137
  social 221
cognitive styles 267–71
  four 269*f*
cognitive–experiential theory (CET) 103, 117–19, 121, 268
  hedonic/affective principle 121
Cohen, S 251
coherence *see* perceptions of coherence
collective intuition 182–3
compassion (MFT) 198
competence, and facial appearance 219
complex domain-relevant scheme (CDRS) 123–4
computerized text analysis software 231
computers
  aesthetics 242
  graphical user interface 244
conceptual leaping 274–5
conditioned learning 119–20, 155
conjunction fallacy 72
conjunction rule 39
connoisseurship 178
conscious competence 87
  vs un/conscious in/competence 87

conscious/explicit *vs* unconscious/implicit processing 106
conscious/unconscious thinking 103–4
consciousness, levels of, in creative process 236*f*
consequential judgments 73
　honest signals 73
consumer choice 240
　and satisfaction 73
　simplicity as a virtue 73
　see also brand name recognition
correspondence-accuracy principle 82
Cosmides, L and Toobey, J, on frequency information 71–2
Covid-19 pandemic 108
　public pronouncements 217
　vaccines 260–2
creative destruction (Schumpeter) 43
creative intuition 229–59
　automated expertise *vs* holistic hunches 248–50
　automating 253–4
　'Eureka' moments in business 233–4
　insight, intuitive 246–8
　insight and 'creative desperation' 244–6
　insight in the real world 237–9
　insight 'sees' 230–1
　intuition 'senses' 229–30
　invention 251–3
　original 'Eureka' moment 232–3
　scientific discovery 250–1
　slow burn, hard work of 242–4
　standard model 234–7
　summary 254
　thinking without thinking 239–42
creative process
　five stages of creative process 236*f*
　see also Standard Model of creative thinking
credit crash *see* financial crash of 2007-8
critical success factors (CSFs) 15
Cronin, James 250–1
Crossan, M, four-I model of organizational learning 183, 246
cue discrimination 90
cue ordering 71
culture, purity concerns 200
Czikszentmihalyi, M, 'flow' and one-pointedness 172

Damasio, A 146, 196
Dane, Erik 11
Darwinian models
　decision-making 34–5
　Malthus essay 239
'Darwinian' moral sense 189–91
de Groot, Adriaan, chess 163, 164–6
debiasing 260, 262, 265–6, 290
decision-making

'automatic system' 104
classical/rational model 8, 34–5
difficult, important, and frequent (DIF) 286–7
explorative success 249
on the fire ground 84–7
intuition and analysis 82, 83, 115–19
proxies 142
quasi-rationality 82–3
systemic bias 265
under radical uncertainty 6–7
under risk and uncertainty 4–5
default-interventionist (DI) mode 113
deliberation-without-attention effect 243
deliberative *see* analytical–rational thinking (system 2)
Deromedi, RK 200
desirability bias 121
diagnosing 267
difficult, important, and frequent (DIF), decision-making 286–7
Dijksterhuis, A 240, 241, 243
Dirac, Paul 242
Dodge, Viper 16
Dodge, Wagner 245, 249
dominant actor intuition 182
dopamine neurons, caudate nucleus 145
dopamine release 150
Dörfler, V 239, 247, 250
Dreyfus, H and S 171
Dreyfus Skill Acquisition Model (SAM) 171–4
Drucker, P 250
du Sautoy, Marcus 253
dual heuristic–systematic model 106–7
dual-process theory 104–8
　cognitive–experiential theory (CET) 103
　cue–outcome relationship 126
　default-interventionist (DI) mode 113
　dual attitudes 108–10
　dual thinking processes 110
　model, habitual *vs* attentive 216
　parallel–competitive (PC) mode 113
　speed of decision-making 122
Duggan, W 237
Dyson, Sir James 248–9, 252

Ebay, beginnings 169
ecological rationality 56, 57–9
　principles 56, 58
economic rationality 58
Eden, Colin 250
Edison, Thomas 183, 235
Einstein, Albert 242
Eisenhardt, K 74
elimination decision-making 60
Eling, K 252
email marketing 120–1

emotional intelligence 155–6
emotional salience 44
  decision-making and 148, 224
  leader behaviours 156
  positive/negative emotions, asymmetry 46
  risk perception 222
  tone 217, 221–4
  see also ventro-medial prefrontal cortex (VMPFC)
empathy 210
  female superiority of 218
Enron, moral code 195–6, 200
entrepreneurship 42–4
  decision-making style 249
  failure rate 42
environment
  validity of 124
  see also climate change
epistemology, declarative vs procedural knowledge 175
Epstein, S, cognitive-experiential theory (CET) 103, 117–18
estate agents 122, 125
ethics
  ethical behaviour in the workplace, promotion 47–8
  ethical consumption 109
  visual imagery 48, 202
'Eureka' moments 230, 232–4
  in business 233–4
Evans, J
  dual-process theory 126
  dual-processing concept 111
evolution
  archaeological record 111
  consequential judgments 73
  Neanderthals 111
  see also Darwinian models; Wallace
evolution, cultural 50, 71–3
  errors in computation 50
  moral foundations theory 197–200
  selection for cognitive activity 83
Expedia 142
experiential model 117–19
experiential (system 1), vs rational (system 2) 119, 121, 202
expertise, expert sense 13, 163–88
  born vs made 171–8
  in business 178–83
  chess 142–3, 163–6, 168
  intuitive 86–7, 125, 171–4
  practice 169–71
  summary 183–4
  10,000 hours 167–8
explicit learning 106
exploitation vs exploration 248

'Face-Trace' technology 122
facial appearance 218–19
  competence perception 219
  criminality perception 224
failure, creation of new knowledge 249
'fairness vs cheating' (MFT) 198
fast and frugal heuristics 57–75
  bounded and ecological rationality 57–9
  recognition-based heuristics 61–5
  rules of thumb 57, 59–60
  simplicity (a virtue) 70–4
  social and reason-based heuristics 65–70
  summary 75
  why it succeeds, sometimes 70–3
fast vs slow thinking 112–13
feedback 287–8
  and learning structures 289
  mirror mechanisms 155–6
  wicked learning structures 125
Fenton-O'Creevy, Mark 19
financial crash of 2007-8 80, 175, 178
firefighting 90–1, 124
  decision-making and intuition 84–7, 249
  escape fire 245–6
  Mann Gulch fire 244–6, 249
flight/fight responses 222–3
flying, intuition in 170–1
Ford, Henry 16
  assembly line 141
  mentalization 211
framing bias 223
fraud, Ponzi scheme 238
frequency information 71–2
functional magnetic resonance imaging (fMRI) 145, 232
functional near infrared spectroscopy (fNIRS) 142
'fuzzy front end' 247
'fuzzy trace theory' 177

gambling 146–50, 223
Gates, Bill 178, 250
gaze heuristic 60, 71
Geithner, Timothy 6
General Mills 234
Gestalt closure task 139f
Gestalt principles of visual perception 138
'Getty kouros' 229–30
Gigerenzer, Gerd 41, 57–9
  brand name recognition 63–4
gist-based reasoning 177
Gladwell, Malcolm 168, 229
Goldstein, Daniel 58–9
Goleman, D 155, 222
GoPro camera 233
Gore, Al 48, 202
Gould, SJ 39

Graham, J 197
graphical user interface 233, 244
Gray, D 264
Greene, Joshua 190, 192
de Groot, Adriaan, chess 163, 164–6
gun homicide/suicide, availability heuristic 44, 45
gut feeling 5, 6, 12–14, 56–79, 117, 120
   absence 148
   mixed blessing 121
   somatic marker hypothesis 149–50
   'sometimes gets it right' (Ch.3) 56–79

Hadamard, J 242
Haerem, T 174
Haidt, J 148, 194, 197
Hammond, Kenneth, cognitive continuum theory 81–3
happiness, expertise and 173
Harding, Matthew, algorithms 23–4
Harrison, EB 229, 238
Harteis, C 244
Harvard Business Review, practice in business 170
headlines, credibility, framing bias and 223–4
hedonic principle
   and associative learning 119–20
   see also affect heuristic
Helmholtz, Hermann 235
heuristic processing, vs systematic processing 107
heuristics 56–79
   1/N rule 60, 70
   affect heuristic 46, 48–9, 121
   anchoring/adjustment 48
   availability heuristic 44, 45
   defined, and example 32–3
   do-what-the-majority-do vs do-what-your-peers-do 65
   example, critical care 59
   fast and frugal 56, 59–60
   intuitive judgements 50
   recognition-based vs reason-based 61–5
   representativeness heuristic 39–40, 42, 49
   social imitative 65–6
heuristics and biases 32–55
   errors and biases 36–8, 123
   purist stance 59
hiring, intuition and 20
Hirshfeld, Alan 232
Hitler, Nazi Germany 199
Hodgkinson, Gerard 125, 269
Hogarth, R 283
Holmes, Sherlock 273
honest signals 73
   and linguistic markers 216–17
Huang, Laura 3
hubris, defined 42–3

Hudson River 'miracle', Sullenberger's flying intuition 170–1
Huggies 201
Hume, David 189
   reasoning on 194
hybrid intelligence 277

IBM–Lexus collaboration 22
ice cream, marketing 200
'if–then' logic 219–20
ignorance-based decision-making 60
IKEA 201
imagining 275
imitation 65, 70
impact
   of Covid-19 vaccines 260–2
   making, through intuition 260–95
   summary/conclusion 290
Implicit Association Test (IAT) 109
implicit learning 105–6, 218
improvisation 249
incubating 236, 271–2
inductive reasoning processes 72
inferring 273
information, representations of, memory 177
information filtering 90
information processing, automatic vs controlled 83
innovation projects
   analysis/intuition 116
   paradoxical thinking 116
insight
   creating conditions for 272–3
   incubating and 271–2
   matchstick problem 230–1
   in the real world 237–9
   vs intuition 229
insula 153
integrating 275
interoception 150–3, 277–9
interpreting 280
intimation 236, 250
intuition
   actor-driven collective 182
   and bias 97
   chess and 164
   collective 183, 282–3
   combining with analysis 97–8, 113–19
   creative see creative intuition
   definitions
      (1, 2 and 3) 9, 11, 12
      Gigerenzer 70
      shared 182
      summary 12
   faster/more consequential decision-making 174

good/bad 284
ineffability 282
laboratory experiments on 137
moral intuition 194
perceptions of coherence 141
in the right hemisphere? 134–5
sense of (Ch.1) 1–31
sometimes gets it wrong (Ch.2) 32–55
sometimes gets it right (Ch.3) 56–79
sometimes wrong but rarely in doubt 20
often gets it right (Ch.4) 80–102
top management team (TMT) 182
traffic light model 98*f*
two-minds model
   (Ch.5) 103–33
      core processes of intuition (Ch.6) 134–62
unbridled intuition 43
virtue of simplicity 74
vs insight 229
see also analysis/intuition
intuition and analysis
   decision-making 82, 83
   intuitive–analytic thinking continuum 217
   quasi-rationality 82–3
intuition science 17–19
intuition-based inquiry 92–8, 95*f*
   in business 96–7
intuitive expertise 86–7, 125
   in business 165–6, 178–83
   chess 163–5
   NATO 174
   nurses' intuition 174–8
intuitive pattern recognition 89–90, 96
invention 251–3
   see also new product development (NPD)
Iowa Gambling Task (IGT) 146–50, 223
Ireland, Duane 248–9
Italian expresso bars 149
iterating 275, 276

James, William, 'secondary consciousness' 104
Jarosz, A 23, 237–8
job performance
   combining intuition and analysis 97–8
   'don't hire for skills hire for attitude' 74
   intuition-based inquiry 96–7
   predictors 68–70, 69*t*
Jobs, Steve
   graphical user interface 233, 244
   mentalization 212
Jordan, Kayla 217
Joseph, C 197
judgment, framing bias 223
judgment-under-uncertainty view 71
Jung, Carl 11

Kahnemann, Daniel
   Nobel Prize 32, 33, 37–8, 104
   System 1 research 123
Kanizsa triangle illusion 138*f*
Kare, Susan 242
Kasparov, Garry 10
Kay, John 6
Kekulé's tail-swallowing snakes 235–6, 272
Kennedy, JF 42
Keynes, JM, decision-making under risk and
   uncertainty 4–5
Khatri, Naresh 18–19
kind-vs-wicked learning structures 124–5
King, Mervyn 6
Kitano, Hiroaki 253
Klein, G, recognition-primed decision-
   making 81, 84, 124, 237, 238,
   245
knowledge, declarative *vs* procedural
   knowledge 175
Koleva, S 201
Kounios, J 232, 272
Kraft, marketing 200

Land camera 234
language, intuitions 106
leader behaviours 156
learning 283
   conditioned learning 119–20
   organizational learning 183
   structures 289
legal decision-making 173–4
   appearances and culpability 224
   intuitive assessments tainting evidence 224
'less is more' 57–8, 73
Lexus, intuitive car 22
Lieberman, M 209, 211, 218, 221
Linda problem, The 38–9, 41–2, 72
Linguistic Enquiry & Word Count 217
linguistic markers 216–17, 221, 231
   of insight/of intuition 231
London Tube, map 233
'loyalty *vs* betrayal' (MFT) 198
Lutz, Bob 16, 19

macaque monkeys, mirror neurons 153–6
machine learning (ML) 21
Madoff, B, fraud 238
magazine headline credibility, framing bias 223–4
Mailer, Norman 241
management skills
   deliberate practice in 170
   learning 172
   top management team (TMT) intuition 182
Mann Gulch fire 244–6, 249

marketing
  mentalization 211–12
  value-based 200–2
Markopolos, H 238
matchstick problem 230–1
Matzler, K 250
Meehl, Paul 21
meme 190
memory
  'fuzzy trace theory' 177
  representations of information 177
mental shot-gun 41
mentalizing
  and mirroring 208–12, 219–20
  see also theory of mind
metacognition 116, 145
metaphors 279–80
  interpreting intuitions 281–2
Microsoft 178, 250
military operations 81, 171, 174
Miller, Chet 248–9
mimicry 216
mind, as adaptive toolbox 56, 57
mirror mechanism 153–6, 209–11
mirror neurons 153–6, 209–11
  approximate location 154f
mood 213–14
moral foundations theory (MFT) 197–200
  five foundations 197–8
  innate preparation 199
  moral mind 199–200
  'original vs current' triggers 199
  System-1, System-2 processing 197–200
moral intuition/sense 189–207
  altruism 70, 190
  in business 200–3
  'Darwinian' model 189–91
  moral intuition 191–4
  moral judgment, rationalist model 189, 194–5
  neurobiology of 196–7
  social intuitionist model of moral judgment 194–6
  summary 203–4
music 114
musicians 126, 167, 171, 242, 253
  10,000 hours 'rule' 167–9
  expertise 168

Nambu, Y 251
NATO Manual, demands placed on officers 174
naturalistic decision-making (NDM) 80–1
Netflix, spending policy 74
neural correlates
  C-system 222f
  X-system 221–2, 222f
neurological disorders 147–9

VMPFC patients 148–9
neuroscience, cognitive 137
new product development (NPD) 15
  'fuzzy front end' 247, 251
  see also invention
Ng, Alvin 18–19
Nobel Laureates 250–1
Nobel Prizes, for intuition researchers 32
noise 285
non-linguistic markers 216–17
nucleus accumbens 150
'nudging' 107–8
nursing theory
  critical success factors 177–8
  intuitive expertise 174–8

Obama, Barack 6
observable frequencies 71
one reason decision-making 60
$1/N$ rule 60
orbitofrontal cortex (OFC) 138–40f
  perceptions of coherence 137–42
organizational learning, four-I model 183
overpass rescue 88

paradoxical thinking, innovation projects 116
parallel–competitive (PC) mode 113, 115
paralysis-by-analysis 6–7
Parikh, J, survey of intuition 136
Pasteur, Louis 273
pattern recognition 142–6
Pavlovian conditioned learning 119–20, 155
Pearce, Jone 3
Pennebaker, J 217
Pentland, A 216
perceptions of coherence 137–42
Persil 201
Petitmengin, Clare 236
photocopying machine 141
photography
  GoPro camera 233
  Land camera 234
phylogeny, imperfections in function 50
Plato, on reason 194
Platt, Lew 15
Poincaré, H 235
Polanyi, M 176
Polaroid Land camera 234
police cadets 171
police work 14–15
Ponzi scheme 238
Popper, Sir Karl 250
positive affect 116
Post-it Notes, 3M 234
practice (makes perfect?) 169–71, 286
Pratt, MG 11

precuneus, approximate location 144*f*
prefrontal cortex (PFC) 138
prejudice 109
primates
    macaque monkeys, mirror neurons 153–6
    what others do – not *why* 211
problem-solving, proxies 142
prospect theory 222
psychology, Standard Model of creative thinking 229, 234, 235–7, 244, 250, 254, 271, 274
'purity *vs* degradation' (MFT) 198

racism 199
Ramachandran, VS, mirror neurons 154
random error/noise 285
rational approach to decision-making 34–5
rational system 119
rationalist model of moral judgment 189, 194–5
reasoning
    gist-based 177
    Hume, Plato 194
Reber, A
    cognitive unconscious 105
    implicit learning 105–6
recognition heuristic 60–2
    as predictor of outcomes 62–3
recognition-based intuition 94*f*
recognition-based *vs* reason-based heuristics 61–2
recognition-primed decision-making (RPD) 80–102, 163
    business decisions 91–2
    a dual model 89
    essential features 88–9
    model 80–96
    origins 81
    variants 89
reflective cognition 222*f*
reflexive cognition 222*f*
representativeness heuristic 39–40, 42
    and availability 49
retailing, supermarkets and 183
Reyna, V, 'fuzzy trace theory' 177
Rich, N 202
right brain 134–5
right hemisphere aSTG 233*f*
Riley, Michael 86
risk
    and emotions 222
    and uncertainty, decision-making 4–5
risk perception 222
risk-seeking, risk-averse 149
Rizzolatti, G, mirror neurons 153
rules of thumb 57, 59–60
    examples 60

'take the best' 67–8
Russell, Stuart, on AI 21

Samba, Codou, top management team (TMT) intuition 182
Sapir, E 212
satisfaction, and consumer choice 73
satisfice, *vs* maximise 36, 58, 60
Satpute, A 221
du Sautoy, Marcus 253
Schulz, H 178
Schumpeter, J 249–50
science of intuition 17–19
scientific discovery, creative intuition 250–1
scissors analogy 58
search-type heuristics 66
selfish genes 190
semantic inferences 41
sense-making 14–15
sequential sampling strategy 69–71
service quality, availability heuristic 47
shadow banking 1–2
Shane, Scott 43
shared intuition 182
Shefy, E 153
Shogi, Japanese variant of chess 143–5
Simon, Herbert 1, 7, 10–12, 104
    bounded rationality theory 7–8, 33
    Nobel Prize 32–3
simplicity as a virtue 70–4
simplification principle 74
simulation 210
Sinclair, M 14
singular evaluation 88
sixth sense/gut feeling 12–14
skill acquisition model (SAM)
    Dreyfus 171–4
    five stages 171–2
    intuitive mastery 172–3
skin conductance/micro-sweating 147–8
Smith, Adam 189
social cognitive neuroscience 221
social imitative heuristic 65–6
social intuition 49, 210, 217–20
    defined 217–18
    facial appearance 218–19
    social brain hypothesis 220
social intuitist model of moral judgment 194–6
social and reason-based heuristics 65–70
social sense 208–28
    honest signals and linguistic markers 216–18
    mentalizing/mirroring 208–12
    overview 208
    reflexive system 1, reflective system 2 (X- and C-systems) 210–11, 221–2*f*
    social intuition 49, 210, 217–20

social sense (*Continued*)
　summary 225
　thin slicing 212–16
　　in business/management 214–16
social thinking, contrasting modes 106–7
socialization/acculturation 106
sociopathy, acquired 196
somatic markers 146–50
　affect and 149
　anticipation of outcomes 149
　hypothesis, neurocircuits 149
　see also gut feeling
South West Airlines, values 202
speed-dating 218
sports
　athletics 169
　brand-specific 201
　deliberate practice in 170
Standard Model of creative thinking 229, 234, 235–7, 244, 250, 254, 271, 274
　challenges, Mann Gulch fire 244–6
　number of stages 229, 254, 271
Stanford Business School 149–50
Stanovich, K
　dual-process theory 126
　System-1, System-2 processing 110
Starbucks 149
Stevanja, J 233
Stierand, M 239
Stigler, G 251
stock market trading 124
Stravinsky, I 242
Strick, M 241–2
Styhre, A 252
Stylerunner 233
suffering 198
Sull, D, and Eisenhardt, K
　intuition rules 74
　simplification principle 74
Sullenberger, C, intuition in flying 170–1
Sundgren, M 252
supermarkets, retailing and 183
Suskind, on AI 21
sweating, skin conductance/micro-sweating 147–8
System 1 consultancy
　AI-based 'Face-Trace' technology 122
　errors and biases 123
　good-vs-bad fallacy 123
　when to trust 123–5
System-1, System-2 processing 103, 105, 110–19
　climate change 201–2
　moral foundations theory 197–200
　reflexive System 1, and reflective System (X- and C-systems) 210–11, 221–2f
　thin slice judgments 213–14

Trump presidency 194
systematic processing, *vs* heuristic processing 107

tacit knowledge 17, 105, 121, 144, 165, 252, 282
　thin slicing 214
'take the best' heuristic
　cue ordering 71
　sequential sampling strategy 67–71
task continuum, cognitive continuum theory 82
task environments, both intuition and analysis 83
taste metaphor 200
team-driven collective intuition 182
10,000 hours rule for expertise 167–8
Tett, Gillian 2
Thanos, J, strategic decision-making 115–16
theory of mind 154, 208–9, 218, 219
　'default network' 219
　see also mentalizing
thieving 208
　burglary, take the best heuristic 67–8
thin slicing 212–16
　in business 214–16
　tacit knowledge 214
Thomson, V, metacognition 116
Todd, Peter 60
Todorov, A 218–19
top management team (TMT) intuition, four types 182
traffic light model for intuition/ analysis 98f
'trolley problem' (VMPFC patient *vs* normal responses) 197
Trump presidency
　Covid-19 public pronouncements 217
　social intuitist model of moral judgment 194
trust 123–5, 224
Tucker, Paul 2
Tversky, Amos 33, 37–8
two-minds model (dual-process theory) 104–33
　core processes of intuition 134–62
　critical voices 126–7
　dynamics 113–17
　experiential mind 117–19
　summary 127
　System-1, System-2 processing 113–15
　when to trust 123–5
　capturing intuitions 135–7
　interoception 150–3
　intuition in the right brain? 134–5
　mirror mechanism 153–6
　pattern recognition 142–6
　perceptions of coherence 137–42
　somatic markers 146–50
　summary 156
Types 1 and 2 processing 103, 105, 110–17
typography 242

uncertainty, risk and 4–5, 149, 222
uncertainty levels 7
unconscious thought theory (UTT) 240–4
unconscious/implicit vs conscious/explicit processing 106
unease, recognition-primed decision-making (RPD) 92–3
US armed forces
   Air Force Office of Scientific Research 171
   decision-making 81
US Federal Reserve, crash of 2007-8 178
USS Carl Vinson 6

value-based marketing 200–2
values-based organizations 202
Vasconcelos, Gabriel, algorithms 23–4
Venn diagram 39
ventro-medial prefrontal cortex (VMPFC)
   approximate location 147*f*
   framing bias 223
   integration of emotions into decision-making 148, 224

'trolley problem' 197
VMPFC disorders 'patients' 147–9, 196–7
X- and C-systems 221–2*f*
visual perception *see* Gestalt principles of visual perception

Wallas, G 235–6, 250
Weick, Karl 245
Welch, Jack 16
Whitney, Meredith 237–8
'wicked' learning structures 124–5
wisdom of crowds 65
Woodman, Nick 233
WorldCom 203
Wundt, W 236

X-system, neural correlates 222*f*
Xerox 233, 244

Yoplait Go-Gurt 234

Zappos 203, 283